PEARSON ALWAYS LEARNING

Felipe Fernández-Armesto

The World: A Brief History
Vol. 2

Custom Edition for Syracuse University
HIS 122

Taken from:
The World: A Brief History, Combined Volume
by Felipe Fernández-Armesto

Cover Art: Courtesy of Photodisc/Getty Images

Taken from:

The World: A Brief History, Combined Volume
by Felipe Fernández-Armesto
Copyright © 2008, 2005 by Felipe Fernández-Armesto
Published by Prentice Hall
Upper Saddle River, New Jersey 07458

This special edition published in cooperation with Pearson Learning Solutions.

Pearson Learning Solutions, 501 Boylston Street, Suite 900, Boston, MA 02116
A Pearson Education Company
www.pearsoned.com

Printed in the United States of America

2 3 4 5 6 7 8 9 10 V092 16 15 14 13

000200010271301352

SE

ISBN 10: 1-256-75231-2
ISBN 13: 978-1-256-75231-8

22 The Exchange of Enlightenments:
Eighteenth-Century Thought   562

PART 9   The Frustrations of Progress to ca. 1900   586

23 Replacing Muscle: the Energy Revolutions   588

24 The Social Mold: Work and Society
in the Nineteenth Century   614

25 Western Dominance in the Nineteenth Century:
The Westward Shift of Power and the Rise of Global
Empires   638

26 The Changing State: Political Developments
in the Nineteenth Century   664

PART 10   Chaos and Complexity: The World in the Twentieth Century   690

27 The Twentieth-Century Mind:
Western Science and the World   692

28 World Order and Disorder:
Global Politics in the Twentieth Century   718

29 The Pursuit of Utopia:
Civil Society in the Twentieth Century   748

MAPS   ix

INTRODUCING *THE WORLD*   x

ABOUT FELIPE FERNÁNDEZ ARMESTO   xix

22 The Exchange of Enlightenments: Eighteenth-Century Thought 562

THE CHARACTER OF THE ENLIGHTENMENT   564

THE ENLIGHTENMENT IN GLOBAL CONTEXT   565

The Chinese Example   566
Japan   567
India   567
The Islamic World   567

THE ENLIGHTENMENT'S EFFECTS IN ASIA   568

The Enlightenment and China   568
Western Science in Japan   569
■ A CLOSER LOOK: A Meeting of China, Japan, and the West   570
Korea and Southeast Asia   571

The Ottomans   571

THE ENLIGHTENMENT IN EUROPE   572

The Belief in Progress   572
New Economic Thought   573
Social Equality   573
Anticlericalism   574

THE CRISIS OF THE ENLIGHTENMENT: RELIGION AND ROMANTICISM   575

Religious Revival   575
The Cult of Nature and Romanticism   576
Rousseau and the General Will   577
Pacific Discoveries   578
Wild Children   579
The Huron as Noble Savage   579

THE FRENCH REVOLUTION AND NAPOLEON   580

Background to the Revolution   580
Revolutionary Radicalism   581
Napoleon   581
■ IN PERSPECTIVE: The Afterglow of Enlightenment   583

CONTENTS

PART 9 The Frustrations of Progress to ca. 1900 586

23 Replacing Muscle: The Energy Revolutions 588

GLOBAL DEMOGRAPHICS: THE WORLD'S POPULATION RISES 589

FOOD: TRANSITION TO ABUNDANCE 590

ENERGY FOR POWER: MILITARIZATION AND INDUSTRIALIZATION 596
Militarization 596
Industrialization 597

INDUSTRIALIZING EUROPE 601

INDUSTRY IN THE AMERICAS 604

JAPAN INDUSTRIALIZES 605

CHINA AND INDUSTRIALIZATION 607

INDIA AND EGYPT 608
■ IN PERSPECTIVE: Why the West? 610

24 The Social Mold: Work and Society in the Nineteenth Century 614

THE INDUSTRIALIZED ENVIRONMENT 616
Palaces of Work: The Rise of Factories 616
Critics of Industrialization: Gold from the Sewers 618

URBANIZATION 620

BEYOND INDUSTRY: AGRICULTURE AND MINING 621

CHANGING LABOR REGIMES 624
Slavery and the Slave Trade 624
Female and Child Labor 628
Free Migrants 629

HUNTERS AND PASTORALISTS 630

ELITES TRANSFORMED 631
■ IN PERSPECTIVE: Cultural Exchange—Enhanced Pace, New Directions 635

25 Western Dominance in the Nineteenth Century: The Westward Shift of Power and the Rise of Global Empires 638

THE OPIUM WARS   640

THE WHITE EMPIRES: RISE AND RESISTANCE   641

METHODS OF IMPERIAL RULE   648
   ■ A CLOSER LOOK: An Ethiopian View of the Battle of Adowa   649

BUSINESS IMPERIALISM   652

IMPERIALISM IN THE "NEW EUROPES"   655

EMPIRES ELSEWHERE: JAPAN, RUSSIA, AND THE UNITED STATES   656

RATIONALES OF EMPIRE   658
   Doctrines of Superiority   658
   The Civilizing Mission   660
   ■ IN PERSPECTIVE: The Reach of Empires   661

26 The Changing State: Political Developments in the Nineteenth Century 664

NATIONALISM   666
   Nationalism in Europe   666
   The Case of the Jews   668
   Nationalism Beyond Europe   669

CONSTITUTIONALISM   672

CENTRALIZATION, MILITARIZATION, AND BUREAUCRATIZATION   673
   In and Around the Industrializing World   673
   Beyond the Industrializing World   676

RELIGION AND POLITICS   680

NEW FORMS OF POLITICAL RADICALISM   681
   Steps Toward Democracy   681
   The Expansion of the Public Sphere   683

WESTERN SOCIAL THOUGHT   684
   ■ IN PERSPECTIVE: Global State-Building   686

CONTENTS

PART 10 Chaos and Complexity: The World in the Twentieth Century 690

27 The Twentieth-Century Mind: Western Science and the World 692

WESTERN SCIENCE ASCENDANT 694
   China 695
   India 698
   The Wider World 698

THE TRANSFORMATION OF WESTERN SCIENCE 700
   Physics 700
   Human Sciences 702
   Anthropology and Psychology 705
   Philosophy and Linguistics 707

THE MIRROR OF SCIENCE: ART 709

THE TURN OF THE WORLD 714
   ■ IN PERSPECTIVE: Science, Challenging and Challenged 714

28 World Order and Disorder: Global Politics in the Twentieth Century 718

THE WORLD WAR ERA, 1914–1945 720
   The First World War 720
   Postwar Disillusionment 724
   The Shift to Ideological Conflicts 726
   The Second World War 729

THE COLD WAR ERA, 1945–1991 731
   Superpower Confrontation 731
   ■ A CLOSER LOOK: Reporting Our Harvest to Chairman Mao 736

DECOLONIZATION 738

THE NEW WORLD ORDER 742
   The European Union 743
   ■ IN PERSPECTIVE: The Anvil of War 744

29 The Pursuit of Utopia: Civil Society in the Twentieth Century 748

THE CONTEXT OF ATROCITIES 749

THE ENCROACHING STATE 750

UNPLANNING UTOPIA: THE TURN TOWARD INDIVIDUALISM 754

COUNTER-COLONIZATION AND SOCIAL CHANGE 757

GLOBALIZATION AND THE WORLD ECONOMY 762

CULTURE AND GLOBALIZATION   766

SECULARISM AND RELIGIOUS REVIVAL   767

■ IN PERSPECTIVE: The Century of Paradox   770

GLOSSARY   G-1

A NOTE ON DATES AND SPELLING   DS-1

NOTES   N-1

CREDITS   C-1

INDEX   I-1

* Indicates Interactive Map Explorations

22.1 The Shape of the Earth **565**

22.2 Napoleon's Empire, ca. 1799–1815 **582**

23.1 World Population Growth, ca. 1700–1900 **592**

23.2 Industrialization, Technology, and Food Manufacturing in the Nineteenth Century **595**

23.3 The Industrialization of Europe by 1914 **602**

23.4 The Politics of Cotton **609**

24.1 The Growth of Manchester, England 1840–1900 **620**

24.2 The Movement of Indentured Labor in the Late Nineteenth Century **627**

***24.3** Ethnic Neigborhoods in Manhattan, ca. 1920 **632;** World Migration 1860–1920 **633**

25.1 Foreign Imperialism in East and Southeast Asia, 1840–1910 **642**

***25.2** The Imperial World, 1900 **644**

25.3 The Scramble for Africa **654**

25.4 Russian and Japanese Expansion, 1868–1918 **657**

26.1 The Peoples of Europe; Nationalities Within the Habsburg Empire **667**

***26.2** Examples of Resistance to European and United States Imperialism, 1880–1920 **669**

26.3 Revolts in the Qing Empire, 1850–1901 **675**

26.4 Muslim Reform Movements in Africa and Arabia in the Nineteenth Century **679**

27.1 Spread of Western Scientific Learning, 1866–1961 **696**

28.1 Europe, the Middle East, and North Africa in 1914 and 1923 **722**

28.2 World War II **730**

28.3 The Alliances of the Cold War **733**

28.4 Decolonization Since World War II **740**

29.1 Genocides and Atrocities, 1900–Present; The Holocaust **752**

29.2 Percentage of Noncitizen Population, ca. 2005 **758**

***29.3** International Trade Flows, ca. 2004 **764**

By the standards of astronauts, say, or science fiction writers, historians seem timid, unadventurous creatures who are only interested in one puny species—our species, the human species—on one tiny planet—our planet, Earth. But Earth is special. So far, we know of nowhere else in the cosmos where so much has happened and is happening today. By galactic standards, global history is a small story—but it's a good one.

Humans, moreover, compared with other animals, seem outward looking. Our concerns range over the universe and beyond it, to unseen worlds, vividly imagined or mysteriously revealed. Not just everything we do but also everything that occurs to our minds is part of our history and, therefore, part of this book, including science and art, fun and philosophy, speculations and dreams. We continually generate stories—new stories—at an amazing rate.

But the present passes instantly into the past. The present is always over, transformed into history. And the past is always with us, tugging at our memories, shaping our thoughts, launching and limiting our lives. So human history may seem narrowly self-interested, but it focuses on a riveting subject that is also our favorite subject—ourselves.

THE WAY OF HUMANKIND

Though the story of this book is a human story, it can never be merely human because, in isolation, humankind does not make perfect sense. Humans are animals, and to understand ourselves thoroughly and to know what, if anything, makes us unique, we have to compare ourselves with other animals. As with other animals, we are best studied in our habitats. We cannot begin to comprehend our own history except in context. Our story is inseparable from the climates where it takes place and the other life-forms that we depend on or compete with. All the elaborate culture we produce generates new, intimate relationships with the environment we refashion and the life-forms we exploit.

We are exceptionally ambitious compared to other animals, consciously remodeling environments to suit ourselves. We turn prairies into wheat lands, deserts into gardens, and gardens into deserts. We fell forests where we find them and plant them where none exist; we dam rivers, wall seas, cultivate plants, extinguish some species, and call others into being by selective breeding. Sometimes we smother terrain with environments we build for ourselves. Yet nothing we do liberates us from nature. As we shall see, one of the paradoxes of the human story is that the more we change the environment, the more vulnerable we become to ecological lurches and unpredictable disasters. Failure to establish a balance between exploitation and conservation has often left civilizations in ruins. History becomes a path picked across the wreckage. This does not mean that the environment determines our behavior or our lives, but it does set the framework in which we act.

We are an exceptionally successful species in terms of our ability to survive in a wide range of diverse climates and landscapes—more so than just about any other creatures, except for the microbes we carry around with us. But even we are still explorers of our planet, still trying to change it. Indeed, we have barely begun to change planet Earth, though, as we shall see, some human societies have devoted the last 10,000 years to trying to do it. We call ourselves masters, or, more modestly, caretakers of creation, but about 90 percent of the biosphere is too far underwater or too deep below the Earth for us to inhabit with the technology we have at present; These are environments that humans have only recently begun to invade and that we still do not dominate.

If we humans are peculiarly ambitious creatures, who are always intruding in the life of the planet, we are also odd compared to other animals in the way we generate change among ourselves. We are an unpredictable, unstable species. Lots of other animals live social lives and construct societies. But those societies are remarkably stable compared to ours. As far as we know, ants and elephants have the same lifeways and the same kinds of relationships that they have had since their species first appeared. That is not to say animals never change their cultures. One of the fascinating discoveries in primatology is that apes and monkeys develop cultural differences from one another, even between groups living in similar and sometimes adjacent environments. In West Africa, chimpanzees have developed a termite-catching technology. They "fish" with stripped branches that they plunge into termite nests but do not use tools to break open nuts. Chimps in a neighboring region ignore the termites but are experts in nut cracking, using rocks like hammers and anvils. In Sumatra in Indonesia, orangutans play a game—jumping from falling tress—that is unknown to their cousins in nearby Borneo. In East Africa, some male baboons control harems while others have one mate after another. In some chimpanzee societies, hunting and meat eating seem to have increased dramatically in recent times.

These are amazing facts, but the societies of nonhuman animals still change little compared with ours. So, alongside the theme of human interaction with the rest of nature is another great theme of our history: the ways our societies have changed, grown apart from one another, reestablished contact, and influenced one another in their turn.

THE WAY OF THIS BOOK

This book, then, interweaves two stories—of our interactions with nature and with each other. The environment-centered story is about humans distancing themselves from the rest of nature and searching for a balance between constructive and destructive exploitation. The culture-centered story is of how human cultures have influenced each other but also been different from each other. Both stories have been going on for thousands of years. We do not know whether they will end in triumph or disaster.

No one book can cover all of world history, and the fabric of this book is woven from carefully selected strands. Readers will see these at every turn, twisted together into yarn, stretched into stories. Human-focused historical ecology—the environmental theme—will drive readers back, again and again, to the same concepts: food, shelter, disease, energy, technology, art. (The last is a vital category for historians, not only because it is part of our interface with the rest of the world, but also because it forms a record of how we see reality and of how we see it change.) In the global story of human interactions—the cultural theme—we return constantly to the ways people make contact with each another: migration, trade, war, imperialism, pilgrimage, gift exchange, diplomacy, travel—and to their social frameworks: the economic and political arenas, the human groups and groupings, the states and civilizations, the sexes and generations, the classes and clusters of identity. In both stories, ideas and imagination play key roles, because most—perhaps all—of the changes we make happen first in our heads. We observe the world as it is, imagine it differently, and try to fend off our fears and realize our hopes.

The stories that stretch before us are full of human experience. "The stork feeds on snakes," said the ancient Greek sage Agathon, "the pig on acorns, and history on human lives." To build up our picture of human societies and ecosystems of the past we have to start with the evidence people have left. Then we reassemble it bit by bit, with the help of imagination disciplined by the sources. Anyone reading a history book needs to remember that interpreting evidence is a challenge—half burden and half opportunity. The subject matter of history is not the past directly because the past is never available to our senses. We have only the evidence about it. This makes history an art, not a science, a disciplined art like that of poetry disciplined by rhyme and meter, or a novel disciplined by character and plot, or a play disciplined by the limitations of stagecraft.

For a book like this, the sources set the limits of my imagination. Sometimes, these are concrete clues to what people really did—footprints of their wanderings, debris of their meals, fragments of their technologies, wreckage of their homes, traces of diseases in their bones. Usually, however, the sources reflect at best, not the way things were but the way people wished to represent them in their arts, crafts, and writings. Most sources—in short—are evidence of what happened only in the minds of those who made them. This means, in turn, that our picture of what went on in the world beyond human minds is always tentative and open to reinterpretation. The historian's job is not—cannot be—to say what the past was like, but rather, what it felt like to live in it, because that is what the evidence tends to reveal.

One of the most admirable historians of the twentieth century, R. G. Collingwood, who was also a professor of philosophy at Oxford, said that "all history is intellectual history." He was right. History—even the environmental and cultural history that is the subject of this book—is largely about what people perceived rather than what they really saw, what they thought or felt rather than what happened outwardly, what they represented rather than what was real. The nineteenth-century philosopher Arthur Schopenhauer, one of the most pessimistic thinkers ever, who drew on Hindu and Buddhist writings for his inspiration, said that history's only subject was "humankind's oppressive, muddlesome dream." He thought it made history pointless. I think it makes it intriguing.

Because the evidence is always incomplete, history is less a matter of describing or narrating or question-answering than it is of problem-posing. No one reading this book should expect to be instructed in straightforward facts or to acquire proven knowledge. The thrill of history is asking the right question, not getting the right answer. Most of the time, we can only hope to identify interesting problems that stimulate debate. And we have to accept that the debate is worthwhile for its own sake, even if we have insufficient knowledge to reach conclusions.

Historians do not even agree about which questions to ask. Some—including me—are interested in huge philosophical questions, such as how does history happen? What makes change? Is it random or subject to scientific laws? Do impersonal forces beyond human control—environmental factors or economics or some world force called fate, evolution, God, or progress—determine it? Or is change the externalization of ideas that people project onto the world? And if it's a mixture of all or some of these, what's the balance?

Some historians ask questions about how human societies function. How and why do societies grow and fragment and take different forms? How do people get power over others? How and why do revolutions happen and states and civilizations rise and fall?

Other historians like to pose problems about the present. How did we get into the mess we're in? Can we trace the causes of our problems back into the past and, if so, how far? Why do we have a globally connected world without global governance? Why is peace always precarious? Why does ecological overkill menace our environment? Having accounted—or failed to account—for the present, some historians like to focus on the future. They demand lessons from history about how to change our behavior or cope with recurrences of past difficulties. Others, again, search to make sense of the past, to find a way to characterize or narrate it that makes us feel we understand it.

Yet others—the majority, and again including me—like to study the past for its own sake and try to identify the questions that mattered to people at the time they first asked them. This does not mean that the sort of history found in this book is useless (although I do not necessarily think it would be a bad thing if it were). For to penetrate the minds of people of the past—especially the remote past of cultures other than your own—you have to make a supreme effort of understanding. The effort enhances life by sharpening responses to the streetscapes and landscapes, art and artifacts, laws and letters we have inherited from the past. And understanding is what we need most today in our multicultural societies and multi-civilizational world.

HOW THIS BOOK IS ARRANGED

After finding the time, accumulating the knowledge, posing the questions, stiffening the muscles, and summoning the blood, the big problem for the writer of a global history textbook is organizing the material. The big problem for the reader is navigating it. It is tempting to divide the world into regions or cultures or even—as I did in a previous book—into biomes and devote successive chapters to each. You could call that "world history," if you genuinely managed to cover the world. But "global history" is different: an attempt to see the planet whole, as if from an immense, astral height, and discern themes that truly transcend geographical and cultural boundaries. In this book, therefore, I try to look at every continent in just about every chapter (there are a couple of chapters that, for reasons described in their place, focus only on part of the world). Each chapter concentrates on themes from the two great global stories: how human societies diverge and converge, and how they interact with the rest of nature.

Because history is a story, in which the order of events matters, the chapters are arranged chronologically. There are 30 chapters—one for each week in a typical U.S. academic year (though of course, every reader or group of readers will go at their own pace)—and ten parts. I hope there is plenty to surprise readers without making the parts perversely defiant of the "periods" historians conventionally speak of. Part I runs roughly from 150,000 to 20,000 years ago, and, on the whole, the periods covered get shorter as sources accumulate, cultures diverge, data multiply, and readers' interests quicken. Of course, no one should be misled into thinking the parts are more than devices of convenience. Events that happened in, say, 1850, are in a different part of this book from those that happened in, say, 1750. But the story is continuous, and the parts could be recrafted to start and end at different moments.

At every stage, some parts of the world are more prominent than others, because they are more influential, more populous, more world-shaping. For much of the book, China occupies relatively more space, because China has, for much of the past, been immensely rich in globally influential initiatives. In the coverage of the last couple of centuries, Europe and the United States get a lot of attention: this is not "Eurocentrism" or "Westocentrism" (if there is such a word), but an honest reflection of how history happened. But I have tried not to neglect the peoples and parts of the world that historians usually undervalue: poor and peripheral communities, the margins and frontiers of the world, are often where world-changing events happen—the fault lines of civilizations, which radiate seismic effects.

HOW THIS BOOK HELPS STUDENTS

Pedagogy that Focuses and Enriches

The pedagogical features in *The World* help students engage with the narrative, provide reinforcement for learning, and enrich their study of world history.

Focus Questions open each chapter and encourage students to think critically while they read.

An Extensive and Integrated Map Program, created by Dorling Kindersley, one of the world's leading cartographic publishers, provides clear and innovative perspectives on both the larger themes and the particular events of world history.

Compelling Visual Sources, tightly coordinated with the text, include images never before published and captions that stimulate inquiry.

A Closer Look sections provide in-depth visual analysis of a specific cultural artifact. Detailed notes draw the viewer into close contact with the object.

Making Connections tables throughout the text offer visual summaries of important concepts. Instead of simply listing facts, these tools help students see connections that span across regions.

In-text Pronunciation Guides, embedded directly in the narrative, provide phonetic spellings for terms that may be unfamiliar to students.

Key Terms are defined in the Glossary and set in boldface type in the text

In Perspective sections end each chapter and ask students to consider the fundamental questions of a time period in world history.

HOW THIS BOOK SUPPORTS TEACHERS AND STUDENTS

An Extensive Teaching and Learning Package

The supplement package has been carefully crafted to enhance the instructor's classroom teaching experience and to provide students with resources that enrich the learning process.

Extensively revised and updated, the **Primary Source: Documents in Global History DVD** is both an immense collection of textual and visual documents in world history and an indispensable tool for working with sources. Extensively developed with the guidance of historians and teachers, the revised and updated DVD-ROM version includes over 800 sources in world history—from cave art to satellite images of the Earth from space. More sources from Africa, Latin America, and Southeast Asia have been added to this revised and updated DVD-ROM version. All sources are accompanied by headnotes and focus questions, and they are searchable by topic or region. The DVD comes with all new copies of *The World*. A stand-alone version can be purchased separately (0-13-178938-4).

myhistorylab www.myhistorylab.com With the best of Prentice Hall's multimedia solutions in one easy-to-use place, MyHistoryLab for *The World: A Brief History* offers students and instructors a state-of-the-art, interactive solution for world history. Organized by the main subtopics of *The World*, and delivered within a course-management platform (WebCT or Blackboard), or as a website, MyHistoryLab supplements and enriches the classroom experience and can form the basis for an online course.

www.prenhall.com/armesto The open-access companion website for *The World* includes study questions, flash cards, and interactive maps.

The **Instructor's Resource DVD** offers class presentation resources, including all of the maps and many of the illustrations from the text, PowerPoint presentations, and Classroom-Response System presentations.

The **Instructor's Guide to Teaching the World** provides everything instructors need to incorporate *The World: A Brief History* into their courses. An extensive Test-Item File, sample syllabi from users of *The World: A Brief History*, and teaching notes authored by David Ringrose, University of California, San Diego, enrich the utility of the Guide.

CourseSmart **CourseSmart Textbooks Online** is an exciting new *choice* for students looking to save money. As an alternative to purchasing the print textbook, students can *subscribe* to the same content online and save up to 50% off the suggested list price of the print text. With a CourseSmart eTextbook, students can search the text, make notes online, print out reading assignments that incorporate lecture notes, and bookmark important passages for later review. For more information, or to subscribe to the CourseSmart eTextbook, visit www.coursesmart.com.

Study on the go with **VangoNotes.** VangoNotes is a digital audio study guide for *The World: A Brief History* that can be downloaded to an mp3 player. Students can study wherever they are or whatever they are doing by listening to the key concepts they need to know for each chapter of *The World.*

VangoNotes are **flexible**; students can download all the material directly to their mp3 players, or only the chapters they need. www.vangonotes.com

Study Guide, Volumes I and II, includes practice tests, essay questions, and map exercises.

Titles from the renowned **Penguin Classics** series can be bundled with *The World: A Brief History* for a nominal charge. Please contact your Pearson Arts and Sciences sales representative for details.

The Prentice Hall Atlas in World History, Second Edition includes over 100 full-color maps in world history, drawn by Dorling Kindersley, one of the world's most respected cartographic publishers. Copies of the *Atlas* can be bundled with *The World* for a nominal charge. Contact your Pearson Arts and Sciences sales representative for details.

DEVELOPING *THE WORLD*

Developing a project like *The World* required the input and counsel of hundreds of individuals. We thank all those who shared their time and effort to make *The World* a better book.

Reviewers

Donald R. Abbott, San Diego Mesa College
Wayne Ackerson, Salisbury University
Roger Adelson, Arizona State University
Alfred J. Andrea, University of Vermont (Emeritus)
David G. Atwill, Pennsylvania State University
Mauricio Borrero, St. John's University
Leonard Blussé, Harvard University
John Brackett, University of Cincinnati
Gayle K. Brunelle, California State University—Fullerton
Fred Burkhard, Maryland University College
Antoinette Burton, University of Illinois
Jorge Cañizares-Esguerra, University of Texas—Austin
Elaine Carey, St. John's University
Tim Carmichael, College of Charleston
Douglas Chambers, University of Southern Mississippi
Nupur Chaudhuri, Texas Southern University
David Christian, San Diego State University
Duane Corpis, Georgia State University
Dale Crandall-Bear, Solano Community College
Touraj Daryaee, California State University—Fullerton
Jeffrey M. Diamond, College of Charleston
Brian Fagan, University of California—Santa Barbara
Nancy Fitch, California State University—Fullerton

Alison Fletcher, Kent State University
Patricia Gajda, The University of Texas at Tyler
Richard Golden, University of North Texas
Stephen S. Gosch, University of Wisconsin—Eau Claire
Jonathan Grant, Florida State University
Mary Halavais, Sonoma State University
Shah M. Hanifi, James Madison University
Russell A. Hart, Hawaii Pacific University
Phyllis G. Jestice, University of Southern Mississippi
Amy J. Johnson, Berry College
Deborah Smith Johnston, Lexington High School
Eric A. Jones, Northern Illinois University
Ravi Kalia, City College of New York
David M. Kalivas, Middlesex Community College
Frank Karpiel, College of Charleston
David Kenley, Marshall University
Andrew J. Kirkendall, Texas A&M University
Dennis Laumann, The University of Memphis
Donald Leech, University of Minnesota
Jennifer M. Lloyd, SUNY—Brockport
Aran MacKinnon, University of West Georgia
Moria Maguire, University of Arkansas—Little Rock
Susan Maneck, Jackson State University

Anthony Martin, Wellesley College
Dorothea Martin, Appalachian State University
Adam McKeown, Columbia University
Ian McNeely, University of Oregon
Margaret E. Menninger, Texas State University—San Marcos
Stephen Morillo, Wabash College
William Morison, Grand Valley State University
Laura Neitzel, Brookdale Community College
Kenneth J. Orosz, University of Maine—Farmington
Michael Pavkovic, Hawaii Pacific University
Kenneth Pomeranz, University of California—Irvine
Phyllis E. Pobst, Arkansas State University
Sara B. Pritchard, Montana State University
Norman Raiford, Greenville Technical College
Stephen Rapp, Georgia State University
Vera Blinn Reber, Shippensburg University
Matthew Redinger, Montana State University—Billings
Matthew Restall, Pennsylvania State University
Jonathan Reynolds, Arkansas State University
Richard Rice, University of Tennessee—Chattanooga

Peter Rietbergen, Catholic University (Nijmegen)
David Ringrose, University of California—San Diego
Patricia Romero, Towson University
Morris Rossabi, Queens College
David G. Rowley, University of Wisconsin—Platteville
Sharlene Sayegh, California State University—Long Beach
William Schell, Murray State University
Linda Bregstein Scherr, Mercer County Community College
Patricia Seed, University of California, Irvine
Lawrence Sondhaus, University of Indianapolis
Richard Steigmann-Gall, Kent State University
John Thornton, Boston University
Ann Tschetter, University of Nebraska—Lincoln
Deborah Vess, Georgia College & State University
Stephen Vinson, SUNY—New Paltz
Joanna Waley-Cohen, New York University
Anne M. Will, Skagit Valley College
John Wills, University of Southern California
Theodore Jun Yoo, University of Hawaii—Manoa

ACKNOWLEDGMENTS

Without being intrusive, I have tried not to suppress my presence—my voice, my views—in the text, because no book is objective, other than by pretense, and the reader is entitled to get to know the writer's foibles and failures. In overcoming mine, I have had a lot of help (though there are sure still to be errors and short-comings through my fault alone). Textbooks are teamwork, and I have learned an immense amount from my friends and helpers at Pearson Prentice Hall, especially my editors, Charles Cavaliere and Gerald Lombardi, whose indefatigability and forbearance made the book better at every turn. I also thank the picture researcher Emma Brown and the members of the production and cartographic sections of the team who performed Herculean labors: Mary Carnis, managing editor; Kathleen Sleys, production project manager; Frank Weihenig, production editor; Marianne Gloriande, print buyer; Maria Lang, designer; Alison Lorber, media editor; and Maureen Diana, editorial assistant. Finally, Kate Mitchell has once again crafted a superb marketing campaign.

I could not have gotten through the work without the help and support of my wonderful colleagues at Queen Mary, University of London; the Institute of Historical Research, University of London; and the History Department of Tufts University. I owe special thanks to the many scholars who share and still share their knowledge of global history at the Pearson Prentice Hall Seminar Series in Global History, which now meets at Tufts University. David Ringrose of University of California, San Diego, was a constant guide, whose interest never flagged and whose wisdom never failed. Many colleagues and counterparts advised me on their fields of expertise or performed heroic self-sacrifice in putting all of the many pieces of the book together: Natia Chakvetadze, Shannon Corliss, Maria Guarascio,

Anita Castro, Conchita Ordonez, Sandra Garcia, Maria Garcia, Ernest Tucker (United States Naval Academy), David Way (British Library), Antony Eastmond (Courtland Institute), Morris Rossabi (Columbia University), David Atwill and Jade Atwill (Pennsylvania State University), Stephen Morillo (Wabash College), Peter Carey (Oxford University), Jim Mallory (Queens University, Belfast), Matthew Restall (Pennsylvania State University), Roderick Whitfield (School of Oriental and African Studies, University of London), Barry Powell (University of Wisconsin), Leonard Blussé (Harvard University), Guolong Lai (University of Florida), and Jai Kabaranda, my former graduate student at Queen Mary, as well as the many good people whose assistance I may have failed to acknowledge.

In making this abridged version of the original book, I have been able to make some small changes as well as many cuts. Readers inspired most of these, and I am especially grateful to the universities that gave me a chance to talk to teachers and students who have used or were going to use the book: Colorado State University; Jackson State University; Northern Kentucky University; Pennsylvania State University; Salem State University; the U.S. Air Force Academy; the US Naval Academy; the University at Buffalo (SUNY); the Ohio State University; the University of Arkansas, Little Rock; and the University of Memphis. I also learned a lot from the comments and feedback from subscribers to the H-World listserv. They are too numerous to name, but I owe special debts for self-sacrificingly generous help to Jack Betterly, Jerry Green, David Kalivas, and Peter Wozniak. I am also indebted to seminar-goers at the Boston Global History Consortium's Global History Seminar at Tufts University. But it has taken a long time to produce the book, and much of the good advice I've had, which came too late or required too much re-thinking for the time available, will only be reflected in future editions, if I am lucky enough to have any.

Felipe Fernández-Armesto
Tufts University
Fall 2007

About Felipe Fernández-Armesto

Felipe Fernández-Armesto holds the Prince of Asturias chair of Spanish Civilization at Tufts University where he also directs the Pearson Prentice Hall Seminar Series in Global History. Fernández-Armesto is a visiting professor of Global Environmental History at Queen Mary College, University of London, and is on the editorial board of the History of Cartography for the University of Chicago Press, the editorial committee of Studies in Overseas History (Leiden University), and the *Journal of Global History*. He has also served on the Council of the Hakluyt Society and was Chairman of Trustees of the PEN Literary Foundation. Recent awards include a Premio Nacional de Investigación (Sociedad Geográfica Española) in 2003, a fellowship at the Netherlands Institute of Advanced Study in the Humanities and Social Sciences, and a Union Pacific Visiting Professorship at the University of Minnesota (1999–2000). He won the Caird Medal of the National Maritime Museum in 1995 and the John Carter Brown Medal in 1999. In 2008, Fernández-Armesto will give the keynote address at the annual meeting of the World History Association.

The author, coauthor, or editor of over 25 books and numerous papers and scholarly articles, Fernández-Armesto's work has been translated into 24 languages. His books include *Before Columbus; The Times Illustrated History of Europe; Columbus; Millennium: A History of the Last Thousand Years* (the subject of a ten-part series on CNN); *Civilizations: Culture, Ambition, and the Transformation of Nature; Near a Thousand Tables; The Americas; Humankind: A Brief History; Ideas that Changed the World; The Times Atlas of World Exploration;* and *The Times Guide to the Peoples of Europe.* Two recent works are *Amerigo: The Man Who Gave His Name to America* and *Pathfinders: A Global History of Exploration* (which was awarded the World History Association Book Prize for 2006).

CHAPTER 22
The Exchange of Enlightenments: Eighteenth-Century Thought

As a portrait painter, the British artist Henry Perronet Briggs made a specialty of theatrical subjects. His study of Raja Rammohan Roy (1774–1833) seems romantic and dramatic, giving the Indian sage a visionary stare and a strange, vaguely oriental outfit, in a setting that seems to recall the Mughal Empire.

IN THIS CHAPTER

THE CHARACTER OF THE
ENLIGHTENMENT

THE ENLIGHTENMENT IN
GLOBAL CONTEXT
The Chinese Example
Japan
India
The Islamic World

THE ENLIGHTENMENT'S
EFFECTS IN ASIA
The Enlightenment and China
Western Science in Japan

Korea and Southeast Asia
The Ottomans

THE ENLIGHTENMENT IN
EUROPE
The Belief in Progress
New Economic Thought
Social Equality
Anticlericalism

THE CRISIS OF THE
ENLIGHTENMENT: RELIGION
AND ROMANTICISM
Religious Revival

The Cult of Nature and Romanticism
Rousseau and the General Will
Pacific Discoveries
Wild Children
The Huron as Noble Savage

THE FRENCH REVOLUTION
AND NAPOLEON
Background to the Revolution
Revolutionary Radicalism
Napoleon

IN PERSPECTIVE: The
Afterglow of Enlightenment

n 1829, a rumor reached the English Bishop of Calcutta. India's most respected thinker, Raja Rammohan Roy (1774–1833), had turned to Christianity. Roy had spent most of his life in Bengal under British rule, except for a period of study in London. He had become an admirer of Western ways, a master of Western languages, a scholar of Western science. As a teacher, he introduced his pupils to the writings of Western philosophers. He translated Western literature into Indian languages. He led movements to abolish female infanticide and the custom that required widows to burn themselves to death on their husband's funeral pyres. He argued for freedom for women.

In short, many observers saw Rammohan as representative of a new phase of global history: the slow but unstoppable triumph, from the late eighteenth century onward, of Western ideas, as Western power spread them around the world. Indeed, there is truth in that image. But it does not do justice to the complexity of Rammohan's thought or to the diversity of the traditions he inherited. He was a scholar of the Veda and of classical Persian literature long before he became a student of Western learning. His liberal, radical, humane, and skeptical notions were confirmed, not created, by Western influence. He sought not to turn India into an Eastern version of the West, but to use Western help to restore what he saw as a golden age of reason from India's own past. He rejected superstition and social abuses, whether they were Indian or Western.

The Western authors Rammohan loved and taught were those connected with the innovative movement of eighteenth-century European thought that we call the **Enlightenment**—writers who elevated reason, science, and practical utility, challenged conventional religion, and sought to expose cant. When the bishop of Calcutta congratulated him on his supposed conversion to Christianity, Rammohan denied it with the kind of irreverent wit he had picked up from European writers: "My Lord, I assure you, I did not abandon one superstition merely in order to take up another." The Enlightenment, indeed, was the source of the most powerful influences that spread from Europe over the world of the nineteenth and twentieth centuries. Even before the eighteenth century was over, the Enlightenment made a home in the Americas, with some modifications, and gripped fingerholds in Asia.

● ● ● ● ●

FOCUS questions _____

- WHAT WAS the Enlightenment and how did it influence Western social, political, and economic thinking?
- HOW DID China and Japan view Europe in the eighteenth century?
- WHY WERE the ideas of Rousseau so influential?
- WHY WAS there a reaction against the cult of reason, and what forms did it take?
- HOW DID Enlightenment ideas influence the course of the French Revolution and Napoleon's policies?
- WHAT INTELLECTUAL trends did Europe, the Americas, Islam, and east Asia have in common in the eighteenth century?

Moreover, the Englightenment was global in its inspiration as well as its effects. Historians have debated about where in northern or Western Europe the Enlightenment started. But this debate misses the fundamental contribution made by the interaction of Western European thought with ideas from overseas, and, in particular, from China.

The best way to approach the Enlightenment may be by first telling a story that expresses its character better than any attempt at a dictionary-style definition. We can then look at the global exchange of influences that surrounded enlightened ideas, the key texts that encoded them in Europe, and the changes that overtook and transformed the Enlightenment during the eighteenth century.

THE CHARACTER OF THE ENLIGHTENMENT

To understand what the Enlightenment was like, a good place to start is Kittis in northern Finland, near the Arctic Circle, where a French scientist, Pierre Louis Moreau de Maupertuis, pitched camp in August 1736. Maupertuis was engaged in the most elaborate and expensive scientific experiment ever conducted up to that time. Traditionally, Western scientists had assumed that the Earth was perfectly spherical. Seventeenth-century theorists, however, led by Isaac Newton in England, argued that it must be distended at the equator and flattened at the poles, owing to centrifugal force (the thrust or sense of thrust you get on the edge of a circle in motion, which tends, for instance, to fling you off a merry-go-round). Meanwhile, mapmakers working on the survey of France had made a series of observations that suggested the contrary. The world seemed to be elongated toward the poles. To resolve the debate, the French Royal Academy of Science sent expeditions—of which Maupertuis's was one—to measure the length of one degree along the surface of the circumference of the Earth. If measurements at the Arctic Circle matched those at the equator, the globe was spherical. Any difference between them either way would indicate where the world bulged (see Map 22.1).

In December 1736, Maupertuis began his measurements with rods made of fir, because it was least likely to shrink from the cold. His readings helped to convince the world that the planet was indeed squashed at the poles and bulging at the equator. On the front page of his collected works, he appears in a fur cap and collar over a eulogy that reads, "It was his destiny to determine the shape of the world."

Like many scientific explorers seared by experience, Maupertuis eventually became disillusioned by science but inspired by nature. He set off believing that every truth was quantifiable and that every fact could be sensed. By the time he died in 1759, he had become something of a mystic. "You cannot chase God in the immensity of the heavens," he concluded, "or the depths of the oceans or the chasms of the Earth. Maybe it is not yet time to understand the world systematically—time only to behold it and be amazed." Perhaps, he speculated, only God exists, and perceptions are illusions of a mind "alone in the universe."

Pierre Louis de Maupertuis (1698–1759), on his return from the Arctic in 1737, seems to flatten the globe in this portrait by the French artist Robert Lervac-Tournières. The hero points the way forward. A map of the area he surveyed in Finland is on the table, with the Laplanders' fur-lined cap he wore on his expedition.

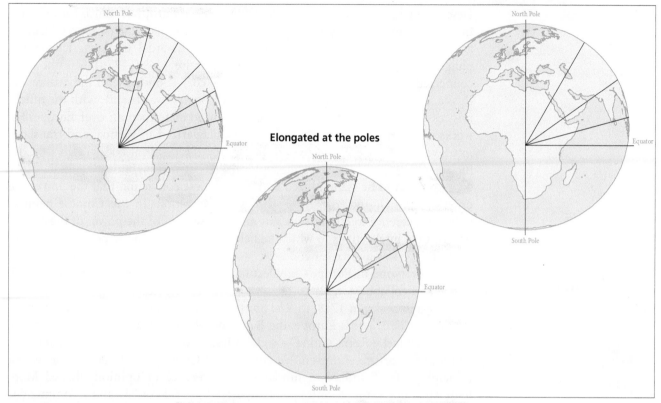

Perfectly spherical

Elongated at the poles

Distended at the equator and flattened at the poles

MAP 22.1 **The Shape of the Earth**

Maupertuis's mental pilgrimage between certainty and doubt, science and speculation, rationalism and religious revelation reproduced in miniature the history of European thought in the eighteenth century. First, in a surge of optimism, the perfectibility of humankind, the infallibility of reason, the reality of the observed world, and the sufficiency of science became common assumptions. In the second half of the century, the Enlightenment flickered as intellectuals rediscovered the power of feelings over reason and sensations over thoughts. Then revolutionary bloodshed and warfare, in which the century ended, seemed to extinguish the torch completely. But embers remained: enduring faith that freedom can energize human goodness, that happiness is worth pursuing in this life, and that science and reason—despite their limitations—can unlock progress and enhance lives.

THE ENLIGHTENMENT IN GLOBAL CONTEXT

During the eighteenth century, despite the long reach of some European empires, China's was, as we saw in Chapter 21, still the fastest-growing empire in the world. China also looked more modern than any society you could find in the West. It was a better-educated society, with over a million graduates from a demanding educational system, and a more entrepreneurial society, with bigger businesses and bigger clusters of mercantile and industrial capital than you could find anywhere else. It was a more industrialized society, with higher levels of production in more specialized concentrations, and a more urbanized society, with denser distributions of population. China's was even—for adult males—a more egalitarian society, in which the hereditary landed gentry had to defer to scholar-bureaucrats who were drawn from every level of rank and wealth.

The Chinese Example

Described with admiration by the Jesuits on whom Europeans relied for information, China excited positive interest among European thinkers. One of China's greatest fans was also one of Europe's most influential thinkers. The French philosopher who wrote under the name Voltaire (1694–1778) was the best-connected man of the eighteenth century. He corresponded with the Empress of Russia, corrected the King of Prussia's French poetry, was friends with the official mistresses of the king of France, and influenced statesmen all over Europe. His works were read in Sicily and the Balkans, plagiarized in Vienna, and translated into Swedish. He saw China, in part, as a source of inspiration for his own art. Confucianism attracted him as a philosophical alternative to organized religion, which he detested. And he sympathized with the Chinese conviction that the universe is orderly, rational, and intelligible through observation. In the Chinese habit of political deference to scholars, he saw an endorsement of the power of the class of professional intellectuals to which he belonged. In the absolute power of the Chinese state, he saw a force for good.

Not everyone in Europe's intellectual elite shared Voltaire's opinion. His colleague and collaborator, Denis Diderot (1713–1784), ridiculed him for believing Jesuit propaganda. In 1748, in *The Spirit of Laws*, a work that inspired constitutional reformers across Europe, the Baron de Montesquieu (1689–1755) claimed that "the cudgel governs China"—a claim Jesuit accounts of Chinese harsh justice and judicial torture endorsed. He condemned China as "a despotic state, whose principle is fear." Indeed, a fundamental difference of opinion divided Montesquieu and Voltaire. Montesquieu advocated the rule of law and recommended that constitutional safeguards should limit governments. Voltaire never really trusted the people and felt that strong, well-advised governments could best judge the people's interests. Montesquieu, moreover, developed an influential theory, according to which Western political traditions were benign, and tended toward liberty, whereas Asian states were despotic and concentrated power in the hands of tyrants. "This," he wrote, "is the grand reason of the weakness of Asia, and of the strength of Europe; of the liberty of Europe and of the slavery of Asia." *Oriental despotism* became a term of abuse in Western political writing. François Quesnay (1694–1774), Voltaire's colleague, who echoed the idealization of China, countered that "enlightened despotism" would favor the people rather than elites. He even persuaded the heir to the French throne to imitate a Chinese imperial rite by plowing land in person as an example to agrarian improvers.

One way or another, whether you favored China or rejected its examples, Chinese models seemed to be shaping European political thought. By the 1760s, a satirist in England could complain that busts of Confucius were replacing those of Plato and Aristotle and that instead of relying on the classics, "we take our learning from the wise Chinese." The dramatist Oliver Goldsmith (1728–1774) composed fictional *Letters of a Chinese Philosopher* to express disapproval of English society.

Meanwhile, Chinese influence was changing elite taste in Europe. Until the eighteenth century, China exercised its artistic influence on the West almost entirely through porcelain, lacquers, and textiles. Now Chinese wallpaper became accessible to a rich elite, and European furniture and dishes were decorated with Chinese themes. The French painter Jean-Antoine Watteau's (1684–1721) designs of Chinese scenes to decorate an apartment for King Louis XIV inaugurated a taste for Chinese-style schemes. It spread through the palaces of the Bourbon dynasty, which ruled France, Spain, and Naples, and was connected by marriage with many

Baron de Montesquieu, from *The Spirit of the Laws*

Voltaire. When Voltaire died in 1778, the sculptor Jean-Antoine Houdon (1741–1828) used the great writer's death mask (a plaster cast of the face made just after a person died) to represent him realistically. But this sculpture remains highly charged with symbolic meaning. Voltaire is robed like an ancient philosopher-sage; his hands are wrinkled with useful toil; a sardonic smile represents his use of irony and humor to challenge the institutions of church and state.

of Europe's other royal families. From Bourbon courts, the Chinese look radiated through Europe. In England, the king's son, the Duke of Cumberland, sailed on a fake Chinese pleasure boat. William Halfpenny's *Chinese and Gothic Architecture* (1752) was the first of many books to treat Chinese art as equivalent to Europe's. The fashionable British architect Sir Willim Chambers designed a pagoda for Kew Gardens in London and Chinese furniture for aristocratic homes, while "Chinese" Thomas Chippendale, England's leading cabinetmaker, popularized Chinese themes for furniture. By midcentury, engravings of Chinese scenes hung even in middle-class French and Dutch homes.

il "Chinoiserie"

Japan

Enthusiasm embraced Japan as well as China. Jesuits, of course, did not praise Japan, whose rulers had expelled them in the 1630s. Since then, Japanese governments had persecuted Christianity. The Japanese policy of excluding foreigners kept Europe ignorant of Japanese life. But the Dutch East India Company's trade with Japan opened a window. Engelbert Kaempfer, a company envoy, published the most influential account of Japan in 1729. His portrait of a people in "slavery and submission" fed into European ideas for centuries to come, but he was also frank about the peace, order, and prosperity he observed. Opinion about Japan in Europe split as it did over China. Montesquieu saw Japan as an oriental despotism. Voltaire saw it as the embodiment of "the laws of nature in the laws of a state."

India

Voltaire found an even better model in India. In 1756, he published *Dialogue Between a Brahman and a Jesuit*. The Brahman speaks with Voltaire's voice. He wants, above all, "a state in which the laws are obeyed." Voltaire's work on India was more profound than his assertions about China and Japan, because he recognized how much Western thought owed to Indian civilization. "It is probable," he averred, "that the Brahmins were the first legislators of the earth, the first philosophers, the first theologians." The study in the West of Asian languages strengthened this contention. The Collège Royal in France introduced Chinese studies in the 1730s, but Jesuit work on Indian languages, especially Sanskrit, facilitated the most remarkable disclosure. In 1786, the English scholar Sir William Jones realized that Sanskrit—the language of the Indian classics—was related to Latin and Greek and probably shared with them a common root.

The Islamic World

Muslim Turkey and Persia, too, influenced Western minds in the eighteenth century, mainly as sources of exotic imagery, and also, in Turkey's case, as a model of good and bad government. Montesquieu added objectivity and credibility to his critiques of Western society in his *Persian Letters* (1721) by pretending that they were the work of a Persian sage. Playwrights favored Turkish settings and characters for social satire. In 1782, Mozart's comic opera, *The Abduction from the Seraglio*, showed Turks outfoxing Europeans and exceeding them in generosity. Turkey was often cited as a model for hygiene, education, charitable institutions, and what a late seventeenth-century traveler praised as "order, ... economy and the regulation of provisions." In 1774, Simon-Nicolas-Henri Linguet pointed out that in Turkey and Persia the Quran protected liberty by restraining the power of rulers. Well-informed observers commended the Ottomans for religious toleration,

Lady Mary Wortley Montagu on the Ottoman Empire, 1717

Concubine. In the eighteenth century, Chinese emperors inaugurated a fashion at the imperial court for having one's portrait painted in Western dress. Here the favorite concubine of the Qianlong emperor (r. 1735–1796) wears a Western suit of armor. The artist, Giuseppe Castiglione, was a member of the Jesuit mission in China from 1730 until 1768. He also helped design the gardens of the imperial summer palace, with their complicated series of fountains that constituted a feat of hydraulic engineering.

respect for laws, customs, and property rights, and benevolence toward minorities—the very virtues that some Enlightenment thinkers thought that Europe lacked.

Nonetheless, during the eighteenth century, European critics of Ottoman life and customs became increasingly strident. Features of government formerly praised as evidence of strength and wisdom—the lack of a governing aristocracy, for instance, the docility of the sultan's subjects, the vulnerability of high office-holders to the sultan's mood—came to be seen as arbitrary and despotic. Turkey, even more than China, became a reference point for denunciations of oriental despotism. "In such distressful regions," wrote a follower of Montesquieu, "man is seen to kiss his chains, without any certainty as to fortune and property; he adores his tyrant; and without any knowledge of humanity or reason, is reduced to have no other virtue but fear."

THE ENLIGHTENMENT'S EFFECTS IN ASIA

European interest in Asia transformed Europe but changed Asia only a little.

The Enlightenment and China

Historians have generally regarded the Chinese attitude to European ideas at the time as arrogant, unrealistic, and restricted by outmoded traditions. But Westerners had always had more to learn from China than the other way round. Even in the eighteenth century, the inferiority of the West was only beginning to be reversed. So it is not surprising that the Chinese were still selective in their receptivity to Western ideas. At the beginning of the century, when Jesuits were already installed as the emperors' favorite astronomers, mapmakers, and technicians (see Chapter 18), one of them, Father Chavagnac, complained that the Chinese still "cannot be persuaded that anything which is not of China deserves to be regarded." Chavagnac found it particularly distressing that Chinese scholars still expressed skepticism when he showed them his map of the world. "They all cried out, 'So where is China?' 'It is this small spot of land,' said I. 'It seems very little,'" was their reply.

Nevertheless, the Jesuits extended their activities at court. "Every day," they claimed in letters home during the reign of the Kangxi emperor (r. 1661–1722), "from two hours before noon to two hours after noon, we were at the emperor's side, lecturing on Euclid's geometry, or on physics, astronomy, etc." The emperor commissioned Jesuits to map inner Asia and commanded the translation of Western mathematical works and all the texts Jesuits recommended on the calendar. The Yongzheng (yung-jheng) emperor (r. 1722–1735) restricted missionaries' freedom to make converts but had himself painted in a Western curled wig and coat. For the Qianlong emperor (r. 1735–1796), European artists painted his favorite concubine dressed in Western armor. Other Jesuits designed his gardens and engineered its fountains and mechanical statues.

Western technology made its biggest impact, perhaps, on war. In 1673, the emperor threatened to expel all Christians from China unless the Jesuits consented to design and manufacture artillery for him. The priests' designs continued in use until the mid–nineteenth century. They supervised gunnery practice, under compulsion, insisting that they were men of peace. In the mid-1780s, when news of hot-air balloons in the West reached the Chinese court, the Chinese immediately inquired about its possible military applications. Nonetheless, Westerners still seemed just clever barbarians to the Chinese, useful in their place, dangerous when they aimed higher.

Western Science in Japan

Admiration for the West penetrated deeper—though still not very deep—in Japan. The shogun Yoshimune (r. 1716–1745) took an interest in science and technology comparable to Kangxi's. From 1720, he allowed Chinese translations of Western books to circulate in Japan. The Japanese scholar Miura Baien (1723–1789) recognized that Western astronomy had revolutionized knowledge of the universe. Like many Western philosophers of the time, he advocated practical utility and technical efficiency above traditional values. "A tiny lantern that lights humble homes," he wrote, "is worth more than gems." Yet it was hard to find ways to promote Western knowledge. Japan's seventeenth-century experience (see Chapter 19) still made its government determined to exclude Christianity and limit foreign access to the country. Since the representatives of the Dutch East India Company were the only Europeans allowed in Japan—and even then only under tight restrictions—access to scientific information was haphazard. Japanese scholars had no way to judge what information was accurate or up to date. The interpreters who negotiated with the Dutch worked exclusively in Portuguese, the traditional language of Western commerce in east Asia. To read Western books, Japanese scholars had to teach themselves Dutch from scratch.

The case of Rembert Dodens's *Crudetboeck*, a Dutch study of plants published in 1554, is instructive. In 1659, a Dutch embassy presented an edition of 1618 to the shogun. Hidden away in the palace library, it was extracted at Yoshimune's command in 1717, in the belief that it might contain useful medical knowledge. It was handed over to a translator, who eventually produced his translation in 1750. The work was by then nearly 200 years out of date. The same translator worked on another supposed guide to plants for 24 years before realizing that it was a zoological work that had no medical information.

title page from a Japanese anatomy text, 1775

A breakthrough came only in 1771, when the dissection of a corpse demonstrated the accuracy of European books of anatomy. A group of enthusiastic beginners in "Dutch studies" started meeting six or seven times a month to puzzle over the meaning of Western books. "After about a year," wrote one of them, "we became capable of reading as much as ten or more lines of text per day if the particular passage was not too difficult."

So China remained the dominant intellectual influence in Japan, and Confucianism remained the foundation of Japanese thought. Most new developments came not from the West but from Japanese reactions against Confucianism. Independently, Japanese thinkers discovered principles similar to those philosophical radicals in Europe and America advocated: the virtues, especially, of universal reason—*ri*, the Japanese called it—approached scientifically, through observation. Ogyu Sorai (1666–1728) advocated experience in place of speculation as the key to truth. "History," he declared, "is ultimate knowledge." Tominaga Nakamoto (1715–1746) went further, doubting the possibility of any universally valid statements because experience seemed too diverse. In 1713, Kaibara Ekken argued that nature was in constant flux and so could only be understood by observation, not by the grand generalizations of Confucian theory. Some radicals embraced an egalitarian theory of human nature. Ishida Baigan (1685–1744), an advocate of reason as the unique means to truth, was one of many teachers who opened their classes to people of modest social backgrounds, in the belief that commoners had the same mental powers as the gentry.

A MEETING OF CHINA, JAPAN, AND THE WEST

Eastern and Western Enlightenments meet in this late eighteenth-century Japanese painting on silk.

In the background, firefighting teams from Japan, China, and Holland tackle the same blaze with their respective techniques. The Dutch seem to be most effective.

The Japanese man, who seems the dominant presence, in this discussion group, is perhaps a self-portrait of the artist, Shiba Kokan, who played a big part in promoting "Dutch learning" in Japan. His position near the European suggests his admiration for Western science.

The unidentified Dutchman displays a book of anatomy—one of the sciences in which the Japanese acknowledged Western superiority. The closeness of the Dutch and Japanese figures is emphasized, while the Chinese participant sits somewhat apart, listening critically.

How does this painting illustrate the global exchange of ideas in the eighteenth century? ●

Korea and Southeast Asia

In Korea and Vietnam, too, national revulsions from Confucianism and Chinese cultural dominance stimulated new thinking. In Korea, the movement called "practical learning" started as a reaction against Confucianism but acquired knowledge of Western technology by way of China. A design for a Western crane, copied from a Chinese book, helped to build a castle. Koreans began to model world maps on Western examples. In the mid–eighteenth century, Yi Ik began a systematic study of Western learning in Chinese books. In the 1780s, Korean intellectuals founded a society to introduce Catholicism into the country. In Vietnam, meanwhile, the most remarkable echo of new ideas from the West appeared in the work of the poet Ho Xuang Huong. "Down with husband-sharing!" she exclaimed when her husband took a second wife. "One [wife] rolls in warm blankets, the other freezes. . . . I've turned into a half-servant, an unpaid maid! Had I known, I would have stayed single."

Other Asian cultures were even less hospitable to Western thought. In Thailand, an exchange of embassies with France in the 1680s stimulated, at first, enormous interest in both countries. For the French, Thailand offered a model of the exotic. For the Thai, the French presented an insight into the Western technical proficiency already admired in China. Kosa Pan, the Thai envoy to France, took home a large collection of European maps, and the French mission to Thailand established an observatory in the royal palace. The king attended lectures by Jesuit astronomers. But Western influence in Thailand receded after a palace revolution there in 1688.

The Ottomans

Inhibited by Muslim religious scruples, the Turks and Persians, too, were slow to open up to the worldwide exchange of ideas. The first printing press in Turkey was only set up in 1729. When the authorities closed it down in 1742, it had produced

---

○ MAKING CONNECTIONS   ○

ENLIGHTENMENT INFLUENCES IN ASIA

COUNTRY/REGION →	EXAMPLES OF INFLUENTIAL IDEAS →	SOURCES →	SOCIAL/POLITICAL/ECONOMIC CONSEQUENCES
China	Western astronomy, mathematics, scientific methods, technology	Jesuit missionaries; European diplomats	Imperial leaders collect Western mechanical devices; use Western-designed artillery
Japan	Western astronomy, mathematics, scientific methods, technology; Japanese concepts of universal reason, scientific observation	Dutch diplomats, merchants; Japanese thinkers (Sorai, Nakamoto, Ekken)	Restrictions on trade and interaction limit exposure to Western ideas, technology; Japanese ideas spread more rapidly as reaction against Confucianism
Korea, Vietnam	Korea: "practical learning"	Korea: reaction against Confucianism and interest in Western technology, religious inspiration	Korea: development of new technology aids in construction, mapmaking; Catholicism introduced by intellectuals
	Vietnam: interest in women's rights	Vietnam: Ho Xuang Huong (writer)	Vietnam: critique of traditional marriage practices

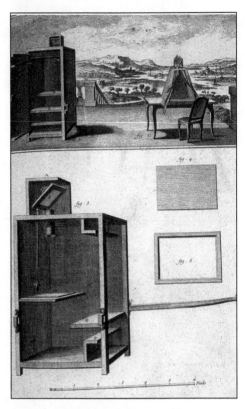

Camera obscura. Denis Diderot's *Encyclopedia* promoted technology and "useful" knowledge—in this case, the construction of a camera obscura, which was the forerunner of modern photography. The camera obscura captured an image by projecting rays of light from an object through a pinprick opening onto the inner wall of a chamber. Painters used this technique to ensure realism in their art.

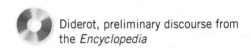

Diderot, preliminary discourse from the *Encyclopedia*

only 17 titles. In 1798, French armies invaded Egypt and Syria, leaving—after their early withdrawal—seeds of Western thinking. Here, as in India, aspects of Western thought were only enthusiastically embraced in the nineteenth century after unmistakable demonstrations of Western military strength (see Chapter 25).

THE ENLIGHTENMENT IN EUROPE

Even in Europe, new thinking met distrust, censorship, and persecution. To understand why—and to identify the defining themes of the thought of the time—the best source is the French *Encyclopedia*, subtitled *Reasoned Dictionary of the Sciences, Arts and Trades*, which appeared in 17 volumes of texts and 11 volumes of illustrations between 1751 and 1772. By 1779, about 25,000 sets had been sold throughout Europe, in the teeth of condemnation by reactionary governments and established churches. This may not seem many, but the ideas the *Encyclopedia* contained reached the entire European elite, one way or another, and circulated in countless spinoff works. Diderot, who masterminded the project, wanted a comprehensive work that would "start from and return to Man," while covering every intellectual discipline along the way. The *Encyclopedia*, he announced, would "assemble the knowledge scattered over the face of the Earth ... that we may not die without having deserved well of mankind."

Of course, the book had a slant. First, its values were practical. It emphasized utility, engineering, mechanics, technology. There was, according to Diderot, "more intelligence, wisdom, and consequence in a machine for making stockings" than "in a system of metaphysics." Second, the writers advocated reason and science as means to truth. Third, although the contributors by no means agreed among themselves on questions of political philosophy, the *Encyclopedia* was generally critical of Europe's monarchies and aristocracies. Drawing on the English thinker, John Locke (1632–1704), most contributors on political questions favored constitutional guarantees of the liberty of the citizen against the state. Many insisted on the "natural equality" of all men. Finally, the work was uniformly hostile to organized religion.

The Belief in Progress

Only optimists could have undertaken such an ambitious project. To make progress credible, someone had to think up a way to understand evil, and explain away the woes of the world. Theologians had never satisfactorily answered the atheists' challenge, "If God is good, why is there evil?" In the seventeenth century, the growth of atheism made the task seem urgent. In 1710, the German philosopher Leibniz (1646–1716) did so. He was the most wide-ranging thinker of his day, combining philosophy, theology, mathematics, linguistics, physics, and law with his role as a courtier in Hanover. He started from a truth witnessed in everyday experience: Good and evil are inseparable, because each is meaningless without the other. Freedom, for example, is good, but must include freedom to do evil. Altruism is good only if selfishness is an option. But of all logically conceivable worlds, ours has, by divine decree, the greatest possible surplus of good over evil. So—in the phrase Voltaire used to mock this theory—"All is for the best in the best of all possible worlds." Even then, believers in progress feared that it was merely a phase, enjoyed by their own times, but exceptional by the standards of history in general. The Marquis de Condorcet (see Chapter 21), for instance, thought he could see "the human race ... advancing with a sure step along the path of truth, virtue, and happiness" only because political and intellectual revolutions had subverted the crippling effects of religion and tyranny. The human spirit was now at last "emancipated from its shackles" and "released from the empire of fate."

New Economic Thought

If you believe in human goodness, you believe in freedom. Pessimists about human nature favor strong, even repressive governments to keep destructive instincts in check. Optimists hope to liberate people to do good. Montesquieu and the authors of the *Encyclopedia* were particularly concerned to recommend political freedom, but economic freedom was an equally important theme.

Free trade was a new doctrine. Long experience of an unfavorable trade balance with Asia had induced two obsessions in Western economic thought: Bullion—gold and silver—is the basis of wealth; and to grow rich, an economy must sell more than it buys. According to the Spanish moralist Tomás de Mercado, what "destroys this abundance and causes poverty is the export of money." All European governments believed this. To evade impoverishment they hoarded bullion, trapping cash inside the realm, limiting imports and exports, regulating prices, defying laws of supply and demand, and founding empires to create markets for their goods.

The consequences were woeful. Overseas investment was restricted, except in imperial ventures. The protection of trade nourished inefficiency and squandered resources. Competition for protected markets caused wars. Money drained out of circulation. These conditions, which inhibited economic growth, were much criticized from the late seventeenth century onward. The eighteenth-century French school of economists known as the physiocrats devised the slogan **laissez-faire** to mean "leave the market to itself." The British economist David Ricardo (see Chapter 21) agreed. "Wages," he recommended, "should be left to the fair and free competition of the market, and should never be controlled by the interference of the legislature." The decisive moment in the shift toward economic freedom came in 1776, when the Scots professor of moral philosophy, Adam Smith, published *The Wealth of Nations*.

Smith had a lofty view of the law of supply and demand, believing that it affected more than the market. "The natural effort of every individual to better his own condition" was the foundation of all political, economic, and moral systems. Self-interest could be left to serve the common good. "It is not from the benevolence of the butcher, the brewer or the baker that we expect our dinner, but from their regard to their own interest." The rich, Smith declared, "in spite of their natural selfishness and rapacity, are led by an invisible hand to make nearly the same distribution of the necessaries of life which would have been made, had the earth been divided into equal portions among all its inhabitants."

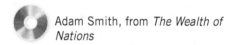
Adam Smith, from *The Wealth of Nations*

The Wealth of Nations appeared in the same year as the Declaration of Independence and should be counted among the United States' founding documents. It encouraged the American Revolution, for Smith said that government regulations limiting the freedom of colonies to engage in manufacture or trade were "a manifest violation of the most sacred rights of mankind." The United States has remained the homeland of economic liberalism ever since.

Social Equality

Smith claimed that freedom would deliver equality. This is not necessarily true, but it was characteristic of the time. Reason suggested that all men are naturally equal. So what about women? Montesquieu saw no reason to exclude them. The ideas we now call **feminism**—that women collectively constituted a class of society, historically oppressed and deserving emancipation—appeared in two works of 1792, the *Declaration of the Rights of Woman and of the Female Citizen* by Marie-Olympes de

Marie-Olympes de Gouges, *Declaration of the Rights of Woman and the Female Citizen*

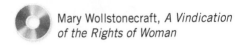

Mary Wollstonecraft, *A Vindication of the Rights of Woman*

Voltaire, "On Universal Toleration"

Gouges and *A Vindication of the Rights of Woman* by Mary Wollstonecraft. Both authors had to struggle to earn their living. Both died tragically. Wollstonecraft died in childbirth in 1797 at the age of 38. De Gouges was guillotined in 1793 during the French Revolution for defending the king and queen of France. Both writers rejected the previous tradition of female championship, which praised women for their domestic and maternal virtues. Instead, they admitted women's vices and blamed male oppression.

Anticlericalism

For most of the philosophers who worked on the *Encyclopedia*, the great obstacle to progress was the Church. They catalogued the crimes of the Church—inquisitions, persecutions, clerical abuses of power. The article on cannibalism referred to articles on the Eucharist, Communion, altar, and such. "We must show that we are better than Christians," wrote Diderot, "and that science makes more good men than grace." Voltaire erected his own temple to "the architect of the universe, the great geometrician" but regarded Christianity as an "infamous superstition to be eradicated—I do not say among the rabble, who are not worthy of being enlightened and who are apt for every yoke, but among the civilized and those who wish to think." Many people in France ceased to mention God and the saints in their wills. Donations to religious foundations dwindled. King Louis XV (r. 1715–1774) abandoned the traditional rites of laying supposedly healing royal hands on the sick, because he found belief in miracles embarrassing.

We can measure the progress of the Enlightenment in anticlerical acts. In 1759, Portugal expelled the Jesuits and confiscated their property. In 1762, Catherine the Great of Russia secularized a great portfolio of church property. Between 1764 and 1773, the Jesuit Order was abolished in most of the rest of the West. In the 1780s, governments in parts of Europe confiscated church lands and forced 38,000 monks and nuns into lay life. In 1790, the King of Prussia proclaimed absolute authority over clergy in his realm, both Protestant and Catholic. Meanwhile, among the European elite, the cult of reason was taking on the characteristics of an alternative religion. In the secret ceremonies of freemasonry, a profane hierarchy celebrated

"The cult of reason was taking on the characteristics of an alternative religion." For Catholicism, reason is a gift of God and can enlighten faith, but eighteenth-century critics in France denounced the Church for smothering reason and encouraging superstition. They also hated the Church for wasting—as they thought—economic resources and supporting an oppressive political order. Many of them advocated deism—belief in God, without the supposed irrational doctrines of Christianity. In 1794, this "cult of the Supreme Being" briefly replaced Catholicism as the official religion of France, in a gaudy ceremony presided over by the head of a group of fanatics who had seized power during the Revolution.
Pierre-Antoine Demachy, Festival of the Supreme Being at the Champ de Mars on June 8, 1794. *Musée de la Ville de Paris, Musée Carnavalet, Paris, France. Bridgeman-Giraudon/Art. Resource, NY*

the purity of its own wisdom, brilliantly portrayed in Mozart's opera *The Magic Flute*, first performed in 1791. In 1794, the French revolutionary government tried to replace Christianity with the cult of the Supreme Being.

To some extent, the success of science encouraged mistrust of religion. From John Locke, eighteenth-century radicals inherited the conviction that it was "fiddling" to waste time thinking about what, if anything, lay beyond the scientifically observed world. The evidence of our senses was all true and—with certain exceptions about sound and color that experiments could confirm—it was all caused by the real objects our senses seemed to disclose to us: The jangling is proof of the bell, the heat of the fire, the stink of the gas. "Freethinking" atheism got a boost from the microbial world, with its apparent evidence of spontaneous generation. The very existence of God—or at least, the validity of claims about God's unique power to create life—was at stake.

John Locke, *Essay Concerning Human Understanding*, 1689

THE CRISIS OF THE ENLIGHTENMENT: RELIGION AND ROMANTICISM

This attitude, however, which we would now call *scientism*, did not satisfy all its practitioners. The Scottish philosopher David Hume (1711–1776) pointed out that sensations are not really evidence of anything except themselves—that objects cause them is just an unverifiable assumption. Many scientists, like Maupertuis, drifted back from atheism toward religion or speculated about truths beyond the reach of science. In 1799, with the aid of a powerful microscope, Lorenzo Spallanzani observed fission—cells reproducing by splitting. He demonstrated that if heating killed bacteria they could not reappear in a sealed environment. He concluded that living organisms did not appear from nowhere. They could only germinate in an environment where they were already present. No known case of spontaneous generation of life was left in the world.

Religious Revival

The churches, moreover, knew how to defeat unbelievers. Censorship did not work. But appeals, over the intellectuals' heads, to ordinary people did. Despite the hostility of the Enlightenment, the eighteenth century was a time of religious revival in the West. Christianity reached a new public. In 1722, Nicolas Ludwig, Count Zinzendorff built the village of Herrnhut (meaning "the Lord's keeping") on his estate in Germany to be a refuge for persecuted Christians. It became a center from which evangelical fervor—or "enthusiasm," as they called it—radiated over the world. Zinzendorff's was only one of innumerable movements to offer ordinary people an affective, unintellectual solution to the problems of life: proof that, in their way, feelings are stronger than reason, and that religion—for most people—is more satisfying than science. As one of the great Christian revivalists, Jonathan Edwards (1703–1758) of Massachusetts, said, "Our people do not so much need to have their heads stored, as to have their hearts touched." His meetings, characteristically, were occasions for congregations to purge their emotions in ways intellectuals found repellent. "There was a great moaning and crying through the whole house," observed a witness to one of Edwards's sermons, "the shrieks and cries were piercing and amazing."

Preaching was the information technology of these movements. Between 1740 and his death in 1758, George Whitfield (or Whitefield—he spelled it both ways) was always on the move, all over Britain and across the American colonies.

Addressing a congregation composed of almost the entire population of Boston, he made the town seem "the gate of heaven. Many wept enthusiastically and cried out under the Word." In 1738, with a "heart strangely warmed," John Wesley (1703–1791) began a mission to the workers of England and Wales, traveling 8,000 miles a year and preaching to thousands at a time. He communicated a mood rather than a message—a sense of how Jesus can change lives by imparting feelings of love. Catholic evangelism was equally stirring and targeted the same enemies—materialism, rationalism, apathy, and formalized religion. One observer compared Alfonso Maria Liguori's (1696–1787) mission among the poor in Naples to the preaching of a biblical prophet. In 1765, the pope authorized devotion to the Sacred Heart of Jesus—a bleeding symbol of divine love.

Music contributed to the mood. In the eighteenth century, God seemed to have all the best tunes—from the hymns that Wesley's brother, Charles, wrote to the stirring settings of Christ's passion by Johann Sebastian Bach (1685–1750). In 1741, George Friedrich Handel wrote *Messiah*, telling the life of Jesus in music so sublime that when the first London performance approached its climax, King George II rose to his feet and heard the "Hallelujah Chorus" standing. The scriptures Handel set made an effective reply to skeptics: "I know that my Redeemer liveth, and though worms destroy this body, yet in my flesh shall I see God." Mozart's music, too, ultimately served the Church better than the Masonic movement. He died in 1791 while writing his great *Requiem Mass*—his own triumph over death.

Cynically, some European monarchs used religious revival to distract people from politics and strengthened churches as institutions of social control. Frederick the Great of Prussia (r. 1740–1786) was a freethinker who liked the company of philosophers at dinner. He employed, for a while, both Maupertuis and Voltaire. But he favored religion for his people and his troops, founding military chaplaincies and requiring religious teaching in schools. He was applying a principle Voltaire uttered: "If God did not exist, it would be necessary to invent him."

The Cult of Nature and Romanticism

The cult of nature was something Christians and their enemies could agree on. Nature seemed both more beautiful and more terrible than any construction of the human intellect. In 1755, an earthquake centered at Lisbon, Portugal, shook even Voltaire's faith in progress. One of Europe's greatest cities, home to nearly 200,000 people, was reduced to ruins. It was the worst natural disaster on record in European history. As an alternative to the return to God, radical philosophers responded to the call, "Return to Nature," which one contributor to the *Encyclopedia*, Baron d'Holbach, uttered in 1770: "She will console you, drive out from your heart the fears that hobble you … the hatreds that separate you from Man, whom you ought to love." "Sensibility" became a buzzword for responsiveness to the power of feelings, which were valued even more than reason. Romantic values included imagination, intuition, emotion, inspiration, and even passion, alongside—or in extreme cases, ahead of—reason and scientific knowledge as guides to truth and conduct. Romantics professed to prefer nature to human works, or, at least, wanted art to demonstrate sympathy with nature.

Exploration in the eighteenth century was constantly revealing new marvels of nature. The influence of American landscapes on romantic minds began with the drawings that two young Spaniards, Jorge Juan and Antonio de Ulloa, made during a scientific expedition to the equator. In work published in 1752, they combined scientific diagrams with images of awestruck reverence for untamed nature. Their

Goethe, *Prometheus*, 1773

drawing, for instance, of the volcanic Mount Cotopaxi erupting in Ecuador, with, in the background, arcs of light in the sky, combines precision with rugged romance. The Andean settings they recorded remained the source of the most powerful romantic images of America. Cotopaxi became a favorite subject of American landscape painters.

The merging of science and romance is apparent in the work of one of the greatest scientists of the age, Baron Alexander von Humboldt (1769–1859). In the 1790s, he began a series of journeys of scientific exploration in America: "to see Nature in all her variety of grandeur and splendour." The high point of his endeavors came in 1802, when he tried to climb Mount Chimborazo—Cotopaxi's twin peak. Chimborazo was thought to be the highest mountain in the world—the untouched summit of creation. Sickened by altitude, racked by cold, bleeding from nose and lips, Humboldt had almost reached the top when he was forced to turn back. His story of suffering and frustration was just the sort of subject romantic writers were beginning to celebrate in Europe. The cult of the unattainable—an unfulfillable yearning—lay at the heart of romanticism.

Romantics also valued the supposedly natural feelings of uneducated people. Their poetry, said the English poet William Wordsworth (1770–1850), was "the language of ordinary men." The music of romanticism ransacked traditional songs for melodies. Its theater and opera borrowed from the antics of street performers. Its prophet was Johann Gottfried Herder (1744–1803), who praised the moral power of the "true poetry" of "those whom we call savages." Its philosopher was Jean-Jacques Rousseau (1712–1778), who taught the superiority of natural passions over cultivated refinement. Its portrait paintings showed society ladies in peasant dress in gardens landscaped to look natural, reinvaded by romance. "The people" had arrived in European history as a creative force.

Cult of the unattainable. Alexander von Humboldt stoops to pluck a botanical specimen near the foot of Mount Chimborazo. His account of his climb to the top of Chimborazo is a poignant litany of the cult of the unattainable so characteristic of romanticism.

von Humboldt, from *Personal Narrative of a Journey to the Equinoctal Regions of the New Continent, 1773*

Rousseau and the General Will

Of the thinkers who broke with the outlook of the *Encyclopedia*, Rousseau was the most influential. He was a restless supertramp with a taste for low life. He changed his formal religious allegiance twice without once appearing sincere. He betrayed all his mistresses, quarreled with all his friends, and abandoned all his children. Addiction to his own sensibilities became the guideline of his life. In 1750, in the prize-winning essay that made his name, he repudiated one of the most sacred principles of the Enlightenment—"that the Arts and Sciences have benefited Mankind." The fact that the topic could be proposed at all shows how far disillusionment with enlightened optimism had gone. Rousseau's assertion of the natural goodness of humankind in its primitive state made Voltaire want "to walk on all fours," like an animal.

Nonetheless, Rousseau's political thinking helped shape the politics of his day and has remained influential. Rousseau regarded the state as a sort of organism, in which the individual identities of the citizens are submerged. At a previous, unknown stage of history, the act occurred "by which people become a people, ... the real foundation of society." "The people becomes one single being.... Each of us puts his person and all his power in common under the supreme direction of the general will." Citizenship is fraternity— equivalent to the blood bond between brothers. The commands of the general will are perfect freedom—social or civil freedom, Rousseau called it—and anyone constrained to obey them is simply being "forced to be free." "Whoever refuses to obey the general will shall be compelled to do so by the whole body."

Rousseau was vague about the moral justification for this dangerous doctrine. The German philosopher Immanuel Kant (1724–1804) provided one. By setting aside one's individual will or interests and exercising reason instead, one can identify goals of a merit everyone can see. Submission to the general will limits one's own freedom in deference to the freedom of others. In practice, however, the general will just meant the tyranny of the majority. Rousseau admitted that "the votes of the greatest number always bind the rest." In Rousseau's utopia, political parties are outlawed because "there should be no partial society within the state." The same logic would forbid trade unions, religious communions, and reformist movements. Yet the passion with which Rousseau invoked freedom made it hard for many of his readers to see how illiberal his thought was. Revolutionaries adopted the opening words of his essay of 1762: "Man is born free and everywhere he is in chains!"

Pacific Discoveries

Underlying the elevation of the common man and woman to be fit for participation in government were influences from surprising directions: the Pacific and the Americas. The Pacific in the eighteenth century stretched between myths: an unknown continent called *Terra Australis*, supposedly awaiting discovery in the south, and the rumored sea passage around America in the northwest. Investigation of those myths became the objective of the English navigator Captain James Cook (see Chapter 19). In 1769, he was ordered to Tahiti in the South Pacific to observe the transit of the planet Venus and returned with a burning vocation to sail "as far as I think it possible for man to go."

from *Captain Cook's Journal During His First Voyage Round the World*

In three voyages of Pacific exploration, he charted New Zealand, the west coast of Alaska, and the east coast of Australia. He also filled in most of the Pacific's remaining gaps on the map. He brought a new precision to mapmaking, using the latest technology for finding longitude—the exquisitely accurate chronometer the English inventor John Harrison (1693–1776) had developed. He exploded the myth of Terra Australis, or at least pushed its possible location into latitudes "doomed to lie forever buried under everlasting snow and ice." His ships brought back sketches and specimens of plants and beasts unknown in Europe.

Cook was the spearhead of a scientific invasion of the Pacific by expeditions from Britain, Spain, France, Russia, and the new United States. Another "new world" became available for Western imperialism to exploit, and another treasury of natural resources was open to enrich Western economies. For intellectual history, the most important discoveries Western explorers made in the Pacific were of its peoples.

Observers dismissed some of them as intellectually insignificant. William Dampier, who published the first description of the aborigines of Australia in 1697, found them "nasty" and repellent. Early painters of the aborigines commonly depicted them crawling on the earth or scampering in the trees like monkeys.

From other parts of the Pacific, however, explorers brought home specimens of manhood, whom admirers instantly classed as **noble savages**—"proof" that to be morally admirable you did not need to be white, Western, Christian, or educated in ways that Europeans recognized as "civilized." In 1774, English society lionized

Omai, who had been a restless misfit in his native Polynesia. Lee Boo, from Micronesia, was another "prince of nature." Visitors to the Pacific found a sensual paradise. Romantic primitivism became inseparable from sexual opportunity. Images of Tahiti as the ravishing home of nymphs filled Westerners' imaginations. Diderot focused on sex to highlight the mutual incomprehension of a Tahitian girl and a French chaplain: "Honest stranger, do not refuse me. Make me a mother."

Wild Children

The disappointments of previous centuries had not put to rest the quest for "natural" man. On the contrary, interest in the origins of language and of political and social life, and the moral effects of civilization was acute, and scholars were anxious to examine specimens of primitive humanity untouched by civilized society. "Wolf children" seemed to supply the raw material for analysis. Carolus Linnaeus (1707–1778)—the Swedish botanist who devised the modern method of classifying species—thought that wild children were a separate species of human beings. Plucked from the woods, wrenched from the wolves and foxes that suckled them, they became experiments in efforts to teach them language and manners.

But all the experiments to "civilize" these children failed. Boys, whom bears supposedly raised in Poland, continued to prefer the company of bears. "Peter the Wild Boy" whom rival members of the English royal family struggled to possess as a pet in the 1720s, hated clothes and beds and never learned to talk. The "savage girl" kidnapped from the woods in France in 1731 preferred raw frogs to food from the kitchen, and for a long time, she imitated birdsong better than she spoke French. The most famous case was the "Wild Boy of Aveyron." Abandoned in infancy in the forests of southwest France, he survived by his own wits for years until he was kidnapped for civilization in 1798. He learned to wear clothes and to dine elegantly, but never to speak or to like what had happened to him.

The Huron as Noble Savage

The most influential source of ideas about the nobility of savagery were the Native American Huron of the Great Lakes (see Chapter 19). Secular philosophers filtered cautionary tales out of missionary accounts of the Hurons' way of life until only an idealized Huron remained. This became easier as real Hurons literally disappeared—virtually destroyed by the diseases to which European contagion exposed them.

The great secularizer of legends about the Huron was Louis-Armand de Lom de l'Arce, who called himself by the title his family had sold for cash, Sieur de Lahontan. Lahontan left France for Canada in the 1680s and set himself up as an expert on its curiosities. The mouthpiece for his freethinking anticlericalism was an invented Huron called Adario, with whom Lahontan discussed the imperfections of the Bible, republicanism, and free love.

The intoxicating potential of the Huron myth was distilled in a comedy, performed in Paris in 1768, in which a Huron excels in all the virtues of noble savagery as huntsman, lover, and warrior. When urged to adopt French dress, he

Omai—the restless young Tahitian who sailed to England with Captain Cook in the 1770s—became the darling of London society. He is shown here painted by Sir Joshua Reynolds, the most fashionable portrait painter of the day, in heroic fashion, in misplaced oriental attire, and bare feet, against a majestic backdrop. In Western eyes, Omai embodied the idea that the untutored, "natural" man could be effortlessly noble.

 Huron women, from the *History of Canada*, 1664

The Enlightenment

r. 1661–1722	Kangxi, Chinese emperor, tutored by Jesuit scholars
1680s	Louis-Armand de Lom de l'Arce leaves France for Canada
1685–1750	Johann Sebastian Bach, composer
1689–1755	Baron de Montesquieu, author of *The Spirit of the Laws* and *Persian Letters*
1694–1778	François Marie Arouet (Voltaire), leading philosopher and admirer of China
1703–1791	John Wesley, founder of Methodism
1712–1778	Jean-Jacques Rousseau, author of the *Social Contract*
1713–1784	Denis Diderot, publisher of the *Encyclopedia*
1720	Chinese translations of Western books allowed to circulate in Japan
1736	Maupertuis's expedition to the Arctic Circle
1740–1758	Preaching career of George Whitfield, emotional preacher
1771	Japanese "Dutch studies" group begins study of Western books

The Declaration of the Rights of Man and Citizen

denounces imitation as fashion "among monkeys but not among men." "If he lacks enlightenment by great minds," comments an observer, "he has abundant sentiments, which I esteem more highly. And I fear that in becoming civilized he will be the poorer." Unhappy in love, the Huron urges the mob to breach the prison fortress of Paris, the Bastille, to rescue his imprisoned lover. He is therefore arrested for sedition.

THE FRENCH REVOLUTION AND NAPOLEON

Believers in the nobility of the savage found it easy to believe in the wisdom of the common man. The Bastille was a symbol of oppression. Seized copies of the *Encyclopedia* were kept there. Voltaire had been briefly and comfortably imprisoned there. Urban myth insisted that hundreds of prisoners of conscience suffered there. In fact, like most organs of the French state, it was rickety, and like the government's treasury, virtually empty. Rebels who broke into it in search of arms on July 14, 1789, found only a handful of inmates.

Background to the Revolution

Historians have looked deep into the pre-Revolutionary old regime in France for explanations of the causes for the revolution that broke out on that day. Yet like most political upheavals, the French Revolution arose suddenly in the particular circumstances of the time and unrolled rapidly in ways previously unforeseeable. The costs of French participation in the American Revolutionary War, which ended in 1783 and added to the state's debts, left the monarchy desperate to increase taxes. By summoning the Estates General, the medieval assembly of the realm, for the first time since 1614 to meet the crisis, royal ministers took a risk. Many deputies arrived resentful, having sat on consultative bodies whose advice the government had dismissed. Most belonged to the literate minority the Enlightenment had affected. They had strong inclinations toward constitutionalism in politics and anticlericalism in religion. All had read the gutter press of the day: scandal sheets about alleged sexual and financial shenanigans at court.

Local assemblies elected the deputies. "Public opinion," King Louis XVI (r. 1774–1792) wrote in one of his schoolbooks, "is never wrong." The regulations for electing the assembly emphasized that "His Majesty wishes that everyone, from the extremities of his realm and from the most remote dwelling places, may be assured that his desires and claims will reach him." As a result, the deputies arrived with "books of grievances," full of the complaints of peasants hungry after bad harvests, venting their rage on big landowners. Most of them demanded lower taxes and relief from traditional obligations of peasants and the traditional privileges of lords—to hunt game, evade taxes, hold markets, mobilize forced labor. In June, the Estates General gave itself the title of National Assembly with the right to "interpret the General Will of the nation." In August, it enacted the Declaration of the Rights of Man and Citizen. "Men are born free and remain equal in rights," this document proclaimed. Sovereignty, said the Declaration, rested not with the king but with the whole people. As in all revolutions, radicals exploited the mood in favor of change to agitate for more change than most people wanted.

Revolutionary Radicalism

In 1790, the revolutionaries enacted a "civil constitution of the clergy" that turned priests into public servants and nationalized church property. The pope rejected it. So did the king, who had never supported radical reform. Once his opposition became known, the king became a virtual prisoner of the assembly. Opponents of the Revolution fled. Foreign powers feared the Revolution might be exported. In March 1792, war broke out, and Austria and Prussia invaded France.

In wartime, anything can happen, and only harsh measures can give governments control over events. In August 1792, the monarchy was overthrown. In 1793, the royal family was executed. Aristocrats, priests, and officials were massacred in urban riots and peasant rebellions. Ruthless revolutionary factions seized power over what remained of the state, while committees of militants and self-appointed "people's tribunals" imposed revolutionary terror. In the bloodiest spell, during June and July 1794, 1,584 heads were chopped off in Paris, and thousands of peasants and workers were killed in the provinces. "It was not," admitted a member of the government, "a question of principles. It was about killing."

So many crimes committed in the name of liberty destroyed the idealism that had launched the Revolution. Take the example of a leading revolutionary propagandist, the Marquis de Sade (1740–1814), who called himself Citizen Sade after the revolutionaries liberated him in 1789 from the Bastille, where his family had begged the government to confine him. His private correspondence exposes his revolutionary enthusiasm as a sham. In contrast to the enlightened idealism he claimed to profess, he had a record of depravity unsurpassed among eighteenth-century sexual athletes. He gave his name—*sadism*—to morbid forms of sexual cruelty. He ejaculated over a crucifix; tortured, imprisoned, and poisoned prostitutes; and—so he claimed—"proved that God does not exist" by inserting consecrated communion wafers in the rectums of people with whom he was going to have anal intercourse. His sexual antics were a distortion of liberty, his egotism a warped version of individualism, his violence a caricature of revolutionary injustice. As if in parody of Rousseau, de Sade thought no instincts could be immoral because all are natural. And as if in parody of Pierre Laplace's elimination of God from science (see Chapter 20), he thought no passions should be condemned because all are governed by chemical forces in the body. In his brief career as a revolutionary spokesman—he ended his days in an insane asylum—he tried to combine extreme individualism with the social solidarity the Revolution demanded.

Napoleon

When revolutions unleash chaos, people often turn to a "strong man." In 1799, a military coup made France's best general a dictator. Napoleon Bonaparte (1769–1821) called himself First Consul of the Republic, then, from 1804, after more victories, Emperor of the French. His military genius and the strength of his armies turned Europe into a playground for his political experiments. French power extended at its height from Spain, and Portugal to Poland and Croatia.

The Fall of the Bastille by the French artist Jean-Pierre Houel (1735–1813). Houel's paintings contributed to the myth that the Bastille, a medieval fortress in the heart of Paris, was a terrifying, cruel, and secretive prison, in which a repressive monarchy tortured its many victims. But when a citizen army captured the castle on July 14, 1789, they found only a small, demoralized garrison and a handful of privileged inmates lodged in comfortable cells, not chained in dungeons. This did not stop Houel from romanticizing the event. Each time he painted a different version of the fall of the Bastille, he enlarged the crowds, increased the flames, and exaggerated the scale of the struggle.

French armies carried revolutionary ideas into Russia, Egypt, and Syria (see Map 22.2). The wars were the nearest thing to world war that the world had yet seen, igniting conflicts in India, where the British seized the opportunity to extend their conquests, and in the Americas, where British armies attacked Buenos Aires in Argentina and burned the White House in Washington. Colonies changed hands in the Caribbean, North America, the Indian Ocean, and South Africa. Haiti achieved independence (see Chapter 21).

Napoleon—until his final defeat in 1815—was one of the most inventive rationalizers of states. He imposed a uniform law code on his conquests, which still forms the basis of the laws of much of Europe, Latin America, and Africa. He abolished ancient states, created new ones, and imposed constitutional government where it had never existed before. He subordinated the Church and created new

MAP 22.2

Napoleon's Empire, ca. 1799–1815

- Territories under direct French control
- other states ruled by Napoleon or members of his family
- other dependent states

elites. He cultivated a romantic image of himself as a meteor that changed the fate of a continent. To the poor, he fulfilled the French Revolution. To the rich, he tamed it. In some ways, he ruled a barbarian empire, descended as much from that of Charlemagne as from Rome. Sometimes he had himself painted as a Roman emperor. Sometimes he was depicted among ancient Germanic gods. Historians have detected opportunism and lack of any general principles in his behavior. A police state operated wherever he ruled.

To the disappointment of idealists who advocated "liberty, equality, and fraternity," the French Revolution had failed to change the world. The wars the Revolution started were the real anvil of change, and Napoleon was their smith and hammer. Henceforth, no form of political legitimacy would be beyond challenge.

The French Revolution

1783	End of the American Revolutionary War
1789	Convening of the Estates General
June 1789	Estates General becomes the National Assembly
July 14, 1789	Storming of the Bastille
March 1792	Invasion of France by Austria and Prussia
January 1793	Louis XVI executed
1799	Napoleon overthrows Directorate

IN PERSPECTIVE: The Afterglow of Enlightenment

The French Revolution opened with noble cries—for the rights of man and the sovereignty of the people. It ended with the sickening scream that forms the last line of the "Marseillaise," calling for troughs full of the "impure" blood of aristocrats, traitors, and foreigners.

In Britain, the statesman and philosopher Edmund Burke was so appalled by the Revolution's excesses that he reached for the comforts of conservatism. In Spain, in the black paintings of Goya, and in Germany, in the private darkness of Beethoven's late music, we can sense another response: retreat into hag-ridden disillusionment. In the *Critique of Pure Reason* of 1781, Kant proposed a rickety, human-scale world of "crooked timber" in place of the grand ruined structures of the Age of Reason.

The Enlightenment was streaked with shadows. In Paris in 1798, Etienne Robert Gaspard displayed a light show in which monstrous shapes loomed at the audience from a screen or flickered eerily across clouds of smoke. In other demonstrations of the wonders of electricity, the real-life forerunners of Frankenstein made corpses twitch to thrill an audience. It was not the sleep of reason that produced these monsters. They were creations of its most watchful hours—the hideous issue of scientific experimentation, the brutal images of minds tortured by revulsion at revolutionary crimes.

The Enlightenment survived in America. The United States' Constitution of 1787 embodied some of the dearest political principles of Montesquieu and the authors of the *Encyclopedia*, substituting the sovereign people for a sovereign government, switching powers from the executive to the legislature, creating constitutional guarantees of freedom, outlawing any "establishment of religion," and expressing confidence in the people's fitness to decide their own fate. Assumptions about human equality—though they did not extend to black people, Native Americans, or women—typified American society. No formal aristocracy was acknowledged. Servants treated employers with a familiarity that shocked Europeans. Money became a more powerful indicator of social distinction than birth. To the surprise of much of the world—and of some Americans—the United States avoided becoming a military dictatorship, unlike so many other supposedly republican and egalitarian revolutions.

Even in Europe, the idea of progress survived. In the nineteenth century, it strengthened on the "march of improvement"—the history

Immanuel Kant defines the Enlightenment

An image of war. Francisco Goya's art began to desert the conventional subjects demanded by his early patrons in the 1790s. Under the dark and bloody impact of the French Revolution, he produced scenes of witchcraft and torture. It was the Spanish War of Independence against Napoleon in 1808–1814, however, that released from his imagination colossal monsters like this: an image of war wading through the land and overshadowing the wreckage of lives.

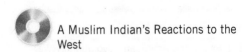
A Muslim Indian's Reactions to the West

of industrialization, the multiplication of wealth, the victories of constitutionalism against tyranny. It became possible to believe that progress was irreversible. Evolution programmed it into nature. It took the horrors of the twentieth century—a catalogue of famines, failures, inhumanities, and genocide—to make people question whether progress was inevitable or even real.

Europeans and the inhabitants of European colonies in the Americas felt growing confidence as a result of their sense that their societies were making scientific and technical progress. Rivals in Asia seemed stagnant by comparison. Western visitors to Turkey in the 1790s felt that the Ottomans had slipped into inferiority through neglect of science, "too stupid to comprehend," an English observer averred, "or too proud to learn." Even China seemed to have sacrificed former advantages. A Dutch envoy in 1794 declared that despite their sometime superiority, the Chinese remained in their " primitive state, without their even seeking, like the Europeans, to make further progress, or to bring their discoveries to perfection. . . . We have consequently so far surpassed them." The former greatness of Asia—it was alleged—had shifted to Europe.

Yet the Enlightenment rippled over the world. Rammohan Roy was not alone in trying to appropriate the scientific learning of the Enlightenment for Indians' use. Indians joined the scientific societies that the British founded in India and founded others of their own. Bal Shastri Jambedkar, a professor of mathematics who collaborated closely with English scientists in Calcutta in the 1830s, published his work in Indian languages and translated useful texts. In the same period, the work of surveying India began increasingly to rely on Indian, not British, experts. Where Western scientific impact led, the influence of Western political, economic, and philosophical thinking followed.

India had privileged access to Western ideas because of the vast number of Westerners whom British imperialism introduced to that country. Other European empires had similar effects in areas they colonized. And, increasingly in the nineteenth century, missionaries and technicians carried the effects of Western intellectual movements beyond the reach of imperialism. Jesuits were instrumental in China. Dutch merchants and ambassadors penetrated Japan. Books communicated Western ideas to parts of the world Westerners in person could hardly hope to remold. The consequences are apparent in most of the rest of this book. Up to this point in our story, the exchanges of culture we have chronicled have been mutually influential or have tended to be dominated by influences exerted on Europe from outside. From this point onward, global history becomes increasingly a story of Western influence.

CHRONOLOGY

r. 1661–1722	Kangxi, Chinese emperor, tutored by Jesuit scholars
1680s	Louis-Armand de Lom de l'Arce leaves France for Canada
1685–1750	Johann Sebastian Bach, composer
1689–1755	Baron de Montesquieu, author of *The Spirit of the Laws* and *Persian Letters*
1694–1778	François Marie Arouet (Voltaire), leading philosopher and admirer of China
1703–1758	Jonathan Edwards, New England preacher
1703–1791	John Wesley, founder of Methodism
1712–1778	Jean-Jacques Rousseau, author of the *Social Contract*
1713–1784	Denis Diderot, publisher of the *Encyclopedia*
1720	Chinese translations of Western books allowed to circulate in Japan
1736	Maupertuis's expedition to the Arctic Circle
1740–1758	George Whitfield, emotional preacher
1771	Japanese "Dutch studies" group begins study of Western books
1752	Publication of Maupertuis's *Letters on the Progress of Science*
1776	Publication of Adam Smith's *The Wealth of Nations;* United States Declaration of Independence
1783	End of the American Revolutionary War
1789	Convening of the Estates General; Estates General becomes the National Assembly
Late 1700s and early 1800s	Romantic movement
July 14, 1789	Storming of the Bastille
1792	Invasion of France by Austria and Prussia; publication of Mary Wollstonecraft's *A Vindication of the Rights of Woman*
1793	Louis XVI executed
1799	Napoleon comes to power in a military coup
1804	Napoleon crowns himself Emperor of the French
1815	Napoleon's final defeat

PROBLEMS AND PARALLELS

1. How was the Enlightenment global in its inspiration, as well as in its effects? How did ideas from overseas, particularly from China, influence the Enlightenment? How did Asian cultures influence writers like Voltaire, Diderot, and Montesquieu?

2. What role did religion play in the development of the Enlightenment? How was preaching the "information technology" of religious revivals in the West?

3. How did Diderot's *Encyclopedia* serve as a vehicle for advancing Enlightenment thinking in eighteenth-century Europe?

Why was Romanticism often seen as antithetical to the Enlightenment?

4. How did influences from the Pacific and the Americas shape the elevation of the "common man"? What does the term *noble savages* mean?

5. Did Napoleon fulfill the Enlightenment or undermine its ideals?

DOCUMENTS IN GLOBAL HISTORY

- Baron de Montesquieu, from *The Spirit of the Laws*
- Lady Mary Wortley Montagu on the Ottoman Empire, 1717
- title page from a Japanese anatomy text, 1775
- Diderot, preliminary discourse from the *Encyclopedia*
- Adam Smith, from *The Wealth of Nations*
- Marie-Olympes de Gouges, *Declaration of the Rights of Woman and the Female Citizen*
- Mary Wollstonecraft, *A Vindication of the Rights of Woman*
- John Locke, *Essay Concerning Human Understanding*, 1689

- Goethe, *Prometheus*, 1773
- von Humboldt, from *Personal Narrative of a Journey to the Equinoctal Regions of the New Continent*, 1773
- From *Captain Cook's Journal During His First Voyage Round the World*
- Huron women, from the *History of Canada*, 1664
- The Declaration of the Rights of Man and Citizen
- Immanuel Kant defines the Enlightenment
- A Muslim Indian's Reactions to the West

Please see the Primary Source DVD for additional sources related to this chapter.

READ ON

S. Cromwell, Crawford *Raja Rammohun Roy and Progressive Movements in India: A Selection from Records, 1775–1845* (1983) is useful. Maupertuis is best approached through his own writings, but there are useful studies by D. Beeson, *Maupertuis* (1992), and M. Terrall, *The Man Who Flattened the Earth* (2002).

On the Enlightenment in general, P. Gay, *The Enlightenment* (1995), is a classic that is still stimulating. J. Israel, *Radical Enlightenment: Philosophy and the Making of Modernity* (2001) is a superb study that emphasizes the Dutch contribution. O. Gunn, *First Globalization* (2003) is a useful introduction to the global context.

A. Çirakman, *From the "Terror of the World" to the "Sick Man of Europe"* (2002) traces changes in the image of the Ottomans in the West. Li Yan and Du Shiran, *Chinese Mathematics: A Concise History* (1987) is fundamental. J. Waley-Cohen, *The Sextants of Beiking* (1999) is a broad survey of Chinese science, with special attention to interchange with the West. F. Wakeman, *The Great Enterprise* (1986) is a good introduction to China in the period.

For the context of Dutch studies, L. Blussé et al., *Bridging the Divide* (2001) is enthralling. J. B. Bury, *The Idea of Progress* (1982) is an unsurpassed classic.

T. Ellingson, *The Myth of the Noble Savage* (2001) is an important revisionist work. M. Newton, *Savage Girls and Wild Boys: A History of Feral Children* (2003) is a fascinating overview of its subject. A. Pagden, *European Encounters with the New World from Renaissance to Romanticism* (1994) is indispensable.

C. L. Johnson, ed., *The Cambridge Companion to Mary Wollstonecraft* (2002) is a mine of information and a valuable guide to work on early feminism.

J. C. Beaglehole's classic *The Life of Captain James Cook* (1992) is still the best biography.

S. Schama, *Citizens* (1991) tells the story of the French Revolution with vision and verve. C. Jones, *The Great Nation* (2003) is excellent on the background of eighteenth-century France. There are so many books about Napoleon: P. Geyl, *Napoleon: For and Against* (1967) is a magisterial survey of the literature.

PART Nine

The Frustrations of Progress to ca. 1900

CHAPTER 23 Replacing Muscle: The Energy Revolutions 588

CHAPTER 24 The Social Mold: Work and Society in the Nineteenth Century 614

CHAPTER 25 Western Dominance in the Nineteenth Century: The Westward Shift of Power and the Rise of Global Empires 638

CHAPTER 26 The Changing State: Political Developments in the Nineteenth Century 664

Ottoman world map. In 1803, the Turkish ▸ Military Engineering School published this world map—the first Ottoman map based on Mercator's projection—in an atlas using European geographical knowledge and map-making techniques.

ENVIRONMENT

since 1800
Global population boom

since ca. 1800
Coal and steam power

CULTURE

1800–1880
Decline of slavery

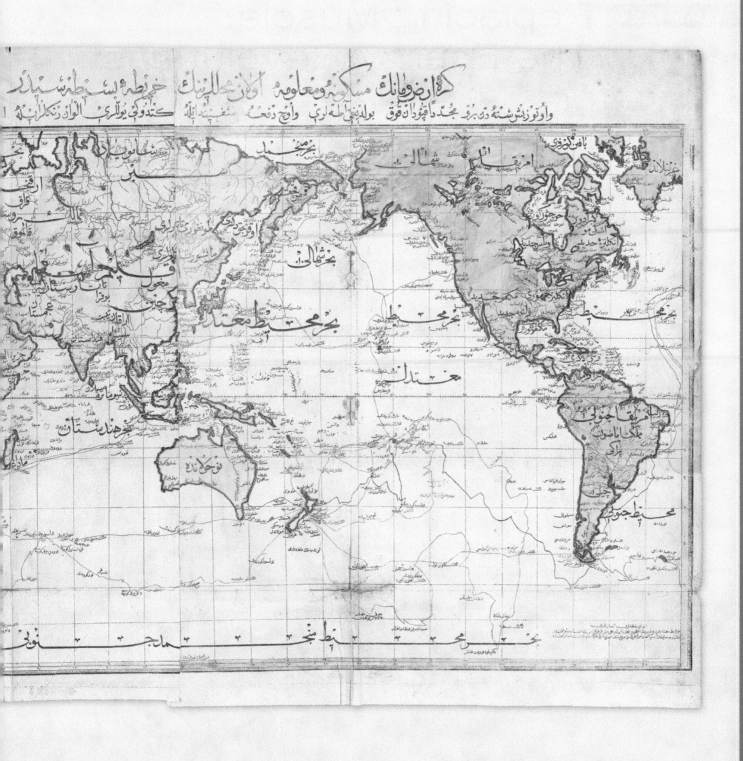

since 1850
Industrialization of food production

ca. 1850
Electricity

1870–1900
Famine and drought worldwide

1840s–1860s
Opium Wars, China

1860s–1910
Mass migrations

1870–1871
Franco-Prussian War

1885
Berlin Conference–Partition of Africa

CHAPTER 23
Replacing Muscle: The Energy Revolutions

Ambroise-Louis Garneray (1783–1857) was among the artists whose heroic whaling scenes helped to inspire Herman Melville's novel *Moby-Dick*. Garneray's depiction of whalers at work in the North Atlantic in 1836 emphasizes the solitary combat between the heroic harpooner and the great, black sea beast, and shows other dangers—the fragile boat, its frantic crew, the spurt of blood from the wounded whale, the foaming sea. In the background, the ship is calm—with fires ready to render the whale's blubber.
Photograph courtesy of the Peabody Essex Museum

IN THIS CHAPTER

GLOBAL DEMOGRAPHICS: THE
WORLD'S POPULATION RISES

FOOD: TRANSITION TO
ABUNDANCE

ENERGY FOR POWER:
MILITARIZATION AND
INDUSTRIALIZATION
Militarization
Industrialization

INDUSTRIALIZING EUROPE

INDUSTRY IN THE AMERICAS

JAPAN INDUSTRIALIZES

CHINA AND INDUSTRIALIZATION

INDIA AND EGYPT

IN PERSPECTIVE: Why the West?

M*oby Dick* is a tale of monsters, the saga of a seaman's revenge against a huge white whale that snapped off his leg: a monstrous man, a monstrous beast, a monstrous obsession. When Herman Melville wrote it in 1851, whalers still hunted in open boats that a whale could crush or smash. Harpoonists had to worry and bleed the whale to death. The crew knelt between decks in blood and blubber to chop and melt the fat before it turned putrid. For the fat was precious: whaling was the world's main source of oil. The world was facing a fat crisis—a shortage of lipids and lubricants. Within a few years, however, a series of innovations solved the problem. In 1859, drilling began to release fossil oil from the depths of the earth. In 1865, the first fully industrial whaling ship was launched in Norway, with explosive harpoons and a steam engine that could tow dead whales into port for quick processing. Even the gigantic blue whale—which previous hunting techniques could not touch—now became prey.

THE WORLD

Meanwhile, the search was on for other sources of fat. Intensive methods to produce feed supported more livestock and boosted supplies of animal fat. New grazing areas opened up. Demand for edible fat drove European powers into tropical colonies to produce palm, peanut, and coconut oil.

• • • • •

Fat made the nineteenth-century world work. It supplied calories for human consumers. It greased the machines of industrialization. It induced empire-building. But the fat crisis was part of a bigger picture: a revolution in energy sources. How people responded to the crisis is the subject of this chapter: industrialization—new ways to release energy and new uses for it. The following three chapters cover the consequences: new forms of imperialism and the effects of industrialization on society and politics.

GLOBAL DEMOGRAPHICS: THE WORLD'S POPULATION RISES

Population growth meant rising demand, which made new sources of energy necessary. In 1800, there were about 950 million people in the world. By 1900, there were about 1.6 billion people (see Map 23.1). Around 1800, only four large areas in the world could be called densely settled—with, say, more than four people per square mile: East Asia, southeast Asia, the Indian subcontinent, and Western Europe. By 1900, parts of Africa and the Americas, especially along the coasts, had comparable densities.

FOCUS questions

- WHY DID the world's population begin to rise rapidly during the nineteenth century?
- WHY DID industrialization increase the world's food supply?
- HOW WAS industrialization related to the growth of military power?
- WHY DID the economies of the United States and Latin America develop in different ways?
- WHY DID Japan and China pursue different policies toward industrialization?
- HOW DID British imperialism affect the economic development of India and Egypt?

In some ways, demographic buoyancy seemed surprising. Improvements in long-range communications made it easier for disease to spread. As people got more crowded together, new eco-niches opened for disease. Growing cities were poorly equipped with drainage and sanitation. Polluted and nutritionally inadequate food was a major problem. Urban epidemics multiplied, culminating in 1917–1919, when an influenza pandemic killed at least 30 million people worldwide. But by then, the rate of population increase was so quick that the disaster hardly made a dent in the world's population.

Nor were rural populations exempt from ecological disasters. Although food production soared in global terms, it was unevenly distributed, and famine killed more people in the nineteenth century than at any other period in recorded history. Political neglect worsened the effects, especially in large empires under distant or indifferent rulers. The most successful crops of the period—the most prolific, the most nutritious—ensnared consumers in overreliance. When fungal disease ruined potatoes in Ireland, for instance, in 1845–1859, or in Belgium and Finland in 1867–1868, millions starved or fled. Famine killed at least 4.3 to 7 million people in India in 1876–1878. Famine in China at the same time was "the most terrible disaster in twenty-one dynasties." In the 1890s, droughts associated with an unusual concentration of El Niño events caused 12 million deaths in India and 20 million in China. Famines triggered plagues. A cholera epidemic killed half the population of Guntur in eastern India after the crops failed in 1833. Smallpox and cholera also followed the great Indian famine of 1896. Nonetheless, population growth recovered from every catastrophe.

FOOD: TRANSITION TO ABUNDANCE

In view of the way famine and disease accompanied population growth, it is tempting to see Malthusian logic (see Chapter 20) linking demographic increase to ecological disaster. But population increase did not conform to Malthus's prophesies. In all parts of the world for which we have data, people practiced forms of population control. In France, they used contraception. In India, they idealized celibacy and restricted remarriage of widows. In Japan and most of Europe, they postponed marriage. Moreover, for unknown reasons, Japanese women began to delay having children until their mid-twenties, some five years later than was normal in Europe at the time. Most households had only one childbearing couple.

New ways to produce food outstripped population growth. In this respect, Malthus's critics, who expected "progress" to prevent dis-

Slum life. Social reformers of the late nineteenth century listed sanitation, children's welfare, and animal abuse as some of the most pressing problems associated with urban conditions. This snapshot, taken around 1900 in New York City, captures all three issues: The ragged children play in a filthy gutter while a dead horse, presumably used to pull a cart or a trolley car, rots just a few yards away.

aster, were right. Food production soared, partly because more land was devoted to it and partly because of more efficient methods of exploitation. In the Philippines and Java, for instance, where population growth had long been static, rates of increase rose to 1 percent a year, largely because women started marrying at under 20 years of age. But this was an adjustment to new conditions that boosted food stocks and generated wealth. Large-scale deforestation released land for food production. Marginal soil was exploited to grow coconuts, not necessarily for food but for their fiber, which was used for matting, and for coconut oil, which was used in everything from cooking to making soap.

Sometimes food production rose simply because farmers applied traditional methods more systematically. For example, in Japan, agrarian output rose without significant increase in the amount of farmed land. In Egypt, wheat and barley production nearly doubled from 1880 to 1900, while the acreage under cultivation increased by less than half. Elsewhere, natural growth occurred, with little or no human effort, adding almost 600 square miles, for instance, to the fertile Yellow River delta in China in the second half of the century. Or human agency intervened. The Netherlands, for instance, reclaimed 11,000 acres from sea and wasteland during the nineteenth century. Partly in consequence, in the second half of the century, the number of Dutch cattle doubled, and pigs increased fourfold.

Beyond question, the greatest extension of the frontier of food production happened in the vast open lands of Argentina, Brazil, Uruguay, Australia, and North America. The incorporation of the North American prairie to raise cattle and grow grain was the most conspicuous large-scale adaptation of the environment for human purposes ever recorded. In 1827, when James Fenimore Cooper wrote *The Prairie*, the region seemed desolate: "A vast country incapable of sustaining a dense population." People called it the Great American Desert. Except in a few patches, the soil was too tough to plow without industrial technology.

The extension of grazing was the first stage in the region's transformation. This was the common experience of previously underexploited grasslands in the period. Much of southeast Australia and New Zealand became sheep-rearing country, though at first more for wool than for meat. Argentina became a major exporter of beef and mutton. But the North American prairie exceeded other areas in productivity, partly because railway construction concentrated large, though temporary, labor forces in parts of the region. When the railways were built, big markets in the Mississippi River valley and along the seaboards of North America became accessible to the products of the prairie.

Grains soon became more important than meat, as wheat and maize replaced native prairie grasses. The change could not have happened without industrial technologies. Steel plows turned the sod of the prairie. Railways transported grain across what would otherwise be uneconomic distances. Houses built from precision-milled lumber and cheap nails spread cities in a region where most construction materials were unavailable. Repeating rifles destroyed vital links in the earlier ecosystem: the buffalo herds and their human hunters, the Native Americans. Grain elevators appeared in 1850. Machinery enabled a few hands to reap large harvests. Wire enclosed farmland against buffalo and cattle. Giant mills processed the grain into foodstuffs.

Rice cultivation in Japan. Hiroshige (1797–1858) specialized in painting comforting images of traditional Japan. Here bent-backed peasants labor virtuously under enriching rain in regularly patterned rice fields, surrounded by benign landscape. In the 100 years after the artist's death, enhanced efficiency enabled the Japanese to harvest more rice without extending the area under cultivation.

 James Fenimore Cooper, from *The Praire*

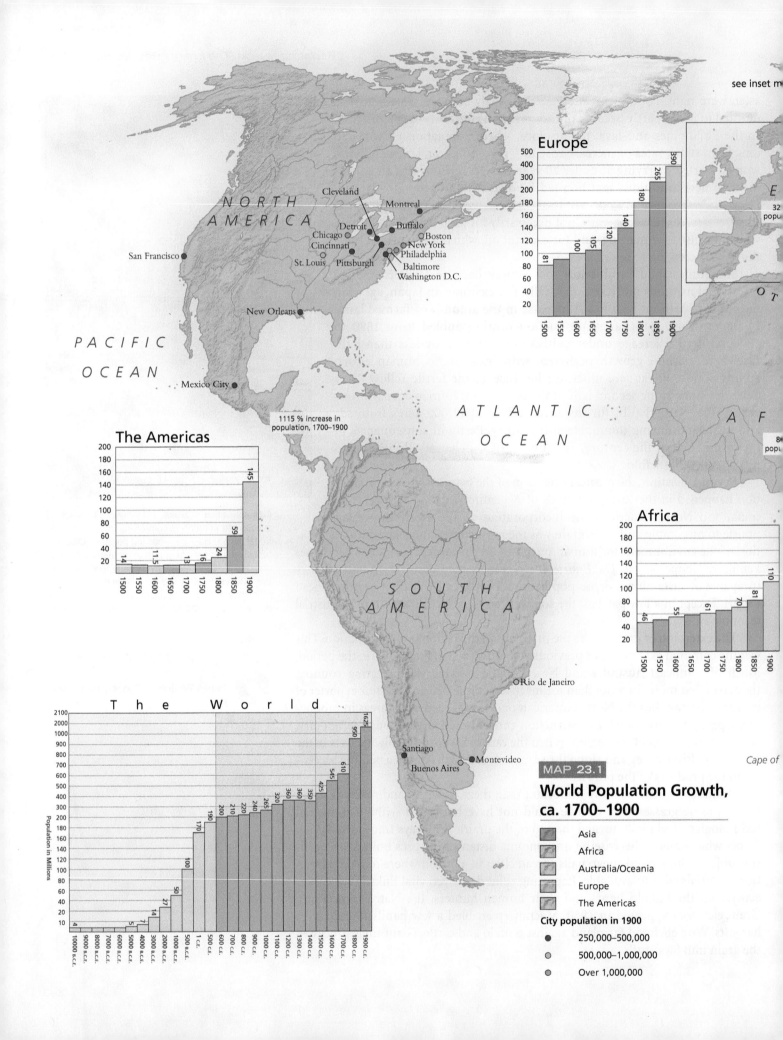

MAP 23.1

World Population Growth, ca. 1700–1900

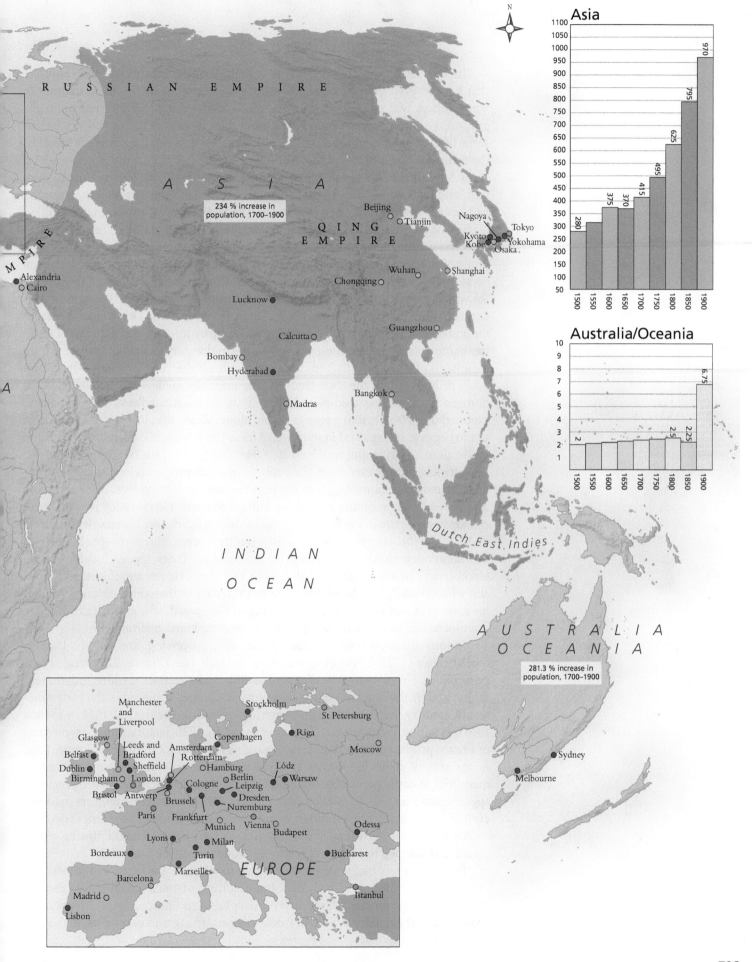

RUSSIAN EMPIRE

A S I A

234 % increase in population, 1700–1900

QING EMPIRE

EMPIRE

Alexandria
Cairo

Beijing
Tianjin

Nagoya
Kyoto
Kobe
Osaka
Tokyo
Yokohama

Wuhan
Chongqing
Shanghai

Lucknow

Calcutta
Guangzhou

Bombay
Hyderabad

Madras
Bangkok

INDIAN OCEAN

Dutch East Indies

AUSTRALIA OCEANIA

281.3 % increase in population, 1700–1900

Asia

Year	Value
1500	280
1550	
1600	375
1650	370
1700	415
1750	495
1800	625
1850	795
1900	970

Australia/Oceania

Year	Value
1500	2
1800	2.5
1850	2.25
1900	6.75

St Petersburg
Stockholm
Moscow
Riga
Copenhagen
Manchester and Liverpool
Glasgow
Belfast
Dublin
Leeds and Bradford
Amsterdam
Rotterdam
Hamburg
Lódz
Warsaw
Sheffield
Birmingham
London
Berlin
Leipzig
Bristol
Antwerp
Cologne
Dresden
Nuremburg
Brussels
Frankfurt
Paris
Munich
Vienna
Budapest
Odessa
Lyons
Milan
Bucharest
Bordeaux
Turin
Marseilles
EUROPE
Barcelona
Istanbul
Madrid
Lisbon

Sydney
Melbourne

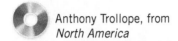

Anthony Trollope, from *North America*

In 1861, Anthony Trollope saw the results: concentrations of food resources that had no precedent or parallel. Trollope was "grieved by the loose manner in which wheat was treated" in Minneapolis—"bags of it upset and left upon the ground. The labor of collecting it was more than it was worth." In Buffalo, he saw some of the 60 million bushels of grain that passed through the city every year. But the transformation of the prairie was only beginning. In 1862, the Homestead Act made land in the West available at nominal prices. By 1900, 500 million acres of farmland had been added. Similar changes occurred in other grasslands. Argentina had been a net importer of grain in the 1860s. By 1900, it exported 100 million bushels of wheat and maize a year. Canada also became a major grain exporter.

Fertilizers increased productivity, too. In Europe, farmers kept their fields constantly productive, alternating beets or turnips with clover or alfalfa, which renew the soil because they recycle nitrogen. Turnips, rutabagas, and potatoes kept cattle alive during the winter, generating more manure. In 1860, British farms still got 60 percent of their fertilizers from animal waste. But the system increasingly needed supplements because the market demanded more and more meat. Turnips, moreover, demand a lot of fertilizer in most soils. The first consequence was the midcentury guano boom, mined from mountains of nitrogen-rich bird-dung on islands off the Peruvian coast, where huge flocks of birds fed on the abundant fish. The normally rainless climate preserved the nitrogen from being washed away. In the 1850s, the main handler of Peruvian guano exported over 200,000 tons a year to Britain alone. Meanwhile, in 1843, new sources of guano began to be exploited in southwest Africa. The first chemical fertilizers came into production: British output rose from 30,000 tons in 1854 to 250,000 tons in 1866.

Farming became ever more of a business, in which producers looked to boost production and make farms bigger to cut relative costs. In consequence, more and more capital went into scientific agronomy. Luther Burbank (1849–1926) was the most extraordinary figure in the field. He started a market-gardening business in California in 1875 and became the world's most inventive—even obsessive—practitioner of hybridization, grafting, and breeding. He produced 1,000 new species, including white blackberries and a fruit that was half apricot, half plum. He was a profligate sensationalist who would destroy hundreds of plants to create one that suited his purposes. But his enormous commercial success encouraged the spread of scientific techniques to improve strains and develop new plants for newly exploited environments.

Industrialization revolutionized preserving, processing, and supply. Lazzaro Spallanzani's (1729–1799) observations of bacteria (see Chapter 22) revealed new possibilities. Simultaneous heating and sealing could keep food edible indefinitely. Stimulated by the demands of the large armies Europe mobilized in the early nineteenth century, huge bottling and canning operations began. By 1836, a French firm was selling 100,000 cans of sardines a year. By 1880, factories on the west coast of France produced 50 million cans of sardines annually. Canning kept more food in the supply chain for longer. It made it possible to transport unprecedented quantities of easily perishable food in bulk over long distances, facilitating regional specialization and economies of scale. In the 1870s, Australian engineers made an even more dramatic breakthrough in preservation techniques: the compressed-gas cooler. Meat from Australia, South America, or New Zealand could now be refrigerated and shipped to Europe at relatively modest cost (see Map 23.2).

Food no longer had to be produced near to where it was eaten. In industrializing areas, agriculture declined. British agriculture virtually collapsed in the last generation of the nineteenth century. All over Western Europe, farmers abandoned growing wheat for dairy products, smoked meats, fruits, and vegetables, in the face of long-range imports.

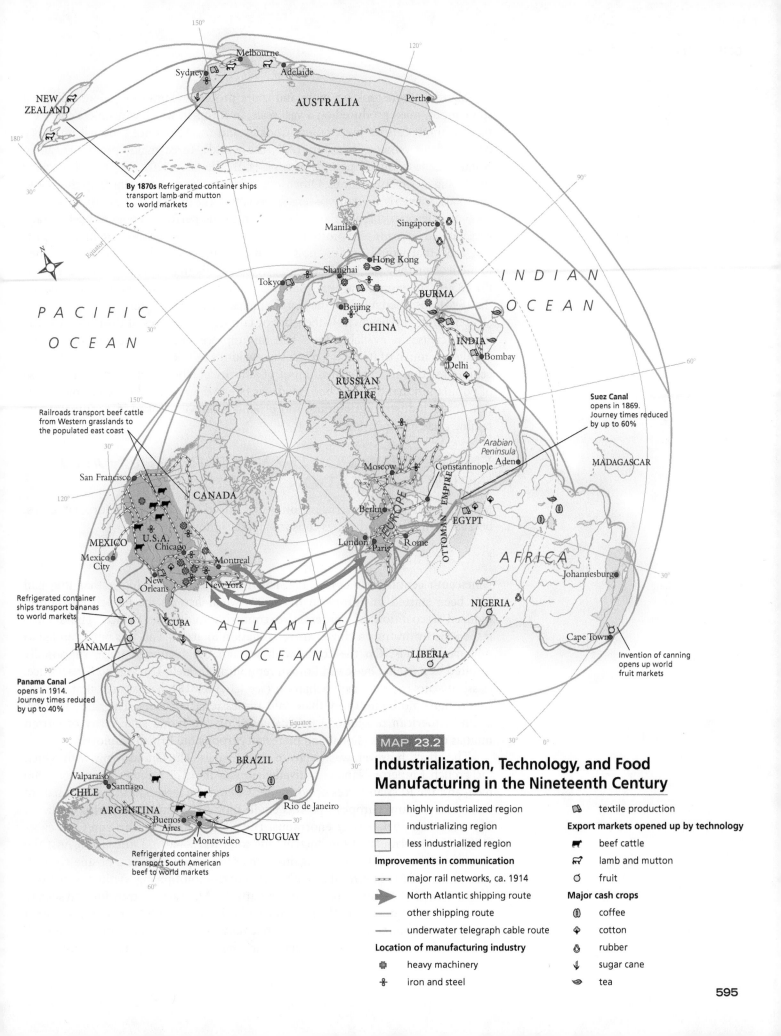

By 1870s Refrigerated container ships transport lamb and mutton to world markets

Railroads transport beef cattle from Western grasslands to the populated east coast

Suez Canal opens in 1869. Journey times reduced by up to 60%

Refrigerated container ships transport bananas to world markets

Panama Canal opens in 1914. Journey times reduced by up to 40%

Invention of canning opens up world fruit markets

Refrigerated container ships transport South American beef to world markets

NEW ZEALAND
AUSTRALIA
PACIFIC OCEAN
INDIAN OCEAN
Melbourne
Sydney
Adelaide
Perth
Manila
Singapore
Hong Kong
Shanghai
Tokyo
BURMA
Beijing
CHINA
INDIA
Delhi
Bombay
RUSSIAN EMPIRE
Arabian Peninsula
Aden
MADAGASCAR
Moscow
Constantinople
EUROPE
OTTOMAN EMPIRE
Berlin
EGYPT
London
Paris
Rome
AFRICA
San Francisco
CANADA
Johannesburg
MEXICO
U.S.A.
Chicago
Montreal
Mexico City
New Orleans
New York
NIGERIA
CUBA
ATLANTIC OCEAN
Cape Town
PANAMA
LIBERIA
BRAZIL
Valparaíso
Santiago
CHILE
Rio de Janeiro
ARGENTINA
Buenos Aires
Montevideo
URUGUAY

MAP 23.2

Industrialization, Technology, and Food Manufacturing in the Nineteenth Century

- highly industrialized region
- industrializing region
- less industrialized region

Improvements in communication
- major rail networks, ca. 1914
- North Atlantic shipping route
- other shipping route
- underwater telegraph cable route

Location of manufacturing industry
- heavy machinery
- iron and steel

- textile production

Export markets opened up by technology
- beef cattle
- lamb and mutton
- fruit

Major cash crops
- coffee
- cotton
- rubber
- sugar cane
- tea

Manufacturers took on more and more processing, until they were delivering some foods, mass produced on a vast scale, in forms in which consumers could eat them without further preparation. Cookies and crackers, once artisanal products, became factory-made items. In 1859, the world's three major producers, all in Britain, made 6 million pounds of cookies. By the late 1870s, the same firms were producing 37 million pounds. Other industries created new foodstuffs. In the 1840s, chocolate, formerly a luxury beverage, became a cheap food in Western Europe. In 1865, the German chemist Baron Justus von Liebig perfected cubes of beef extract, which could be made into broth by adding water. Moral crusaders sought a low-protein food that would reduce "passion" and promote chastity. They thought they found it when the American Reverend Sylvester Graham invented breakfast cereals in the 1830s. These products were suitable for industrial production methods and, by the 1890s, absorbed much of the world's increased output of grain.

For all its inefficiencies—the scars of famine, the failures of distribution—the huge increase in available food had an unprecedented impact on the world. Because so much of it was the result of new kinds of science and technology, it was achieved with a relatively small input of additional labor. Part of the vast increase of population that the food boom fed was free to engage in other economic activities. Trade, industry, agriculture, and urbanization were linked in a mutually sustaining cycle of expansion.

ENERGY FOR POWER: MILITARIZATION AND INDUSTRIALIZATION

Militarization and industrialization were linked to the midcentury fat crisis, because armies and industries consumed large amounts of fat.

Militarization

Nineteenth-century armies were big. The trend to make them bigger than they had ever been started in Europe in the 1790s when fear of the French Revolution induced a coalition of conservative countries to invade France. The French responded by drafting a citizen army or "nation in arms." This was not intended to militarize society. On the contrary, it was an old-fashioned ideal, supposedly inspired by ancient Greek and Roman republican models. During the Renaissance, classical scholars, such as Machiavelli (see Chapter 18), had argued that citizens would fight more effectively than paid professional warriors. The same idea lay behind American revolutionaries' insistence on the moral superiority of citizen militias over the professional and mercenary troops the British employed.

Karl von Clausewitz, from *On War*

The effect, however, was to create mass armies. The Grand Army with which the French Emperor Napoleon invaded Russia in 1812 numbered over 600,000 men, and the Russian forces opposing him were even larger. In the second half of the century, many European powers could mobilize armies numbering millions. The effects on warfare were enormous. The German theorist Karl von Clausewitz (1780–1831) formulated the doctrine of "total war"—waged not just against the enemy's armed forces but also against the entire population of a hostile country (see Chapter 26). The results made war worse—multiplying victims, spreading destruction, and encouraging preemptive attacks. Mass armies transformed society by taking young men from their homes, gathering them in barracks, drilling them in military discipline, and teaching them loyalty to the state. "Peasants," it was said, "became Frenchmen" through service in the army. Armies became forges of national identities.

The economic consequences of militarization were, perhaps, even more significant. Wartime logistics generated innovations in production, supply, and communications. Huge production lines, for instance, first appeared in state bakeries that produced dry bread for navies. These bakeries inspired the factory system of production that was necessary for large-scale industrialization. Armies concentrated huge numbers of men, straining food supplies and transport resources. Navies consumed unprecedented amounts of iron and steel for shipbuilding and of coal to keep the ships going. Every serviceman had to be fed. Margarine was invented for the French navy. Canning was a response to war. Canned milk was developed in the American Civil War (1861–1865). Massive armed forces demanded unprecedented quantities of mass-produced munitions. Every gun and cartridge had to be greased. In 1857, the issue of cartridges supposedly greased with pig and beef fat sparked a major rebellion among the native troops of Britain's Indian army. To the Muslims, pigs were unclean. To the Hindus, cows were sacred. (In fact, the cartridges were greased with vegetable oil.)

An early Union ironclad on the Mississippi River during the Civil War. Although the British and French navies already had ships built entirely of iron by 1860, U.S. naval experts were reluctant to believe that these vessels could be effective. But the Union navy put iron plates on wooden ships and began building iron-hulled vessels in 1862, in response to Confederate plans to launch similar ships and buy others from Britain.

Industrialization

Fossil fuels fired industrialization. Peat and coal were extracted from the ground on an unprecedented scale. Oil followed (and in the twentieth century, natural gas). In effect, mining and drilling for coal and oil released buried sunlight, accumulated millions of years ago when plants and creatures—which store energy from the sun in the carbons that form their bodies—were buried and crushed. A few pounds of coal can produce as much heat as an acre of timber. So the first effect of the release of coal from the ground was to liberate woodland for farming. The second was to provide energy for new forms of power.

Coal and steam were inextricably linked. Steam powered the pumps that drained the mines. Coal fueled the furnaces that produced the steam. Iron and steel were inescapably part of the picture. They were the materials from which the machinery was made to convert coal to energy and steam to power—the rods and the pistons, the cogs and casings of the engines. Coal produced the heat that fused the ores and forged the metals. The metals in their turn enclosed the spaces in which the coal burned.

Fuel consumption and production leaped. Japanese coal production had always been modest, but it rose from 390,000 tons in 1860 to 5 million tons in 1900. Increases of a similar order of magnitude occurred in Belgian and Spanish coal mines over the same period. The most productive coalfield in the world was already that of South Wales in Britain. Here, in the same period, output soared from 11.4 million to 35.1 million tons a year. German coal was of problematic quality, but nineteenth-century developments made its exploitation worthwhile. Over 100 million tons were being mined annually by 1900.

But what was all this extra energy for? Statistics seem to dominate the story of industrialization whenever historians tell it. Economic historians like to measure industrial change in terms of productivity figures. These are sometimes suggestive, sometimes spectacularly revealing. Machinery in Britain by the 1830s, for instance, could produce in 135 hours the same amount of cotton that took 50,000 hours to spin by hand. This helps to explain the appeal of industrialization. But it also

Power to rival nature's. Philippe-Jacques de Loutherbourg, born in France in 1740, made his career as a painter in England, where his work as a stage designer helped to add a showy, theatrical quality to his art. His painting of the great ironworks of Coalbrookdale in the English Midlands shows the rural setting typical of early industrial sites and displays the "sublime," "picturesque," and "romantic" qualities for which he became famous. The smoke and flames from the forge are more on the scale of a volcano than of a factory.

Fanny Kemble, from *Records of a Girlhood*

points to a paradox. In an age of increasing population, more muscle power was becoming available worldwide. So why bother to mechanize?

In part, the explanation lies in the geography of industrialization. On the whole, it happened earliest and fastest in regions where labor was relatively expensive: in areas such as Europe and Japan, where the size of the workforce was relatively modest compared with, say, China and India; or in the United States, which, despite the huge increase in its population, was still underpopulated in the nineteenth century. Second, industrialization was a function of demand. Population increase accounted in part for increasing demand, but so did the multiplication of sources of wealth—the new resources unlocked from the soil, the enormous expansion of financial institutions, the growth in the money supply as governments took on increasing responsibilities and minted cash to pay for them. The growth in the money supply worldwide would have been hugely inflationary if production and trade had not increased proportionately and absorbed its effects. Although mechanization stripped workers of employment in traditional industries and in unindustrialized parts of the world, it generated new wealth and, therefore, new employment opportunities in other activities and other areas. Trade and capital were essential extra spokes in the cycle that linked food, population, and industry. They provided incentives to mechanize and money to invest in mechanization.

Economic circumstances alone, however, cannot explain industrialization. It was more than an economic phenomenon. For contemporaries who took part in it, the appeal of industry was a form of enchantment. Like magic, it multiplied power and effected dazzling transformations. A passenger aboard the first commercially viable locomotive train—George Stevenson's *Rocket* in Britain, which achieved a speed of 35 miles per hour in 1829—called it a "magical machine with its flying white breath and rhythmical unvarying pace. When I closed my eyes the sensation of flying was delightful." A witness of the unveiling of one of the century's most impressive technologies—Sir Henry Bessemer's process for turning iron into steel in 1856—described the event with the slack-jawed awe of a sorcerer's apprentice: "Out came a volcanic eruption of such dazzling coruscations as had never been seen before. When combustion had expended all its fury, most wonderful of all, the result was steel!"

Industrial technology represented, for its early witnesses, the triumph of imagination over nature. Admirers of mechanization saw it as romantic—a perspective we have lost today. The English artist Turner (1775–1851) painted the speed of the locomotive. The German composer Mendelssohn (1809–1847) turned the noises of steam navigation into music. The British author Samuel Smiles (1812–1904), who convinced the English-speaking world of the virtues of industrialization, called the steam engine "the noblest machine ever invented by man." Engineers became heroes. Smiles wrote their lives in the style of romances of chivalry or even of fairy tales.

There were martyrs as well as heroes. One hundred workers died digging two miles of a railway tunnel I. K. Brunel (1806–1859) designed in Britain. And, of course, industrialization had its enemies. It threatened livelihoods in traditional crafts. Moralists condemned techniques that forced workers into soulless rhythms of work in the backbreaking, disease-breeding environments of factories and mines, and as we shall see in Chapter 24, their laments were justified. For some people, railways desecrated the countryside or damaged and stole the land. Nostalgia for the fate of the land inspired artists, novelists, and reactionary social movements (see Chapter 26) wherever industrialization occurred.

Even industrialists often seemed uncommitted to what we should now call entrepreneurial spirit. In England, "captains of industry" typically devoted wealth to buying country estates and building huge country houses in imitation of traditional landed aristocrats. Their managers, who could not afford country estates, imitated the longed-for way of life in so-called garden suburbs. French industrialists commonly affected scorn for entrepreneurship. In 1836, a member of a great textiles dynasty of northern France went on a pilgrimage "to obtain illumination from the Holy Ghost, so that we should never undertake anything in business above our strength, lest we should be troubled by hazardous speculations." François Wendel died a multimillionaire in 1825, having become, he said, an iron master and owner of profitable businesses "against my will." Another French magnate, Jules Siegfried, engraved "To work is to act" on his cufflinks, but retired from manufacturing textiles at the age of 44. In Japan (as we shall see), entrepreneurs insisted that they worked for honor or patriotism rather than profit. Again, they sought to imitate the warrior aristocracy. Even in the United States, Cornelius Vanderbilt (1794–1877), the owner of steamships and railroads, liked to see himself as a "knight of industry" and had himself depicted in a church window dressed in medieval armor. In the southern states, manufacturers aped planters' lifestyles. Industrialization, in short, succeeded only where people could reconcile it with traditional values.

Even regions with few or no factories or mechanized production methods, such as China, India, and South America, got railways, steamships, and electric telegraphs. The first successful experiment in steam locomotion was carried out in 1804, when Richard Trevithick carried ten tons of iron along nine miles of tracks in Britain. The local paper predicted "a thousand instances" of uses "not yet thought of." Trevithick's designs were too slow and cumbersome to be commercially useful, but viable railways soon spread around the world with amazing speed. Although the

Indian railway. When it began to operate in 1881, the Darjeeling Railway in northwest India ran 55 miles from the port of Calcutta, mounting steep slopes to reach the tea-growing regions. This loop, photographed in the late nineteenth or early twentieth century, shows one of the devices the British engineers who built the railway used to conquer the sharp ascent. The tea the trains carried eventually went to England, supplying a cheap stimulant for the workforce of British industry.

web of railways was densest in industrial regions, the rails also stretched across vast distances of the unindustrialized world, delivering to ports and factories ingredients for machines to turn into saleable goods, and food and drugs to keep the workers at their tasks. The first line across the American continent opened in 1869. By 1900, the United States had nearly 170,000 miles of track. Most of the network linked regions of primary products to centers of industrial processing and consumption.

Among the most intensive scenes of railway building in the mid–nineteenth century were India and Cuba—colonial lands where the ruling powers discouraged manufactures and exploited their basic products to serve industries in Britain and Spain, the "home countries." India's case is especially spectacular. Railway construction began in 1852. Fifty years later, India had nearly 42,000 miles of track—more than all the rest of Asia put together. One hundred fifty million pounds of British capital made the enterprise possible. In terms of labor, however, this was a genuinely Indian enterprise, with over 370,000 Indians a year working on the lines by the 1890s. Indian contractors, who supplied workers and, in most cases, supervised the work, made the biggest fortunes in railway construction. Jamsetji Dorabji Naegamwalla (1804–1882) was the most successful of all. He was an illiterate carpenter in a British-run dockyard when, in 1850, he realized the potential of the railways. He employed thousands of Indians and a handful of European engineers, ensuring the smooth running of the operations the government confided to him. When a viaduct he built collapsed in 1855, he bullied the authorities to let him rebuild it at extra cost and waive their usual demand for cash securities in advance. Unlike most British contractors who worked on railway construction, he made money and retired in 1870 to enjoy his wealth.

The development of steam-powered shipping kept pace with that of the railways. In 1807, the first commercial steamboat, built by Robert Fulton, navigated the Hudson River, traveling 150 miles upriver from New York City to Albany in 32 hours. The first regular transatlantic steam service began in 1838. Ten or 12 days instead of 6 weeks became the normal length of an Atlantic crossing between Western Europe and North America.

Intersecting rail and shipping lines was the scaffolding of the world, along which trade and travelers could clamber to every part of it. James Hill, who built the cathedral of St. Paul, Minnesota, founded a steamship line that linked the great food-producing and consuming belt of the world, from Vladivostock to Vancouver on Canada's Pacific coast. The railways made a startling difference. They wrenched trade in new directions. They made it possible for land-based systems of communications to carry freight on a scale previously possible only by sea. The world's great hinterlands, far from seas and ports and even navigable rivers, in the innermost parts of the continents, could be integrated into an increasingly global economy.

Electricity began to rival steam power. In the 1830s and 1840s, the English amateur physicist Michael Faraday demonstrated the possibilities of electric lighting. The biggest contribution arose from one of his first gadgets: an electromagnetic induction machine made in 1831. The following year, the American Samuel Morse used Faraday's discovery to transmit messages. The first long-range telegraph line linked Washington, D.C., to Baltimore, Maryland, in 1844. Submarine cables to transmit telegraph messages crossed the Atlantic in 1869, shrinking the ocean to the dimensions of a pond. An electric age was

Population, Food, and Energy

1780–1831	Karl von Clausewitz, developer of theory of "total war"
ca. 1800	Global population: 950 million; areas with regions in excess of four people per square mile: East Asia, southeast Asia, India, Western Europe
1804	First successful railroad locomotion
1807	First commercial steamboat
1850s	British imports of guano reach 200,000 tons per year
1850–1900	500 million acres added to U.S. farmland
1860–1900	Japanese coal production rises from 390,000 to 5 million tons; British coal production rises from 11.4 million to 35.1 million
1866	British output of chemical fertilizers reaches 250,000 tons
1869	First transcontinental railroad in United States; first telegraph messages cross the Atlantic
1870s	Australian engineers develop compressed-gas cooler
ca. 1900	German coal production reaches 100 million tons annually
	Argentina exports 100 million bushels of wheat per year; global population: 1.6 billion; new areas with regions in excess of four people per square mile: Americas, Africa

○ MAKING CONNECTIONS ○

INDUSTRIALIZATION AND MILITARIZATION

INDUSTRIAL DEVELOPMENT →	MILITARY ADAPTATION →	EFFECTS
Food technology: preservation, production, innovation	To supply massive armies of nation-states: canning of food, beverages; automated production lines for baked goods; new products like margarine to supply naval personnel	Extension of ability to provision large-scale armies/navies across continents and oceans; projecting military power; ability to manage colonies more effectively
New energy sources: fossil fuels	Coal-generated energy and steam power fuel industrialized production of weapons, ammunition	Largest industrial nations (Europe, U.S.) develop massive armies, navies equipped with weapons and ammunition that are more deadly
Transportation technology	Railroads, steamships used to transport troops and supplies rapidly across oceans, continents	Tighter control of homelands, colonies through technologically advanced military forces
Electrical technology	First practical application focuses on communication—telegraphy, used by military forces to coordinate troop movements	Ability to maintain control of large-scale armies on battlefields or across continents and oceans via telegraph messages

about to succeed the age of steam. The gasoline-fueled internal combustion engine, invented in the 1890s, also pointed the way to a further stage of locomotion without rail tracks. It would have as transforming an impact on the twentieth century as the steam engine had on the nineteenth.

INDUSTRIALIZING EUROPE

One way to measure the spread of industrialization is to map the distribution of steam-powered businesses. By these standards, Europe developed early and mightily. In the first half of the nineteenth century, Britain, Spain, Italy, and Belgium all doubled their steam-driven industrial capacity. France and Russia tripled theirs. In what is now the Czech Republic (but what was then part of the Austrian Empire), capacity grew fivefold, and Germany's capacity multiplied by six.

Industries transcended traditional national boundaries. In 1830, the Englishman John Cockerill's core business was manufacturing textiles in Belgium. He set up a factory in Liège to manufacture his own equipment. He diversified into weaving in Germany and Russian-ruled Poland and into producing cotton yarn in Spain. He went into mining in various European countries to obtain raw materials for his engineering factories and into international banking to finance his operations. He even had a sugar plantation in the Dutch colony of Surinam in South America. When his empire collapsed in 1837, he built railways in Russia.

From 1815 to 1914, city growth came to exceed army growth as the motor of change in Europe. Industrialization helped shape what remains, on the map, a conspicuous feature of the modern world: a zone of densely clustered industrial cities from Belfast in Northern Ireland and Bilbao in northwest Spain to Rostov and St. Petersburg in Russia (see Map 23.3). By 1900, nine European cities had more than a million people. Most of the population of Britain and Belgium had forsaken agriculture for industry and rural life for the cities. The rest of industrializing Europe

MAP 23.3

The Industrialization of Europe by 1914

Land use 1914

- mountainous area/wasteland
- agriculture and stock rearing
- forest
- industrial area

Resources

- coalfield
- oil
- potash

Manufacturing industry

- textiles
- iron smelting
- machinery
- shipbuilding

Population growth

- city with population over 500,000 in 1850
- city with population over 500,000 in 1914
- city with population under 500,000 in 1914
- principal railways 1914

Scale varies with perspective
6,220 km (3,870 miles)
5,980 km (3,720 miles)

1891 Trans-Siberian railway to Vladivostok

showed the same drift to the towns. The Russian Empire remained an overwhelmingly peasant country, but two-thirds of the inhabitants of St. Petersburg, Russia's capital, were former peasants.

Still, European industrialization tended to be concentrated in particular areas. Only little Belgium was a fully industrialized country in the sense of having industry evenly scattered throughout its territory. Southern Britain actually lost industrial capacity, which became concentrated in northern and central England and along the river Clyde in Scotland. In France, the northeast had most of the country's industry. In Switzerland, it was in the north. In Germany, most industry was located in two regions: the Ruhr in the west and in Silesia and Saxony in the east. Italy's industries were concentrated in the north in Piedmont and Lombardy and focused on the cities of Turin and Milan. In Russia, the two favored areas were in St. Petersburg and in the Donets Basin to the north of the Black Sea. In Spain, only the Basque Country and Catalonia were industrialized.

To try to understand why neighboring areas responded differently to the opportunity to industrialize, the Low Countries are a good place to look. If Britain was, as is commonly said, the first industrial nation, Belgium was the second. Belgian entrepreneurs concentrated on iron and steel production, for which Belgium was well supplied with raw materials. By 1870, Belgian furnaces were producing on average a third more iron than those of Britain, over half as much again as those of Germany, and more than double those of France. Zinc and glass were other Belgian specialties. Belgium was also well served by railways. Its 1,800 miles of track in 1870 constituted a substantial network for such a small country.

The Netherlands, meanwhile, remained overwhelmingly agricultural. Its industrial sector was dedicated to food processing, especially to making candy, using the cane sugar from Dutch colonies in the Caribbean and the Dutch East Indies and the beet sugar Dutch farmers produced. Dutch firms supplied 80 percent of the British market for condensed and powdered milk by 1900 and the Netherlands was Europe's biggest manufacturer of margarine. Despite the traditional importance of shipbuilding, Dutch iron and steel production only began to catch up with European averages in the 1890s.

So why were the two countries, which had similar histories and cultural profiles, so different? If anything, the Netherlands had historic advantages: a large colonial empire and a tradition of overseas trade—both of which, according to economic theorists in the nineteenth century, should have stimulated industrial development. Dutch coal was mainly anthracite and hard to mine—but similar limitations did not restrain industry in Germany. If there is such a thing as an industrial or capitalist spirit, it is unlikely that it should have been prevalent in one country and not in its neighbor. Indeed, when global conditions changed in the late nineteenth and twentieth centuries, the Netherlands did turn to industrialization.

In the nineteenth century, however, the two countries' economies were complementary: Belgium specialized in heavy industries, while the Netherlands specialized in producing and processing food for industrializing markets, including those of Belgium. The patchiness of industrialization, in short, was essential to industrialization's success. It was part of a pattern of specialization in which some regions supplied food and raw materials while others concentrated on manufacturing. If some places had comparative advantage in resources, others had comparative advantage in finance and access to markets, or a relatively disciplined or suitably educated labor force. The system was reproduced at a global level, as large areas of the world became suppliers of primary produce to industrializing economies.

Ankle-deep in coffee on a plantation in Brazil in the early twentieth century. The freshly harvested beans are tipped into troughs to be washed. Business imperialism continued to promote long-range ecological exchange as global trade increased, making South American coffee a major product alongside coffee from southeast Asia, and sending Brazilian rubber trees to southeast Asia.

Domingo F. Sarmiento, *"Civilization and Barbarism"*

INDUSTRY IN THE AMERICAS

The United States was a surprising industrializer, with a long history of supplying raw materials—pelts and skins, whaling products—for other people's industries. The southern states produced raw cotton for mills in Britain, and tobacco and sugar, which contributed to the world economy mainly as mild drugs to make workers' dreary lives more bearable. The Midwest had, by the mid–nineteenth century, an obvious future as a source of food for the world. The rest of the American interior had vast stocks of lumber, agricultural land, and mineral deposits. The states' main manufactures in the eighteenth century had specialized in the partial processing of raw products, such as turning sugar into molasses and rum.

Still, in other ways, the United States was a suitable arena for industry. High per capita incomes meant money for investment. A large merchant marine connected with global markets. Mechanization could make up for the shortage of labor. Slavery, lawful in almost half the country until 1865, tied down a lot of labor unproductively, raising labor costs elsewhere. Nor did the abolition of slavery do much for this problem, because most former slaves remained in the South as sharecroppers or subsistence farmers. On the other hand, high immigration rates from Europe (see Chapter 24) supplied enough manpower to make factory systems viable and ensured growing domestic demand for industrial products. There was plenty of coal and iron. High tariffs were designed to shut out European products and protect native industry. By the 1890s, factories in the United States produced twice as much as those of Britain and half as much again as the whole of Europe.

Nothing like this industrialization happened in the rest of the Americas. Canada became an agricultural country, thanks to the domestication of its prairie, but not an industrial one. Fewer than 500,000 Canadians, out of some 7 million, worked in industry in 1900, and a third of those processed timber and food.

Most of Latin America was even less industrialized. The wars of independence left much of Latin America exhausted and divided (see Chapter 22). The newly independent nations, after spending heavily to fight Spain, had to maintain big armies in wariness of each other and to suppress domestic discontent. They lacked the north's incentive to mechanize. Latin America had plenty of ex-slaves, Indians, and illiterate laborers. In a sense, the region never fully emerged from colonial-style exploitation. Its elites became the exploiters of their own peasants, whereas until the emancipation of the slaves, the United States hardly had any dependent peasants, and none of them lived in the areas that industrialized. In North America, small farmers were their own bosses. Big North American ranchers used the mobile labor of "cowboys."

Free trade, which most of the independent Latin American states practiced, favored industrializing economies that could produce cheap goods and condemned Latin American economies to underdevelopment. Having fought Spanish monopolists under the banner of free trade, the new countries were unable to protect their native industries, such as they were, against European imports. They became locked into a role as producers of primary products: the ore, timber, and rubber that supplied the factories of Europe and the United States; the foods and fertilizers that fed the workforces; the tobacco and coffee that provided the stimulants that fought workers' need for sleep; the sweets that kept their blood sugar up. The grasslands of South America never followed the grain-rich, city-sprinkled model of the North American prairie, not even in Argentina, which had plenty of prairie-like land—the pampa—that still remains ranching country. The pampa was too far from most centers of population. The success of the United States became a standing reproach to the economically frustrated countries to its south.

Much of Latin America became a continent of disillusioned hopes. In 1857, Carlos Barroilhet, who did more than anyone else to explain the merits of guano to the world, prophesied that Peru was destined to be "at once the richest and happiest nation on Earth," but by the 1880s, guano—much depleted by overexploitation—was considered a "curse." Competition from African guano and chemical superphosphates undermined a monopoly on which governments had staked all their economic plans. Brazil, similarly, lost its rubber monopoly when British businessmen smuggled out some plants and replanted them in Malaya. Late nineteenth-century Brazil relied more on coffee—another asset subject to increasing global competition—than rubber. Mexico lost its potentially most valuable territories—unmined gold and silver, untapped oil—in war with the United States in 1846–1848. In 1900, Argentina seemed still—in some ways, more than ever—a land of promise. Frozen meat exports and a meat-extract processing industry made the dominance of ranching in the pampa seem like a wise strategy. According to an "oath to the flag" that educational reformers introduced in 1909, Argentina was simply "the best land in the world," which would know "no history without a triumph." But its economy remained at the mercy of foreign investment and precarious global markets, and its promise was never fulfilled.

JAPAN INDUSTRIALIZES

Commodore Perry sailed into Tokyo Bay on July 8, 1853. His mission was to persuade or oblige the Japanese to open their ports to trade with the United States. He meant business in every sense of the word. He had four heavily armed ships with him. "The universal Yankee nation," wrote the expedition's interpreter, Samuel Williams, had arrived to end Japan's "apathy and long ignorance" with the example of "a higher civilization." Nevertheless, what Williams actually saw in Japan conformed only in part to the stereotype of a country consigned to backwardness by isolation. Japan's modernization had already begun, and the country was well poised to invest in innovative technologies: rich, urban, with a long history of commercial growth and a large middle class.

The project for the elites of late nineteenth-century Japan was to create an industrial economy like those in Europe and the United States. Japan would become the "floating wharf of the Pacific." "We need industry to attain the goal of becoming a rich nation," declared the government in 1868.

Japanese views of American naval technology

At first, unfair terms of trade held Japan back. Western powers imposed "unequal treaties" that allowed them to sell products in Japan cheaply and exempted their nationals from having to obey Japanese laws or be judged in Japanese courts. The trade balance remained adverse—Japan imported more than it sold abroad—until the 1880s. In 1884, only 176 nongovernment factories employed more than 50 people, and only 72 were steam powered. By 1899, however, Japan was able to break out of the unequal relationship and revise the terms of trade with the West, while imposing terms on China after defeating that country in 1895. Japan's total foreign trade increased tenfold between 1877 and 1900. The emperor

The Tokyo terminus of the new Tokyo-Yokohama railway line, built in 1872 with the aid of foreign engineers. From a series of prints called "Famous Places on the Tokaido: A Record of the Process of Reform," it was published only seven years after the Meiji Restoration opened Japan to foreign trade and ideas in 1868.

presided at the opening of the first long-distance railway in 1872. Nearly 5,000 miles were added by 1900. At the century's end, 50 cities had telephone exchanges, handling 45 million calls a year.

There were surprising successes. Buttons, previously unknown in Japan, became a major export by 1896. The textile-producing area of Britain inspired Japanese entrepreneurs to reorganize their country's cotton production. Cotton yarn production swelled more than sixfold to 250 million pounds—25 percent of Japan's total industrial output—by 1900. This was a remarkable achievement, because cotton textiles were one of the world's most competitive sectors. But women's labor kept costs down.

Two strategies were essential: first, expanding traditional economic activities and reinvesting the profits in new industries; and second, heavy investment by the state to kick-start industrial enterprises. Exports of traditional Japanese products, especially raw silk and tea, paid for industrialization, taking up what would otherwise have been China's expanding markets. By 1900, Japan exported practically as much silk as China.

Meanwhile, the strategy of involving state finance in the establishment of industry began to pay off at the cost of huge losses for the treasury. In the 1880s, state enterprises sold off mining interests and textile centers to private companies. Shipyards, established to build warships in the 1850s and 1860s, diversified into civil engineering and the production of iron and steel for industry. The foundations of wealth were available at cut price. Great corporations, of the kind that still dominate Japanese economic life, such as Mitsui and Mitsubishi, were able to take advantage, thanks to connections with the government and to the wealth they had accumulated during under the Tokugawa shoguns (1603–1868).

Japan's was industrialization Japanese style—not a copy of that of the West. Japanese responded to the West by trying to adapt rather than ape, equal rather than imitate. Western theorists of the merits of private enterprise and enlightened self-interest were well known in Japan, but the Japanese preferred to see business as a form of service to the community and the state. They knew the laws of supply and demand, but preferred to regulate consumption for moral reasons. Industrialists claimed to have patriotic motives. Fukuzawa Yukichi (1835–1901) convinced samurai of the merit of trade "for profit and for Japan." His books and pamphlets sold 10 million copies in Japan in his lifetime. Eiichi Shibusawa, who spent a long time as the government minister responsible for industrial development, confessed that he began by thinking that only the military and political classes were honorable. "Then," he wrote, "I realized that the real force of progress lay in business."

These mental habits and convictions made collaboration between the state and the private sector easy. The Western division between the state and private enterprise did not apply. Industrialists collaborated with government to restrain domestic demand and prioritize strength for war. Governments responded with contracts and concessions. In part this was because influential Japanese misunderstood Western models. Okuba Toshimichi, who visited manufacturing cities in Britain in the 1870s, reported that there was "no instance" in Europe where "a country's productive power was increased without the patronage and encouragement of its officials." This was not a false observation, but the inference he drew was misleading. The engine of Western capitalism—unless you count Russia as Western—did not need the state to stoke it, only to keep hands off the damper.

Nonetheless, the overall achievement of industrialization in Japan was remarkable. Compared with the beginning of the nineteenth century, Japan's national output of manufactured goods, raw materials, and agricultural products had quadrupled, and the proportion contributed by industry had at least doubled.

CHINA AND INDUSTRIALIZATION

As so often in Chinese history, peasant rebellion, rather than foreign example, was the spur to change. Western industrialization should have alarmed Chinese officials and intellectuals in the first half of the nineteenth century. It eroded Chinese domination of the global economy and reversed the military balance of power—with effects that China painfully felt, as we shall see in the next chapter. But influential Chinese did not develop their response until 1861. They called it "**self-strengthening.**"

In 1860, two events brought on a sense of crisis. First, huge areas fell into the hands of peasant revolutionaries, notably the Taipings, who mounted a serious threat to the Qing dynasty from 1852 to 1864. Second, an Anglo-French army occupied Beijing. The immediate pretext for this invasion was an apparently trivial matter of diplomatic procedure, but the background included a series of incidents that convinced the Westerners that they had to humble China to secure freedom of action for Western merchants and missionaries (see Chapter 25).

While smarting under their humiliations, China's elites took comfort from the outcome. The Western barbarians had no intention of trying to wrest the mandate of heaven from the Qing. Their aims were commercial, and the Chinese could buy their goodwill with trade. Barbarian skills could be employed to strengthen China. As an official memorandum of early 1861 put it, China had the chance "to snatch good fortune out of disaster, to transform weak to strong...." Civil servants reporting to the emperor insisted that the technology that gave the barbarians a present advantage was all of Chinese origin, anyway. They were largely right.

China would have to relearn its old skills from the foreigners. Shipbuilding and munitions manufacture were technologies China could adopt from Europe. "Now that we know what they depend on for victory," agreed Prince Gong, the emperor's chief minister, "we should try to master it."

Because European soldiers of fortune and merchants helped the Chinese government suppress the Taiping rebellion, General Li Hongzhang could inspect Western munitions closely. "If China were to pay attention to these matters," he concluded, "she would be able to stand on her own a hundred years from now." He called for a revolution in values that would elevate technicians and engineers above scholars and writers. "Seek machines that make machines and men who make machines."

As in Japan, the early impact of mechanization was confined to munitions. The Jiangnan arsenal opened in 1865 to manufacture guns and ships. It also had a translation department charged with keeping up to date with Western knowledge in armaments. But it never managed to produce rifles that were as good or as cheap as imported models. Its ships cost twice as much as those available from competitors abroad. A naval yard inaugurated in 1866 built 40 ships, none of which performed well.

Li Hongzhang (1823–1901). The Chinese states-man and general Li Hongzhang was the chief negotiator of the treaty that ended the first Sino-Japanese War in 1895. In 1896, he also negotiated a treaty that granted Russia the right to build the Trans-Siberian railroad across northern Manchuria.

Zeng Guofan (dzung gwoh-fahn), the model administrator responsible for modernizing China, went on insisting that imperial rule and rites were perfect. "Propriety and righteousness" came above "expediency and ingenuity." After his death in 1872, the focus of self-strengthening switched to civilian industries, the infrastructure, and the economic basis of a strong state: civil steamships, mechanization of coal mining and textile manufacture, and the telegraph system. A railway-building boom, paid for with foreign capital, followed in the 1880s, linking coal mines and agricultural hinterlands to the ports. Yet China remained a preindustrial power. Private investment was channeled through state-run monopolies in all these fields.

In war against Japan over who would dominate Korea in 1894–1895, the difference between the belligerents showed. On paper the Chinese navy, which had cost more than Japan's, looked more formidable—bigger and more heavily armed —than the Japanese navy. But when battle began, the Chinese guns had only three rounds of ammunition each. Most of their ships avoided action. The Japanese captured or sank those that did fight.

China and the West were mutually blinded by perceptions of each other's barbarism. From 1840, the Opium Wars (see Chapter 25) exposed China's weakness and dispelled the Western respect for the empire and its people that had featured so prominently during the Enlightenment (see Chapter 22). In China, it was heresy to acknowledge the West as civilized. For Westerners, the Chinese were Asiatic barbarians to be treated with contempt. For most of the Chinese elite, the big problems were those of longest standing: the peasant uprisings; the unrest of Muslim minorities, whose rebellions the Qing repressed with difficulty; the erosion of state power to provincial bosses. Carefully measured deference to selective Western superiority seemed the best course. "Chinese essence, Western practice" became the government's slogan after the humiliating defeat in the Sino-Japanese war of 1894–1895.

In the 1880s, the tea trade shrank in the face of Indian competition. Although Chinese silk exports remained significant, new exports from China were geared to an industrializing world: primary foodstuffs intended for processing abroad, skins and straw, hog bristles and timber, coal and iron ore. Much of the trade supplied Japanese industries that were outstripping those of China. The era of dominance for China through its luxury products was largely over.

INDIA AND EGYPT

In the nineteenth century, India deindustrialized. India's traditional industries, particularly cotton textile weaving, began to collapse in the 1820s. The disappearance of the great courts and armies of the Mughal era (see Chapter 21) left India without the motors of demand that once drove its economy. Indians had to turn back to the land.

The British made matters worse. They bureaucratized tax collection—cutting out native Indian capitalists. From an industrial giant, India became a producer of raw materials for the British Empire: tea, coffee, quinine, opium, jute, cotton. Early in the century, while the balance of trade with China was still unfavorable, Britain's trade drained cash from India's economy. Industrialization elsewhere lowered prices for Indian products. Millions of Indian laborers emigrated in the second half of the century, most to work on construction projects or plantations elsewhere in the British Empire. India still had a favorable trading balance with its Asian trading partners, but not with Britain. The machinery of British cotton mills pulverized Indian manufactures. By the end of the nineteenth century, British-made textiles accounted for over a third of India's total imports. India bought two-fifths of Britain's cotton exports (see Map 23.4). The British set the tariffs to favor their own exports. British firms effectively monopolized India's shipping, insurance, and international banking.

The British built a new economic infrastructure in India: dams, bridges, tunnels, roads, harbor installations, and, above all, railways. But the railways moved troops, administrators, travelers, and the primary goods the empire demanded. They did not contribute, as they did in Europe or North America, to industrialization.

In most of the rest of the world, industrial models of development had little appeal. Rulers wanted to get their hands on modern munitions—generally by buying them from the West—and to hire Western technicians to train their armies. Elsewhere, rulers or elites welcomed Western investment to build railways and bridges, but rarely tried to compete with Western manufactures.

The big exception was Egypt. Its population had grown rapidly from 2.5 million inhabitants in 1800 to 6.8 million in 1882. The passage of French Revolutionary armies through the country in 1798–1799 was an experience Egypt shared with much of Europe. While they were in Egypt, French officials opened factories for guns, gunpowder, food, and beer. After they departed, Mehmet Ali (1769–1849)—who, from 1805, was nominally the viceroy or khedive (heh-DEEV) for the Ottoman Empire but was, in effect, an independent monarch and the founder of a dynasty that ruled Egypt until 1953—brought in the services of Western, mostly French, experts to reproduce the activities already characteristic of industrializing Britain: cotton mills, munitions factories, steelworks, shipyards, a printing press. One of his French hired hands, Louis-Alexis Jumel, introduced a new strain of cotton that proved amazingly successful as the basis of fine textiles. In 1826, Mehmet Ali imported 500 steam-powered looms from Britain. About ten years later, Egypt was producing 1,200,000 bolts of cotton cloth a year. The industry was a state monopoly. In 1839, however, Britain forced Egypt to abandon protective tariffs when they blocked Mehemet Ali's attempt to overthrow the Ottoman Empire with

MAP 23.4

The Politics of Cotton

→ raw cotton from U.S. to Britain

→ cotton textiles to India

→ raw cotton from India to Britain

⬧ cotton-producing region

▱ textile town

▭ major cotton-producing states

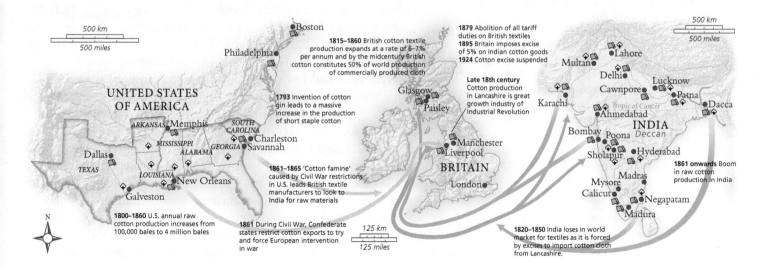

1815–1860 British cotton textile production expands at a rate of 6–7% per annum and by the midcentury British cotton constitutes 50% of world production of commercially produced cloth

1793 Invention of cotton gin leads to a massive increase in the production of short staple cotton

1861–1865 'Cotton famine' caused by Civil War restrictions in U.S. leads British textile manufacturers to look to India for raw materials

1800–1860 U.S. annual raw cotton production increases from 100,000 bales to 4 million bales

1861 During Civil War, Confederate states restrict cotton exports to try and force European intervention in war

Late 18th century Cotton production in Lancashire is great growth industry of Industrial Revolution

1879 Abolition of all tariff duties on British textiles
1895 Britain imposes excise of 5% on Indian cotton goods
1924 Cotton excise suspended

1861 onwards Boom in raw cotton production in India

1820–1850 India loses in world market for textiles as it is forced by excises to import cotton cloth from Lancashire.

UNITED STATES OF AMERICA — ARKANSAS, Memphis, MISSISSIPPI, ALABAMA, GEORGIA, SOUTH CAROLINA, Charleston, Savannah, TEXAS, LOUISIANA, New Orleans, Dallas, Galveston

Boston, Philadelphia, Glasgow, Paisley, Manchester, Liverpool, BRITAIN, London

Multan, Lahore, Delhi, Cawnpore, Lucknow, Patna, Karachi, Ahmedabad, Dacca, Bombay, Poona, Deccan, INDIA, Sholapur, Hyderabad, Mysore, Madras, Calicut, Negapatam, Madura

The Suez Canal. The French artist Edouard Rion (1833–1900) went to Suez to record Egyptian life for the French illustrated press just before the opening of the canal. Engravings of many of his paintings—including this bustling interpretation of the inaugural procession of ships through the canal in November 1869—appeared as illustrations to the account of the canal's construction written by Ferdinand de Lesseps, the canal's promoter and chief engineer.

French support. As a result, the Egyptian cotton industry dwindled, and Egypt, like the American South, became a major exporter of cash crops—sugarcane and raw cotton. Continuous irrigation was required to force the extra output needed to support the military and government facade of a modern state from the land. The peasants were impoverished and overburdened, and the opportunity to modernize on the Western European model slipped from Egypt's grasp.

Egyptian intellectuals remained faithful to Western models of development, and Khedive Ismail (r. 1863–1879), Mehemet Ali's grandson, tried to revive his grandfather's program. Ismail proclaimed Egypt part of Europe. Borrowing money at outrageous interest from European bankers, he built docks, sugar mills, an opera house in Cairo, and a school for girls. He had the Suez Canal driven across Egypt using French engineers and French capital. The canal opened in 1869 and, by connecting the Mediterranean to the Red Sea, reduced the sailing time from Europe to India and the Far East from months to weeks. But his extravagances bankrupted the state. In 1875, Britain purchased Ismail's shares in the canal. In 1879, his European creditors forced him to abdicate. Much of Egypt's revenue was assigned to repay foreign debts, and 1,300 foreign bureaucrats arrived to manage the country's finances and armed forces. In September 1881, the handful of native Egyptian officers still left in high ranks rebelled under the slogan "Egypt for the Egyptians."

Britain responded by occupying the country "to save," as a British official claimed, "Egypt from anarchy, and all European nations interested in Egypt from incalculable losses in blood and treasure." Egypt became a British dependency with a puppet government and a large British garrison until after the Second World War.

IN PERSPECTIVE: Why the West?

In 1800, China was probably about eight times as productive as Britain. By 1900, Britain produced about three times as much as China. In 1800, Britain and Germany combined contributed less than 5 percent of global industrial production. By 1900, those two countries alone accounted for nearly a third of that output. China's share in the same period fell from over a third to barely 6 percent (see Figure 23.1). Industrialization had dwarfed a giant and hoisted jacks-of-all-trades to the top of the beanstalk. Why did the West beat the rest—or most of the rest, if we include Japan—to the benefits of industrialization?

The West had few of the advantages commonly alleged. Traditional Western values, which were those of the landed aristocracy and the church, were industrialization's antibodies, training elites to have contempt for trade. Factories went up in a world where, according to the English essayist William Hazlitt (1778–1830), "people were always talking of the Greeks and Romans." Nor did Europe's supposedly scientific culture breed industry. The late eighteenth-century inventors of industrial processes—coke smelting, mechanized spinning, steam pumping, and the steam-driven loom—were all self-taught artisans or entrepreneurs with little or no formal scientific training. Science had no inbuilt practical vocation until the late nineteenth century. It

Industrialization in Global Context

1798–1799	French armies occupy Egypt
Nineteenth century	India deindustrializes
1800–1850	Dramatic increase in steam-driven industrial capacity in Europe
1805–1849	Rule of Mehmet Ali in Egypt, proponent of industrialization
1839	Britain forces Egypt to end protection of cotton industry
July 8, 1853	Commodore Perry sails into Tokyo Bay
Mid-nineteenth century	Japanese industrialization focuses on military technology
1860	Peasant revolutionaries take control of large parts of China
	Anglo-French army occupies Beijing
1861	China begins "self-strengthening" program
1877–1900	Japan's foreign trade increases tenfold
1890s	United States produces twice as much steel as Britain
1895	Japan defeats China in war over Korea
1900	Nine European cities have populations of more than a million

would be fairer to say that industry hijacked European science—bought it for useful research, diverted it to social responsibility. Nor is it enough—though it is important—to say that the distribution of coal and iron privileged some economies for industrialization. In some places outside the West and beyond Western control, coal and iron reserves were left unexploited. In others, such as New England and parts of northern Spain and Italy, industrializers found ways to compensate for the lack of them.

The West's real advantage was commercial. Commerce makes specialization possible. Without extensive systems of long-range trade, large concentrations of labor dedicated to manufacturing particular items or producing particular primary products are impossible. In the eighteenth and nineteenth centuries, Western Europe and North America were excellent environments for banking and what would now be called financial services industries, thanks to the climate of economic liberalism, and the commitment of states to foster commerce. Europe was not unique in this respect. Capitalism and commercial entrepreneurship were also ingrained in many communities and ruling elites in Asia. In China, however, commerce did not enjoy the same level of support from the state. Moreover, China was slow to change this attitude in the nineteenth century.

The pace of commerce is a function of the size of the market. European populations experienced exceptionally high growth rates in the nineteenth century. The population of Europe more than doubled to over 400 million in 1900. The populations of Belgium, Britain, and Germany all rose faster than the average. The United States had 76 million people by 1900—making it the most populous state in the Western world. Taken together, the demographic trends of the nineteenth century represented a shift in the global balance of resources in favor of the West. The continent, which had about a fifth of the world's population at the start of the century, had about a quarter by its end. The traditional pattern of global history, in which the hugely populous and productive societies of East and South Asia predominated, was ending or over. In some ways, the population figures mask an even greater shift: The extra people that Europe and the United States acquired produced hugely disproportionate increases in wealth, thanks to giant strides in the output of food and manufactures.

Westerners, finally, came from behind. That is where innovation usually comes from, because leaders in any field have little interest in promoting

Share of World Manufacturing Output, 1750–1900

	1750	1800	1830	1860	1880	1900
Europe	23.1	28.0	34.1	53.6	62.0	63.0
China	32.8	33.3	29.8	19.7	12.5	6.2
India	24.5	19.7	17.6	8.6	2.8	1.7

FIGURE 23.1 SHARE OF WORLD MANUFACTURING OUTPUT, 1750–1900

Derived from B. R. Tomlinson, "Economics: The Periphery," in Andrew Porter (ed.), The Oxford History of the British Empire: The Nineteenth Century, *Oxford 1990, p. 69 (Table 3.8).*

CHRONOLOGY

1780–1831	Karl von Clausewitz, developer of theory of "total war"
1798–1799	French armies occupy Egypt
Nineteenth century	India deindustrializes
ca. 1800	Global population: 950 million; areas with regions in excess of four people per square mile: East Asia, southeast Asia, India, Western Europe
1800–1850	Increase in steam-driven industrial capacity: Britain, Spain, Italy, Belgium doubled; France, Russia tripled; Czech Republic increased fivefold; Germany increased sixfold
1804	First successful railroad locomotion
1805–1849	Reign of Mehmet Ali in Egypt, proponent of industrialization
1807	First commercial steamboat
1839	Britain forces Egypt to end protection of cotton industry
Mid–nineteenth century	Japanese industrialization focuses on military technology
1850–1900	500 million acres added to United States farmland
1850s	British imports of guano reach 200,000 tons per year
July 8, 1853	Commodore Perry sails into Tokyo Bay
1860	Peasant revolutionaries take control of large parts of China; Anglo-French army occupies Beijing
1860–1900	Japanese coal production rises from 390,000 to 5 million tons; British coal production in South Wales rises from 11.4 million to 35.1 million
1861–1865	American Civil War
1861	China begins "self-strengthening" program
1866	British output of chemical fertilizers reaches 250,000 tons
1869	First transcontinental railroad in United States
1870s	Australian engineers develop compressed-gas cooler; Belgium leads world in iron- and steel-making equipment
1877–1900	Japan's foreign trade increases tenfold
1890s	United States produces twice as much steel as Britain
1895	Japan defeats China in war over Korea
Late nineteenth century	Belgium and Netherlands develop increasingly complementary economies
1900	German coal production reaches 100 million tons annually; Argentina exports 100 million bushels of wheat per year; global population: 1.6 billion; nine European cities have populations of more than a million

change. Economies like those of India and China, which had productive traditional industries and enormous reserves of labor, felt no call to mechanize.

Industrialization was disastrous for many who took it up. Like the ancient adoption of farming, it had adverse consequences for nutrition, health, and what we would now call quality of life. It nourished oppression and tyranny. So why did people accept it—why, indeed, did they relish it so much that almost every community that has had the chance to industrialize over the last 200 years has opted to do so?

Industrialization had one obvious benefit—it released land for food production. It was no longer necessary, for instance, to maintain forests to provide wood for fuel. Forests in England halved between 1800 and 1900. The conservation policies of eighteenth-century Japan (see Chapter 20) were abandoned. In the nineteenth century, the carefully husbanded woodlands that formerly covered much of the islands of Honshu, Kyushu, and Shikoku largely vanished as coal replaced wood as a source of fuel, and Japan devoted more land to agriculture. The opposite happened in much of New England, where the rock-ribbed soil, which had largely been under the plow in 1800, began to revert to forest as food production shifted westward in the 1820s and 1830s.

Second, as we shall see in Chapter 24, the long-term consequences of industrialization tended to spread the benefits widely. In its early stages, mechanization increased the burden of labor for the workers who operated the machines. But it was labor saving for others. And technical improvements gradually liberated even the machine workers to enjoy increased leisure.

Finally, it is worth dwelling for a moment on the example of agrarianization. As readers of earlier parts of this book know, early farming communities adopted new production methods despite adverse short-term effects. In part, this was because most people—especially those most likely to suffer, because they were poor and powerless—had no say in decision making. Industrialization, like farming, was an elite option. It appealed to people whose power it increased. It enabled the controllers of industrial wealth to join or replace existing elites, and it empowered industrialized and industrializing communities to dominate the rest of the world and extort or exploit its resources.

PROBLEMS AND PARALLELS

1. How did fat—oil from animals, plants, and minerals—make the world of the nineteenth century work? What other sources of energy were exploited in the nineteenth century?

2. How did the population explosion of the nineteenth century lead to new ways to exploit and use the Earth's resources? Why did population increase not conform to Malthusian logic?

3. Why was the incorporation of the vast, open lands of Argentina, Brazil, Australia, and North America so important?

4. How did industrialization revolutionize the world's food supply?

5. How did militarization and industrialization put intense pressure on the world's energy sources in the nineteenth century?

6. What are the explanations for nineteenth-century industrialization? Why did industrialization have social consequences?

7. Why did Japan industrialize more rapidly than China? How did industrialization affect India and Egypt?

DOCUMENTS IN GLOBAL HISTORY

- James Fenimore Cooper, from *The Praire*
- Anthony Trollope, from *North America*
- Karl von Clausewitz, from *On War*
- Fanny Kemble, from *Records of a Girlhood*

- Domingo F. Sarmiento, *"Civilization and Barbarism"*
- Japanse Views of American naval technology

Please see the Primary Source DVD for additional sources related to this chapter.

READ ON

C. A. Bayly, *The Birth of the Modern World* (2004) is an insuperable survey of global history in the nineteenth century. E. A. Wrigley, *Peoples, Cities and Wealth: The Transition of Traditional Society* (1989) provides an overview of some of the most conspicuous issues. P. N. Stearns, *The Industrial Revolution in World History* (1998) is an introductory essay.

On food, F. Fernández-Armesto, *Near a Thousand Tables* (2003) is a short, general history. J. Burnett, *Plenty and Want* (1988) surveys the topic for Britain. J. Goody, *Cooking, Cuisine and Class* (1982) is an ingenious, anthropologically informed work that opens up comparative perspectives. P. N. Stearns, *Fat History* (2002) studies attitudes to fat in France and the United States. On famine, M. Davis, *Late Victorian Holocausts* (2002) is important and challenging.

On the domestication of the prairie, W. Cronon, *Nature's Metropolis* (1991) is essential reading. R W. Paul, *The Far West and the Great Plains in Transition* (1998) is an excellent study. W. Cronon et al., eds., *Under an Open Sky* (1993) includes some important essays. On fertilizers W. M. Mathew, *The House of Gibbs and the Peruvian Guano Monopoly* (1981) is a most helpful monograph. On Burbank, F. W. Clampett, *Luther Burbank* (1926) provides a rather uncritical outline.

On the militarization of society, E. Weber, *Peasants into Frenchmen* (1979) is a classic study. P. Paret, *Clausewitz and the State* (1985) is a useful study of Clausewitz's work in social and political perspective.

G. R. Taylor, *The Transportation Revolution* (1951) is an old but still authoritative study of the infrastructure of industrialization. On the industrialization of Europe, T. Kemp, *Industrialization in Nineteenth-century Europe* (1969) provides an overview. D. Landes, *The Unbound Prometheus* (1969) is a classic survey. P. N. Stearns, *Lives of Labor* (1975) takes a comparative approach focused on workers' experience.

On Britain and France, P. O'Brien and R. Quainault, eds., *The Industrial Revolution and British Society* (1993), and P. O'Brien and C. Keyder, *Economic Growth in Britain and France* (1978) are in some respects correctives of the still important classic study, P. Mathias, *The First Industrial Nation* (1969). T. Zeldin, *France 1848–1945*, 2 vols. (1973) is a wonderful book: sensitive and stimulating with an impressively original method. For Germany, T. Pierenkemper and R. Tilly, *The German Economy during the Nineteenth Century* (2005) is a good brief introduction. J. Mokyr, *Industrialization in the Low Countries* (1976) is basic. E.

H. Kossmann, *The Low Countries 1798–1914* (1978), and J. C. H. Blom and E. Lamberts, eds., *History of the Low Countries* (1998) provide useful overviews. J. L. Van Zanden, *The Economic Development of the Netherlands since 1870* (1996) includes a brief history of Dutch industrialization. J. de Vries and A. van de Woude, *The First Modern Economy* (1997) is an influential survey of pre–nineteenth-century Dutch economic history. Spain is superbly covered by D. Ringrose, *Madrid and the Spanish Economy* (1983), and N. Sanchez-Albornoz, ed., *The Economic Modernization of Spain* (1987). For Italy, J. Cohen and G. Federico, *The Growth of the Italian Economy* (2001) is an efficient introduction. D. C. North, *The Economic Growth of the United States* (1966) is a venerable and reliable work. G. J. Kornblith, ed., *The Industrial Revolution in America* (1998) contains some stimulating essays. M. Girouard, *The Return to Camelot* (1981), and D. C. Lieven, *The Aristocracy in Europe 1815–1914* (1993), are helpful on the survival of an aristocratic ethos in the industrializing West.

J. Batou, ed., *Between Development and Underdevelopment* (1991) is an important collection on attempts at industrialization in the extra-Western world in the nineteenth century.

R. Bin Wong, *China Transformed: Historical Change and the Limits of European Experience* (2002) is of fundamental importance; L. Aiguo, *China and the Global Economy since 1840* (1999) is a helpful introductory work. India is covered in D. Kumar, ed., *The Cambridge Economic History of India, II* (2005), and I. J. Ker, *Building the Railways of the Raj* (1998). M. B. Jansen, ed., *The Cambridge History of Japan* V (1995), and S. Sugiyama, *Japan's Industrialization in the World Economy* (1988) deal with Japan; S. Hanley and K. Yamamura, *Economic and Demographic Change in Preindustrial Japan* (1967) is valuable on the background and takes a critically acute approach to controversial issues in historical demography. On the Middle East, R. Owen, *Cotton and the Egyptian Economy* (1969), and *The Middle East and the World Economy* (1993). C. Issawi, ed., *The Fertile Crescent, 1800–1914* (1988) is a useful economic overview of the Middle East with many documents. P. J. Vatikiotis, *The History of Modern Egypt* (1991) is an outstanding survey.

Debate on the reasons for the West's great leap forward is mainly conducted in K. Pomeranz, *The Great Divergence* (2001); A. Gunder Frank, *ReOrient*; D. Landes, *The Wealth and Poverty of Nations* (1999); and J. Goody, *The East in the West* (1996).

CHAPTER 24
The Social Mold: Work and Society in the Nineteenth Century

Akira Kurosawa's epic movie of 1954, *The Seven Samurai*, was set in the Japan of the sixteenth century, but it depicted the predicament of the samurai in modern times. By the nineteenth century, the samurai had become an obsolete class, whose prestige and wealth had been diminished by social, economic, and political changes. But in their own eyes, and in those of most Japanese, they still embodied timeless values of honor and courage. In the movie, the seven find work as mercenaries, defending villagers from bandits. In the process, they teach the peasants the art of war, thus rendering themselves—and by extension, all samurai—useless.

IN THIS CHAPTER

THE INDUSTRIALIZED
ENVIRONMENT
Palaces of Work: The Rise of Factories
Critics of Industrialization: Gold from the Sewers

URBANIZATION

BEYOND INDUSTRY: AGRICULTURE
AND MINING

CHANGING LABOR REGIMES

Slavery and the Slave Trade
Female and Child Labor
Free Migrants

HUNTERS AND PASTORALISTS

ELITES TRANSFORMED

IN PERSPECTIVE: Cultural
Exchange—Enhanced Pace, New
Directions

As the police closed in, four rebels struggled in bitter March cold through mountains south of Osaka, Japan. When the first one faltered, his companions cut off his head. The second hanged himself. Only Oshio Heihachiro and his son were left. When the police caught up with them, Oshio's son wanted to flee, but, screaming, "Coward! Coward!" Oshio stabbed him to death, set fire to the house where they were hiding, slashed his own throat, and perished amid the flames on May 1, 1837.

In Japan, Oshio has always been regarded as a hero, despite, or perhaps because of, his horrific suicide. He was a member of the hereditary warrior caste—a proud samurai—who had grown up believing that nobles' obligations to the poor were more important than their privileges over them. As a magistrate, he rooted out secret practitioners of Christianity—which still had followers 200 years after Japan banned it—and exposed scandals in the administration. He then retired, after a mystical vision, to found a small school.

His was a new kind of revolt in Japanese history. For the first time, samurai made common cause with the poor against the middle class. As had happened before in Japan, and in every society dependent on one staple crop, the 1830s was a decade of rice failures and famine. In 1837, as people died of starvation in Osaka, the state granaries were well stocked, and the officials who ran them got rich by shipping rice to the capital. Oshio petitioned local officials to open the warehouses, but they threatened him with prosecution for meddling where he had no official status.

He bought firearms and hired an artillery expert to train his men in their use. He then issued a summons to revolt, promising to "visit Heaven's vengeance" on the officials and merchants, and calling on peasants to burn the tax records on which the authorities relied. He stressed, sincerely, that he did not aim to seize power, only to right injustice.

● ● ● ● ●

Oshio's call was echoed in surprising places. In Bengal in India, for instance, a landlords' agent, Titu Mir, led a peasant revolt against moneylenders, tax collectors, and rent gougers in 1831. In England, at about the same time, conservative aristocrats saw workers and landowners as natural allies in a struggle to save the old economy of the land against the new economy of capital. In North America, some slave owners appealed to their slaves to fight alongside them against would-be liberators who wanted to subordinate the states to the federal government. In Latin America, aristocratic rebels recruited peasants to fight in civil wars. In France, middle-class intellectuals dreamed of leading the masses to progress. In the Ottoman Empire, Butrus Bustani, a Western-influenced aristocrat, spoke up for rebellious peasants in Lebanon. In Russia the great novelist Count Leo Tolstoy (1828–1910), renounced his wealth and adopted a peasant's way of life.

New wealth from commerce and industry threatened traditional society, diminishing aristocracies, elevating bourgeoisies, ruining peasants, creating industrial working classes, and eliminating traditional forms of labor such as slavery and serfdom. Traditional resentments—of merchants by aristocrats, of profiteers by peasants—grew. Global wealth gaps gaped ever more widely, turning some regions and peoples into suppliers of staple products for consumers thousands of miles away.

JAPAN

FOCUS questions

- HOW DID industrialization change society and the economy?
- WHY WAS Marx wrong in predicting that industrialization would lead to violent revolution?
- WHY WERE the slave trade and slavery abolished in the nineteenth century?
- WHY WERE some aristocracies able to adapt to the changes industrialization brought?

Even in unindustrialized societies, economic status rivaled age-old ways of determining people's place in society—parentage, ancestry, birthplace, learning, strength, sanctity. Where industry flourished, social change was even more convulsive. Instead of identifying with communities that embraced people at all levels of rank and prosperity—neighborhoods, cities, provinces, sects, families, clans, big households, ethnic groups—people, uprooted and regrouped in industrial centers, came to define themselves in terms of wealth or what they increasingly called class. Nineteenth-century observers in the West believed that the world was being redrawn on class lines. Some governments even adopted class as a way to categorize people as nobles, bourgeois, peasants, or workers. Karl Marx (1818–1883) championed a new theory of history: that all change was part and product of inevitable **class struggles** that pitted the rich against those whom they exploited. This chapter is about the spaces people occupied in this changing world: the way their work altered and shifted, the new relationships they developed, the shaken kaleidoscope of class and rank.

THE INDUSTRIALIZED ENVIRONMENT

Machines created unprecedented differences of power and wealth: between regions and countries, of course, but also, within industrializing regions, between classes, sexes, and generations.

Palaces of Work: The Rise of Factories

Work moved from country to city, from outdoors indoors, from homes and small workshops into factories and mines, from relatively healthy to relatively unhealthy environments that were often deafening, exhausting, and alienating. In the past, small groups of workers had shared intimate surroundings: workshops in which a few equals or near equals collaborated, or households in which a master craftsman marshaled apprentices who lived together like a large family. Now seismic social upheavals raised factories, like "smoking volcanoes" (as contemporaries said), burying the world of artisans and flattening traditional social hierarchies.

Factories reorganized work and reordered life. For their admirers, factories represented proof of progress, a magical extension of human power over nature, a romantic adventure. In 1802–1803, for instance, the German artist, C. A. G. Goede, traveling through industrializing landscapes between the cities of Birmingham and Shrewsbury in England, marveled at "mountain and valley in flames" for miles around, "beautifully lit by the gleaming glow of coal." Mechanization made people feel godlike. The ways early nineteenth-century artists painted factories are full of echoes of volcanic imagery.

Early depictions, moreover, show factories in harmony with nature, sited in the countryside for convenient access to raw materials. Philippe-Jacques de Loutherbourg painted Coalbrookdale in England in 1801, with furnaces ablaze in a cozy pastoral setting. In 1830, Karl Schurz painted steelworks, near Cologne in Germany, in the style of a farmyard scene against a background of rolling hills.

Factories were creations of the imagination. Architects sought models from the ancient world and fiction, raising fantasy buildings, bristling with turrets, battle-

Unthreatening industry. William Ibbitt's engraving of industrial Sheffield, in northern England, in the mid–nineteenth century, depicts the towering factories that rival the city's churches, the outpouring smoke, and the huge sprawl of the growing city. But, nestling in nature, industry seems at ease with the environment, and traditional rural life is undisturbed in the foreground.

ments, spires, and domes, to be what contemporaries called cathedrals of work or castles of industry. "These palaces house no pharaohs, no orgies, but are a means of life for hundreds of families," said a Spanish newspaper in 1855. The words express belief in the nobility of work and reveal the power-hunger of industrialists who based their claims on merit rather than wealth. **Paternalism** leaps from the page.

One of the problems for historians of industrialization is to explain why people left the land for factories. Most probably had no choice. The mechanization of agriculture reduced the amount of work available. Economies of scale concentrated more land in fewer hands. Global specialization shifted food production and industrial raw materials out of the industrializing world, leaving some rural workforces unemployed. Factory owners had to compete with one another for labor, as industries multiplied and businesses crowded the marketplace.

Some entrepreneurs had vision or vocation, religious or charitable. Samuel Smiles spoke of the spirit of industry as "the gospel of work." Henry Heinz (1844–1919) of Pittsburgh epitomized that spirit. His early ambition was to be a Lutheran minister. When he made a fortune from his canned and bottled food business, Heinz chose a famous slogan: "57 Varieties," not because there were really 57 of them—there were soon many more—but because the number came to him in a vision. His vast factory in Pittsburgh resembled a church.

 Samuel Smiles, from *Self-Help*

His employees worked hard. In 1888, entry-level employees got five cents an hour for a ten-and-one-half-hour day—lower wages than many other local employers paid. But Heinz provided generous benefits. His workers, for instance, got free uniforms, medical and dental care, and, if they handled food, a daily manicure. There were hot showers, a gymnasium, a roof garden, and a reading room. Heinz had carriages to take workers for rides in the park and hired trains for outings. He provided lectures, concerts, and free courses. There were four dances a year and a Christmas party, where Mr. Heinz welcomed Santa Claus. Critics branded this style of management as paternalist and self-serving, but Heinz's methods had a genuinely benevolent message: Capital and labor were not enemies but natural allies. Management—not exploitation and profiteering—was the key to success.

Critics of Industrialization: Gold from the Sewers

Philanthropic industrialization showed that industry could spread the benefits of prosperity widely and increase leisure for workers as well as bosses. Most bosses, however, did not share Heinz's devotion to good works. And with the rush to industrialize came evils. Outside the few exemplary factories and model industrial towns, in the streets and slums that the concentration of labor created, the effort to erect a romantic environment for industrial society was a horrible failure.

Industrialization uprooted lives, disrupted families, and imposed bleak working conditions in cities rife with filth and disease. Visiting the British city of Manchester in 1835, Alexis de Tocqueville, considered the greatest social analyst of his time, recoiled from factories that "keep air and light out of the human habitations which they dominate; they envelop them in perpetual fog; here is the slave, there is the master; there is the wealth of some, here the poverty of most." Yet she wrote, "from this filthy sewer, pure gold flows."

Karl Marx and Frederich Engels, from *The Communist Manifesto*

Karl Marx foretold that industrialization would worsen class warfare. At first, in the 1830s and 1840s, it looked as if he must be right. Workers, Marx thought, must soon discover their power, realize that their labor was the source of society's wealth, and demand their share of prosperity. The result would be a bloody revolution, in which the working class, or **proletariat,** would overthrow the bourgeoisie. "Workers of the world arise," he proclaimed in 1848, "you have nothing to lose but your chains!" Riots, if not rebellions, were commonplace in industrializing cities.

Yet, in the world's most industrialized societies, Marx's warnings went unfulfilled. Workers soon had more than chains to lose. Increasingly, they had a stake in their societies. In the second half of the nineteenth century, reformers responded with a new concept: "public health"—sewers and clean water provided by municipal authorities. Town planning showed the power of industrial capitalism to "improve." The uniformity of the grid plan for city streets evoked an ideal of social equality. Governments stepped up their services to citizens, especially by regulating health, education, and food supply.

Meanwhile, moral restraint, Christian good works, and "enlightened self-interest" blunted the fangs of industrial capitalism and helped to ensure that workers benefited from the wealth industries created. Warned, perhaps, by prophets like Marx and the social movements he helped inspire, or driven by the energy of the market, employers raised wages and improved working conditions. Cheap food, better pay, and declining disease smothered or diminished revolutionary inclinations. Prosperity bought out proletarian rage. As William Cobbett (1763–1835), a leading English reformer, observed, "You can't agitate a man on a full stomach."

Businesses and governments were not purely benevolent. States wanted to be able to recruit large, effective armies. Employers realized that good wages and healthy workforces enhanced production and increased demand for their products. Churches championed workers to forestall revolution.

The United States is the most remarkable case, because Marx expected revolution to start there. Instead, socialists in America were the first to sell out to capitalism. Rather than leading the world into socialism, America led the world in revulsion from it. Industry soaked up all the new labor that immigration and population rise created. The frontier (see Chapter 23) sucked rebels and malcontents out of industrializing areas. Cheap land in the West enabled even poor settlers to achieve prosperity. The American dream became a nightmare for socialists, diverting the hopes of the poor from revolution to self-enrichment.

Socialists yearned for a better future. Other critics of industrialization yearned for a lost past. Artisans smashed machinery to defend their jobs. Romantics deplored a world that the English priest and poet Gerard Manley Hopkins (1844–1889) described as "seared with trade, bleared, smeared with toil." Ironically, escapees from industrialization were often also its beneficiaries. G. Poldi-Pezzoli, an Italian industrialist, collected medieval art. In Barcelona, the architect Antoni Gaudí (1852–1926) created fantasy buildings for captains of industry. The machine age enabled the rich to live out their romantic fantasies in comfort.

When factory workers got home, however, they would often find the "loathsome wretchedness" that Dr. Philip Kay described in Manchester in 1832 in houses "dilapidated, badly drained, damp." Or the worker might be confined to one of the cellar dwellings swilling with filth from the street and from underground. Disease got trapped in the bad ventilation.

Reformers stressed the effects of an industrial environment on workers' morale. In Barcelona, Jaume Balmes thought workers worse off than ancient slaves. Moral criticism reflected the values of the critics, and workers did not necessarily share it. Philip Kay watched the tenants of vile housing "wallow in the unrestrained licence of animal appetite." For workers, the vices he cited were rational survival strategies. Gambling was a form of investment for people with no spare cash to save. Alcohol was a lubricant for dreary lives. Popular songs—the genuine utterances of the working classes—mocked middle-class prudery and praised pleasures that moralists attacked, including drink, gambling, idleness, and sex.

Bosses—according to critics of industrialization—were in moral danger, too. A Barcelona newspaper warned owners that "the mechanics in your factories … must not be confused with the machines you have in your workshops." This mixture of conscience and common sense was typical of the Catholic response to industrialization. Pope Leo XIII (r. 1878–1903) tried to save workers from seduction by socialism. He would not undermine a social hierarchy in which the church had a strong vested interest, but he encouraged Catholics to found their own trade unions. He could not endorse socialism, but he condemned naked individualism.

There had been gigantic concentrations of people before, especially in China, but never had so much population, in so many places, been gathered together in big cities.

In the industrializing world, this was hardly surprising. Owners needed to concentrate labor and communications. Steam power and improved transport moved production nearer to markets, making cities even bigger. The result was a new way to organize life around specialized production processes. Former villages, such as Manchester and Birmingham in Britain and Essen in the Rhineland, became great cities.

At first, industrialization created flimsy cities that bred disease and disorder. In the 1840s, works such as Edwin Chadwick's *Sanitary Conditions of the Labouring Population* in Manchester, or Jaume Salarich's survey of working-class health in Barcelona in the 1850s, described the effects of the textile mills: labored breath, profuse sweat, exhaustion, gastric trouble, poor circulation, mental weariness,

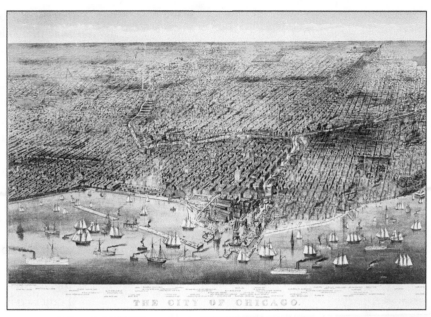

Instant metropolis. In the second half of the nineteenth century, exploitation of the North American prairie and the development of commerce on the Great Lakes turned Chicago from a small fort and trading post into a vast city. This image was made in 1892, when the city shaped its World's Fair to mark the 400th anniversary of the European discovery of the New World.
Dagli Orti (A)/Picture Desk, Inc./Kobal Collection

Edwin Chadwick, from *Sanitary Conditions of the Labouring Population*

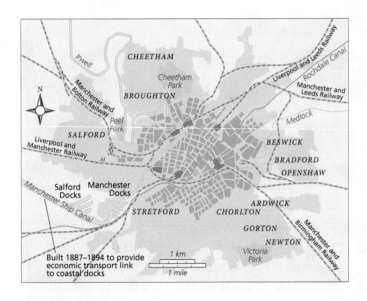

MAP 24.1

The Growth of Manchester, England, 1840–1900

- - - - railway
- ▨ railway station
- ▨ park
- ▨ built-up area 1840
- ▨ growth of city 1840–1900

Most Populous Cities in 1900

Name	Population
1. London, United Kingdom	6,480,000
2. New York, United States	3,437,000
3. Paris, France	3,330,000
4. Berlin, Germany	2,707,000
5. Chicago, United States	1,717,000
6. Vienna, Austria	1,698,000
7. Tokyo, Japan	1,497,000
8. St. Petersburg, Russia	1,439,000
9. Manchester, United Kingdom	1,435,000
10. Philadelphia, United States	1,418,000

United Nations; United States Census Bureau

nervous prostration, corrosion of the lungs, poisoning from machine oils and dyes. Slums clung to city centers. Shanties spread around city edges (see map 24.1).

Food is an even more basic index of the standard of living than hygiene and housing. Growing towns make fresh foods relatively expensive and hard to obtain. As late as 1899, R. See-bohm Rowntree found that most working families in northern England were inadequately fed. Their normal diet was monoto-nous, with only occasional treats of meat and fish. Unlike their rural counterparts, they could not grow vegetables or keep a pig. Some lived almost entirely on oatmeal.

URBANIZATION

Madcap urbanization also happened in parts of the world that played only a minor or marginal role in industrialization. Min-ing, for instance, created mushroom-growth towns, such as San Francisco and Kimberley and Johannesburg in South Africa. In 1871, diamonds were found on a farm at Kimberley. By 1900, 100,000 miners worked there. Gold turned Melbourne, on Australia's farthest Pacific edge, from a village in 1837, the year Queen Victoria came to the throne, into the third largest city in the British Empire, with over 800,000 people, by the time she died in 1901.

Trade, meanwhile, stimulated ports all over the world. The most conspicuous examples were where industrialization was taking off. New York, for instance, grew from 60,000 inhabitants in 1800 to nearly 3.5 million by 1900. But outside the industrializing world, ports from which primary produce was shipped overseas also grew. Cotton trade boosted Alexandria on Egypt's Mediterranean coast from only a few thousand people in 1800 to about 250,000 by 1900. Lagos in Nigeria boomed in the late nineteenth century because of palm oil and cocoa. Buenos Aires grew rapidly thanks to the refrigerated meat trade. Calcutta, a small settlement in 1800, had more than 750,000 people in 1900, because of its role in exporting the dyes and coarse fibers of Bengal. In the 1850s Shanghai became the port of choice for European merchants in China. Thanks to its role in exporting opium, the pop-ulation of Izmir on the Mediterranean coast of Turkey grew at a rate of 2 percent a year from the 1840s, to house more than 200,000 people by the 1880s. Izmir illus-trates how a new kind of cultural life became possible. It had French-built boule-vards and British gas lighting. There were 5 newspapers, 17 printing houses, a large public library, and one of the first theaters in the Ottoman Empire.

Earlier cities were fearsome places, heavily policed, filled with rootless populations, and stalked by diseases. Now they acquired facilities for recre-ation, education, and welfare that are only possible where many people con-gregate and large resources concentrate. Towns were remodeled or enlarged on new principles of urban planning. Paris and Vienna acquired the boule-vards familiar today. Grids of rationally planned streets were added to Madrid and Manhattan. In Cairo and Alexandria, new quarters enveloped the chaotic old cities in networks of straight streets. Opera houses arose in places as remote as Cairo and Manaus, the center of the rubber-producing region in Brazil. New roads, sewerage, water-supply systems, public baths, large stores, street lighting, cafes and clubs, sporting facilities, and trolleys and buses multiplied. New kinds of public spaces arose on cast-iron arches: so-called crystal palaces—glass-covered markets, railway stations, green-houses, shopping arcades. London's Crystal Palace, scene of the first great

Universal Exposition of 1851, housed a display of the world's industrial arts. Madrid's main market, built in 1870, enclosed more than 100 acres in a pyramid of glass.

New urban spaces permitted new kinds of social activity. Mass education was a remarkable development. In some places investment by the state spurred education, partly because states wanted to train people for soldiering. In Japan in 1880, 35 percent of girls—and 70 percent of boys—went to school. Compulsory universal education, introduced in many European countries and the United States during the nineteenth century, was in one respect the most remarkable development of all, for it defied two cherished beliefs: the doctrines of parental responsibility for children and individual freedom.

Opera in the jungle. The nineteenth-century rubber boom turned Manaus, in the Brazilian rain forest, into a grand, rich city, with this enormous opera house that attracted famous singers and musicians from Europe. But Manaus was ruined toward the end of the century when rubber production shifted to the British colonies in Malaya.

BEYOND INDUSTRY: AGRICULTURE AND MINING

But the spread of industry and the growth of towns skipped huge areas of the globe, which remained largely a world of peasants, even in the West. Yet even unindustrialized and deindustrialized regions experienced pressures for social change.

⊙ MAKING CONNECTIONS ⊙

INDUSTRIAL TRANSFORMATIONS IN THE NINETEENTH CENTURY

ECONOMIC / POLITICAL TRANFORMATIONS →	SOCIAL CHANGES →	CHANGES IN DAILY LIFE
Development of industrial/factory-based employment	Urbanization, increased population density; increased labor specialization, formal division of work and leisure time	Work moves from country to city, outdoors to indoors; from homes and small workshops to factories and mines; large, impersonal work environments, bleak working conditions
Salary-based labor system	Shift from proprietorship to large-scale enterprises where power is concentrated in small number of factory and mine owners	Plentiful workers relatively powerless to negotiate unless organized; strict organization of daily routines
Urbanization and mixture of factory–residential districts	Proximity of work offset by increase in air and water pollution; grimy surroundings, lack of public sanitation in high-density cities	Increased exposure to epidemics of cholera, dysentery, and chronic diseases such as tuberculosis
Increased power of municipal, national governments to regulate	Development of idea of "public health" to stem disease, child mortality rates, epidemics, etc.	Increased town planning, public sanitation by 1900 lead to longer life spans, increased livability of cities
Growth of global trade	Increased movement of goods and traders in port cities all over the world; generation of wealth	Foreign goods and luxury items as well as technological innovations spread rapidly in industrialized countries

Peasants from Adjara. The region of Adjara, in present-day Georgia, straddles the southeastern shore of the Black Sea and was contested by the Ottoman and Russian empires throughout the nineteenth century, with Russia gaining the upper hand in 1878. Soon thereafter, the port of Batumi was developed into a major seaport and rail terminus, and commercial agriculture quickly transformed the lives of the peasantry. Farmers, like the ones shown here on their way to market, produced crops, such as tea, for consumption throughout the Russian Empire, and crops, such as corn, for both local markets and export abroad.

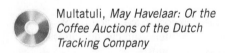

Multatuli, *May Havelaar: Or the Coffee Auctions of the Dutch Tracking Company*

In the country, work in ever-larger fields, employing ever-less labor, displaced traditional agriculture, with its communal habits, companionship, and shared rituals. Revolutions in tenure arose as the brokers or middlemen who sold peasants' crops to merchants began to invest in land themselves, using their control of credit to obtain holdings cheaply. Agriculture, like industry, became increasingly a specialized activity, with particular crops concentrated in favored regions.

The American Midwest, Australia, and Argentina could produce meat and grain with methods that involved relatively little labor, thanks to mechanized harvesting and, for ranching, small, specialized, and free-spirited workforces—cowboys or, in Argentina and Uruguay, *gauchos*. Elsewhere, however, peasants had to be induced or compelled into growing labor-intensive crops. In the East Indies, for instance, the Dutch, in collaboration with native elites, forced peasants to grow coffee, whether their land was suitable for it or not. In Egypt, too, world demand for cotton forced peasants to provide a product they could not eat, at prices they could not influence. Peasant landholdings tended to split under the strain. By the end of the century, Egypt had some 2 million landless peasants, who were subject to forced labor in the irrigation works and conscription into the army.

The Ottoman Empire became a net exporter of crops for the first time in history, thanks to the grapes and opium of western Anatolia, where exports increased by more than 500 percent between 1845 and 1876. Private owners took over state landholdings, while much land passed from the hands of peasants into those of tribal or local chiefs, city merchants, moneylenders, and officials. Sixty percent of the soil of Ottoman Syria—once a peasant land—was officially reclassified as large estates in the early twentieth century. Many estate owners were outsiders—Armenians, Greeks, and Jews.

In West Africa, palm-oil production, formerly the work of gatherers of wild plants, became, from the 1840s, a focus of systematic farming. Harvesting palm fruits, pounding the nuts to extract the oil, and getting the product to market were labor intensive. Typically, a group of independent farmers would combine under an elected leader. In Nigeria, families could operate small palm-oil farms. But as time went on, merchants grabbed land and started slave-operated plantations. Much of the profit went into private armies to fight for power or seize more slaves. Labor was wrenched out of food production to keep up the flow of oil. Transporting and marketing the oil enriched a growing commercial class.

In southern Bengal, indigo planting was the big new opportunity. But it required capital investment, which forced peasants to borrow. Getting a loan—said a magistrate in 1830—reduced the borrower to "little better than a bond slave to the factory." In the second half of the century, jute—a cheap fiber for making rope and bags—became dominant. Peasants abandoned rice to grow jute on plots of an acre or two. But reliance on a single export crop left them at the mercy of the market and led to impoverishment and high levels of debt, incurred to tide them over hard times.

The **caste system** gripped India more tightly than ever, as the British imposed forms of discrimination that were supposedly traditional because they were enshrined in ancient texts, but that people had not practiced much. In southern India, especially, British policy favored the concentration of the best agricultural land in the hands of a few dominant families, reducing many peasants to abject poverty. Western immigrants could also end up joining the losers in the global marketplace. In the mid–nineteenth century, the Portuguese government began settling poor white farmers in Angola to extend Portuguese control of the native Africans. Most of these settlers abandoned export crops and struggled to feed their families, living in hovels, and dressing in rags. The fate of black peasants in Angola was even worse: dispossession and enslavement. In the 1870s, Portugal officially abolished slavery, but not until the early twentieth century did the authorities make serious efforts to stop the illegal export of slaves.

The erosion of independence and of local prosperity was a common—but not universal—consequence of specialization. In the second half of the century, Thailand, formerly a self-sufficient country, began to specialize in a few exportable commodities: rice, tin, and teak. The Thai stayed on the land, increasing output by extending the amount of land under cultivation. They left commerce to Chinese immigrants. The amount of capital investment required for growing rice was modest, and, among foreigners, Chinese supplied most of it. Thailand never succumbed to foreign "business imperialists" (see Chapter 25). Relative to other staple foods, rice earned good profits for the people who grew it. Only about 50 percent of the export price went to the middleman, miller, and shipper.

As well as the fruits of increasingly specialized agriculture, the unindustrialized world also supplied raw minerals in ever-larger quantities. The local impact was often intense. The Kimberley diamond mines in South Africa were a good example. "Every foot of the blue ground," said Cecil Rhodes (1853–1902), one of the big early investors in the enterprise and a champion of the British Empire in Africa, "means so much power." Mines meant power to their owners. To workers, they signified the destruction of traditional life. As soon as diamonds were discovered, black African workers wrenched from agrarian and pastoral communities poured in, struggling to re-create the layouts and routines of their home villages in the squalid, lawless vicinity of the mines. Black mine workers were forbidden to acquire licenses to establish their own diggings. Though nominally not slaves, they could be fined or flogged for desertion of employment, and their wages were never more than a fifth of what white miners earned for similar work.

Although miners in Europe and North America were better treated, mines could wreak comparable havoc in the industrializing world. The Río Tinto copper mines in Spain recruited thousands of Spanish and Portuguese workers in the 1870s and 1880s. The company aimed to practice the sort of productive benevolence associated with the best factories. But decent housing and modest health care and schooling did little to ease the feelings of alienation understandable in uprooted communities or the impatience workers felt at the company's paternalism. Living conditions were always overcrowded, because the building program could not keep up with the demand for labor. The environment was literally poisonous, as sulphurous fumes hung over the area whenever the wind fell. Most of the British staff—the management and most of the top technicians were Britons—were housed in what would now be called a gated community, where ordinary workers and local people were forbidden to enter.

The face of Africa, scarred and pitted by colonial exploitation. Open-cast diamond mining in the "blue earth" at Kimberley, South Africa, in 1872. At that early stage—not much more than a year after the first diamond was discovered on the De Beers's farm—the diggings were checkered with the square plots of individual prospectors. The inability to dig deep enough to find diamonds on small plots led to the consolidation of these shallow digs into bigger holdings and to the formation of the De Beers Mining Company in 1874. By 1914, the Kimberley pit had become the largest man-made crater ever dug.

Industrialization, Mechanization, and Urbanization

Nineteenth century	Factories in the United States and Western Europe reorganize work and reorder workers' lives
1842	Poor living conditions in Manchester detailed in Edwin Chadwick's *The Sanitary Condition of the Labouring Population*
1844–1919	Henry J. Heinz, industrialist and proponent of paternalist management
1845–1876	Ottoman agricultural exports increase fivefold
1848	Publication of Marx's and Engels's *The Communist Manifesto*
1851	London's Universal Exposition held at Crystal Palace
1870	New central market built in Madrid
r. 1878–1903	Pope Leo XIII, advocate of social reform
ca. 1900	Cotton cultivation in Egypt contributes to the creation of 2 million landless peasants
	Population: Izmir, 200,000; Alexandria, 250,000; Calcutta, more than 750,000; Melbourne, 800,000; New York, 3.4 million, London, 6.5 million

CHANGING LABOR REGIMES

The virtual disappearance of slavery—and the total disappearance of plantation slavery in the Americas—was perhaps the most surprising episode of the nineteenth century. Almost every pre-industrial society we know about has considered slavery normal and legitimate—a suitable status for supposedly inferior people, for captives, or for those unable to survive except as a master's chattel. Nineteenth-century Western science produced strong, new justifications for slavery: Certain races were inferior to others. Black people were, according to some anthropologists, more like apes than Europeans.

Slavery and the Slave Trade

On the other hand, slavery repelled believers in three doctrines of growing appeal in the world, especially in the West: evangelical Christianity, egalitarianism, and economic liberalism. According to evangelical Christians, Jesus' message of universal love outlawed slavery. According to egalitarians, all people were equal, and it was nonsense for anyone to be born into slavery. For economic liberals, and especially for those who believed in free trade, slavery was irrational, because people worked better when they did so freely and for wages.

Impeccable in theory, the free-trade doctrine did not seem to be borne out in reality. On the contrary, the world economy relied, as it had relied for centuries, on compulsion to work. In much of Africa, slaves were both a vital labor force and a major export product. In the tropical and subtropical latitudes of the Atlantic-side New World, they were the only labor force available. Trade in slaves sustained shipping in Europe and America. In Liverpool, Britain's leading port, a quarter of the ships were engaged in the slave trade around 1800. Cotton manufacture in Europe, the rum industry of New England, and the arms trade to Africa would all be jeopardized without slavery. In the long run, mechanization might make slavery out of date. But no one could foresee this in the early nineteenth century. On the contrary, the kind of plantation environment in which slavery was entrenched seemed unsuitable for mechanization. In any case, in slave-owning societies, slavery was part of culture and tradition. People practiced it not because it was profitable but because it was part of the fabric of life. So it was not just economics that eliminated slavery. The rise of a new morality changed cultural assumptions. Reformers dismantled the system despite the dictates of tradition, ideology, economics, and what passed for science.

Cotton plantation, USA

They started with the slave trade. This was an easier target than slavery, because it did not involve problems of how to compensate slave owners or dispose of liberated slaves. In the 1790s, in Europe and America, a wave of sentiment against the slave trade broke against the fears and obstacles that vested interests raised. But in 1803, Denmark outlawed the trade. Britain and the United States followed. The abolition of the slave trade became a British national crusade. Indeed, it became a way to justify British imperialism and inspired wars, in which thousands of native slave-traders and their families, who thought they were engaged in a traditional and lawful activity, died. Meanwhile, Britain paid rulers in Africa and the Indian Ocean to stop dealing in slaves.

Reformers expected the abolition of the slave trade to lead to the disappearance of slavery. Demographic trends suggested this possibility. As we saw in Chapter 20, plantation slave populations in the eighteenth century normally had high death rates and low birthrates. But abolition had two unforeseen effects that combined to frustrate the abolitionists' predictions.

First, abolition made slaves more expensive and, therefore, gave new life to the slave trade. The total number of slaves shipped across the Atlantic from Africa to the Americas in the nineteenth century was about 3.3 million. Slavers made great fortunes, charging premiums for the risks they faced in running the gauntlet of the British Navy's patrols. By the 1830s, Pedro Blanco of Cadiz in Spain reckoned that if he could save one vessel in three from capture he could make a profit. At his slave-holding camp in West Africa, he could keep 5,000 slaves at a time. He permanently employed a lawyer, 5 accountants, 2 cashiers, 10 copyists, and a harem of 50 African slave girls.

Second, abolition of the slave trade made slave owners more careful of their slaves. As a result, numbers of slaves began to grow through natural reproduction. When Spain ended the slave trade in 1818, it allowed owners a period of grace during which they could import slave women of fertile years, so that "by propagating the species, the abolition of the commerce in slaves should be less noticeable in future." Meanwhile, in the southern United States, the number of slaves multiplied from under 1 million at the start of the century to almost 4 million by 1860. The upward trend was unstoppable. Even when federal law banned the trade after 1808, world demand for cotton drove the rise of slavery in the South.

Slaves played surprisingly little part in their own liberation. Though rebellions were frequent, plantation societies learned to live with them, absorbing the costs of suppression or confining the runaways to roles that were troublesome rather than fatal to planter control. The big exception was Haiti, the French colony called Saint-Domingue where rebellious slaves seized power in the 1790s. The French Revolution, igniting expectations about "the rights of man" (see Chapter 22), provided Haitian slaves with an ideology of liberation. Yet controversy in Haiti early in the Revolution focused not on whether slavery was right or wrong but on whether free black and mixed-race people should have the right to vote. The slave revolt that began in 1791 seems to have started outside revolutionary circles—with rumors that the king of France had freed the slaves, with voodoo ceremonies, and with a slave leadership barely connected with free black people, some of whom also rebelled against white rule.

In 1792, a new phase began, when Léger-Félicité Southonax arrived as the representative of the French Republic with orders to pacify the colony. The following year, impelled by revolutionary fervor and the worsening security situation, with the British poised to invade, he freed the slaves of the northern province—creating at a stroke, he said, "200,000 new soldiers for the republic." He promoted the most talented black officer, Toussaint L'Ouverture (1746–1803), who, in effect, seized power in 1797.

After the French captured L'Ouverture in 1802, Haitian resistance became desperate. In 1804, L'Ouverture's successor, Jean-Jacques Dessalines, proclaimed "Independence or Death." In a remarkable reversal of the white man's usual rhetoric, he denounced the French as barbarians:

> What have we in common with that bloody-minded people? Their cruelties compared to our moderation—their color to ours—the extension of seas that separate us—our avenging climate—all plainly tell us they are not our brethren. . . . Let them shudder . . . at the terrible resolution we are going to make—to do to death any native of France who shall defile, with his sacrilegious footstep, this land of liberty.

The Haitians officially won their liberty in 1825 at the cost of agreeing to pay a crippling indemnity to compensate French property

Slavery in the Nineteenth Century

1790s	Abolitionist sentiment on the rise in Britain and the United States
1791–1803	Haitian Revolution
1800	1 million slaves in the United States
1800–1900	3.3 million slaves shipped from Africa to the Americas
1803	Denmark outlaws slave trade
1807	Britain outlaws slave trade
1808	Importation of slaves banned in United States
1823	Spain outlaws slavery
1825	Haiti wins official independence
1834	Slavery abolished in the British Empire
1848	France outlaws slavery
1860	4 million slaves in the United States
1863	Emancipation Proclamation (United States)
1885	Egypt outlaws slavery
1886	Cuba outlaws slavery
1888	Brazil outlaws slavery

owners. They excluded white colonists, depriving their country of capital investment and technical expertise. They also sent tremors of fear through other planter societies.

Even without the Haitian example, emancipation of slaves was likely to follow the abolition of the slave trade. In the 1820s and 1830s, some Spanish-American republics led the way, not because they were peculiarly virtuous, but because slavery played a relatively small part in their economies. The British Empire as a whole did not ban slavery until 1834. It took the Civil War (1861–1865) to free the slaves of the southern United States—and even then the federal government's Emancipation Proclamation in 1863 was more a practical response to war conditions than an act of morality. Spain freed its slaves—but not those of its colonies—in 1823. France decreed emancipation in 1848 and the Netherlands in 1863. The Spanish colony of Cuba held out until 1886 and the Empire of Brazil until 1888. Outside the world of plantations, slavery survived longer. Persia signed an anti-slave-trade treaty with Britain in 1882 but never enforced its terms. Egypt made slavery illegal in 1885. Formal laws against the slave trade were proclaimed in the Ottoman Empire in 1889 and in Zanzibar in 1897—which, as part of an Omani trading empire that had ousted the Portuguese from much of East Africa (see Chapter 21), throve as a slave-trading center.

Slavery was not the only form of forced labor to dwindle in the nineteenth century. There was also serfdom in which peasants were tied to the land they worked and could be sold along with, but not apart from, it. In Europe, wars in the aftermath of the French Revolution shifted the frontiers of serfdom eastward, forcing the emancipation of the peasants of central and eastern Germany. The Habsburg monarchy finally granted all former serfs freedom and land in 1853–1854. In Thailand, almost the entire male population was bound by forced labor laws, which the government abolished bit by bit throughout the century.

Even Russia, where most people were still serfs, joined the trend. Peasant violence in the 1840s and, in 1855, defeat in the Crimean War by Turkey, France, and Britain helped to concentrate minds in favor of reform. Russia also felt the pressure of a European model of economic change: recognition that the empire had to enter the railway age and reorganize for industrialization. The Czar proclaimed emancipation of the serfs in 1861.

In Japan, meanwhile, peasants became participants in an enlarged marketplace as communications improved and cities grew. Individual farms tended to replace the traditional village collectives in which all the village families had worked the land in common and shared the harvests. There were crosscurrents. New regulations favored landowners, especially by limiting traditional tenants' rights in common land. But the peasants' lot generally improved. In 1868, the government promised, "the common people, no less than the civil and military officials, shall be allowed to pursue their own individual callings so that there may be no discontent." In the 1870s, government decree freed the dependent peasants and workers of Japan. In 1877, when disaffected samurai attempted a rebellion of the type Oshio Heichiro had tried to launch in 1837, the peasants were on the other side, drafted into the government's army, armed with guns, and drilled in obedience.

In some parts of the world, convicts became a substitute for slave labor. "Hard labor" became a way to exploit criminals' potential for work and to exact retribution from them on behalf of society. In Japan, criminals worked in the notorious Ashio copper mine. Governments in Europe deported hundreds of thousands of convicts—often for minor crimes—to remote, previously uncultivated lands. Australia alone, for instance, absorbed over 150,000 British convicts between 1788 and

Tippu Tip, "the biggest slaver of them all," whose activities on behalf of Sultan Barghash of Zanzibar (see Chapter 25) almost succeeded in preempting European imperialism, before he became a collaborator in the empire-building efforts of King Leopold II of the Belgians. In the opinion of Jerome Becker, one of Leopold's agents in the Congo in the 1880s, "From his [Tippu's] immense plantations, cultivated by thousands of slaves, all blindly devoted to their master, and from his ivory trade, of which he has the monopoly, he has in his duplex character of conqueror and trader, succeeded in creating for himself in the heart of Africa a veritable empire."

1868. Some Pacific Islands, Siberia, former slave-holding states in the United States after the Civil War, and French Guiana in northwest South America relied on convict labor to sustain their economies.

The slaves' main successors worldwide, however, were millions of **coolies:** laborers, mainly from poor communities in India and China, conned or coerced at miserable wages as contracted or indentured workers for some of the era's most demanding work on sugar plantations, tropical mines, and colonial railway-building projects (see Map 24.2). Technically, the Chinese government required that every recruit from Chinese jurisdiction should enter "freely and voluntarily" into his agreement with his employers and shippers. In practice, officials connived in what were effectively deportations or abductions. In the 1860s and 1870s, French recruiters shipped some 50,000 laborers from India to the Caribbean, where, Indian government officials complained, the French "tried everything they could to keep Indians in perpetual servitude." A British report of 1871 characterized the condition of Chinese and Indian laborers in British Guiana in South America as the new slavery. A Chinese government inquiry in 1873 found that "the lawless method by which the Chinese were—in most cases—introduced into Cuba, the contempt there shown for them, the disregard of contracts, the indifference about working conditions, and the unrestrained infliction of wrong, constitute a treatment which is that of a slave, not of a man who has consented to be bound by a contract." After Spain abolished slavery in Cuba in 1886, slave catchers stayed in business—hunting down runaway Chinese workers. There were perhaps 25,000

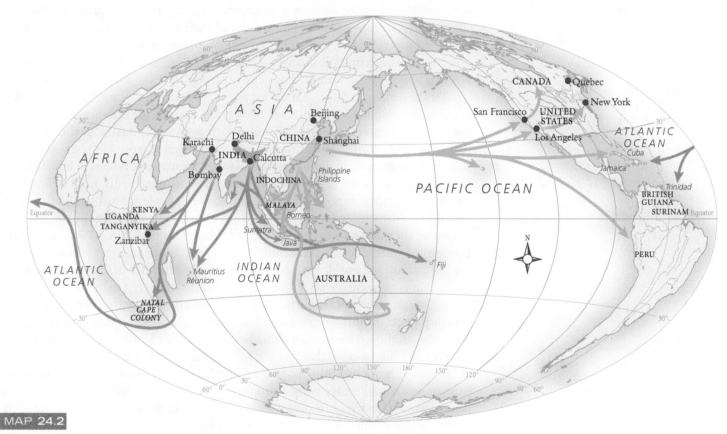

MAP 24.2

The Movement of Indentured Labor in the Late Nineteenth Century

core area of Indian migration   →   Indian migrants

core area of Chinese migration   →   Chinese migrants

Chinese in California in the 1850s. The Central Pacific Railroad employed 10,000 of them. From 1868, by agreement with China, 16,000 arrived annually. Many went to factories in San Francisco, where "Little China" had nearly 50,000 residents by 1875. Violence and immigration controls followed.

From 1834, when the British Empire abolished slavery, until the eve of the First World War in 1914, 4 million workers, mainly from India and China, kept the empire supplied with cheap labor. France conquered Indochina from the 1850s to the 1880s in part to solve the problems of a labor shortage elsewhere in the French Empire.

Chinese immigrants, USA, 1909

Female and Child Labor

So although slavery was abolished in most places and formal serfdom disappeared from Europe, other forms of forced and dependent labor survived and spread. In industrializing economies, it is doubtful how far wage labor was morally superior to slavery. Unlike the masters of slaves, factory owners did not have the right to sell their workers or, at least in theory, sexually abuse them. But work in the factories and mines of the West and its colonies was highly disciplined, unless and until governments allowed workers to organize in trade unions and bargain collectively for their wages. Women and children joined the workforce. Child labor was, of course, entirely forced labor, as was much of the work that women did. Both categories contributed to the success of industrialization. In Germany in 1895, nearly 700,000 workers were under 16 years of age. In France in the 1890s, 32 percent of the manufacturing workforce were women. Well over half the industrial workforce in late nineteenth-century Japan were women, mostly from rural backgrounds, living in supervised dormitories and sending most of their meager pay back home to their village relatives. The biggest source of employment for women was the result of other social and economic changes. Urbanization increased demand for domestic servants and for retail staff in shops and markets.

Trends similar to those of the West were visible in patches wherever industrialization occurred. In Ottoman-ruled Syria and Lebanon, for instance, 85 percent of the workforce in silk reeling, the only steam-powered industry in the area, was female in 1914. Women were dragged into new forms of work in the unindustrialized or deindustrialized worlds, too. Indian tea plantations relied on female labor to pick the tea leaves, partly because women were supposedly nimble fingered, partly because they were cheap to hire and easier to exploit. Most families came to depend on women's wages. In West Africa, men took over much of the work of pounding the palm nuts to extract their oil, which was traditionally women's work. But women were diverted into selling oil and food. Their menfolk benefited. As in the industrializing world, the new economic opportunities of the era led men to assert claims to women's labor and to the proceeds that labor earned.

Although some women turned to jobs outside the home to escape the domination of parents or husbands, it is hard to resist the impression that women were—as usual—employed where men could best exploit their labor. In a German factory, a survey in 1900 revealed that half the women employed claimed that they worked because their husbands could not earn enough to support their families. The problems of balancing factory work and family life were formidable—especially since factory workers married relatively young, typically in their early twenties in highly industrialized countries, such as Britain and Germany, in the late nineteenth century. Even women who stayed at home worked harder, as factories and mines sucked in their menfolk and deprived wives of their husbands' help at home. In the cities, prostitution boomed, often employing, in effect, enslaved women.

In the long run, industrialization led Westerners to reevaluate womanhood and childhood. Women and children were perceived as ideal for certain industrial tasks but were also treated as marginally efficient workers. Gradually, mechanization took them out of the labor market. Society rationalized the process by representing it as a form of liberation and even of elevating the status of women and children. Womanhood was placed on a pedestal. Children were treated as a distinct rank of society whereas formerly they had often been seen as little adults, or as "enemies" who needed discipline, or simply as negligible, even expendable, given the high rates of child mortality.

These were uniquely Western cults, barely intelligible in cultures where women and children were still men's partners in production. The status looked enviable in artists' and advertisers' images of delicate femininity or angelic childhood. But there were disadvantages. Societies that freed children from the workplace tried to pen them inside schools. For many children, and for parents who needed their children's wages, compulsory education was a form of tyranny. The romantic ideal of childhood was more often forced than coaxed into being. Schools were repressive and designed to mold pupils according to adult agendas.

Women liberated from work were assigned a role and rights that resembled, in some respects, those of children. Stiflingly male dominated, middle-class homes confined women. Henrik Ibsen (1828–1906) brilliantly captured the atmosphere in 1879 in his play, *A Doll's House*, which depicts the married household as an oppressive pen from which a woman must struggle to escape. For middle-class women, the fall from the pedestal could be bruising. In 1858, the British artist Augustus Egg painted an adulteress in three terrible stages of decline and destitution. Great composers devoted operas to sexually promiscuous heroines who came to a bad or a sad end—Verdi's *La Traviata* (1851), Bizet's *Carmen* (1875), and Puccini's *Manon Lescaut* (1891), and *La Bohème* (1896). The fallen woman became the favorite villain or victim of the age.

For peoples formerly enslaved, only a modified form of freedom emerged. Even in Haiti, the army kept slaves at work. In areas of previously slave-staffed plantations, a labor crisis followed emancipation. It was met by enforcing new sources of labor and going back to an older pattern of tenure with peasants, renting the land and sharecropping, forced to give landlords a percentage of their harvests. Liberated slaves were too numerous to command much power in a free labor market. In the British West Indies, they made up 80 percent of the population. In the French and Dutch Caribbean, the proportions were 60 and 70 percent respectively. Poor European immigrants supplied the labor that industry needed in the United States, while Indian and Chinese coolies in the Caribbean kept labor there relatively cheap. For most black people in the United States, part of the consequence of emancipation was economic misery and subjection to "color bars": In many states white people excluded them not just from the right to vote and equal opportunities in employment but also from supposedly public spaces and services. Black Americans were subjected to the petty humiliations, enforced by violence if necessary, of exclusion from white churches, schools, restaurants, hotels, athletic and recreational facilities, hospitals, and even streetcars, railroad cars, drinking fountains, cemeteries, and park benches.

Free Migrants

Massive migration of free labor was the final feature that helped to reshape the world's labor force. Population increase combined with improved, cheap, long-range communications to make unprecedented migration rates possible.

Russian and Chinese migration into northern Asia—Siberia and Manchuria—illustrates this well. Russia's population exceeded 167 million in 1900—an increase

Tea picker. Tea was an imperial beverage in the nineteenth century. First, Britain encouraged mass production of tea in India to undermine Chinese exports. Then the British introduced the crop to Sri Lanka, where this harvester is shown at work in a photograph from the 1890s. This "Ceylon tea" is now prized, but it was originally a cheap, inferior beverage to help keep British industrial workers alert.

 Henrik Ibsen, from *A Doll's House*

New Labor Patterns

1788–1868	150,000 convicts shipped from Britain to Australia
1850s	25,000 Chinese live and work in California
1853–1854	Serfs in Habsburg Empire emancipated
1860s and 1870s	French ship 50,000 Indian laborers to the Caribbean
1861	Serfs in Russia emancipated
1870s	Japanese workers and peasants freed by official decree
1880s	5.25 million immigrants arrive in the United States
1890s	32 percent of French work force is female; 1 million settlers move to Siberia; 14 million people emigrate from China
1890–1920	Migration adds 18.2 million people to U.S. population
1895	700,000 German workers under 16 years of age
1914	30 percent of the population of Argentina is foreign born

Italian immigrants. The photographs Lewis Hine (1874–1940) took of immigrants arriving at Ellis Island in New York City in 1904–1905 launched his career as one of the most socially influential photographers in U.S. history. This shot of an Italian mother and her children, which Hine hand colored, typifies his talent for capturing the dignity and promise of the poor and oppressed.

of nearly 20 million since 1880. Siberia relied on convict labor until the 1870s, but by the end of the century, almost all the migrants there were free. Nearly 1 million settlers entered Siberia during the 1890s while the Trans-Siberian Railway was under construction (see Chapter 23). About 5 million followed early in the twentieth century, when the railway was complete. Chinese colonization of Manchuria increased after 1860 when the Qing relaxed the rules restricting it. China, indeed, was still the world's most prolific source of long-range colonists. The age-old Chinese diaspora in southeast Asia gathered pace, rising to a total of almost 14 million in the 1890s, and leaping further in the years before the First World War.

Meanwhile, the steamship trade, which also facilitated coolie migration, helped to populate under-exploited frontiers in the Southern Hemisphere and the North American West, and to provide labor for American industrialization. Europe, because of its exceptional rise in population, was the main source of free migrants. "New Europes," areas with similar climates and environments to those the migrants left behind, were the most attractive destinations. There were areas of this kind in North America, the southern cone of the Americas—Brazil, Argentina, Chile, and Uruguay—Australia, New Zealand, and South Africa.

Most transatlantic migrants headed for the United States, which gained more than 128,000 migrants in the 1820s, and over 500,000 in the 1830s. Numbers tripled in the next decade, mostly from Germany, Britain, and Ireland. A further leap in the 1880s brought the total to over 5.25 million, from all over Europe and especially from Scandinavia, Italy, Central Europe, and the Russian Empire. This was the manpower that fueled continental expansion and industrialization.

From 1890 to 1920, migration brought a net gain of 18.2 million people to the United States—more than in the entire previous history of the country (see Map 24.3). In combination with industrialization, this turned the United States into a major world power. After 1892, the United States subjected immigrants to quotas and questioned them for suitability. Political undesirables and the morally suspect were excluded, as were those suffering from infectious diseases, such as syphilis and tuberculosis. Canada and some South American countries, especially Argentina, also made huge gains. By 1914, when 13 percent of the population of the United States was foreign born, the corresponding figure in Argentina was 30 percent. Nearly half Argentina's immigrants came from Italy and nearly a third from Spain. Most of the rest were Eastern Europeans.

HUNTERS AND PASTORALISTS

When the pattern of world population settled after the shake-up, former parts of it had vanished or shrunk. After slaves, the numbers of pastoral and foraging peoples diminished the most. In some places, mechanized agriculture wiped them out or penned them in reservations where they were doomed to decline. In others, they were converted to settled ways of life. Alternatively, the unfamiliar diseases that contact with outsiders introduced diminished or destroyed them. They survived only in environments too unappealing for better-armed peoples to contest, such as the harsh Kalahari, where San hunters of southern Africa fled to elude their black and white persecutors, or in the vast but merciless Australian interior, where aboriginals retreated from white settlers, or in the Arctic. Occasionally, the hesitations of potential enemies saved them: inhibitions that were sometimes romantic, sometimes practical, sometimes a bit of both. In 1884, for instance, when the Swedish government was considering the fate of the Sami—the reindeer herders of the far north—some theorists argued that the pastoralists were relics of an inferior race, whom the laws of nature doomed to extinction. Opponents countered that Sami culture was "the only one suited to expansive regions of the country." The "small peoples of the north," as Russians called them, benefited from the perceptions of romantics who saw them as embodiments of the ideal of the noble savage (see Chapter 22) or as survivors from an earlier phase of their own peoples' past.

Most pastoralists and foragers, however, lacked such protectors. Railways carved up the lands of the hunter peoples of the North American West. Reservations broke up their communities. Phoney treaties shifted them onto marginal lands where survival was hard. Massacres harassed them into submission. Rifles and machine guns enabled generals to exterminate native peoples "like maniacs or wild beasts." Free rations of cattle bought off the survivors of wars. In 1872, an American army officer reported of the Shoshone of the Great Plains: "Their hunting grounds have been spoiled, their favorite valleys are occupied by settlers and they are compelled to scatter in small bands to obtain subsistence." He described the same depths of demoralization and beggary to which other Native American peoples of the mid- and far west had plunged.

Similar ruthlessness solved the problem of what to do with foragers in the grasslands of South America. In the 1840s, an Argentine president decided that white competition doomed his country's Indians "to disappear from the face of the Earth." In the 1880s, machine guns fulfilled his prophesy when the discovery of gold in the far south of Argentina turned the remotest limits of the American hemisphere into contested territory. Professional manhunters charged around five dollars for every Indian they killed. At the opposite end of the hemisphere, in the Aleutian Islands off the coast of Alaska, missionaries and bureaucrats saved the native fishing communities from extermination by Russian conquerors but could not mitigate the effects of diseases to which the inhabitants had no resistance. An epidemic in 1838–1839 wiped out half the population. When Russia sold Alaska to the United States in 1867, another wave of looters arrived, with another alien culture, imposed by force.

Less dramatically, but equally effectively, governments in the Old World induced nomads to change their way of life. Mehmet Ali, the khedive of Egypt (see Chapter 23), turned nomadic Arab tribal leaders into landowners, mobilized the desert warriors, and seized their horses. The former nomads shifted to the towns or became "lost among the peasants." Russian governments forced Muslim Khazaks and Kirgiz nomads in Central Asia into agriculture by confining them to land grants too small for them to graze their flocks.

An Auracano chief in native dress with the Andes behind him, painted in 1853. The native peoples of the extreme southern cone of the Americas fought off Spanish conquistadores and resisted the Chilean and Argentine republics until industrially produced machine guns defeated them in the late nineteenth century.

ELITES TRANSFORMED

Industrialization created proletariats. The dwindling of slavery, serfdom, and foraging transformed rural lives and work patterns. Migration and new forms of social control shook up the role and distribution of the world's labor. At the top end of society, the changes of the period were almost as traumatic for those they touched. While peasantries and working classes suffered, the era of industrialization transformed aristocracies or, at least, severely tested them. They survived by diversifying from an emphasis on landed estates into new economic activities. When they failed to adapt, they perished.

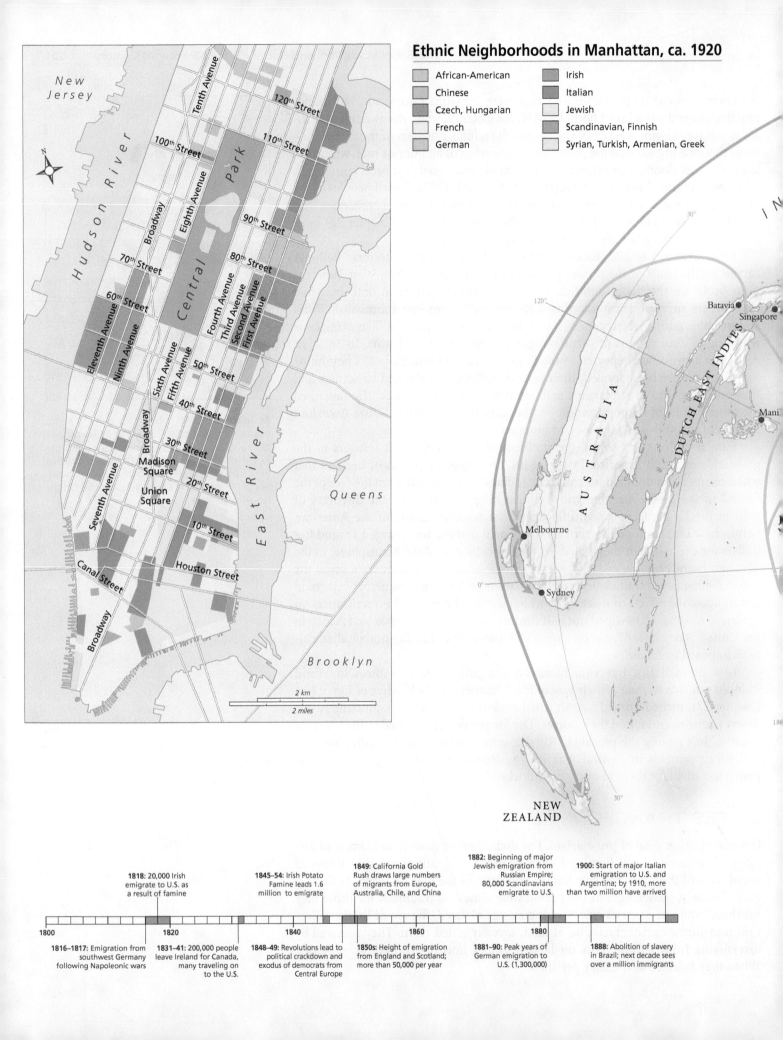

Ethnic Neighborhoods in Manhattan, ca. 1920

- African-American
- Chinese
- Czech, Hungarian
- French
- German
- Irish
- Italian
- Jewish
- Scandinavian, Finnish
- Syrian, Turkish, Armenian, Greek

New Jersey

Hudson River

Central Park

Tenth Avenue
120th Street
100th Street
110th Street
90th Street
Broadway
Eighth Avenue
80th Street
70th Street
Fourth Avenue
Third Avenue
Second Avenue
First Avenue
60th Street
Eleventh Avenue
Ninth Avenue
Sixth Avenue
Fifth Avenue
50th Street
40th Street
Broadway
30th Street
Madison Square
20th Street
Seventh Avenue
Union Square
10th Street
Houston Street
Canal Street
Broadway

East River

Queens

Brooklyn

2 km
2 miles

Batavia
Singapore
Mani

DUTCH EAST INDIES

AUSTRALIA

Melbourne

Sydney

30°
120°
0°
30°

NEW ZEALAND

1816–1817: Emigration from southwest Germany following Napoleonic wars

1818: 20,000 Irish emigrate to U.S. as a result of famine

1831–41: 200,000 people leave Ireland for Canada, many traveling on to the U.S.

1845–54: Irish Potato Famine leads 1.6 million to emigrate

1848–49: Revolutions lead to political crackdown and exodus of democrats from Central Europe

1849: California Gold Rush draws large numbers of migrants from Europe, Australia, Chile, and China

1850s: Height of emigration from England and Scotland; more than 50,000 per year

1881–90: Peak years of German emigration to U.S. (1,300,000)

1882: Beginning of major Jewish emigration from Russian Empire; 80,000 Scandinavians emigrate to U.S.

1888: Abolition of slavery in Brazil; next decade sees over a million immigrants

1900: Start of major Italian emigration to U.S. and Argentina; by 1910, more than two million have arrived

1800   1820   1840   1860   1880

MAP 24.3

World Migration, ca. 1860–1920

Transatlantic migration
- to North America
- to South America and the Caribbean
- to Europe from the Americas

Other European migration
- to Australia and New Zealand
- to North Africa

Asian migration
- to the Americas and Australia
- Russian migration into Siberia
- Indian migration within British Empire
- transcontinental railroad
- major exporters of people
- major importers of people

MAP EXPLORATION
www.prenhall.com/armesto_maps

Elite uniforms. The Freemason's Lodge of Freetown, in Sierra Leone in West Africa, presents an address to the Duke of Connaught, a son of Queen Victoria, on December 15, 1910. The white ladies, in their tea dresses under the canopy, and the top brass with ceremonial swords and pith helmets, look positively informal by the standards of the black dignitaries, who wear what appears to be full court dress in the heat of the tropical day. It would be hard to find a more telling image of determination to defy the environment.

Thorstein Veblen, from *The Theory of the Leisure Class*

In Japan, the government abolished samurai privileges in the 1870s. A military draft for all able-bodied men in 1873 eliminated the main legal distinction—the right to bear arms—between samurai and commoners. Japan now had no warrior caste. Many samurai benefited from the abolition of distinctions within their own class. Lower samurai were now free to accumulate wealth and honor. Professions that had formerly been considered socially beneath them, such as merchants and civil servants, opened up to the gentry, and many of them became dependents of the government. They also served as officials and as officers in the new European-trained army and navy or invested in new industries. Others merged into the ranks of the commoners.

Traditionally, in China merit had been the means to attain high social rank. But rich families had an advantage because they could afford good schooling for their sons and tended to monopolize access to the scholar elite in the nineteenth century. "The gentry are at the head of the common people," said imperial instructions to magistrates, "and to them the villagers look up." The impoverished landowners of China shook off the ties of extended kin and the traditional social obligations of their status. Thanks to their efforts to find new sources of wealth, by engaging in trade, or by exploiting the labor of poor neighbors and tenants on their land, they found themselves demonized as "evil gentry."

The British aristocracy survived the collapse of land prices by diversifying into commerce, by marrying American heiresses, and by absorbing into its ranks the "beerage"—the new class of wealthy entrepreneurs, such as those who owned the massive, mechanized breweries that supplied the workers' beer.

The sons of the **new rich** acquired the habits, friends, and tastes of gentlemen at the numerous new and expensive schools—called "public" in Britain only because they sought to be of public importance—and the growing universities. Old blood allied with new money. Industrialization shifted the balance of power and wealth away from landed estates and into cities. But landowners could also benefit by mining coal and iron ore on their estates or by leasing or selling the land on which to build towns and docks. The third Marquess of Bute (1847–1901) did all these things and left an estate equivalent to several hundred million dollars today. As early as the 1840s, about a sixth of England's landed gentry earned a significant part of their wealth in business, mainly through manufacturing, banking, and railways. Aristocracies were becoming middle class while the middle class was adopting aristocratic tastes.

Every industrializing economy had its new rich and its declining aristocracies. In Spain, Pérez Galdós satirized the decline of old money in one of his best novels, *Mercy* (1897), about hard times for an aristocratic family, who were maintained by their maid's talents as a beggar. In Russia, Chekhov's play *The Cherry Orchard* (1904) features an old landed family compelled to sell its estate, and the upwardly mobile entrepreneur who buys them out, after enduring years of their contempt.

In the United States, "old" money, which was in truth not very old, was more vulnerable to intrusion by the new rich because the country had no landed aristocracy and no titled nobility. Nonetheless, in 1899, Thorstein Veblen proposed in *The*

Theory of the Leisure Class that America had acquired an elite basd on inherited wealth. In the 1870s and 1880s, Samuel Ward McAllister attempted to create high society, based on the admission of supposedly suitable people to entertainments given by socially exclusive hostesses in New York City—exclusive, that is, according to McAllister himself. "We want the money power," he explained in 1872, "but not to be controlled by it." In effect he was admitting that the American aristocracy was open to new money, and indeed, merchants and railroad men's sons and daughters got into McAllister's list of America's "First Four Hundred."

Outside the West, westernization made the rise of a new class easier by spreading values and tastes distinct from those of traditional aristocracies. In the 1870s, one Angolan chief looted his own people to build a medieval-looking castle. In the 1890s, another hired an ex-slave who had worked for the Portuguese as a maid to teach him European etiquette. Almost everywhere, Western dress became the uniform of the world's elite—at least for men. Formal suits with top hats were the uniform of male power, whether among well-to-do of West Africa or the Maori chiefs of New Zealand. The self-reinvented samurai who staffed the Japanese government chopped off the topknots from their hair and clamped shiny top hats to their heads.

IN PERSPECTIVE: Cultural Exchange—Enhanced Pace, New Directions

Industrialization restored a kind of uniformity to Western society. A gap opened between the developed and underdeveloped worlds. The technology gap became a wealth gap between the regions that supplied commodities and those that turned them into manufactured goods. These worldwide inequalities were bigger, and would prove more enduring, than the internal class differences that divided industrializing societies.

Meanwhile, exchanges of culture crossed the world with greater intensity and speed than ever before. No example was more obviously attuned to the pace of industrialization than the standardization of time. Until the nineteenth century, every place determined its own time of day according to the sun and set its clocks accordingly. But the railway made it impossible to maintain this "natural" time. People could move too fast. The railway schedules became too complex. In 1852, an electric telegraph system was set up to transmit the time at the Royal Observatory in Greenwich across Britain. In 1880, Greenwich time became the official standard time for the whole country. In 1884, the same standard became the basis for a sequence of time zones covering the globe. Cultural exchange got faster and more complicated than ever, in part because people could travel farther and more frequently than formerly. The world's first travel agent, Thomas Cook and Company, was founded in Britain in 1841. By 1900, Cook's was selling 3 million travel packages a year, mostly to working- and middle-class tourists within Britain. But Cook's also took luxury travelers, big-game hunters, businesspeople, and even officials of the British Empire across the world.

Cultural exchange, however, was not one-way Westernization. What Europeans considered exotic became fashionable in the West. The Japanese-inspired style that

Cultural exchange. The fashion for Japanese art and taste in the late nineteenth-century West extended to women's clothing. Paintings of Westerners in Japanese kimonos—like these American women painted in San Francisco around 1880—demonstrate the fashionable appeal of Japan. Note the view of Mount Fuji in the background on the left-hand panel.
Photograph courtesy of the Peabody Essex Museum

 Japanese impressions of American culture, 1860

CHRONOLOGY

1791–1803	Haitian Revolution
1800	1 million slaves in the United States
1800–1900	3.3. million slaves shipped from Africa to the Americas
1807	Britain outlaws slave trade
1808	United States bans importation of slaves
1825	Haiti wins official independence
1834	Slavery abolished in the British Empire
1838–1839	Epidemic wipes out half of the native population of the Aleutian Islands
1842	Edwin Chadwick's *The Sanitary Condition of the Labouring Population*
1845–1876	Ottoman agricultural exports increase fivefold
1848	France outlaws slavery; publication of Marx's and Engels's *The Communist Manifesto*
1850s	25,000 Chinese live and work in California
1853–1854	Serfs in Habsburg Empire emancipated
1860s and 1870s	French ship 50,000 Indian laborers to the Caribbean
1861	Serfs in Russia emancipated
1863	Emancipation Proclamation (United States)
1870s	Japanese workers and peasants freed by official decree; samurai privileges abolished
1880s	5.25 million immigrants arrive in the United States; bounty offered for killing Indians in Argentina
1885	Egypt outlaws slavery
1886	Cuba outlaws slavery
1888	Brazil outlaws slavery
1890s	32 percent of French work force is female; 14 million people migrate from China
1890–1920	Immigration adds 18.2 million people to U.S. population
ca. 1900	Cotton cultivation in Egypt contributes to the creation of 2 million landless peasants
	Population: Izmir, 200,000; Alexandria, 250,000; Calcutta, more than 750,00; Melbourne, 800,000; New York, 3.4 million; London, 6.5 million
1914	30 percent of the population of Argentina is foreign born

Western designers called "Japonisme" was the most striking case. Monet (1860–1926) portrayed his wife in a kimono. Puccini, the leading operatic composer in 1900, put Japanese, Chinese, and even Native American music in his operas. These exchanges took in wider influences, too. In the 1890s, Dvořák was among the first European composers to draw on African-American music. European painters and sculptors began to discover what they called primitive art from Africa and the South Seas. Some exchanges bypassed the West altogether. In the 1890s, Chief Mataka of the Yao—deep in the East African interior—made his people don Arab dress, launched Arab-style ships on Lake Nyasa, planted coconut groves and mangoes, and rebuilt his palace in the mixed Arab–African Swahili style (see Chapter 21). "Ah!" he exclaimed, "now I have changed Yao to be like the coast!"

Although cultural transmissions increasingly crisscrossed the world, one route the big new influences came from was the United States, heralding trends that would dominate the twentieth century. This was new. North America had previously followed European and Latin American cultural leadership. In politics, as we shall see, the United States launched, nurtured, or revised some ideas of enormous and growing influence in the world—including, notably, democracy and socialism—but no significant movement in the arts, literature, science, or philosophy started in the United States before the 1890s. Then, however, the flood began, as European composers discovered American ragtime. It was a small beginning, but it was the herald of the dawn of an "American century" in which the United States was increasingly to be the source of worldwide trends in popular culture, entertainment, the arts, taste, food, technology, and ideas.

PROBLEMS AND PARALLELS

1. What were the advantages and disadvantages of modernization and industrialization in Japan and Europe in the nineteenth century? Who were the winners and losers from this process?

2. How did industrialization change daily life for the average urban dweller? Did these changes improve life or make it more difficult? What does the term *paternalism* mean? Why did Karl Marx's prediction of a workers' revolution not come to pass?

3. How did large-scale urbanization transform social, economic, political, and cultural life in the nineteenth century? What types of organizational structures, architecture, and municipal systems developed to cope with highly concentrated populations? How did machines change the way people viewed the environment?

4. What forms of labor replaced slavery in the nineteenth century? How did industrialization change women's and children's lives?

5. How did massive migration of free labor reshape the world's labor force?

DOCUMENTS IN GLOBAL HISTORY

- Samuel Smiles, from *Self-Help*
- Karl Marx and Frederich Engels, from *The Communist Manifesto*
- Edwin Chadwick, from *Sanitary Conditions of the Labouring Population*
- Chinese immigrants, USA, 1909
- Multatuli, *May Havelaar: Or the Coffee Auctions of the Dutch Tracking Company*

- Cotton plantation, USA
- Henrik Ibsen, from *A Doll's House*
- Thorstein Veblen, from *The Theory of the Leisure Class*
- Japanese impressions of American culture, 1860

Please see the Primary Source DVD for additional sources related to this chapter.

READ ON

My version of the story of Oshio Heicharo is based on I. Morris, *The Nobility of Failure* (1988).The best general survey of the nineteenth-century world is C. A. Bayly, *The Birth of the Modern World* (2003).

T. Hunt, *Building Jerusalem* (2004), and A. Briggs, *Victorian Cities* (1993) deal with urbanization in the British state and empire. J. Merriman, ed., *French Cities in the Nineteenth Century* (1981) is a good survey of France; C. Chant and D. Goodman et al., eds., *European Cities and Technology: Industrial to Post-industrial City* (1999) is a valuable six-volume collection of essays and documents. Peter Hall, *Cities in Civilisation* (1998) is particularly good on urban culture. On the effects on health, D. Brunton, *Health, Disease, and Society in Europe* (2004) is a highly useful collection of documents. R. J. Evans, *Death in Hamburg* (1987) is an impressive case study.

On working conditions in the industrializing world, P. Stearns, *Lives of Labor* (1975) is particularly good. J. Burnett, ed., *Useful Toil* (1994) is a valuable collection of English working-class autobiographical materials. A. Kelly, *The German Worker* (1987) does a similar job for Germany. R. C. Alberts, *The Good Provider* (1973) is a lively biography of Heinz. G. Marks and S. M. Lipset, *It Didn't Happen Here* (2000) is a useful attempt to explain the failure of socialism in the United States.

M. Lynch, *Mining in World History* (2004) is a magisterial survey, with emphasis on technological aspects. S. Kanfer, *The Last Empire* (1995) is an enjoyable history of De Beers. D. Avery, *Not on Queen Victoria's Birthday* (1974) studies the Río Tinto case.

On rural conditions in the unindustrializing world, S. Bose, *Peasant Labour and Colonial Capital* (1993) is an outstanding study of Bengal; for Thailand, J. C. Ingram, *Economic Change in Thailand* (1971) is excellent. On Africa, M. Lynn, *Commerce and Economic Change in West Africa* (2002), and W. G. Clarence-Smith, *Slaves, Peasants, and Capitalists in Southern Angola* (1979) are important. J. McCann, *Green Land, Brown Land, Black Land* (1999) surveys sub-Saharan Africa with emphasis on the ecological effects of economic development. C. Issawi has published a series of invaluable works, rich in documents, on the Middle East, notably *The Economic History of the Middle East* (1966) and *An Economic History of Turkey* (1980), which can be supplemented with R. Kasaba, *The Ottoman Empire and the World Economy*; P. Richardson, *Economic Change in China* (1999) is a good introductory survey on that country.

For changes in labor regimes, H. Thomas, *The Slave Trade* (1999) and D. Northrup, *Indentured Labor in the Age of Imperialism* (1995) are fundamental. The eight volumes of P. J. Kitson and D. Lee et al., eds., *Slavery, Abolition, and Emancipation* (1999) make an invaluable collection of mainly literary and theoretical source materials. S. Miers and R. Roberts, eds., *The End of Slavery in Africa* (1988) and P. C. Emmer and M. Morner, eds., *European Expansion and Migration* (1992) are useful collections. P. Kolchin, *Unfree Labor* (1990) compares America and Russia.

CHAPTER 25
Western Dominance in the Nineteenth Century: The Westward Shift of Power and the Rise of Global Empires

Unequal combat in the Opium Wars. The British ironclad *Nemesis* blows Chinese war junks to smithereens with impunity, on January 17, 1841, off Guangzhou. The print was circulated at the British shipbuilders' and arms-makers' expense, partly to advertise their wares.

IN THIS CHAPTER

THE OPIUM WARS

THE WHITE EMPIRES: RISE AND
RESISTANCE

METHODS OF IMPERIAL RULE

BUSINESS IMPERIALISM

IMPERIALISM IN THE "NEW
EUROPES"

EMPIRES ELSEWHERE: JAPAN,
RUSSIA, AND THE UNITED STATES

RATIONALES OF EMPIRE
Doctrines of Superiority
The Civilizing Mission

IN PERSPECTIVE: The Reach of
Empires

On February 10, 1842—Chinese New Year's Day—General Yijing (yee-jing) consulted the oracles in the Temple of the War God. China was at war with Britain. Yijing could succeed, the oracle warned, only if "you are hailed by humans with the heads of tigers." A few days later, a band of aboriginal recruits arrived dressed in tiger-skin caps. The general was delighted and distributed similar caps throughout the army. All his ways to secure victory had a touch of desperation. He contemplated attacking the British ships with monkeys strapped with firecrackers to their backs. But the monkeys died of starvation.

CHINA

The campaign was chaotic. Chinese troops mistook and fought their own men. The supply department failed, inflicting unendurable hunger on the army. Commanders received rewards for writing reports on nonexistent victories. Embezzlers raided the war chest. Only a fraction of the army arrived in time for the battle. They faced, moreover, a new kind of "barbarian." The British forces had state-of-the-art munitions—products of early industrialization—and steam-powered gunboats. They could recruit men—"black devils," as the Chinese called them—from India, where Britain was building up an empire. The Chinese could not stop the invasion.

At first glance, the outcome looks like a triumph for modernity. Ancient methods and magic failed in the face of professional forces equipped with industrially produced equipment. The dynamic out-thrust of a go-ahead Western nation shattered an inward-looking, self-satisfied empire.

• • • • •

Such conclusions would be unfair. Chinese respect for omens did not usually cloud rational judgment or obstruct military efficiency. The deficiencies of organization and generalship in Yijing's command were not unique to, or typical of, Chinese warfare. The Chinese government was negotiating with France to buy the latest Western military and naval technology, but the war broke out before the Chinese could acquire it.

Nevertheless, the conflict revealed how much the balance of power in the world had shifted. For most of recorded history, China had been the source of world-shaping technological innovations, the "central country," with the strength to influence or dictate politics far from its own borders and shores. Britain had spent most of history on the edge of Eurasia—literally, a marginal part of the world—absorbing influences from outside rather than radiating its own influence to the rest of the world. Now the positions were reversed. Thanks in part to the substitution of machine power for manpower, a small country like Britain could defeat a giant such as China. Thanks to the exploration of the wind systems of the world and the development of technologies of long-range communications, a position on the edge of the West had turned from a disadvantage into an advantage. From the shores of the Atlantic, powers in Western Europe and North America could use seaborne communications to mesh together ambitious and vast territorial domains. The broader context of General Yijing's failures reveals a further vast shift in global history: an economic shift—upheaval in the traditional balance of wealth and reversal in the traditional structures of trade.

FOCUS questions

- WHY DID China cease to be the world's richest nation in the nineteenth century?
- WHY WAS the West able to subjugate so much of the world?
- HOW DID African states resist Western imperialism?
- WHAT WAS business imperialism?
- WHERE WERE the "New Europes"?
- WAS THE United States an empire in the nineteenth century?
- HOW DID social Darwinism justify imperial rule?

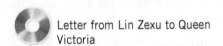
Letter from Lin Zexu to Queen Victoria

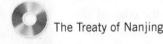
The Treaty of Nanjing

THE OPIUM WARS

A trade dispute, indeed, had provoked the war of which Yijing's campaign formed part. At the center of the dispute was opium. The opium trade represented a breakthrough into a market in which, previously, most foreigners had virtually nothing to sell. Because narcotics are addictive, they create their own captive markets and command high prices. This makes them ideal commodities for relatively poor producer economies seeking outlets in rich economies.

The annual value of the opium that reached China rose fivefold in the 20 years preceding the mid-1830s. As the trade increased, it caused alarm in China, much as today's global traffic in heroin and cocaine alarms the West.

Chinese statesmen blamed opium for demoralizing, enfeebling, and impoverishing large numbers of Chinese. The drain of revenues also threatened one of China's historic sources of strength: its favorable balance of trade with the rest of the world. The situation became acute in the 1830s, because Britain abolished trading monopolies among its own subjects and opened free trade with China. The Chinese emperor, therefore, appointed Commissioner Lin to end the opium trade.

In February 1839, Lin drafted a summary of Chinese thinking for British readers. "Our great, unified Manchu Empire," Lin wrote, "regards itself as responsible for the habits and morals of its people and cannot rest content to see any of them become victims to a deadly poison. For this reason we have decided to inflict very severe penalties on opium dealers and opium smokers…. What it is here forbidden to consume, your dependencies must be forbidden to manufacture. When that is done, not only will the Chinese be rid of this evil, but your people too will be safe. For so long as your subjects make opium, who knows but they will not sooner or later take to smoking it?" Lin also appealed to something the British understood: commercial considerations. "The laws against the consumption of opium are now so strict in China that if you continue to make it, you will find that no one buys it and no more fortunes will be made. Rather than waste your efforts on a hopeless endeavour, would it not be better to devise some other form of trade?"

In the spring and summer of 1839, Lin flushed all the opium he could find into the sea. He was unable, however, to secure promises from the British merchants that they would withdraw from the trade, and in January 1840, the imperial court suspended trade with Britain. The British acknowledged that China could punish its own subjects for smoking opium. But to ban the trade itself was unlawful interference in the freedom of commerce and to confiscate opium from British merchants was an outrage against private property. In the summer of 1840, a British expeditionary force blockaded China's ports, reopening trade by force. The following year, British warships, with opium vessels in their wake, sacked China's coastal and river towns. The British hardly noticed General Yijing's counterattack of 1842.

In the Treaty of Nanjing, which ended the war, China ceded Hong Kong to Britain, opened five other ports to British trade, and paid an indemnity of 21 million silver dollars (equivalent in purchasing power today to around $2 billion). Henceforth, British officials, not Chinese, would settle disputes between British and Chinese subjects. Britain would have what we now call "most favored nation" rights in China. British subjects would automatically enjoy any privileges and immunities that China conceded in future to other foreigners. The United States, France, and Sweden soon persuaded or forced the Chinese to grant them similar treaties.

To the Westerners' surprise, the subsequent growth of trade still favored the Chinese, at least until the late 1860s. Tea was a more valuable drug in the West than opium was in China, and the market for it was bigger and faster growing. Britain's official deficit with China rose from under $20 million in 1842 to nearly $55 million in 1857. It took more British incursions and invasions from 1856 onward to wrest from China terms of trade weighted in Westerners' favor. In 1860, the Taiping rebellion virtually paralyzed the Chinese state. A French and British task force found it easy to march to Beijing, burn the imperial summer palace, and exact the terms the Westerners wanted from the Chinese government (see Chapter 23).

Henceforth, foreigners dominated China's trade and bought up the best real estate in the major trading centers (see Map 25.1). In 1880, for instance, two British steamship companies handled 80 percent of China's shipping business. The effects of the wars partly account for this leap to Western ascendancy. In the background, other influences piled up. First, industrialization in the West compensated for China's size and enabled Western economies to overtake China's in wealth. Second, imperialism in other parts of the world increased the resources available to Western powers.

The rise of the West to economic superiority over China—and of some Western powers to economic dominance within China—was one of the major reversals of history. Since then, the world has experienced an abnormal situation, in which—until the last few years, at least—China has been stagnant and, by the technical standards of Western powers, backward or underdeveloped, while historical initiative—the capacity for some groups in the world to influence others—has been concentrated in the West. Whereas for centuries China had been the only country to occupy the position of a *superpower*—a state exceeding in strength that of all rivals combined—Western states have been the main contenders for that role. Britain exercised it briefly in the nineteenth century, and the United States has enjoyed it—briefly again, so far—in the late twentieth and early twenty-first centuries.

Destroying opium. Commissioner Lin destroyed the opium he confiscated from Western—chiefly British—merchants at Guangzhou in 1839 by mixing it with lime and flushing it into the sea or, in the example here, setting it on fire.

THE WHITE EMPIRES: RISE AND RESISTANCE

The change occurred in the context of a new feature of global history in the nineteenth century: the rise—beginning, like industrialization, in Western Europe and rapidly including Russia, the United States, and Japan—of enormous empires that virtually carved up the world among them. Previously, most of the big empire-building initiatives in the world had originated in Asia, and the empires expanded by land into territories that bordered on those of the conquerors. Such was the nature of the empires of the Persians, Arabs, Chinese, Indians, and Mongols whose stories have dominated much of this book. Chinese rulers had never sent fleets beyond the Indian Ocean or armies beyond Central Asia (see Chapter 15).

Alongside the great empires, smaller imperial ventures had also set out to control trade rather than production, to dominate sea-lanes and harbors rather than

MAP 25.1

Foreign Imperialism in East and Southeast Asia, 1840–1910

Area of control or influence

Russian

Japanese

French

British

Dutch

American

Portuguese

German

1898 date of acquisition by foreign power

Leased territory	Treaty ports
◇ Japanese	◎ Japanese
◇ French	◎ French
◇ British	◎ British
◇ Portuguese	◎ American
◇ German	● open port

Qing Empire at its greatest extent ca. 1850

Foreign attacks on China

→ British (Opium War 1840–1842)

→ Anglo-French campaigns 1858–1860

→ French 1883–1885

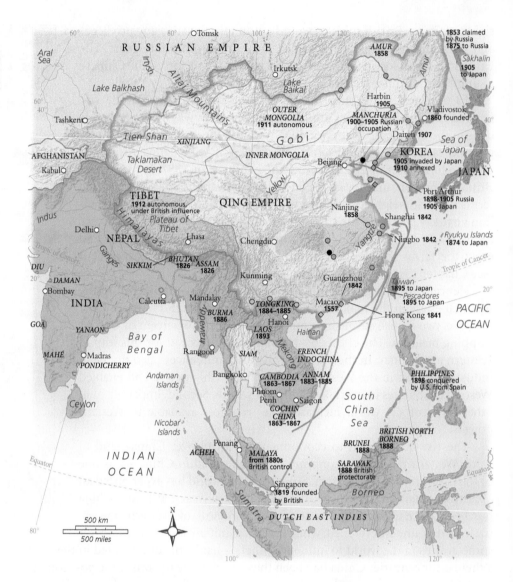

large stretches of land. Most European imperialism had been of this character. Until the eighteenth century, as we saw in Chapter 21, no empire except Spain's had been able to combine these roles on a large scale. Europeans overseas had generally depended on local collaborators in existing economic systems. Now their relationship with the world they had entered changed, as they exploited the advantages of industrially equipped armies and navies to control the production of the key commodities of global trade. The combination of land and sea empires became commonplace.

As in industrialization, Britain established an early lead in imperialism. The first world war—different, of course, from the First World War of 1914–1918—began during the French Revolution in the 1790s (see Chapter 22) and ended with the final defeat of Napoleon in 1815. The British government had already begun to think globally, locating colonies in strategic positions along the world's trade routes. While continental European powers fought each other, Britain wrested colonies from France, Spain, and Holland and seized stations to control global communications by sea, including Malta and other Mediterranean islands, South Africa, parts of the Dutch East Indies, French islands in the Indian Ocean, and islands and coastal positions in and around the Caribbean.

Other governments had, as yet, no such vision. China was self-absorbed, barely aware of events in the wider world. Japan was still proudly ignorant of global events—content to rely on Dutch informants. Even the French closed windows to the world in the early nineteenth century. First, France withdrew from Egypt, then abandoned the effort to reconquer Haiti from rebellious slaves, then, in 1803, sold to the United States its claims to the vast territory known as Louisiana. The British could consolidate the conquests they had already made, thanks to a long period of peace with other European countries that lasted for almost 40 years after the fall of Napoleon.

For other powers, the empire-building process really took off in the second half of the century (see Map 25.2). In Africa, seven European powers colluded to seize 10 million square miles of territory. The Pacific was sliced up in similar fashion. In southeast Asia, only Thailand eluded European, Japanese, or American imperialism. Even in parts of the world largely exempt from the rule of these empires—Latin America, and east and southwest Asia—local governments had to accept economic domination and political interference.

Existing empires enlarged. The extent of land under French rule doubled between 1878 and 1913. The total territory of all European empires more than doubled to more than 20 million square miles over the same period, while the total population of their empires increased from a little over 300 million to over 550 million people (see Figure 25.1). New empires emerged: those of Germany, Italy, and Belgium. These were new countries, outcomes of European rebellions and wars: Belgium only came into being in 1830, while Italy and Germany were forged by the unification of many smaller states in the 1860s. Italy's empire was built up by a state with no direct access to the Atlantic. Italy used the Mediterranean as a route to expand into North Africa and the Levant, and the new Suez Canal, which opened in 1869, as a means of access to conquests in East Africa. Portugal acquired a "third" African empire in Angola and Mozambique to replace those it had lost in the Indian Ocean and Brazil. The Netherlands withdrew from West Africa to consolidate a huge empire in Indonesia. Some parts of Europe took little part: the Scandinavian powers and Spain engaged in the outreach of this period only modestly, while the Habsburg Empire, centered in Austria and Hungary, with limited access to the sea, showed no interest in overseas expansion. Russia's vast land empire left it little scope and energy for maritime adventures (see Chapter 21). With these exceptions, however, it is fair to speak generally of "European" global imperialism.

In part, we need to understand European expansion against the background of demographic change. Over the eighteenth and nineteenth centuries as a whole, despite big rises in population in parts of Asia, Europe's share of world population rose from around a fifth to over a quarter, whereas Africa's share of world population dropped to little more than 8 percent by 1850. The reasons for this are unknown. It seems, however, that while plague (see Chapter 14) receded from Europe, sub-Saharan Africa's killer diseases—malaria, sleeping sickness, yellow fever—remained rampant, and in North Africa plague lingered until at least the 1830s. The decrease of population in Africa altered its role in the world.

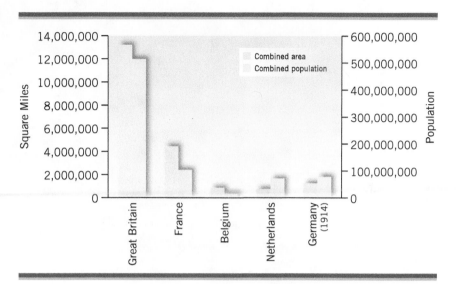

FIGURE 25.1 EUROPEAN EMPIRES: AREA AND POPULATION, CA. 1939

Niall Ferguson, Empire: The Rise and Demise of the British World Order and the Lessons for Global Power, *New York: Basic Books, © 2003, p. 242.* Reprinted by permission of Basic Books, a member of Perseus Books Groups.

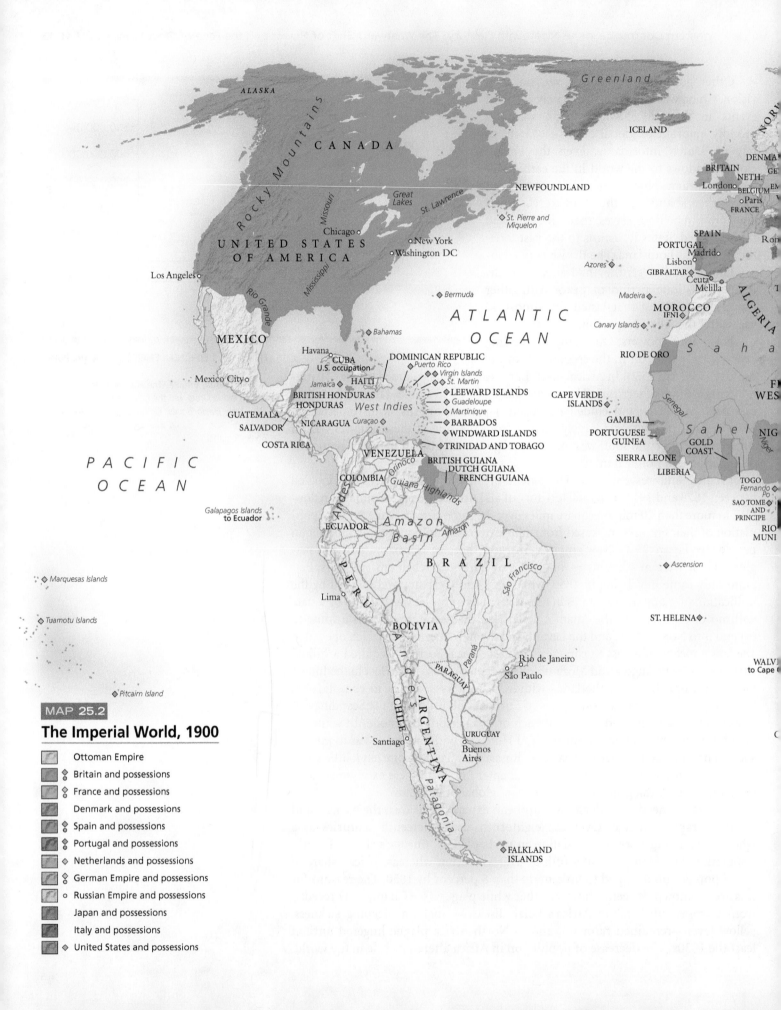

Greenland

ALASKA

ICELAND

CANADA

DENMA
BRITAIN
NETH. GE
Londono BELGIUM EM
oParis
FRANCE

Rocky Mountains

Great
Lakes

St. Lawrence

NEWFOUNDLAND

Missouri

SPAIN
PORTUGAL Ron
Madrid
Lisbon
GIBRALTAR Ceuta
Melilla

St. Pierre and
Miquelon

Chicago

UNITED STATES
OF AMERICA

New York
Washington DC

MOROCCO
IFNI

Azores

ATLANTIC
OCEAN

Los Angeles

Rio Grande

Mississippi

Bermuda

Madeira

Canary Islands

Sahа

MEXICO

Bahamas

ALGERIA

RIO DE ORO

F
WES

Havana
CUBA
U.S. occupation

DOMINICAN REPUBLIC
Puerto Rico
Virgin Islands
St. Martin

CAPE VERDE
ISLANDS

Senegal

Mexico City

Jamaica
HAITI

LEEWARD ISLANDS
Guadeloupe
Martinique

Sahel

GAMBIA

NIG

BRITISH HONDURAS
HONDURAS

West Indies

PORTUGUESE
GUINEA

GOLD
COAST

GUATEMALA
SALVADOR
NICARAGUA
Curaçao

BARBADOS
WINDWARD ISLANDS
TRINIDAD AND TOBAGO

SIERRA LEONE

LIBERIA

COSTA RICA

TOGO
Fernando
Po

PACIFIC
OCEAN

VENEZUELA
BRITISH GUIANA
DUTCH GUIANA
FRENCH GUIANA

SAO TOME
AND
PRINCIPE

COLOMBIA

Orinoco

Guiana Highlands

RIO
MUNI

Galapagos Islands
to Ecuador

ECUADOR

Amazon
Basin

Amazon

Ascension

Marquesas Islands

PERU

BRAZIL

São Francisco

ST. HELENA

Lima

Tuamotu Islands

BOLIVIA

WALV
to Cape

Rio de Janeiro
São Paulo

Paraná

PARAGUAY

Pitcairn Island

Andes

CHILE

ARGENTINA

URUGUAY
Buenos
Aires

Santiago

Patagonia

FALKLAND
ISLANDS

MAP 25.2

The Imperial World, 1900

Ottoman Empire
Britain and possessions
France and possessions
Denmark and possessions
Spain and possessions
Portugal and possessions
Netherlands and possessions
German Empire and possessions
Russian Empire and possessions
Japan and possessions
Italy and possessions
United States and possessions

Percentage of Earth's Land Surface
Controlled by Colonial Empires in 1914

- Independent: 29.8%
- Chinese: 6%
- Ottoman: 1.5%
- Russian: 15%
- Portuguese: 1%
- Spanish: 1%
- French: 7.7%
- Belgian: 1.6%
- Italian: 1.8%
- German: 1.6%
- Japanese: 0.4%
- United States: 7.6%
- Dutch: 1.4%
- Danish: 1.5%
- British: 21.5%

645

The Battle of Omdurman. "Whatever happens, we have got the Maxim gun and they have not," wrote a British cynic about combat between modern Western armies, armed with machine guns, repeating rifles, and heavy artillery, and their non-Western foes who still fought with spears, swords, and shields. This contemporary commemorative panorama of the British victory over the Sudanese at the Battle of Omdurman revels in the slaughter wrought by irresistible technical superiority. Almost 11,000 Sudanese were killed and at least 16,000 wounded in this battle, at a cost of 48 British lives—half of which were lost when a British colonel insisted on fighting one anachronism with another by launching a cavalry charge.

For European intruders, it came to make more sense to take over African soil and exploit its products and potential directly, instead of milking the continent for slave labor.

Europe still did not have enough manpower to dominate the world. Industrial technology, however, made up much of the shortfall. Victim-peoples of Western imperialism found it hard to resist invaders borne on steamboats, fortified by quinine, and armed with steel guns. In the last quarter of the century, machine guns, especially the Maxim gun, patented in 1884, made a huge difference because unlike heavy artillery, they could be easily transported almost anywhere. In 1880, General Roca machine-gunned his way through the Native American defenders of the pampa in Argentina. In 1881, a similar campaign of extermination began against the Yaqui Indians in northwest Mexico. The government expropriated their lands, giving 1 million acres to a frontier rancher and over 1.2 million acres to a U.S. construction company. In 1884, French guns silenced opposition to their takeover of Indochina. British gunships blasted the southeast Asian kingdom of Burma out of existence in 1885. In 1893, white settlers in what is now Zimbabwe in southern Africa shot the spear-armed Ndebele warriors to pieces. In a typical gesture of despair in 1895, Ngoni priests in Mozambique in East Africa threw away their bone oracles after defeat by invincibly well-armed Portuguese. In 1898, at the battle of Omdurman, the British mowed down the forces of a Sudanese leader. The Sudanese lost 11,000 dead and 16,000 wounded. British losses are usually put at 48 killed, 382 wounded. Like all technological advantages, the West's military superiority could not be permanent, but it was vital while it lasted.

Still, it would be a mistake to attribute the empires' dominance to technology alone, any more than to demographics alone. Despite medical advances, disease could still defeat white armies in tropical climes throughout the century. In South Africa in 1879, it killed twice as many British soldiers as were lost in combat to the Zulus. In Cuba in 1898, during the Spanish-American War, three times as many Americans fell to disease as to enemy action. Partly because of the ravages of disease, it took France 13 years of brutal warfare, from 1882, to conquer Vietnam, even with an army of 35,000 men. Nor did Western armies always have things all their own way on the battlefield. During wars against the Sikhs of northwest India in the 1840s, the British found that the defenders could almost match their firepower. In 1876, an alliance of Sioux and Cheyenne almost annihilated a cavalry force at the Little Bighorn. In 1879, a Zulu army surprised a British force at Isandlhwana in South Africa. Of 1,800 British troops, only about 350 escaped alive.

Underequipped native defenders on colonial frontiers could prolong the wars with guerrilla tactics, keeping the British out of Afghanistan in the 1840s and 1870s and harassing the French in Algeria. In the East Indies, the Dutch lost 15,000 men subduing resistance in Java in the 1820s. It later took them 30 years, from 1873, to bring the sultanate of Aceh in northern Sumatra under control, thanks to fierce native guerrillas and killer diseases.

Two cases illustrate the possibilities of successful native resistance in conventional warfare. The Maori wars in New Zealand lasted from 1845 to 1872, on and off. Maoris repeatedly got the better of the British by devising tactical and technical responses to the invaders' superior firepower, copying the volley-firing discipline of European troops. Indeed, the Maori were among the most effective users of muskets. In the 1830s, musket-armed Maori conquered the Chatham Islands, southeast of New Zealand, dispossessing and slaughtering the native fisher folk.

Ethiopia proved to be even more robust. Emperor Menelik II (r. 1889–1913) came to the throne as a passionate modernizer with a love of gadgets. He used revenues from expanding trade to buy Western arms. By the mid-1890s, he had 100,000 modern rifles. He also reformed the army's supply services, while upholding the traditional methods of recruiting soldiers, via the warrior aristocracy and local chiefs, and the traditional ideology of crusade. He proved that an African state could compete with European empires in the scramble for Africa.

Menelik conquered an empire of his own in the south and along the upper Nile to the west. He scattered garrisons in conquered territory, imposed Christianity on pagan communities, and introduced the customs of his native province of Shoa. In 1896, Italy attempted to take over his empire. At the battle of Adowa, the Italian army crumbled in the face of Ethiopian firepower. The Italians lost a third of their 18,000 men killed, plus a further 1,500 wounded and 1,800 captured. Ethiopia emerged from the scramble for Africa as the only enlarged native African state.

Ethiopia is a reminder that even in the nineteenth century imperial expansion was not a white privilege. Other native African states tried it but succumbed to conquest by Europeans. Khedive Ismail of Egypt (r. 1863–1879), for instance, was, for a time, one of Africa's most successful native imperialists. He realized that steam power could open up the African interior and that he could exploit Western sympathies to help him create an empire among the remotest reaches of the Blue and White Niles. Posing as the policeman of slave-trading routes, he would raise finance for empire-building among antislavery philanthropists in Britain and France. He employed Europeans to lead armies and administrators into what he called the "province of Equatoria," in Central Africa. But the difficult environment and vast distances defeated him. His armies were overwhelmed or isolated. Along the Red Sea and Blue Nile, he encountered invincible resistance from the native states. Meanwhile, his ambitions bankrupted Egypt, and his westernizing ways helped provoke a nationalist rebellion. In 1882, Britain took control of the Egyptian government (see Chapter 23). What remained of Ismail's conquests became the Anglo-Egyptian Sudan—in effect, an unruly part of the British Empire.

In northwest Africa, meanwhile, the sultan of Morocco, Mulay Hassan (r. 1873–1894) tried to preempt European imperialism by claiming dominion over the Sahara, as ruler of "all the tribes not subject to another sovereign" and of "the land of all the tribes who mention the sultan in their prayers." These were unrealistic pretensions. The desert peoples acknowledged "no other chief than Allah and Muhammad." After Mulay Hassan's death, rebellious sheikhs and jealous European powers weakened his empire until, in 1904, France and Spain partitioned Morocco between them.

A European view of the battle of Adowa. In contrast to the Ethiopian version of the battle depicted on the Closer Look on page 649, the European press managed to invest the Italian defeat with the heroic quality of a last stand against overwhelming odds. In this typical example from a British newspaper, *The Graphic*, the light is falling on the Italians' gleaming uniforms, which convey an impression of civilization and almost of sanctity, in contrast to the demonic savagery of their Ethiopian attackers. The Italian troops are surrounded by spent cartridge cases. The kneeling soldier on the right, with his transfixed look and prayerful posture, is trying to reload despite a mortal wound. Outlined against the gunsmoke, on a rearing horse, General Baratieri, the Italian commander, raises his helmet in a last salute to rally his doomed troops.

⦿ MAKING CONNECTIONS ⦿

TECHNOLOGY AND IMPERIALISM

TOOLS AND TECHNOLOGY →	REGION OF DEVELOPMENT/DATE OF INVENTION →	EFFECTS
Invention of chronometer	Britain / 1770s	Allowed for precise location of longitude, increasing security of long-range navigation; effective planning of voyages
Steelmaking technology	Britain and Western Europe / 1730s–1800s	Increased productivity in steelmaking creates more products; more effective small arms and artillery
Rifles and breach-loading artillery	Britain and Western Europe / 1840s–1900	Combined with better materials (see above) to improve weaponry
Tropical-weight clothing	Britain and Western Europe / 1850s–1900	Allowed more mobility, comfort in tropical zones for colonial military and officials
Quinine pills, powders, and other medicines	Europe (1750); large-scale use by 1850	Used to stave off effects of malaria; helped increase mobility of European colonial officials and soldiers in Africa/Asia
Steam power	Britain / 1769–1900 (continuously improved)	Powering ships, railroads, vastly increased speed over wind-propelled sails or horsepower on land
Machine guns	Europe / 1860s–1900 (continuously improved)	Allowed for annihilation of native resisters of colonialism in Latin America, Central America, Indochina, Africa, and Burma

The sort of empire Mulay Hassan imagined in North Africa, Said Barghash (r. 1870–1888), sultan of the island of Zanzibar in East Africa, dreamed of in the heart of the continent. "Chosen," he claimed "by Providence to found a great African kingdom which will extend from the coast to the great lakes and beyond to the west," he realized that he needed to conciliate European powers. He therefore posed as a foe of the slave trade—but, along with ivory, slaves were the wealth of the region he claimed. Instead of relying, like Khedive Ismail, on European officers, Barghash employed African and Arab agents to represent him in the African interior. They were often implicated in slaving, which was a provocation to the Europeans. Barghash's system was doomed. By the time he died, Britain and Germany had dismembered and shared out his territories. Zanzibar became a British protectorate in 1890.

METHODS OF IMPERIAL RULE

White imperialism relied almost everywhere on native collaborators. Far from being passive playthings of white superiority, native Asian, African, and Pacific states were participants in the process and native peoples were its exploiters and manipulators, as well as its victims. Without native help in policing and administration, the Western colonial empires could never have functioned.

India, for instance, had fewer than 1,000 British administrators in the 1890s in a country of 300 million people. European observers considered Java, with 300 Dutch administrators for 30 million people "overgoverned." British troops in India never numbered more than 90,000 men—0.03 percent of the population. The rest of the Indian army, more than 200,000 men, was made up of Indian troops under British officers. Though empires sometimes shipped large armies to their colonies for conquests or to repress rebellions, they could never afford to keep such forces in place for long.

AN ETHIOPIAN VIEW OF THE BATTLE OF ADOWA

In the Battle of Adowa in 1896, the Ethiopians under the command of Emperor Menelik II (r. 1889–1913) annihilated an invading Italian army. An Ethiopian painting from early in the twentieth century shows the victors in a more positive light than in the European version of the same battle on page 647.

Menelik calmly directs his troops. He is dressed in imperial regalia and accompanied by officials and holy men who survey the action from underneath umbrellas that signify their rank. The umbrellas are dark colored as a sign of mourning that Christian blood was being shed by both sides.

Astride a white horse, and protected by a halo painted in the national colors of Ethiopia, St. George leads Menelik's army.

Ethiopian firepower includes cannon, machine guns, and repeating rifles.

Legendary Ethiopian heroes, clad in traditional dress, slash the Italian infantry with swords.

With his horse facing backward, the Italian commander, General Baratieri, appears ready to order a retreat.

How does this painting provide a different perspective on nineteenth-century imperialism from the version that most Westerners believed in at the time?

The most common device for harnessing native cooperation was what the British called **indirect rule** (or *dual role* as the Dutch called it, or *association* to use the term the French applied in Indochina). "The keynote of British colonial method," said Frederick Lugard (1858–1945), the official largely responsible for developing the system of indirect rule in Africa, was "to rule through and by the natives." As a British parliamentary committee recommended in 1898, "Adopt the native government already existing; be content with controlling their excesses and maintaining peace between them."

Lugard exaggerated in claiming that this was a uniquely British method, which "has made us welcomed by tribes and peoples in Africa." On the contrary, it was how most empires succeed and have succeeded throughout history. Europeans were welcome in many places that became regions of indirect rule because of the *stranger effect* (see Chapter 16). Some cultures are disposed to grant what may seem surprising power to outsiders—sometimes because of the high esteem accorded to the exotic and strange, and sometimes because of a shrewd calculation: The foreigner is useful, because outsiders can be—or appear to be—objective. So, as long as they retained local power, many native elites were willing to grant the topmost level of authority to European intruders and pay them to exercise it.

Indirect rule worked particularly well in British colonies because British administrators, even though they were usually middle class, had an aristocratic outlook and education and came from an old monarchy. They could sympathize with traditional elites and aristocracies and could even sense that they had more in common with them than with many of their fellow Britons. Especially after 1877, when Queen Victoria officially took the title of Empress of India, British administrators sought to link the traditional Indian elite to the crown with aristocratic trinkets: coats of arms, lavish ceremonies, knighthoods, and other titles. Indirect rule was more than a charade, however. Local, regional, and subordinate native rulers retained real power. More than one-third of India was divided among states ruled by Indian princes, and native sultans ruled virtually the whole of Malaya.

Friendly native chiefs administered parts of German East Africa (modern Namibia). Traditional local rulers and autonomous sultanates survived in the Dutch East Indies. Even the French republic ruled through native monarchs in Cambodia, Laos, and Vietnam, while Morocco and Tunisia were French *protectorates* under puppet Arab monarchs. In their tropical African possessions, the French delegated awkward jobs, such as tax collecting, to native chiefs.

The British far preferred to rely on traditional aristocracies rather than on the "educated natives" whom the French favored. But educated natives, especially interpreters, were indispensable. Even though most colonial regimes privileged some particular set of laws—usually those of their own mother country—in practice many competing systems of traditional and customary law applied in vast territories inhabited by many different historic communities. Locals, who knew their way around the native cultures, were vital guides. In the 1860s, 4,000 of them served in the administration of the British-ruled parts of India. Twenty years later, Indians occupied nearly two-thirds of the jobs.

An alternative strategy to indirect rule or reliance on native administrators was to ship collaborators in from far away. When Frederick Lugard marched into Uganda in East Africa in 1890, his forces included many African Muslims. When Henry Morton Stanley claimed the lower Congo in Central Africa for King Leopold II of the Belgians in 1880, he found a French outpost commanded by a black Senegalese sergeant, dressed "in dirty African rags," who declared "in all seriousness that, being the only White man there, he was glad to see others arrive to keep him company." In Sierra Leone in West Africa, Britain established a colony of freed slaves from the Caribbean, who created an imitation of England in their capital at Freetown, with garden parties, lecture circuits, concerts, and a temperance union to combat alcoholism. Sawyer's bookshop in Freetown sold such English middle-class manuals of behavior as *The Ballroom Guide* and *Etiquette and the Perfect Lady*.

In other places, local allies enabled the Europeans to rule. The British fought the Zulus with the help of other peoples of South Africa and recruited Hausa gunners from Nigeria to keep order in West Africa. The French conquerors of Tukolor on the Niger River in West Africa in 1889 incorporated thousands of other Africans into their army. Then, when their native soldiers rebelled, the French enlisted the conquered Tukoloros against them. In the 1890s, the British Empire nurtured the Kingdom of Lozi in southern Africa while pulverizing the neighboring Ndebele people into submission. The Lozi king acquired a portrait of Queen Victoria, visited London to great acclaim, and became a satisfied client of white imperialism.

Women were among the most important native collaborators. "White" women were in short supply in the European colonial territories in the first half of the nineteenth century, but relations between European men and native women could be advantageous to both parties, opening useful local links for the colonizers and, for local groups, exploitable channels of communication with the incoming elite. The future British field marshal Sir Garnet Wolseley (1833–1913) wrote as a young officer to his mother from India that with a native concubine he could supply "all the purposes of a wife without any of the bother." Concubinage, however, virtually ceased in India after native soldiers rebelled against British rule in 1857, which panicked the British into distancing themselves further from native society. Female emigration from Europe also increased in the late nineteenth century. In the Dutch East Indies, less than a quarter of the European settler population was female in 1860. The proportion had risen to well over a third by the end of the century. India saw a similar rise in the numbers of British women. In former times, the children of sexual alliances between natives and newcomers had often cemented the alliances on which empires relied. In the nineteenth century, that became harder, because racism classed "half-breeds" as inferior and kept them on the margins of the communities from which they sprang.

White Man's Burden. The Indian Civil Service (ICS) was the highly paid, professional bureaucracy that governed Britain's Indian Empire. Until the 1920s, its members were overwhelmingly British. This dinner menu for members of the ICS in 1904 looks lavish and self-indulgent at first but reveals much about the difficulties of governing distant empires: the range of activities for which the civil servants felt responsible; the differences in development in the largely rural India of the day; nostalgia for the tastes of home; and the self-mocking humor that helped English administrators cope with their jobs.
© *The Trustees of the British Museum*

BUSINESS IMPERIALISM

The most indirect form of imperial rule was economic control, which left government in local hands but bought up resources, skimmed off wealth, introduced foreign business elites, reduced economies to dependency, and diverted wealth and political influence abroad. Industrialization made business imperialism possible. A wealth gap between primary and secondary producers gave the rich of the industrialized countries surplus capital with which to buy up the productive capacity of much of the rest of the world. Though the evidence is insufficient, scholars debate whether large-scale foreign enterprises frustrated economic growth and industrialization in regions where business imperialism was rife.

Latin America registered the most obvious effects. In a sense, colonialism never really ended in Latin America. Native communities, or "indios," as they were called, constituted most of the population in most of the region, but they never exercised a fair share of power or acquired a fair share of wealth. Instead, they became the quasi-colonial victims, the exploited human "resources" of their countries' own elites. These elites, though they drove out the representatives of the Portuguese and Spanish crowns, continued themselves to represent European culture—to speak the languages and maintain the customs and privileges of the European conquerors.

Moreover, in the second half of the nineteenth century, foreign investors became a powerful extra elite tier in much of Latin America. A new form of colonial-type dependency arose, this time on international big business. Overwhelmingly, the investors were Europeans, from the major imperial powers of the day—Britain, Germany, and France—and from the United States. In the **Monroe Doctrine** of 1823, the United States had unilaterally decreed a ban on European colonialism in the New World. Thanks in large part to European agreement, the ban worked, and European powers stayed out of most of mainland Latin America for most of the time. But business imperialism almost became the forerunner of reimposed European rule. In 1864, France installed a puppet ruler in Mexico, on the pretext of securing Mexican debts owed to European creditors. Popular rebellion, the need for troops in Europe, and United States' diplomacy drove the French away in 1867, but the involvement of foreign business in the Latin American economy kept growing.

British investments in Latin America rose from $425 million in 1870 to $3,785 million by 1913. This added up to two-thirds of the total foreign investment in the region. British companies controlled over half the shipping in Argentina and Brazil and most of South America's railways. By 1884, Europeans owned two-thirds of Chile's nitrates—the valuable new fertilizers of the period (see Chapter 23). Argentina's foreign trade almost trebled in the last three decades of the century. Foreign capital led the boom. Similar developments occurred throughout Latin America. Like other forms of imperialism, business imperialism was a collaborative project between locals and strangers: local elites and foreign capitalists. In 1870, a British firm opened for business in Rosario, Argentina's second largest city, to provide water and drainage. The local authorities demanded high levels of investment and a high share of the yield for themselves. In Brazil, British power in the coffee market aroused many complaints, but Brazilians owned or acquired most plantations, and the government accepted underdevelopment and economic inferiority to foreigners as inevitable.

Francisco García Calderón, from *Latin America: Its Rise and Progress*

Business imperialism. Even countries that "business imperialism" condemned to produce primary products for the industrialized world could experience industrialization of their own. Some cotton-growing countries, for example, sought to become textile manufacturers. This early twentieth-century photograph of a factory in Ecuador shows automated spinning under way on the right and cylinders full of carded cotton on the left.

Hostility to foreigners was rarely effective. A pattern emerged: Local interests attracted foreign investment. This led to foreign control of key technologies for producing and transporting primary commodities. The consequence was dependence on foreign markets and financiers and, often, political control by foreign businessmen. In 1870, for instance, Costa Rica contracted out its railway-building program to an engineer from the United States. A few years later, his nephew began using the railway to ship bananas to North America. His firm eventually grew into the United Fruit Company—a conglomerate so rich and monopolistic that it became more powerful in the early twentieth century than any government in Central America. The United States itself, meanwhile, was an important arena for European businessmen, who invested massively in industry and construction projects.

The scale and success of business imperialism raise a further question: Was all imperialism really economic? Imperialism was the result of capitalism and industry: a drive for markets. Between 1850 and 1859, the value of world trade increased by 80 percent. During the last quarter of the century, world trade roughly doubled in volume and increased in value by a third. Between 1870 and 1900, world industrial production roughly quadrupled. World shipping nearly doubled to about 30 million tons.

There were cases of profitable imperialism. Between 1831 and 1877, revenues from the Dutch East Indies covered a quarter of Dutch state expenditure. Phosphates in Morocco, diamonds in South Africa, and gems, ivory, and rubber in the Congo enriched, respectively, France, Britain, and the king of the Belgians. It used to be thought that the Portuguese Empire in Africa was a silly extravagance for such a poor country, but it seems to have been acquired as an act of economic calculation. Russia's expansion into Central Asia was—in part at least—directed toward lands that could grow cotton for Russia's textile industries. Indochina yielded coal, zinc, and tin for French industry.

Few parts of Africa with exploitable resources were left out of the global economy. Traditional traders were exterminated or became extinct. Some suffered because they were slavers, others because they got in the way of armed greed. King Leopold II proclaimed war on slave traders in the Congo. But his real aim was to cloak his ruthless ivory and rubber grabbing in moral rhetoric. The native palm-oil traders of the Niger delta in West Africa were innocent of slaving, but British merchants impoverished them. Driven into rebellion in 1895, the natives apologized for their attack on the representatives of the British Niger Company, "particularly in the killing and eating of parts of its employees.... We now throw ourselves entirely at the mercy of the good old Queen [Victoria], knowing her to be a most kind, tenderhearted and sympathetic old mother." The face of Africa was scarred and pitted with roads, railways, and mines, or scratched and scrubbed for plantations and new crops. The scramble for Africa was, in part, a scramble for resources (see Map 25.3).

It is tempting to see greed as the spur to empire-building. But political competition drove imperialism, too. Patriotic pride and the pursuit of glory inspired imperialists who were indifferent to economics. Like other external wars, imperial adventures were ways to export unrest. In Britain, the empire rewarded otherwise potentially rebellious groups. The Scots and Irish, who tended to

 Jules Ferry, from *Le Tonkin et la Mere-Patrie*, 1890

The New European Imperialism: Africa and Asia

Nineteenth century	European population explosion fuels economy and creates surplus population for global migration; Africa's population declines
ca. 1815–1835	Value of opium exported to China increases fivefold
Summer 1840	British blockade Chinese ports in response to Chinese suspension of
1842	Treaty of Nanjing ends Opium War
1850–1859	Value of world trade increases by 80 percent
1857	End of Mughal rule in India
1860–1861	Anglo-French force occupies Beijing
1863–1879	Khedive Ismail attempts to build an Egyptian Empire
1869	Suez Canal opens
1870–1900	World industrial production quadruples; world shipping doubles; world trade doubles in volume
1870s	French face increased guerrilla warfare in Algeria
1877	Queen Victoria takes title of Empress of India
1878–1913	Total territory of European empires doubles to 20 million square miles; population of European empires expands from 300 million to 550 million
1880–1914	Most of Africa brought under European control
1884	Maxim machine gun patented
r. 1889–1913	Emperor Menelik modernizes Ethiopian army and expands empire in Africa
1890s	300 Dutch administrators oversee the government of 30 million Indonesians on Java
1896	Battle of Adowa
1898	Battle of Omdurman

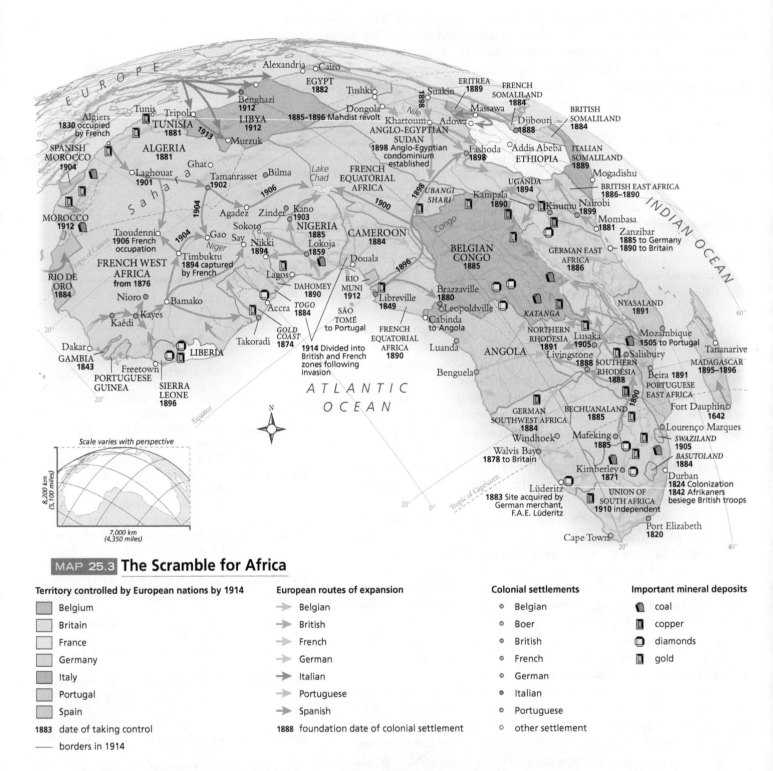

MAP 25.3 **The Scramble for Africa**

Territory controlled by European nations by 1914

- Belgium
- Britain
- France
- Germany
- Italy
- Portugal
- Spain

1883 date of taking control

—— borders in 1914

European routes of expansion

- → Belgian
- → British
- → French
- → German
- → Italian
- → Portuguese
- → Spanish

1888 foundation date of colonial settlement

Colonial settlements

- ◦ Belgian
- ◦ Boer
- ◦ British
- ◦ French
- ◦ German
- • Italian
- ◦ Portuguese
- ◦ other settlement

Important mineral deposits

- ◣ coal
- ▯ copper
- ◉ diamonds
- ▨ gold

resent English rule, were disproportionately represented in the ranks of British colonial officials and merchants. The empire gratified the working class, and popular culture celebrated it. "C is for colonies," trumpeted *An ABC for Baby Patriots*, "Rightly we boast/That of all great countries/Great Britain has the most." The "Great Game"—Anglo-Russian rivalry in Central Asia—drew Russia deeper into Asia to forestall the expansion of British India. Rivalries among European powers prompted the scramble for Africa.

In some ways, however, competition among the great powers did more to frustrate empires than promote them. Iran and Afghanistan stayed independent, partly by playing off the British against the Russians. Thailand staved off colonialism by balancing French and British power. China was so weakened by the end of the century that it seemed ripe for partition among European powers and Japan, but they could not agree on how to divide it.

IMPERIALISM IN THE "NEW EUROPES"

Some lands were subjected to empire because they were **"New Europes"**—regions similar in climate to much of Europe and, therefore, exploitable for European colonization. Most of these regions—in South Africa, Canada, New Zealand, and Australia—belonged to the British Empire or, like Chile and Argentina, were influenced by British business imperialism.

South Africa had already become a New Europe. In some ways, it was less oppressive than those elsewhere in the world, for here, at least, the European settlers allowed the native peoples to survive, so that they could exploit their labor. In most other regions of similar climate—in the South American cone of Argentina, Chile, and Uruguay, the North American West, Australia, and, with less success, in New Zealand—white settlers waged wars of extermination against the native inhabitants. Australia and New Zealand were exploited at first mainly for sheep raising. But refrigeration enabled both countries to export meat and dairy products to Britain. Gold rushes, meanwhile, attracted huge investment and coaxed large cities into being in Australia, California, and South Africa.

Canada was exemplary among the New Europes. During the century that followed the end of the War of 1812, in which the Canadian colonies repelled attacks from the United States, the population grew—modestly by the standards of other parts of the Americas—tenfold to about 8 million people. The vast territorial expansion across the continent to the Pacific included much unproductive territory. The Canadian prairies produced grain but never as much as those of the United States. A railway crossed the continent on Canadian territory, but it carried less freight and fewer passengers than the parallel railways in the United States. Yet merely to survive, alongside a United States that frequently seemed to be threatening to annex it, was an achievement for Canada. Even though the Atlantic-side Canadian provinces, with their English-speaking inhabitants, had little in common, commercially or culturally, with the mainly French settlements in Quebec, all of them combined in a confederation in 1867. Canada incorporated the Pacific coast in 1871 and created a state with potential for social welfare, cultural pluralism, constitutional flexibility, prosperity, and peace. The main casualties were the native peoples. Ignored in the constitution, brushed aside in the westward drive, by the early twentieth century, they had declined at a rate similar to that of most Native Americans of the United States, to a total of around 100,000 people.

Sydney. New Europes rapidly came to look like old Europe. George Street, Sydney, Australia, photographed in 1899, looks like a commercial street in a prosperous English provincial city of the same era.

The system Britain had established in Canada was really a variant of indirect rule, with elected colonial leaders exercising direct power instead of native chiefs and traditional aristocracies. Demographics, combined with improved communications, made this possible. Toward the end of the nineteenth century, Britain's other colonies of white settlers in Australia and New Zealand were approaching population thresholds—about 4 million and about 750,000, respectively—that enabled them to have the same status as Canada in the British Empire. South Africa, the last of Britain's New Europes, was more of a problem. Unlike the other colonies, it still had a native majority. It had even more mineral wealth than Australia—by the end of the century, South Africa was the world's main supplier of gold and diamonds. It also had a sizable community called *Boers*, white citizens, mainly of Dutch ancestry, who had to be forced into collaboration with the British in a series of wars, ending in 1902. Effectively, Britain bought their loyalty by giving them power over black South Africans. As one of the Boer leaders wrote, rejecting British desire to grant civil liberties to "every civilized man" regardless of color, "I sympathize profoundly with the Native races of South Africa, whose land it was long before we came here to force a policy of dispossession on them. . . . But I don't believe in politics for them."

French imperial planners imagined Algeria in North Africa as a New Europe, too, or a sort of Old World America, where France could encourage American levels of input and achievement among the colonists, while penning the native races—Arabs and Berbers—in doomed desert reservations. Algeria was a "promised land," to be farmed "with gun in hand," as Alexis de Tocqueville (1805–1859) put it. Algiers would become like a town in the American Midwest—"Cincinnati in Africa." Tocqueville believed that Algeria, with its rich coastlands along the Mediterranean and its untapped resources, would play a crucial role in the future of France. The best the natives could hope for was to be absorbed by their conquerors. In 1850, 130,000 Europeans lived in Algeria. There were more than 500,000 by 1900.

EMPIRES ELSEWHERE: JAPAN, RUSSIA, AND THE UNITED STATES

Japan, Russia, and the United States lagged only slightly behind Western Europe in imperialism as in industrialization.

Japanese intellectuals began to envy European empires in the late eighteenth century, when Honda Toshiaki, a leading Japanese scholar of Western literature, argued that Japan needed long-range shipping, munitions, and an empire of its own. Colonies could be stripped of resources and their populations exploited for labor. Overseas empires were like unified nationhood, parliamentary constitutions, codified laws, industrial economies, trousers, and bow ties: signs of modernization, qualifications for admission to the circle of the great powers.

The era of Japanese adventures overseas coincided almost exactly with the great age of Western imperialism. A sense of urgency drove Japan to compete for the diminishing living space that rival empires claimed. Japan's population began to grow in the late nineteenth century. Soldiers and businessmen allied to advocate empire. For samurai who had lost their social privileges, external wars were a means of discipline, a purifying ritual for a society polluted by change at home. Victory in the war of 1894–1895 against China (see Chapter 24) equipped Japan with the foundations of an empire: possession of Taiwan and the Pescadores Islands, semicontrol of Korea, and a springboard for further expansion at Russian and Chinese expense (see Map 25.4).

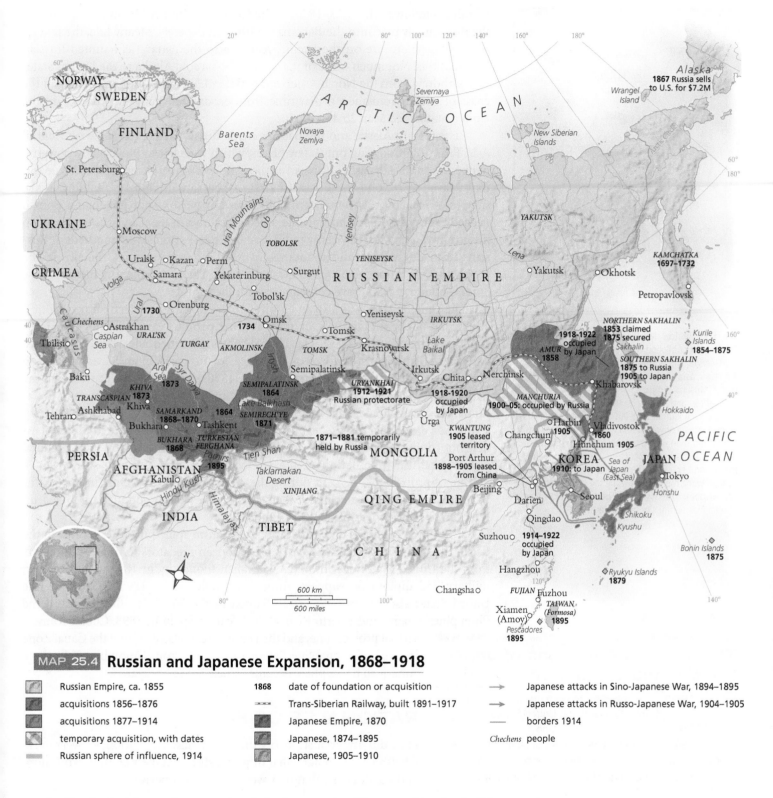

MAP 25.4 Russian and Japanese Expansion, 1868–1918

Russian Empire, ca. 1855	**1868** date of foundation or acquisition	→	Japanese attacks in Sino-Japanese War, 1894–1895
acquisitions 1856–1876	Trans-Siberian Railway, built 1891–1917	→	Japanese attacks in Russo-Japanese War, 1904–1905
acquisitions 1877–1914	Japanese Empire, 1870	—	borders 1914
temporary acquisition, with dates	Japanese, 1874–1895	*Chechens* people	
Russian sphere of influence, 1914	Japanese, 1905–1910		

In Siberia, Russians, of course, already had an empire. They continued to build up their land empire in Europe on their western and southern frontiers. Russian imperialism took a huge leap in the Napoleonic Wars (1799–1815), with the annexation of Finland from Sweden in 1809 and the consolidation of Russia's hold on Poland and the Baltic states. The colonization of "New Russia"—southern

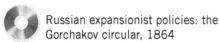

Russian expansionist policies: the Gorchakov circular, 1864

The first satirical Muslim journal in the Russian Empire was published from 1905 to 1917 in Tbilisi, Georgia, the administrative capital of Russian Transcaucasia. Although the Russian Empire had many Muslim subjects, they were divided into competing and often mutually hostile national groups. This journal targeted educated Azerbaijani readers, many of whom had more in common with Shiite Iran than with the Sunni Islam practiced by other Muslims in the Caucasus. The cover page of the November 22, 1909, issue shows the Russian bear growling menacingly while the symbol of Turkish wisdom, the legendary popular philosopher Mullah Nasreddin, sleeps unaware.

The Imperial Ambitions of Japan, Russia, and the United States

1803	Louisiana Purchase transfers vast territory from France to the United States
1809	Russia annexes Finland
1823	United States issues the Monroe Doctrine
1830–1860	Russians struggle to conquer Chechens
1867	Purchase of Alaska from Russia by the United States
1890s	Russian imperialism focuses on the Far East
1894–1895	Japan defeats China, takes Taiwan
1898	United States annexes Hawaii, seizes Philippines, Guam, and Puerto Rico after defeating Spain
1904	United States acquires Panama Canal

Ukraine—followed. In 1853–1856, in the Crimean War, Britain and France halted the Russian advance into the Balkans at Ottoman expense. Meanwhile, the fantasy of a seaborne empire on the Pacific, reaching to the Antarctic, haunted Russian imaginations. Not much came of it. In 1867, Russia sold Alaska to the United States and withdrew from the North American mainland. But the Aleutian Islands off the coast of Alaska remained a maritime frontier, divided between Russia and the United States (see Map 25.4).

Retreat from Alaska and the Balkans made Russia focus even more on Central Asia. From 1868, sparing only a few places, which were left to particularly powerful or obedient native dynasties, Russian armies enforced a new system of direct rule and direct taxation beyond the Oxus. In 1891, a new law limited landholding in the steppes of what is now Kazakstan to 40 acres per person—far less than a nomad needed to survive. Russia, meanwhile, ruled Chechnya in the Caucasus by terror, on the grounds, as a Russian viceroy put it, that "One execution saved hundreds of Russians from destruction and thousands of Muslims from treason." Finally, in the 1890s, Russian imperialism concentrated on the Far East, where it met Japanese empire-building, with grave consequences for the future.

The United States was also an empire. Americans were perfectly frank about it and proud of expanding their territory at other people's expense. They called this America's "manifest destiny." The United States absorbed Mexicans, Canadians, and Native Americans by force or the threat of it. The United States' great leap across the continent began in earnest in the 1830s, with attempts to sweep all the native peoples of the Midwest and Southeast into what is today the state of Oklahoma. It was a genocidal act that the Cherokees called the Trail of Tears, in which thousands died from disease, exposure, and starvation. Many United States planners hoped that it would kill off most Native Americans. Indeed, by 1900, the total Native American population of the United States was recorded as 237,196—a decline of probably 50 percent during the nineteenth century. Only in the Southwest did Indians escape eclipse. Meanwhile, in the 1840s, conquests gobbled up Mexican territory north of the Rio Grande.

Toward the century's end, American imperialism spilled into the oceans. In the Pacific, the Hawaiian kings had fended off European predators for years. But traders from the United States overthrew the Hawaiian monarchy in 1893 with American military and diplomatic support. Annexation followed in 1898. Meanwhile, the United States also annexed American Samoa in the South Pacific and seized the Philippines, Guam, and Puerto Rico, after defeating Spain in 1898. Cuba became a virtual protectorate, and the United States also acquired the Canal Zone in 1904 after enabling Panama to secede from Colombia. The whole American hemisphere became "Uncle Sam's backyard."

RATIONALES OF EMPIRE

How did imperialists justify their activities? Two rationales were overwhelmingly popular: what imperialists called their **civilizing mission**, and the doctrine that they were naturally superior.

Doctrines of Superiority

The most influential doctrine originated in the search for a scientific way to explain the diversity of nature. A theory originally conceived to apply to biology got wrenched out of its original background and applied to society.

In 1800, Haydn's "Creation Oratorio" proclaimed in ravishing music the biblical account of how the planet got filled with so many different plants and creatures. God had created the world and everything in it in six days. It was a metaphor, designed to reveal more than literal truth. Most people who thought about it knew that the planet was immensely old—fossils discovered in the eighteenth century had proved that—and that life developed slowly, growing in complexity, from simple, primitive forms. What remained unknown—the "mystery of mysteries," as Charles Darwin (1809-1882) remarked in the 1830s—was how those life-forms changed, or how God changed them, into the amazing variety visible in nature.

Darwin's earliest scientific interests were in sponges and beetles— life-forms regarded as primitive. In 1839, he got a chance to extend his observations when he accepted a post as the resident scientist on a round-the-world mission by the British navy. In Tierra del Fuego at the southern tip of South America, he was shocked to see how little material culture or intellectual or spiritual life the natives had. "Man in his natural state," Darwin reported, was "so beastly, so vile." He was surprised that the inhabitants could endure the freezing climate in virtual nakedness. He guessed that their bodies must have adapted to the environment. He began to see humans for what they are—well-adapted animals.

Later in the voyage, further revelations occurred off the northwest coast of South America, in the Galápagos Islands, where the diversity of species, and the differences among species from island to island, seemed almost inexplicable. "I never dreamed," he wrote, "that islands would be so differently tenanted. Temples filled with the varied productions of God and Nature … filled me with wonder." Clearly, conditions from island to island must have encouraged life-forms to develop in different ways. When Darwin got home, two circumstances crystallized his thinking.

First, he devoted himself to the study of domestication: how farmers, stock-breeders, and pigeon fanciers, for instance, select to ensure that the offspring of their animals will inherit favored characteristics. Maybe nature functioned in the same way, favoring characteristics suitable to particular environments. Ill-adapted specimens of plants or animals would tend to die earlier and have a shorter fertile life span than more successful specimens. The fittest would survive longest and breed most.

Second, Darwin's personal circumstances affected his theories. He had married his cousin and their children were sickly. When his favorite daughter died, it became "impossible," he said, "for me ever to feel joy again." He began to hate God. In his later years, he ceased to go to church and subscribed to an atheist organization. He thought his own family demonstrated that nature was "clumsy, wasteful, blundering, low, and horribly cruel," or rather, indifferent to sentiment. Nature would allow only strong, well-adapted specimens to survive and pass on their characteristics to their offspring. He held the struggle for life in awe, partly because his own children were victims of it. "From the war of nature, from famine and death," he wrote, "the production of higher animals directly follows."

Darwin published that opinion in *The Origin of Species* in 1859. As his theory became accepted, other thinkers proposed terrible refinements that came to be known as **Social Darwinism.** Nature decreed "the survival of the fittest" and the extinction of the weak. Conflict is natural and, therefore, good. Nature decrees the rule of more evolved races and individuals over "degenerate" people—what we would now call the underclass—who represented throwbacks to some more primitive stage of evolution. It would be unfair to blame Darwin for the consequences. He advocated the unity of humankind and denounced slavery.

Nevertheless, no clear line divided social Darwinism from scientific Darwinism. Darwin was the father of both. As early as 1839, he claimed that "When two races of men meet, they act precisely like two species of animals. They fight, eat

A Fuegian on the frontispiece of Robert Fitzroy's *Narrative of the Surveying Voyage of HMS Adventure and Beagle* (1839). "Nothing," wrote Darwin in his *Beagle* journal, "is more likely to create astonishment than the first sight in his native state of a barbarian—of man in his lowest and most savage state. One's mind hurries back over past centuries, and asks, could our progenitors have been men like these, men who do not appear to boast of human reason. I do not believe it is possible to describe or paint the difference between savage and civilized man…. It is greater than between a wild and domesticated animal." The remarkable environmental adaptation that made the Native American inhabitants of Tierra del Fuego, at the tip of South America, able to withstand the cold was one of the observations that influenced Darwin's thinking about a theory of evolution.

Herbert Spencer, *Illustrations of Universal Progress*, 1864

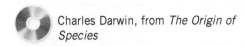

Charles Darwin, from *The Origin of Species*

Rudyard Kipling, *The White Man's Burden*

Thomas Babington Macauley, from *Minute on Education*, 1835

each other. . . . But then comes the more deadly struggle, namely: which have the best fitted organization or instincts (i.e., intellect in man) to gain the day?" Black people, Darwin speculated, would have evolved into a distinct species had European imperialism not ended their isolation. As it was, he thought, black people were doomed to extinction. Many people used Darwin's theories to justify the inequalities of their day: a world stacked in order of race.

A French anthropologist, the Count de Gobineau (1816–1882), arrayed humankind in order of excellence, with white people at the top, black people at the bottom, and others in between. Craniologists proved to their own satisfaction that the skulls of black people resembled those of apes. "No full-blooded Negro," stated the *Encyclopedia Britannica* in 1884, "has ever been distinguished as a man of science, a poet, or an artist, and the fundamental equality claimed for him by ignorant philanthropists is belied by the whole history of the race." The governor of the Dutch East Indies in 1850 thought "the right of rule" was "a characteristic of the pure white race." Some black Africans and Eskimos in Europe and the United States were actually displayed in zoos and exhibitions.

The Civilizing Mission

Alternatively, "the basic legitimization of conquest over native peoples," a French administrator insisted, "is the conviction of our superiority, not merely our mechanical, economic, and military superiority, but our moral superiority." Sir Francis Younghusband, who led a British military expedition to Tibet in 1902, claimed to have witnessed evidence of European superiority over Asian and African peoples due to "that higher moral nature to which we have attained."

A British administrator in South Africa was surely right when he observed "how thin is the crust that keeps our Christian civilization from the old-fashioned savagery—machine guns and modern rifles against knob sticks and spears ... do not add much to the glory of the superior races." But Europeans, white North Americans, and Japanese seemed determined to seize other people's land and wealth. To some extent, this was a reaction to historic positions of inferiority—Europe's with respect to Asia, Japan's with respect to China and Korea, that of the United States to most of the rest of the world.

The civilizing mission seemed inapplicable to much of the colonial world, and especially to India, whose civilization was older and, arguably, richer than that of Europe. But in 1835, the British historian and legislator Thomas Macaulay dismissed Indian civilization as "absurd history, absurd metaphysics, absurd physics, absurd theology." A single shelf of a good European library, he claimed, "is worth the whole native literature of India and Arabia." The English, he predicted, would be to the Indians as the Romans, in their day, had been to the ancient Britons. English would be the new Latin. "Indians in blood and color" would become "English in tastes, in opinions, in morals and in intellect."

Civilization was undeniably a property of Chinese and Japanese societies. Western admiration for China never died out entirely, though the Opium Wars did much to subvert it. Japan's potential to catch up was obvious from the 1870s onward (see Chapter 24). For Westerners, therefore, China and Japan were potential rivals, who could be recruited or resisted. Many Europeans adopted a defensive attitude to what they called "the Yellow Peril." In 1900, the German Emperor Wilhelm II (r. 1888–1918) exhorted German members of an international task force sent to Beijing to rescue European residents from Chinese rebels, "You should give the name of German such a cause to be remembered in China that for a thousand years no Chinaman shall dare look a German in the face."

On the whole, it is hard to assess imperialists' claims to have governed for the benefit of their victims. Under the grasping rule of King Leopold II of the Belgians, 10 million people in the Congo died in massacres or from callous neglect. Native peoples who perished to make room for white empires in the Americas and Australia had no opportunity to count blessings. The British Empire spent much blood and treasure in suppressing the slave trade (see Chapter 24). But even this was not an exclusively benign business. In 1879, in southern Sudan, General Charles Gordon, who was in charge of antislaving operations there, was sickened by the skulls and skeletons his men's work left: slavers' women slaughtered to stop them breeding, thousands of slaves abandoned to starve when caravans were destroyed.

For those who suffered from it, imperialism was often a path to hell paved with the good intentions of white people who stumbled under the burdens of their self-imposed imperial responsibilities. Outside Europe, North America, and a few other lucky locations, the last three decades of the nineteenth century were an age of famine, exceeding all others up to that time for mortality and perhaps for every other kind of measurable severity. Thirty million people may have died in India and an equal number in China. In some respects, imperialism helped people find food for survival. Cheap iron plows from Europe increased food production in West Africa. It is hard, however, to exempt European imperialism from some of the blame for mismanaging the consequences of famine. Humanitarian sentiment, like food, was plentiful in their countries, but they found no way to turn their surplus of either to practical use.

Earlier, native states had handled famine relatively well. China coped with protracted crop failure in 1743–1744. In India in 1661, the Mughal Emperor Aurangzeb (see Chapter 21) "opened his treasury" and saved millions of lives. Western countries—with the exception of the Russian Empire, where crop failures killed millions around the middle Volga and in Ukraine in 1878–1881—seemed able to save people from famine in the late nineteenth century if they so wished. The American Midwest suffered as badly as almost any other part of the world from drought in 1889–1890, but relief was well organized, and deaths were few.

The civilizing mission, New Guinea, 1919. The British missionary stands in a position of authority, on the right. The white women are relaxed and wear hats. The New Guineans are presumably receiving instruction, but it might as well be orders. Almost everything in the scene is mysterious. Is a class or a religious service taking place? Why do only females, not males, hold books? Why is the lady in the black hat seated facing the back of her chair?

Edward Morel, *The Black Man's Burden*

IN PERSPECTIVE: The Reach of Empires

At the start of the nineteenth century, the English poet and artist William Blake could still draw Europe as one of the Graces among equals in the dance of the continents. But during the century, unprecedented demographic, industrial, and technological strides transformed Europe's place in the world. The result was European dominance. By 1900, European powers ruled much of the world, and European political influence and business imperialism controlled much of the rest.

It was, by the standards of world history, a brief phenomenon. By 1900, Japan and the United States had overtaken many European countries in industrial strength and in their capacity for war. In the twentieth century, European empires would collapse as spectacularly and as quickly as they had arisen (see Chapter 28). Meanwhile, even under imperialism, people continued to make their own history,

CHRONOLOGY

Nineteenth century	European population explosion fuels economy and creates surplus population for global migration; Africa's population declines
1803	Louisiana Purchase transfers vast territory from France to the United States
1809	Russia annexes Finland
1812–1814	War of 1812
1823	United States issues the Monroe Doctrine
1830s–1860s	Russians struggle to conquer Chechens
1839	Charles Darwin begins around-the-world expedition
1842	Treaty of Nanjing ends Opium War
1845–1872	Maori Wars in New Zealand
1850	130,000 Europeans live in Algeria
1850–1859	Value of world trade increases by 80 percent
1857	End of Mughal rule in India
1863–1879	Khedive Ismail attempts to build an Egyptian Empire
1867	Purchase of Alaska from Russia by the United States; Canadian Confederation is formed
1869	Suez Canal opens
1870–1900	World industrial production quadruples; world shipping doubles; world trade doubles in volume
1877	Queen Victoria takes title of Empress of India
1878–1913	Total territory of European empires doubles to 20 million square miles; total population of European empires expands from 300 million to 550 million
1880–1914	Most of Africa brought under European control
1884	Maxim machine gun patented
r. 1889–1913	Emperor Menelik modernizes Ethiopian army and expands empire in Africa
1890s	Russian imperialism focuses on the Far East
1894–1895	Japan defeats China
1898	Battle of Omdurman; United States annexes Hawaii and seizes Philippines, Guam, and Puerto Rico from Spain
1899–1902	Boer War
1900	500,000 Europeans live in Algeria, 4 million live in Australia, 1 million live in New Zealand
1904	United States acquires Panama Canal

thanks to systems of indirect rule and the empires' reliance on collaborators. Still, the nineteenth remains a century of a "European miracle": the sudden, startling climax of long, faltering commercial outthrust, imperial initiatives, and scientific progress.

Despite their defects, the empires were of immense importance in global history as arenas of cultural exchange. As we saw in Chapter 23, imperial commerce followed the lines laid down by the effects of industrialization, dividing the world into specialized areas of primary production and manufacturing, encircling the Earth with steamship routes and railroads. As Chapter 24 made clear, these arteries carried culture as well as commerce. Empires intensified the process of exchange. Like distorting mirrors, the colonies reflected imperfect images of Europe around the world.

Cultural exchange happened despite climate and distance. Indian thinkers and writers gave a discriminating welcome to Western influence. The first great Indian advocate of Western ideas, Raja Rammohan Roy (1772–1833), was a child of the Enlightenment (see Chapter 22). Yet the roots of his rationalism and liberalism came from Islamic and Persian traditions. The next great figure in Roy's tradition, Isvarcandra Vidyasagar (1820–1891), did not learn English until he was on the verge of middle age. When he argued for the remarriage of widows or against polygamy, or when he advocated relaxing caste discrimination in the schools, he found ancient Indian texts to support his arguments. But he dismissed the claims of pious Brahmans who insisted that every Western idea had an Indian origin. He resigned as secretary of the Sanskrit College of Calcutta in 1846 because of opposition to his program to include "the science and civilization of the West" in its curriculum. "If the students be made familiar with English literature," he claimed, "they will prove the best and ablest contributors to an enlightened Bengali renaissance." And, indeed, Indian writers did inject Western influences into their work with revitalizing effect. The British in India were like many foreign, "barbarian" conquerors before them, adding a layer of culture to the long-accumulated sediments of the subcontinent's past.

Today, what were once British colonies still have legislatures and law courts modeled on those of England, universities copied from Scotland, and sports that colonists from England's public schools spread. The French Empire spread French culture, Parisian cuisine, and the Code Napoleon (see Chapter 22). Africa became the great growth land of Christianity, thanks to the missionaries who followed or carried the flags of European empires. In much of the ex-colonial world, European languages—English, Spanish, Portuguese, French, Russian—remain the language of first choice. The colonial worlds reciprocated the exchange. Mughal style adorned nineteenth-century British buildings. The industrialists of Paisley in Scotland copied Indian patterns for their textiles. Curry from India has become virtually an English national dish, as has Indonesian rijstafel in Holland and North African couscous in France.

From the end of the nineteenth century, images and works of art looted from empires affected European imaginations and gave artists new models to follow. Despite the barriers to understanding that pseudoscientific racism erected, far frontiers kept increasing the white world's stock of examples of noble savagery (see Chapter 22). In the twentieth century, as we shall see, social scientists found, among the subject peoples of empire, disturbing new perceptions: new ways to see not only the "primitives" and "savages" but also themselves and the nature of human societies.

PROBLEMS AND PARALLELS

1. Why did the British and other foreign powers gain significant control of the Chinese economy by the late nineteenth century?

2. Why were European powers able to control so much of Asia, Africa, the Pacific, and the Middle East in the nineteenth century?

3. How did the Maori and Emperor Menelik of Ethiopia resist European imperialism?

4. What methods did Europeans use to govern native peoples in their colonial possessions? What does the term *business imperialism* mean? How did Europeans justify imperialism?

5. What were the imperial ambitions of Japan, Russia, and the United States in the nineteenth century?

DOCUMENTS IN GLOBAL HISTORY

- Letter from Lin Zexu to Queen Victoria
- The Treaty of Nanjing
- Francisco García Calderón, from *Latin America: Its Rise and Progress*
- Jules Ferry, from *Le Tonkin et la Mére-Patrie*, 1890
- Russian expansionist policies: the Gorchakov circular, 1864

- Herbert Spencer, *Illustrations of Universal Progress*, 1864
- Charles Darwin, from *The Origin of Species*
- Rudyard Kipling, *The White Man's Burden*
- Thomas Babington Macauley, from *Minute on Education*, 1835
- Edward Morel, *The Black Man's Burden*

Please see the Primary Source DVD for additional sources related to this chapter

READ ON

On the Opium War, A. Waley, *The Opium War Through Chinese Eyes* (1979) is a lively collection of sources. J. Y. Wong, *Deadly Dreams: Opium, Imperialism, and the Arrow War (1856–1860) in China* (1998) is excellent on the consequences and on the second Opium War.

J. Darwin, *After Tamerlaine* (2007) is a brillant essay in the global history of empires. H. L. Wesseling, ed., *Expansion and Reaction* (1978) contains groundbreaking papers on imperialism. H. L. Wesseling, *The European Colonial Empires* (2004) is the best overall survey. The same author's *Divide and Rule: The Partition of Africa* (1996) and T. Pakenham, *The Scramble for Africa* (1991) are outstanding in different ways—the first for impeccable judgement, the second for thrilling vividity. On Britain, W. R. Louis, ed., *The Oxford History of the British Empire*, vol. iii (2001), ed. by A. Porter, is sweeping in its coverage. D. R. Headrick, *Tools of Empire* (1981) is important on the technology of imperialism. A. Knight, *The Mexican Revolution*, vol. i (1990) is a model work from which I drew the details on the Yaqui. J. Belich, *The New Zealand War* (1998) is a brilliant work that reset the agenda of the study of colonial warfare.

On Africa, *The UNESCO History of Africa*, vol. vii (1990) and *The Cambridge History of Africa*, vol. vi (1985) offer expert general surveys. G. Prins, *The Hidden Hippopotamus* (1980) is a sensitive, anthropologically informed study of Lozi history. N. R. Bennett, *Arab Versus European: Diplomacy and War in Nineteenth-Century Central Africa* (1986) is useful, especially on Zanzibar. The details on Ma el-Ainin come from J. Mercer, *Spanish Sahara* (1976).

On Johor, J. Gullick, *Malay Society in the Late Nineteenth Century* (1987) is invaluable. Many novels of Bankimcandra Chattopadhyaya are available in English, as are those of Jorge Mármol. On business imperialism, D. C. M. Platt, *Business Imperialism* (1977) is the indispensable introduction. A. de Tocqueville, *Writings on Slavery* is the source of the material on that writer. On the Russian Empire, D. Lieven, *Empire* (xxx), is the best survey.

On Darwin, the best books are the provocative A. Desmond and J. Moore, *Darwin* (1994), and E. J. Brown, *Charles Darwin* (1996) of which two volumes have appeared so far. M. Bates and P. S. Humphrey, eds., *The Darwin Reader* (1956) is a good introduction to Darwin's writings.

CHAPTER 26

The Changing State: Political Developments in the Nineteenth Century

Nene, leader of Maori in Hokianga in northern New Zealand, took the name Tamati Waka after Thomas Walker, his British godfather, when he was baptized a Christian in 1839. Nene sought to befriend and, if possible, exploit the British. He sided with them in the Maori wars of the 1840s, achieving fame as the Maori "who did more than any other to establish the queen's authority," meaning Queen Victoria of England.

IN THIS CHAPTER

NATIONALISM
Nationalism in Europe
The Case of the Jews
Nationalism Beyond Europe

CONSTITUTIONALISM

CENTRALIZATION, MILITARIZATION,
AND BUREAUCRATIZATION
In and Around the Industrializing World
Beyond the Industrializing World

RELIGION AND POLITICS

NEW FORMS OF POLITICAL
RADICALISM
Steps Toward Democracy
The Expansion of the Public Sphere

WESTERN SOCIAL THOUGHT

IN PERSPECTIVE: Global State-Building

n 1882, a British visitor wandered into an ill-mapped area in New Zealand's North Island. James Kerry-Nicholls thought he was still in the British Empire. Instead, he found an "extensive region ruled over by the Maori king" where "an absolute monarch ... defied our laws" and "ignored our institutions." The region is still known as the King Country. In the early 1880s, it occupied over a fifth of the North Island and had a population of some 7,000, who simply ignored British orders. Invited to parley with the British in the year of Kerry-Nicholls's visit, King Tawhiao listened patiently to their proposal to give up his independence in exchange for land. "I will remain," said the king, "in the place where my ancestors and my fathers trod. . . . You can remain on your side, and administer affairs, and I will remain on my side."

NEW ZEALAND

The King Country was the last stronghold of a movement that had originated in the 1850s to unify the Maori into a single state to confront British aggression and stop chiefs from ceding Maori land. Twenty-six Maori tribal groups had come together in 1858, numbering in all perhaps 25,000 or 30,000 souls, to elect a king. The groups had no ties of kinship or traditional alliances with each other. "Do not be concerned for your own village," said one native prophet to his people. "No, be concerned for the whole land." In 1861–1863, the British tried to destroy this new state, sending in armies up to 14,000 strong, with mortars and cannon. But after defeats and inconclusive engagements (see Chapter 25), they gave up. The King Country settled into uneasy coexistence with the British Empire.

Presumably, the Maori got the idea of a unitary state by imitation from the British. Their purpose, as one Maori leader explained, was "that they should become united, ... like the Pakehas," as they called the white men. The idea of switching from armed to peaceful resistance was attributed to native prophets, but perhaps it owes something to Christian missionaries and the model of Jesus' kingdom (which was, as the Bible says, "not of this world"), or maybe even to the secular notion of civil disobedience that some Western intellectuals at the time advocated to effect peaceful change.

● ● ● ● ●

The political inventiveness of the Maori illustrates general features of the way nineteenth-century states grew and changed. New states emerged out of traditional groupings, such as chiefdoms and tribes. Old states made themselves more systematic by eliminating political anomalies, devising constitutions, codifying laws, rationalizing institutions, breaking the power of rival sources of authority (clergies, aristocracies, city councils, or heads of tribes or clans), and imposing centralization or, at least, increasingly consistent methods of administration, on their subjects. *Modernization* is, strictly speaking, a meaningless word, since every era produces its own modernity, but we can use it as a label for these processes because they produced states similar to those that prevail in today's world.

- WHY WAS Westernization often equated with modernization in the nineteenth century?
- WHY WAS nationalism so potentially disruptive?
- WHY DID some African and Asian states succeed in resisting Western imperialism?
- HOW DID the growth of armies and bureaucracies increase the power of states?
- WHAT ROLES did nineteenth-century socialists want government to play?
- WHY DID organized religion and the state come into conflict in the nineteenth century?

Some models of state development or refashioning began in Europe and North America and spread through the world during the "white man's" outreach—by example or the power of imperialism. The process did not end where white rule ended, and some instances probably happened independently of white initiative. Examples we have already met illustrate this: the reforging of Japan and Egypt in response to European industrialization and imperialism, the success of Ethiopia in the scramble for Africa, and the Sioux's efforts to create an empire in the North American prairie. As we shall see in this chapter, some states modernized far from the frontiers of European empires or the reach of European influence.

Nevertheless, the story of state modernization and of how and why it happened must begin in the West, partly because some features of modern states emerged there first. For much of the world, modernization really was *Westernization*, the conscious imitation of the world's most powerful, most prosperous states: Britain, France, Germany, and the United States. From the West, models of state development unfolded and were imitated around the world. Here theories about politics and society were formulated that achieved global importance and global impact. From this point in the story of the world, Westernization is a conspicuous global theme.

We will look at its clearest manifestations—nationalism, constitutionalism, militarization, centralization, and bureaucratization—before turning at the end of the chapter to some of the other influential but, for the time being, frustrated political movements of the period—religiously inspired utopianisms, democracy, and other forms of political radicalism that radiated from the West.

NATIONALISM

Nationalists claimed that a people who shared the same language, historic experience, and sense of identity made up a nation, an indissoluble unit, linked (to quote a Finnish nationalist) by "ties of mind and soul mightier and firmer than every external bond." Nationalists believed that everyone must belong to a nation of this kind and that every nation had to assert its identity, pursue its destiny, and defend its rights. "The voice of God" told Giuseppe Mazzini (1805–1872), the republican fighter for Italian unification, that the nation was the essential framework in which individuals could achieve moral perfection.

Odd as this notion seems, many people believed it. In the nineteenth century, nationalism triumphed in the West. The American and French Revolutions stimulated it. So did the Napoleonic Wars. Belligerents who wanted their people to fight encouraged it. Nationalism spread from the West to touch or transform much of the world.

Nationalism in Europe

Almost all European states contained more than one nation. Many European nations straddled the borders of states. **Nationalism** was therefore potentially disruptive. German nationalists yearned to unite all German-speaking people in a single state. French nationalists wanted to meld France's historic communities into a unified force and secure France's "natural frontiers" by incorporating all the land west of the Rhine and north of the Alps. Spain remained a "bundle" of nations—notably, Castilians, Catalans,

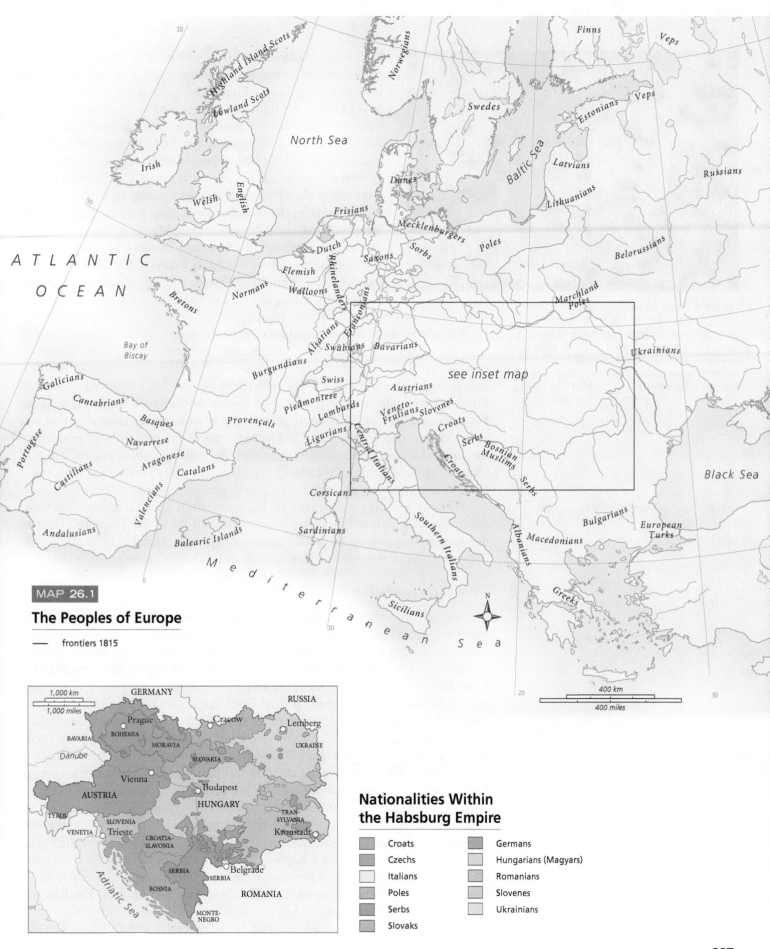

MAP 26.1

The Peoples of Europe

— frontiers 1815

Nationalities Within the Habsburg Empire

- Croats
- Czechs
- Italians
- Poles
- Serbs
- Slovaks
- Germans
- Hungarians (Magyars)
- Romanians
- Slovenes
- Ukrainians

The era of Jewish emancipation allowed European Jews more freedom and a wider recognition of their faith and culture. This painting by G. E. Opitz portrays the dedication of a new synagogue in Alsace in eastern France in 1820.
George Emanuel Opitz (1775–1841), Dedication of a Synagogue in Alsace, ca. 1820. The Jewish Museum/Art Resource, NY.

Joseph Mazzini on nationalism

Basques, and Galicians—unsure whether they wished to become a single Spanish nation. British statesmen kept talking about England, forgetting that the English, Irish, Scots, and Welsh were supposed to have combined in a British nation. Italian nationalists wanted to convert their peninsula from a "geographical expression" into a state. In Central Europe the Habsburg monarchy juggled minorities that often quarreled with each other, privileging Germans, Hungarians, and, to some extent, Czechs and Poles, in areas where they predominated, acknowledging in various ways other groups that had more or less distinct homelands, such as the Slovenes, Croats, and Romanians (see Map 26.1). Even more than that of the Habsburgs, the Ottoman Empire in southeast Europe had conflicting nations within its borders. The Greeks achieved independence from the Ottomans in 1830, Romania and Serbia did so by 1878. Bulgaria, though technically subject to Turkey until 1908, functioned as a sovereign state from the 1880s.

Some large states that enclosed many nations tried to stir themselves into consistency, usually by oppressing minorities. Government campaigns of "Russification" in the Russian Empire or "Magyarization" in Hungary meant, in practice, suppressing historic languages and sometimes persecuting minority religions. In Britain, the Highlanders of Scotland—a nation with its own language, religious traditions, and ways of life—were sent into exile in a vicious campaign that was called "clearances." Governments in London proposed to deal with the problem of the cultural and religious distinctiveness of the Irish by implanting an "agent of civilization"—an English Protestant clergyman—in every Irish parish. This was a failed attempt to wean the Irish from Catholicism.

Without bringing fulfillment to big communities, nationalism threatened minorities with destruction or repression. Some of them, like Finns and Poles in the Russian Empire or Slavs and Romanians in the Habsburg Empire, could respond with counter-nationalisms of their own. The Jews were not so lucky.

The Case of the Jews

The Jews had no national homeland. Their rising population seemed to provoke or aggravate **anti-Semitism**. So did changes in Jewish society and its relationship to the world around it. The triumph of enlightened principles in the French Revolution and their spread in the Napoleonic Wars extended the "rights of man" to the Jews. Except in Spain and Portugal and in the Russian Empire, governments relaxed official legal and financial disabilities against Jews. Many European Jews discarded the traditional exclusiveness of the ghetto in favor of assimilation into secular society. Heinrich Heine (1797–1856), a German Jew, filled his poetry with Jewish self-awareness but regarded Christian baptism as "a ticket into European culture." Part of Jewish self-emancipation was to adopt the dress and manners of host societies and conform to their way of life. From 1810, a reform movement that started in Germany brought these new ways into the synagogues. The very success of Jews in blending into gentile society seemed to excite anti-Semitism. This growing and conspicuous community, anti-Semites claimed, might take over the world.

When the world's biggest synagogue opened in Berlin in 1866, the chief rabbi preached in German about his hopes of a "common Messiah" to unite all nations in brotherhood. This seemed overoptimistic. There were two options. The first was for Jews to espouse Jewish nationalism—which some did as anti-Semitism grew. They turned to the search for a homeland, in Africa, perhaps or Palestine. The second possibility, which most Jews embraced, was to join in the nationalism of the country in which they lived. The young Walter Rathenau (1867–1922), whose family owned the largest electricity-producing firm in Germany, believed that German Jews could help Germany achieve world supremacy.

Assimilation, however, was always risky for unconverted Jews, unless they were immensely rich. In the prayer book of French Jews in the 1890s, France was praised as the country "preferred by God," and the French, according to the country's chief rabbi, were "the chosen race of modern times." None of this prevented French anti-Semitism, as became all too clear in the case of a Jewish officer in the French army accused of spying for the Germans in 1893. Captain Alfred Dreyfus was obviously innocent, but the French gutter press bayed for his blood, in effect because he was Jewish. He was led into imprisonment crying, "Long live France!" and after his innocence was proved, he won medals fighting in the French army.

Nationalism Beyond Europe

Beyond Europe, nineteenth-century nationalism is hard to distinguish from resistance against European imperialism (see Map 26.2). But by 1900, many independence movements in European empires overseas had adopted nationalism as their

MAP 26.2

Examples of Resistance to European and United States Imperialism, 1880–1920

Anti-colonial uprisings
and incidents

🌿   anti-British
🌿   anti-Dutch
🌿   anti-French
🌿   anti-German
🌿   anti-Italian
🌿   anti-Portuguese
🌿   anti-Russian
🌿   anti-Spanish
🌿   anti-American
——   boundary at 1914

MAP EXPLORATION

www.prenhall.com/armesto_maps

An Argentine gaucho. The painter Eduardo Morales specialized in romantic landscapes of his native Cuba. Here he portrays an Argentine cowboy, a gaucho, and the landscape of Argentina itself in a similar romantic style. The man's horse, however, seems groomed for a formal riding contest, with forepaw raised in a tradition more appropriate for depicting rulers and warriors than cowboys.

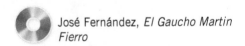

José Fernández, *El Gaucho Martin Fierro*

own ideology. Rebels proclaimed as "nations" countries, such as "the Philippines," "Indonesia," "Algeria," and "India," that had never existed and that housed many different historic nations.

This phenomenon started in the Americas. Though the Creole elites shared a common identity as "Americans," their desire to exercise power in states of their own creation exceeded their willingness to remain united. Spanish-American unity was a Humpty Dumpty, smashed by its fall in struggles against Spanish rule between 1810 and the 1820s. Paraguay and Uruguay fought to stay apart from Argentina and Brazil. Bolivia and Ecuador rejected union with Peru. In the 1830s, large states that had emerged from the independence wars dissolved into small ones. Gran Colombia split into Colombia and Venezuela. The United Provinces of Central America crumbled into Guatemala, Honduras, Nicaragua, Costa Rica, and El Salvador. The fissures continued to spread, detaching Texas and California from Mexico and almost detaching Yucatán as well in the 1840s.

Brazil, meanwhile, like the United States, emerged formally united but, unlike the United States, was fragile in the short term (see Chapter 21). Offshore currents in the South Atlantic divided coastal Brazil into two zones, between which it was hard to communicate. The ranch-rich São Paulo region in the south was a law unto itself. The interior was a wild west of mining, slaving, and logging with its own boss class. Northern Brazil was the domain of coffee and sugar planters. Unity survived destructive civil wars in the 1830s only because the regions were incapable of collaborating in revolt and because the emperor supplied a symbol of legitimacy. Ethnic diversity added to the complexity of regional divisions. Brazil had more black people than other Latin American states, but as slave labor became harder to obtain, the country needed more free immigrants of diverse origins.

In the second half of the century, nationalist sentiment in the Latin American states increased, partly in detestation of interference from the United States, and the countries fought each other. In Argentina, nationalism tended to get distracted by romantic identification with the *gauchos*—the rugged cattle drovers of the pampa. In Brazil and Paraguay, the romantic sympathy took the form of yearning for an idealized "Indian" world, though poetry written in praise of the Indians excited little political activity on Native Americans' behalf. The first fully independent Mexican state in 1822 based the official symbol of its nationhood—an eagle devouring a snake atop a cactus—on an Aztec carving. In Colombia, Ecuador, and Venezuela, the landscape inspired nationalist poetry and art.

In sub-Saharan Africa, too, the nationalist idea was implanted, at least in part, from the United States. It started in Liberia, a colony of ex-slaves founded in 1821 as a private venture by philanthropists, with help from racists who wanted to rid the United States of black people. Liberia proclaimed its independence in 1847, with a constitution based on that of the United States. One of the earliest Liberian presidents, Stephen A. Benson, perceived "the makings of a great nation" in the colony in 1856. In 1872, Edward Blyden, an outstanding black intellectual who had settled in Liberia, proclaimed "Africa for the African."

West African missionaries helped to spread nationalism, imagining national churches similar to those that Protestants maintained in Europe. Black intellectuals saw the political potential of this model. James Africanus Horton, for instance, a black doctor from Sierra Leone, pointed out in 1868 that "We have seen European nations who in long years past were themselves as barbarous and unenlightened as the negro Africans are at present, and who have exhibited wonderful improvement within the last century. This should urge the Africans to increased exertions, so that their race may, in course of time, take its proper stand in the world's history." Talk of nationalism began to have real political effects in West Africa. In 1871, Fanti chiefs in what is now Ghana founded a confederation "to advance the interest of the whole Fanti nation."[11]

North of the Sahara, meanwhile, nationalism emerged as the Ottoman Empire retreated and European imperialism threatened. In the second half of the nineteenth century, Egyptian intellectuals began to give the Arabic word *watan*—which originally meant something like "birthplace"—the sense of the European term *nation*, with the same romantic associations. One of the most influential of them was Ali Mubarak Pasha (see Chapter 23), who published a nationalist novel in 1882, the year when opponents of British and French influence rose up with the cry, "Egypt for the Egyptians!"

To some extent, Western empires encouraged nationalism around the world, regarding its spread as evidence of successful Westernization and of the fulfillment of Westerners' supposedly civilizing mission. In the early 1850s, a British statesman, Lord Grey, believed that by bringing the chiefs of Ghana together, Britain had turned "barbarous tribes. . . . into a nation." British administrators in Canada assumed that nation making was an obligation of empire. Even without official collaboration, Western empires tended to have this effect. In colonial settings, budding nationalists could read and learn about what was going on in Europe. Many of them went to Europe to study or attended European-style schools at home. To them, nationalism seemed a way to confront traditional elites allied with or controlled by outsiders.

José Rizal (1861–1896), for instance, the great spokesman of Filipino nationalism in the late nineteenth century, crammed his writings with allusions to classical, Spanish, English, and German literature, but he also searched for inspiration in the poetic traditions of his homeland. Spanish observers noticed Rizal's patriotic poetry as early as 1879 and identified him as "a man who bears watching, a rare and new kind of man. . . . for whom the mother country is the Philippines, not Spain." He spent his last years in exile, charged with conspiring with other nationalists to make the Philippines independent. When he returned to Manila and was shot by the Spaniards as a rebel, he struck out the words "Chinese half-breed" on his death warrant and wrote "pure native" instead.

Rizal's subversive novels showed how literature could help forge nationalism in colonial environments. Equally powerful were the novels that another culturally ambiguous figure whom we met in the last chapter, Bankimcandra Chattopadhyaya in India, wrote. Bankim often chose politically inflammatory themes for his fiction while serving the British as a deputy magistrate. This was typical of the nationalists who formed the Indian National Congress in 1885. Most of the founder members and early recruits belonged to the civil service or the legal profession. Most of the leading figures were graduates of British-style universities in Calcutta, Bombay, and Madras.

Western models promoted the growth of nationalism worldwide. Nevertheless, other influences were also at work. Japan became a model for Asian nationalists

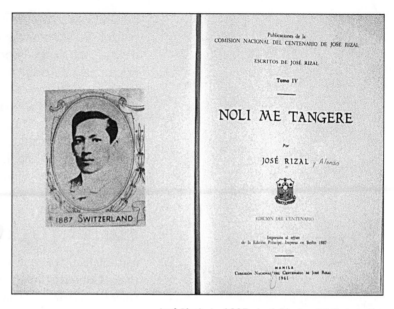

José Rizal. In 1887, José Rizal published, in the form of a novel, what he called "the first impartial and bold account" of the Filipino independence movement and the injustice that inspired it. "Felicity," Rizal wrote, "is proportional to liberty." He compared Spanish rule to a wooden bridge—vulnerable to wind and rot.

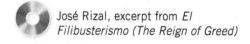
José Rizal, excerpt from *El Filibusterismo (The Reign of Greed)*

because its success demonstrated that Asian nations could rival or surpass Western powers. Vietnamese nationalism fed on memories of age-old resistance to the Chinese as well as on opposition to the French in the nineteenth century. To some extent, nationalism happened independently wherever big empires provoked subject-peoples to react or rebel. The Russian, Habsburg, Chinese, and Ottoman Empires all faced similar problems. Chinese nationalism was itself an expression against the ruling Qing dynasty, even though the emperors' Manchu origins were now 200 years in the past (see Chapter 21). Opponents of the regime appealed to Chinese "purity." The first rebellion of the movement that called itself "nationalist," in Guangzhou in 1895, was an attempt to found a Chinese state free of Manchu domination.

CONSTITUTIONALISM

Nationalism was one way to justify the new structures of power or challenge old ones. **Constitutionalism**—the doctrine that the state is founded on rules that rulers and citizens make together and are bound to respect—was another.

Constitutionalism was not confined to Europe, but Europe was its great battleground. After the French Revolutionary Wars, most European states tried to prevent another such explosion by sanctifying existing frontiers and outlawing or restricting constitutional reforms. By mutual agreement, they intervened to repress each other's revolutions. The system worked well, and revolutionaries achieved freedom to act only when the European powers fell out among themselves. The nineteenth century was, therefore, a great age for monarchies. All the new European states of the period—Belgium, Greece, Romania, Serbia, Bulgaria—were kingdoms or principalities. Republics that fell during the Napoleonic Wars—in Venice, Genoa, and the Netherlands—were not restored. Even in Latin America, some states toyed with plans for monarchical systems. Mexico and Haiti had monarchs for a time. Brazil's monarchy survived until 1889.

Most European monarchies, however, eventually granted or accepted constitutions, or enlarged the numbers and nature of those of their subjects admitted to the political process. Constitutionalism not only redistributed power; it also changed how people thought about the state—no longer the domain of the ruler, but of the rule of law, to which the monarch and government were themselves subject. Constitutionalism did not necessarily embody the idea that the people were sovereign, but it at least implied that more than one person and more than one class shared sovereignty. In Britain, for instance, though no written constitution was ever granted, a series of Reform Acts turned parliament from an enclave of the aristocracy and gentry into an assembly that was also representative of the middle class and even, from 1867, of the more prosperous workers.

On the fringes of Europe, the Ottoman and Russian Empires staved off constitutionalism with difficulty. In 1864, the Russian monarchy permitted district assemblies with representatives from all classes to meet, while judges became at least nominally independent of the government. The Ottoman court convened an assembly of provincial representatives in 1845, but the sultan quickly abandoned this experiment in constitutionalism. In 1876, a constitutional revolt made the executive responsible to the legislature. "All Ottoman subjects," the new constitution decreed, "regardless of whether they possess property or fortune, shall have the right to vote." Religious liberty and equality before the law were enshrined. The constitution lasted only a few months before the sultan reimposed his authority, but resentment festered among the educated classes.

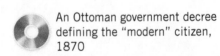

An Ottoman government decree defining the "modern" citizen, 1870

Constitutionalism spread, along with other Western ways, to Japan, where in 1882, the decision to draw up a constitution was based on the results of a fact-finding mission to Europe. Because Japan was now industrializing, the framers of the constitution thought that they had to accommodate the middle classes. Sovereignty remained the prerogative of the "sacred and inviolable" emperor, who would govern "with the consent" of a representative assembly, elected by a franchise restricted to those rich enough to pay property taxes. The constitution also enshrined what we now call civil and human rights—to hold and transfer property, to speak and associate freely, to practice religion without hindrance, and to be tried under the law. The emperor, however, could suspend these rights in emergencies. Political parties had a role in running the assembly but not the country. Because it was considered vital for the emperor to remain "above politics," he appointed ministers, on the advice of senior statesmen without reference to party.

In other parts of the world, constitutionalism rarely achieved power. Copycat constitutions accompanied the independence of all the new Latin American states, but they were usually mere formalities that disguised the rule of military strongmen, dictators, and oligarchies. The same can be said of Liberia's constitution. Nonetheless, there were attempts to create effective constitutions. In the North American Southeast, under the influence of German missionaries, and the inspiration of their chief, Sequoia (1770–1843), the Cherokee people established their own republic alongside the United States, with representative institutions and laws codified in a written version of their own language. The Cherokee state flourished until the United States crushed it and expelled its people in the 1830s. The Fanti confederacy in West Africa, as James Africanus Horton described it, was "the pivot of national unity, headed by intelligent men, to whom a great deal of the powers of the kings and chiefs are delegated.... Through it the whole of the Fantee race can ... boast of a national assembly." The chiefs elected a king-president. Education and road maintenance were among the government's responsibilities.

Although constitutionalism was Western inspired, traditional societies often had similar systems or conceptions of government of their own that limited rulers' power or subjected them to control by aristocratic or popular assemblies. When, for instance, the war leader Atiba reconstructed the Kingdom of Oyo in central Nigeria in the 1850s, he looked back to his people's traditions, restoring the rites of ancient gods and instituting worship of royal ancestors, even though he and most of his people were nominally Muslims. He enjoyed such grandiose titles as Owner of the World and of Life and Companion of the Gods. But the king could not act without the support of the council of representatives of noble families, who nominated officials and had the right to demand his self-sacrifice by ritual suicide. In Ghana, the king of the Asante was known as "He Who Speaks Last" because, although he made policy decisions, he listened first to the views of the chiefs.

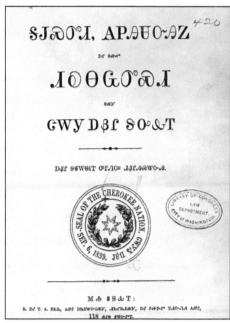

Constitution of the Cherokee Nation. Sequoia (ca. 1770–1843) developed a writing system for the Cherokee language in 1809, in which each of 85 symbols stands for a syllable. In 1839, a Cherokee assembly used it to write the Constitution of the Cherokee Nation, which provided for all land to be common property and for a chieftain, legislature, and judiciary to be elected by all males over 25 years old, descended from "Cherokee men by free women." Black people and Cherokee men who were part black, however, were explicitly denied a vote.

 The Constitution of the Empire of Japan, 1889

CENTRALIZATION, MILITARIZATION, AND BUREAUCRATIZATION

Whether monarchical or republican, constitutional or absolutist, nineteenth-century states tended to become more centralized, as industrialization and militarization boosted the power of governments.

In and Around the Industrializing World

In the Ottoman Empire, for instance, Sultan Mahmud II (r. 1808–1839) reorganized the army on European lines in 1826 and used his new troops to wipe out the

Janissaries, the old, politically unreliable military corps. The army became the spearhead of movements of political reform and the guardian of what increasingly—as the multinational empire shrank—felt like a Turkish nation-state. Under the next sultan, a new bureaucracy took over tax collecting, which the state had farmed out to local agents. Muhammad Ali in Egypt (see Chapter 23) had launched a similar program as early as 1820, conscripting peasants into an army he called the New Order. To recruit and pay for the army, he overhauled the administration, dividing Egypt into 24 provinces and creating layers of bureaucracy that reached from the capital into every village. Rulers in Libya, Tunisia, and Morocco created similar bureaucracies that functioned alongside traditional authorities.

In the industrializing world, the most spectacular cases of restructured state power were those of Germany, Italy, the United States, and Japan. In the 1860s, all of these countries experienced unifying wars won by industrialized regions. Germany and Italy had long been divided among many different states. Japan had a long history as a unitary state, but the central government had lost control of remote provinces. The United States was still a new state, but its constitution had never really settled a crucial issue: whether the separate states had permanently and irrevocably renounced their sovereignty in favor of the federal government. When some of the slave-holding states seceded from the Union, the federal government contested it.

China underwent a "restoration" in the 1860s after old-fashioned rebellions—Muslim risings on the edges of the empire, peasant revolutions at its heart—and the invasions by Britain and France recounted in Chapter 25 (see Map 26.3). The restoration did not involve the radical recrafting that circumstances really required, and decentralization continued in defiance of the trend in the industrializing world. The Chinese government sold offices—wrecking the ancient examination system as a method for filling official positions by merit. Partly to maximize sales, the government appointed magistrates for short terms, so local administration tended to fall into the hands of petty officials who, once appointed as magistrates' underlings, remained in their jobs indefinitely.

Centralization did not always or even primarily mean extending the power of central institutions. It was also a matter of overcoming traditional provincial, regional, and communal loyalties with a common sense of allegiance to the state. Governments used universal military service (see Chapter 23) to create a statewide sense of political community, usually in combination with efforts to spread nationalist feelings. Japan's army, typically, became a nursery for reeducating young men in a new version of samurai values, focused on obedience to the emperor and self-sacrifice for the state.

The Japanese army, in consequence, felt no loyalty to the civil government and remained, in effect, outside and above the constitution. A similar pattern can be discerned in Spain and Latin America, where the wars of the early nineteenth century militarized huge proportions of the populations. Armies became the agents of independence and in some cases of modernization, the guardians of the state and, therefore, the arbiters of constitutional conflicts. All countries that used their armed forces to mobilize the entire society risked suffering, or did suffer, similar consequences: Militarized societies produced politicized armies. The United States was fortunate that by the time of its Civil War (1861–1865) its civil institu-

"Honored dead." The reality of the field of Gettysburg was litter-strewn and squalid, with gaping, crumpled corpses. Photography helped to take romance out of depictions of war.

tions and traditions were strong enough to survive the trauma. Civil conflict in the United States never led, as it has done in most countries, to military dictatorship. Britain, too, escaped the danger by keeping its army small and avoiding conscription until 1916 during the First World War.

As well as bringing armies into politics, militarization made wars worse. The Prussian military theorist Carl von Clausewitz (1780–1831) thought the only rational way to wage war was "to the utmost. . . . He who uses force unsparingly, without reference to the bloodshed involved, must obtain a superiority." The ultimate objective was to disarm the enemy permanently. This encouraged belligerents to fight for unconditional surrender when they were winning, to resist it obstinately when they were losing, and to impose harsh terms in victory.

In combination, the improved technology of war, the doctrines of militarism, and the transformation of society into a battleground all made the horrors of war worse. Photographers and chroniclers of the American Civil War and the Franco-Prussian War of 1870–1871 introduced a new awareness of war's consequences. The novels of Emile Zola (1840–1902) depicted bloody hospitals, decaying dead,

MAP 26.3

Revolts in the Qing Empire, 1850–1901

- Qing Empire
- tribal risings
- Muslim revolts
- area of Northwestern Muslim rising 1863–1873
- area controlled by Taiping rebels 1853–1863
- → Taiping rebellion
- area of Boxer uprising 1900–1901
- Guizhou Muslim uprising 1854–1872
- → opium trade

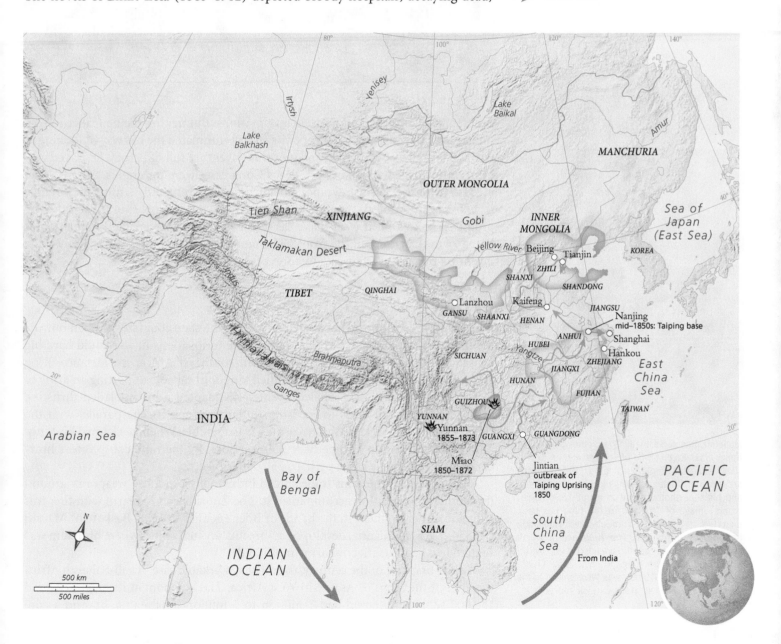

Asante King. Reminiscences of the greatness of the Asante kings persisted after defeat by the British in the late nineteenth century. In this photograph of the 1890s, King Agyeman Prempeh I, borne by slaves, sits on his litter under the royal umbrella, surrounded by drummers and praise singers. Shortly after the photograph was taken, the British arrested and exiled him and provoked a further—and, for the Asante, disastrous—war by demanding custody of the Asante's sacred golden stool.

Modernization personified. The clothes suggest an upper-class Englishman of the era and an expensively educated English schoolboy. But the faces are those of Chulalongkorn, the king of Thailand, and his son, photographed in about 1890. Westerners' image of Thailand at the time has been distorted, thanks to the much-loved Hollywood and Broadway musical *The King and I*, which depicts an exotic court, presided over by an unbending patriarch king. In fact, King Chulalongkorn (r. 1868–1910), was Westernized in his sentiments as well as in his outlook and policies. See p. 678.

gangrenous wounded, and frenzied amputations. But neither the new doctrines of militarism nor the new awareness of its effects eliminated the old way of looking at war as a chivalrous, romantic, and glorious adventure full of heroes, flags, and colorful uniforms. So wars went on. Peace Congresses were for cranks. Alfred Nobel (1831–1896), the Swedish weapons magnate who invented dynamite, took refuge in extravagant projects for world peace. War would "stop short instantly," he promised in 1890, if it were made "as death-dealing to the civilian population at home as to the troops at the front." The best hope he could see for peace was the invention of germ warfare or a weapon of mass destruction.

Beyond the Industrializing World

It is tempting to suppose that similar effects on the state could not happen outside the industrializing world. But relatively simple innovations in war could have big consequences in pre-industrial societies. In southeast Africa, for instance, King Shaka reorganized the Zulus into a unified kingdom capable of putting an army of 50,000 men into the field. Shaka invented or adapted a heavy-bladed thrusting spear and developed drills to accustom infantry to use it. The parallel with the effects of firearms drill on Western armies is irresistible. When he claimed his kingdom in 1816, his clan had perhaps 350 warriors. By the time conspirators murdered him in 1828, he ruled perhaps 250,000 subjects.

In any case, as the arms trade spread industrially produced weaponry around the world, militarization accompanied it. The Zulus began to rearm with firearms after encountering them in the hands of Boer enemies in 1838. Baskore of Maradi (r. 1854–1875) in Nigeria, developed a bureaucracy in Katsina, where his realm was centered, to keep an effective army mobilized.

In the first half of the century, the most remarkable case in sub-Saharan Africa was that of the kings of Asante in West Africa. The kingdom at its height covered 150,000 square miles and had 3 million to 5 million inhabitants. Beyond a core area around the capital, Kumasi, where the ruler's war companions ruled their own followers without much interference from the court, a central treasury that also ran the kings' own commercial transactions—mining, slave trading, and hunting for ivory—regulated tribute, taxes, and tolls. Early in the century, the kings adopted Arabic as a language of record keeping, which thereafter was done on paper instead of in the old form of piles of shells and coins. The Asante usually redesignated traditional rulers of conquered peoples as captains of the Asante king and placed agents alongside them to keep them in order. Bureaucrats were at the disposal of the king. "We are willing to prove to your majesty," ran the declaration of office of the highest treasury official, "our devotion to your person by receiving your foot on our necks, and taking the sacred oath that we will perform all your commands. Our gold, our slaves and our lives are yours, and are ready to be delivered up to your command."

But Ethiopia was the most successful case of political modernization in sub-Saharan Africa. In the third quarter of the century, Ethiopia emerged from a long period of internal war and weak leadership. The emperors never enjoyed

○ MAKING CONNECTIONS ○

STATE MODERNIZATION IN THE NINETEENTH CENTURY

TYPE OF DEVELOPMENT/IDEOLOGY →	CORE IDEA/PURPOSE →	SCOPE AND RESULTS
Nationalism	Uniting people who shared same language, historic experience, and sense of identity into a cohesive state	Worldwide; positive effects include increased self-government, popular sovereignty; negative effects include repression of minorities (ethnic, religious, racial) within larger states; promotion of assimilation
Constitutionalism	Belief that state is founded on rules that rulers and citizens create and are bound to obey within a legal framework	Worldwide; beginning in Britain, United States, and Europe; vigorously opposed because of the implication that sovereignty was shared by more than one person/one class; threatened divine right of monarchy and aristocracy; eventual spread to Middle East and Asia
Centralization	Overcoming traditional provincial, regional, communal loyalties by fostering allegiance to the state; often extending power of central institutions	Worldwide, especially in quickly developing regions; often propelled by civil wars (United States, Japan, Germany, Italy) and in areas threatened with fragmentation
Militarization	Use of armed forces to mobilize populations; boosts power of governments to tax and spend on a large scale	Worldwide, especially in industrializing regions and colonial territories; use of larger armies, advanced technology expands warfare to civilian population, increases military and civilian casualties; arms race for improved technologies
Bureaucratization	Systemizing tax collecting, census taking, and regulation; often relying on regional governors to exercise local authority	Worldwide, in old empires (Ottoman), new industrial states (United States, Germany, Britain), and regions with progressive rulers (Ethiopia, Thailand, Asante kingdom); improved ability to harness economic systems to government goals

Nationalism, Constitutionalism, Militarization, Centralization, and Bureaucratization in the Nineteenth Century

ca. 1800–1850	Asante kings centralize and bureaucratize their kingdom
1805–1872	Giuseppe Mazzini, Italian nationalist
1810	Beginning of Jewish reform movement
ca. 1810–1820s	Wars of independence from Spain fought in Latin America
1820	King Shaka controls most of southeast Africa
1821	Founding of Liberia
1822	First fully independent Mexican state
1830	Greece gains independence from Ottoman Empire
1830s	Large Latin American states dissolve into smaller ones
1832	Great Reform Act becomes law in Britain
1839	Constitution of the Cherokee Nation
1845	Ottoman sultan convenes an assembly of provincial representatives
1861–1896	José Rizal, Filipino nationalist
1864	Creation of district assemblies in Russia
1870s–1880s	King Chulalongkorn of Thailand (Siam) modernizes his state
1878	Romania and Serbia gain independence from Ottoman Empire
1889	Japanese constitution created by imperial decree
1893	French Captain Alfred Dreyfus accused of spying for the Germans
1895	Nationalist rebellion in Guangzhou region of China
Late nineteenth century	Ethiopia undergoes political modernization

uncontested legitimacy or universal obedience, but at least they had credible programs of reunification. The system of government was loosely federal, with regional rulers exercising authority without reference to the center, except for paying tribute and defending the country from invaders.

In the 1870s, as a result of victories against Egyptian invaders, Emperor Yohannes IV (r. 1872–1889) began to build up a huge supply of captured modern weapons and to reorganize the army so that it had a professional core. When Menelik II (r. 1889–1813) became emperor, he concentrated on creating a militarily efficient state, armed with the best guns he could buy from Europe. He established garrisons in remote parts of the empire, dominating the country, stimulating markets, and spreading Christianity. At his death, the empire had postal, telegraph, and telephone services and a rail link to the Red Sea. The emperors imported technical know-how from Europe. Alred Ilg, a Swiss engineer, was Menelik's chief aide, attending to everything from the palace plumbing to foreign policy. Menelik also used Italian technical advice and arms shipments before the outbreak of conflict with Italy in 1896. As a result of all these changes, Ethiopia, uniquely among native African states in the late nineteenth century, not only repulsed European invasion but also participated in imperial expansion on its own account alongside European powers (see Chapter 24).

Thailand was a southeast Asian state that modernized even more thoroughly than Ethiopia and also achieved the distinction, unique in its region, of avoiding European conquest. In the 1830s, Prince Mongkut, who already had a reputation as an outstanding Buddhist scholar and reformer, came into contact with French Catholic and American Protestant missionaries and immediately appreciated that Thailand had a lot of catching up to do if it were to survive in a Western-dominated future. When he became king in 1851, he began reforms, inaugurating a government newspaper, printing laws, and—in a break with a tradition—allowing his face to be seen in public. He permitted his subjects to petition him, gave women rights to choose marriage partners, and educated his successor, Chulalongkorn, in a Western as well as a traditional curriculum.

Chulalongkorn (r. 1868–1910) inherited a bigger empire than any that southeast Asia had ever seen. But it was decentralized: a tributary empire at its edges, with hundreds of traditional communities, all with their own peculiar relationships to the throne. Chulalongkorn placed royal princes in charge of government departments, bypassing the old customs by which ministers succeeded by hereditary right. In the 1870s and 1880s, royal commissioners brought outlying autonomous regions of the Thai Empire under control of the central administration. In 1897, the king went to Europe and professed himself "convinced that there exists no incompatibility" between the acquisition of Western know-how "and the maintenance of our individuality as an independent Asiatic nation." Although Western examples inspired his reforms, he presented them as triumphs of Buddhist morality.

Bureaucratic centralization occurred in every continent. Until the British invasions of the 1840s, the Sikh state in the Punjab in northern India was creating a bureaucracy, surveying the territory it occupied, and introducing a consistent scheme of taxation. In the Central African highlands, King Mutesa (r. 1857–1884) of Buganda in what is now Uganda imported European weapons to equip his own servants and clients and Christian missionaries to strengthen his bureaucracy. He was able to concentrate unprecedented power in his own hands. In West Africa, the empire of Sokoto survived throughout the nineteenth century, in part because it created a bureaucracy to replace the local power of chiefs. The kingdoms of Fouta Toro and Fouta Jalon became elective monarchies, relying on Muslim clergy as servants of the state (see Map 26.4). Tawhiao, the proud Maori who alarmed James Kerry-Nicholls in New Zealand, had counterparts in state creation all over the world.

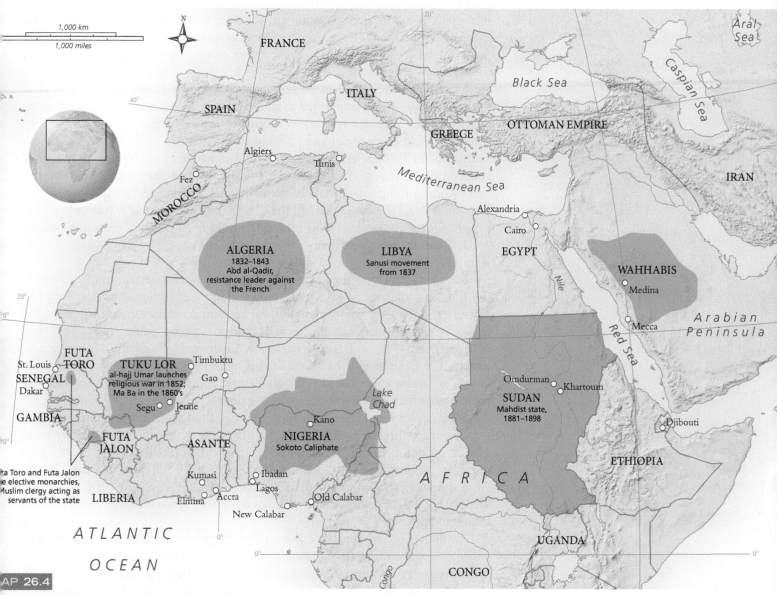

AP 26.4

uslim Reform Movements in Africa d Arabia in the Nineteenth Century

▮ Islamic reform movement

RELIGION AND POLITICS

State power mopped up rivals. Nationalism, militarization, and centralization eclipsed other traditional allegiances. Aristocracies, as we have seen, were on the wane anyway in most places (see Chapter 24). Religion, however, was more problematic. In the nineteenth century, morality, family life, and the spaces in which social relationships were forged—the household, educational institutions, and the workplace—became arenas fiercely contested between religious institutions and states. In the West, civil marriage was the state's most important intrusion. Most countries with codified law made provision for it. Education was another battleground, usually resolved by compromise, because clergy were too cheap and too valuable as teachers to eliminate from schools. States that had not already done so, in some cases, even took over existing religions, funding them and appointing clerics. Japan's ancient popular religion, Shintoism, which had always been a chaotic mix of local nature and ancestor cults, became a national organization under imperial leadership with the emperor as chief priest, largely because nineteenth-century intellectuals in Japan perceived state control of religion to be one of the strengths of Western powers.

Europe and the Americas became arenas of state–Church competition. Pope Pius IX (r. 1846–1878) responded to challenges to Church authority and Christian belief with defiance. He refused to submit to force or defer to change. He condemned almost every social and political innovation of his day. When Italy occupied Rome in 1870, he retreated into virtual seclusion in the Vatican. For a godly vocation undiluted by compromise, his fellow bishops that same year rewarded him by proclaiming papal infallibility in religious doctrine and morals. His successor, Leo XIII (r. 1878–1903) turned the Church into a reforming institution, a privileged critic of abuses of secular power. But after Leo's death, the Church became much more conservative. Clergy in every faith were always prepared to collaborate with repression and authoritarianism on the political right.

Meanwhile, religion resisted a challenge from atheism that science claimed to validate. Darwin's theory of evolution (see Chapter 25) suggested, to some of its advocates, a new God-free explanation for life. Impersonal evolution threatened to replace divine Providence as the motor of change. If science could explain a problem as "mysterious"—to use Darwin's word—as the diversity of species, it might be able to explain everything else. Religious doubts multiplied among Western elites. From the 1870s, "humane" or "ethical" societies aimed to base moral conduct on humane values rather than on the fear of God or the dogmas of religious institutions.

Christianity was stirred in response rather than shaken. Evangelizing movements spread Christian awareness in the new industrialized, urban workforces. In 1867, the English poet Matthew Arnold stood on Dover Beach and heard in his mind the "melancholy, long, withdrawing roar" of the "the Sea of Faith." But in 1896, the Austrian composer Anton Bruckner died while writing his great "Ninth Symphony," a dark document of religious doubts smothered in a glorious finale of resurgent faith.

Among many instances of the continuing vitality of Islam as a source of political inspiration in the nineteenth century, none was more spectacular than the movement Muhammad Ahmad proclaimed in the Sudan in 1881. Calling on followers to "put aside everything that resembles the customs of Turks and infidels," he came to see himself as the *Mahdi*—the successor of the Prophet Muhammad, the restorer of the faith, whose coming would herald the end of time. His typical follower was, as the British admitted (in lines by the great poet

Pope Leo XIII, *Rerum Novarum*, 1891

Matthew Arnold, *Dover Beach*

of the British Empire, Rudyard Kipling [1865–1936]) "a pore benighted 'eathen, but a first-class fightin' man." The Mahdi himself had a different explanation for his success: "Every intelligent person must know that Allah rules. If ... you persist in denying my divine calling, ... you are to be killed." The Egyptian and British governments were unable to suppress the movement until 1898, when a crushingly well-armed British force slaughtered the Mahdists at the Battle of Omdurman (see Chapter 25).

Religion remained a revolutionary force in the world. In 1847, a conflict known as the Caste War broke out in Yucatán in Mexico. Maya rebels threatened to kill all white people. Government supporters retorted with threats to exterminate the Maya. The rebels' rallying point was the so-called Talking Cross of the shrine of Chan Santa Cruz—an oracle proclaiming divine sanction and success for the rebel cause. In the 1850s and 1860s, holy men launched religious wars in West Africa. In 1860, for instance, Muslim preachers roused the peasants of Sine against their king, who said he wanted to do with subject-peoples "as we have always done. These people are my slaves. . . . I will take their property, their children and their millet." In Ethiopia, Emperor Tewodros II (r. 1855–1868) appealed to Christians as a Messiah, and to Muslims as a Mahdi, before behaving like a Western modernizer and secularizing church property.

In Japan in the 1860s, a woman who claimed to be divine inspired thousands of peasants to rebel. She preached equality and peasant solidarity. In China at around the same time, a failed examination candidate, who came to see himself as a "brother of Jesus," led a rebellion that, as we saw in Chapter 25, almost overthrew the Qing Empire. In 1866, a woman who called herself the Virgin of the Rosary led a rebellion in Bolivia. In the North American plains, meanwhile, the Ghost Dance was a Native American ritual to bring the dead back to life. In the 1880s, prophets associated it first with a project to bring on the end of the world, then with a plan to invoke divine help against the white invaders. Most Ghost Dancers never intended violent resistance, but settlers called in the United States' cavalry who massacred Sioux Ghost Dancers at Wounded Knee in 1890.

On the whole, despite the vigor of religiously inspired politics, religion lost out in its conflicts with secular states. The charms religious zealots such as the Mahdi issued did not work against the machine gun. Sacred notions of political authority succumbed to new kinds of legitimacy that nationalists, constitutionalists, and bureaucrats advocated.

NEW FORMS OF POLITICAL RADICALISM

Popular revolutionary movements of religious inspiration were not new. But more subversive ways of thinking about the state were building up strength for the future.

Steps Toward Democracy

In the West, enthusiasm for democracy became a major force for change independent of any sect. The United States—perhaps because men steeped in reverence for both the classics and Christianity founded it—was the laboratory of democracy for the nineteenth-century world. Democracy as we understand it today—with a representative legislature, elected on a wide suffrage, and political parties—was, in effect, an American invention. Despite major imperfections—slaves, Native Americans, and women were excluded—democracy developed early in the new republic. By the early 1840s, almost all adult, white, free males could vote.

Stump Speaking. George Caleb Bingham (1811–1879) chronicled the life of the Missouri valley in the mid–nineteenth century in his accomplished, well-observed paintings. He was also active in politics on behalf of Andrew Jackson, which gives his political scenes an edge of personal commitment. Typically, as here in *Stump Speaking* (1853–1854), a politician's passion contrasts with the attitudes of his audiences—variously cool, critical, idly curious, sneering, bored, or depraved.
George Caleb Bingham (American, 1811–1879), Stump Speaking, 1853–54. Oil on canvas, 42 1/2 × 58 in. The Saint Louis Art Museum, Gift of Bank of America. Photo © The Saint Louis Art Museum.

Alexis de Tocqueville, from
Democracy in America

In Europe, however, democracy seemed at first to be one of America's "peculiar institutions," like slavery, that it would be best to avoid. Why should elites share power with poorly educated masses who tended to vote for demagogues and charlatans? The bloodshed of the French Revolution seemed to show that the "common man" was untrustworthy. In consequence, the first half of the nineteenth century was a time of democratic retreat in most of Europe, as rulers withdrew or diluted constitutions that they had conceded in the crises of the Napoleonic Wars. The new constitutions that did emerge in Europe at this time were designed to create alliances among monarchs, aristocrats, churches, and the middle classes and, thus, to defend traditional privileges by enlarging support for them. Whenever possible, the birth of working-class organizations was aborted, radical presses censored, demonstrators shot. In Britain, the Reform Act of 1832, often hailed as a first step toward democratic progress, actually disenfranchised working-class voters.

Nevertheless, the model of the United States became increasingly attractive as the young country proved itself. European radicals who visited America returned enthused. The first influential apologist for American democracy was a German, Karl Postl, who in 1828 recommended a "system which unites the population for the common good." Between 1835 and 1840, Alexis de Tocqueville published *Democracy in America*. His aristocratic self-confidence in the face of popular sovereignty helped reconcile Europeans to democratic change. While most Europeans of his class felt the menace of the revolutionary mob, Tocqueville saw "the same democracy ... advancing rapidly toward power in Europe." Properly managed, the result would be "a society which all men, regarding the law as their work, would acknowledge without demur." Where rights were guaranteed, he wrote, democracy would "shelter the state" from tyranny, on the one hand, and lawlessness, on the other. Democracy became the first American cultural product to conquer Europe—even before jazz, rock music, casual manners, fast food, and tight jeans. In the late nineteenth century, most European countries modified their constitutions in a democratic direction and enlarged the franchise. Though France,

Switzerland, and Spain were beacons of universal male suffrage, the most conspicuous concentration of states with democratic franchises was in the former Ottoman dominions in the Balkans. In Greece, Bulgaria, Serbia, and Romania, the right to vote was more widely shared than in Britain or Scandinavia. This was understandable. The newest states, repudiating the empires that preceded them, had the least historic baggage to discard in adopting democracy.

There was, however, no uniform march of progress toward practical democracy in most of Europe. On the contrary, democracy remained marginal throughout the century, for effective democracy is not just a matter of how many people have the right to vote. Everywhere small groups tried to manipulate mass electorates. In Romania, the constitution was often suspended or ignored. In Britain, the biggest single extension of the franchise in 1884–1885 was accompanied by a redistribution of parliamentary seats to preserve the existing parties' shares of power. Constitutional reform in Europe never completely pried open the world of the dominant political caste and its recruits. The aristocracy retained formal power. When Germany introduced universal male suffrage in 1871, it was only for elections for one chamber of the national legislature, the Reichstag, whose power was limited.

The Expansion of the Public Sphere

Even where there was little or no democracy, more people got involved in what historians and sociologists now like to call the **public sphere**: in clubs, institutions, and associations outside the home, in arenas of debate in cafes and bars, and in places of worship. Public readings of newspapers made even illiterate people politically informed. In Cuba, this was the normal entertainment for workers in factories while they rolled cigars. In Barcelona in 1852, a friar found factory workers listening to children reading aloud from "political journals which generally spread subversive doctrines, mocked holy things ... spoke ill of the proprietors and government, and preached socialism and communism." Catholic clergy provided reading material for factories to deflect workers from hearing too much inflammatory or revolutionary propaganda.

The public sphere was widest and most developed in North America and parts of Europe. That is why democracy got a foothold in those regions. But there were outposts and echoes elsewhere in the world. Although the number of people who took part in political life in Latin America was relatively small, they contested power with great commitment and sustained ferocious debates in the press. In Brazil, the proliferation of political clubs, newspapers, and rallies preceded the abolition of slavery in 1888 and the proclamation of the republic in 1889. In the late nineteenth century, most Argentine intellectuals regarded their country as a democracy.

In Japan, the spread of education (see Chapter 24) enlarged the public sphere. Examinations replaced samurai privileges as a means to recruit state officials. Even in China, the political class expanded, thanks in part to the creation of hundreds of provincial academies to train officials. On the whole, the Qing responded to crisis by resisting social or political change and clinging to the notion that the inherited order of society was sacred. The terms of public debate, however, were enlarged. At the height of the crisis caused by rebellion and Anglo-French invasion in the 1860s, Feng Guifen (fung gway-fun) (1809–1874), director of one of the largest provincial academies, advocated the professionalization of the civil service and popular election of village headmen. The government, however, shelved his proposals.

 Feng Guifen on Western strength

WESTERN SOCIAL THOUGHT

The clash of political visions in the nineteenth-century West was part of a worldwide tension between secularism and religiosity in everyday conceptions of life and the world. Were men apes or angels? Would the goodness inside them emerge in freedom or was it corroded with evil that had to be controlled? In 1816, the English writer Thomas Love Peacock gathered fictional philosophers in the setting of his comic novel, *Headlong Hall.* "Mr. Forster, the perfectibilian," expected "gradual advancement towards a state of unlimited perfection," while "Mr. Escot, the deteriorationist," foresaw, with gloomy satisfaction, "that the whole species must at length be exterminated by its own imbecility and violence." These extremes of optimism and pessimism echoed real debates. In France, for instance, Louis Blanc (1811–1882) believed that the state could eliminate human wickedness, while his contemporary, Alphonse Karr, thought that attempted reforms only made things worse. The politics of fear and hope pitted rival kinds of radicalism—reformist philosophies that claimed to get to the root of the world's problems—against each other.

Robert Owen, *Address to the Workers of New Lanark,* 1816

Socialism was an extreme form of optimism. Socialists advocated the ideals of equality and fraternity that those Enlightenment thinkers who believed in the perfectibility of human nature had proclaimed (see Chapter 22). Early socialist communities in Europe and America practiced sharing and cooperating. Charles Fourier (1772–1837) planned a settlement called New Harmony, where even sexual orgies would be organized on egalitarian principles. In Texas in 1849, Étienne Cabet (1788–1856) founded a town he called Icaria, where abolishing property and forbidding rivalry would prevent envy, crime, anger, and lust.

These experiments and others failed, but the idea of reforming society as a whole on socialist lines appealed to people unrewarded or outraged by the unequal distribution of wealth in the industrializing world. Economic theorists maintained that since workers' labor added the greater part of the value of most commodities (see Chapter 24), the workers should get the lion's share of the profits—or so some socialists inferred. This was a capitalist's kind of socialism, in which ideals carried a price tag. Louis Blanc convinced most socialists that the state could impose their ideals on society. John Ruskin (1819–1900) echoed these arguments in England. For him "the first duty of a state is to see that every child born therein shall be well housed, clothed, fed and educated," and he relished the prospect of increased state power to accomplish it.

Meanwhile, Karl Marx (1818–1883) predicted the inevitability of socialism's triumph through class conflict. As economic power passed from capital to labor, so workers—degraded and inflamed by exploitative employers—would seize power in the state. "Not only," he announced, "has the bourgeoisie forged the weapons that bring death to itself. It has also called into existence the men who are to wield those weapons—the modern working class, the proletarians." The transition, he believed, would be violent. The ruling class would try to hold on to power, while the rising class struggled to gain it. So he tended to agree with the thinkers of his day who saw violence as conducive to progress. In part, the effect was to inspire revolutionary violence, which sometimes succeeded in changing society, but never seemed to bring the communist utopia into being or even into sight. All Marx's predictions, so far, have proved false. Yet the brilliance of his analysis of history ensured that he would have millions of readers and millions of followers.

While mainstream socialists put their faith in a strong, regulatory state to realize revolutionary ambitions or sought to capture the state by mobilizing the masses, revolutionary violence sidetracked others. Some of these "anarchists," as they called themselves, turned to the bloodstained ravings of Johann Most

Noble workers. Giuseppe Pelizza's painting *Il Quarto Stato*, completed between 1899 and 1901 expresses the grandeur and grind at the heart of Socialism. The workers advance heroically united, but with the look of automation, with individuality suppressed. Pelizza was convinced that artists were workers who had a social responsibility to educate, elevate, and inspire other workers.
G. Pellizza da Volpedo, The Fourth Estate. *Milano, Galleria Civica D'Arte Moderna.* © Canali Photobank.

(1846–1896), the first great ideologue of terror. The entire elite—including their families, servants, and all who did business with them—were, for Most, legitimate targets of armed struggle, to be killed at every opportunity. Anyone caught in the crossfire was a sacrifice in a good cause. In 1884, he published a handbook on how to explode bombs in churches, ballrooms, and public places, where the "reptile brood" of aristocrats, priests, and capitalists might gather. He also advocated exterminating policemen on the grounds that these "pigs" were not fully human. The bombs of terrorism exploded in elite ears. Social outcasts and the chronically disaffected formed pacts to assassinate rulers, provoke revolutions, fight the state, and defy the repressive realities of politics and economics.

In most European countries in the late nineteenth century, socialists built up mass organizations for political and industrial action. They believed their triumph was determined by history. The questions that divided them were whether that triumph should be triggered violently, pursued democratically, or engineered by industrial action.

Opponents of socialism included philosophical pessimists, who believed humans could not be reformed, and that only law and order could redeem their wickedness. Between extreme optimism and extreme pessimism, centrist political thinking developed. In the nineteenth century, the English philosopher Jeremy Bentham (1748–1832) devised the most influential form of centrist thinking, called **utilitarianism**. Bentham proposed a new way to evaluate social institutions without reference or deference to their antiquity or authority or past record of success. He thought good could be defined as a surplus of happiness over unhappiness

Religion, Utopianism, Democracy, and Political Radicalism in the Nineteenth Century

1748–1832	Jeremy Bentham, proponent of utilitarianism
1772–1837	Charles Fourier, created planned community of New Harmony based on egalitarian ideals
1788–1856	Étienne Cabet, founded utopian community of Icaria
1806–1873	John Stuart Mill, combined individualism with social reform
1811–1882	Louis Blanc, argued that the state could eliminate human wickedness
1818–1883	Karl Marx, predicted socialism's inevitable triumph
1835–1840	Publication of Alexis de Tocqueville's *Democracy in America*
ca. 1840	Almost all adult white males can vote in the United States
1844–1900	Friedrich Nietzsche, rejected liberalism and religion
r. 1846–1878	Pope Pius IX, opponent of social and political innovation
1847	Caste War begins in southeast Mexico
1881	Muhammad Ahmad calls on Muslims in the Sudan to join his reform movement

John Stuart Mill, from *On Liberty*

and that the aim of the state was "the greatest happiness of the greatest number." For Bentham, social utility was more important than individual liberty. His doctrine was thoroughly secular. Bentham's standard of happiness was pleasure, and his index of evil was pain. His views, therefore, appealed to the irreligious. But the greatest happiness of the greatest number means sacrifices for some. It is strictly incompatible with human rights, because the interest of the "greatest number" will always tend to leave some individuals without benefits.

Modifying, then rejecting utilitarianism, Bentham's disciple, John Stuart Mill (1806–1873), adopted a scale of values with freedom at the top. Liberty, he thought, is absolute, except where it interferes with others. "The only purpose," he wrote, "for which power can be rightfully exercised over any member of a civilised community, against his will, is to prevent harm to others," not to make him happier. For Bentham's "greatest number," Mill substituted the individual. "Over himself, over his own body and mind, the individual is sovereign." Mill's individualism, however, never excluded social priorities. "For the protection of society," the citizen "owes a return for the benefit." He can be made to respect others' rights and to contribute a reasonable share of taxes and services to the state. Freedom and social priorities, however, did not commend themselves to everybody. Philosophical opponents of liberalism—the most eloquent of whom was Nietzsche (1844–1900)—favored "heroes" and "supermen" to solve social problems. Dictators in the next century would adopt these ideas.

Meanwhile, Benthamism was amazingly influential. The British state was reorganized along lines Bentham recommended. The penal code was reformed to minimize unhelpful pain. The government bureaucracy was restaffed with administrators who had passed competitive exams. Capitalist and libertarian prejudices could never quite exclude public interest from legislators' priorities, even under nominally right-wing governments. Benthamism made social welfare seem like the job of the state. In promoting social welfare, Germany led the way, introducing pensions, health services, and education for all in the 1880s. The German policy is often seen as an attempt to preempt the appeal of socialism—as indeed it was. But it was also the outcome of a trend, begun during the Enlightenment, of philosophical respect for the common man. Australia and New Zealand copied German initiatives in an attempt to create a common identity for settlers—an identity, moreover, distinct from those of the snobbish and class-ridden society that migrants from Britain had left behind. A worldwide consensus in favor of a socially responsible state gradually emerged. The main disagreements, which would be bloodily fought out in the following century, were over how far that responsibility extended.

IN PERSPECTIVE: Global State-Building

All the transformations of nineteenth-century states need to be understood against a common background: the declining credibility of traditional forms of authority, as conflicts overthrew old supremacies and economic change enriched new aspirants to power. During the changes that followed, the sphere of the state enlarged. States had still not penetrated vast areas of the globe, but these regions were now the exception—underpopulated and relatively inaccessible environments. In most of the rest of the world, the state had arrived: imposed from outside by imperialist invasions, or created from within by monarchs or elites, usually in imitation of Western powers. In parts of the world with long experience of states, such as Japan, Egypt, and Thailand, governments had extended their reach. States took on new responsibilities as their power increased. Education, as we have seen, received a boost from militarization. States interfered more and more in religion and family life. It even became increasingly accepted that the state was responsible for the total well-being of its citizens.

After all the wars, reforms, constitutional conflicts, radical thinking, and administrative tinkering, how strong were the states and empires that covered most of the world by 1900? Had they reformed for survival? Or were they, as socialists thought, doomed to disappear? Old rivals of the state—religious institutions and allegiances—had proved remarkably strong. And although local, regional, and tribal loyalties were in retreat, they had only been checked, not destroyed. As we shall see, they would often reemerge in the twentieth and twenty-first centuries. In 1900, it looked as if some states, such as Japan, the United States, and the British Empire, had met the challenges of the century successfully and recast themselves in lasting form. Others, such as the Ottoman Empire and China, looked vulnerable. In between were superficially strong states, such as the German, Russian, and Habsburg Empires, which were to prove surprisingly fragile when tested in the twentieth century. While white empires continued to grow, the days of their supremacy were numbered. Their power was founded on technological superiority, which was a wasting asset. Nonwhite powers in Asia and Africa had already demonstrated that they could copy the trick, either by buying European technology, as Ethiopia had, or, like Japan, launching their own industrialization programs.

CHRONOLOGY

1748–1832	Jeremy Bentham, proponent of utilitarianism
1772–1837	Charles Fourier, created planned community of New Harmony based on egalitarian ideals
ca. 1800–1850	Asante kings centralize and bureaucratize their kingdom
1805–1872	Giuseppe Mazzini, Italian nationalist
1806–1873	John Stuart Mill, combined individualism with social reform
ca. 1810–1820s	Wars of Independence from Spain fought in Latin America
1811–1882	Louis Blanc, argued that the state could eliminate human wickedness
1818–1883	Karl Marx, predicted socialism's inevitable triumph
1820	King Shaka gains control of most of southeast Africa
1821	Founding of Liberia
1822	First fully independent Mexican state
1830	Greece gains independence from Ottoman Empire
1830s	Large Latin American states dissolve into smaller ones
1832	Great Reform Act becomes law in Britain
1835–1840	Publication of Alexis de Tocqueville's *Democracy in America*
1844–1900	Friedrich Nietzsche, rejected liberalism and religion
1845	Ottoman sultan convenes an assembly of provincial representatives
r. 1846–1878	Pope Pius IX, opponent of social and political innovation
1847	Caste War begins in southeast Mexico
1861–1896	José Rizal, Filipino nationalist
1870s–1880s	King Chulalongkorn of Thailand modernizes his state
1873–1901	British conquest of Kingdom of Asante
1878	Romania and Serbia gain independence from Ottoman Empire
1881	Muhammad Ahmad calls on Muslims in the Sudan to join his reform movement
1889	Japanese constitution created by imperial decree
1893	French Captain Alfred Dreyfus accused of spying for the Germans
1895	Nationalist rebellion in Guangzhou region of China
1896	Battle of Adowa
Late nineteenth century	Ethiopia undergoes political modernization

To maintain its power in the world, Europe needed peace at home. Only brief wars broke that peace in the nineteenth century. For almost 40 years after the defeat of Napoleon in 1815, no major war flared on Europe's home ground. The wars of the midcentury to 1870 were short and did not overstrain the belligerents. After 1870, short-term military service became the universal fashion in the West—with the major exceptions of Britain and the United States but including almost all of Latin America—and Japan, as states sought to give more male citizens experience of military service. Armies therefore had to make up in technology what they lacked in professional ability, because most recruits did not serve long enough to become skilled soldiers. Ever more efficient means of mobilizing armies were called on, as railways linked front lines to barracks and bases all over Europe. Ever more accurate and long-range weapons were required to compensate for soldiers' lack of expertise in firing them. The result was an arms race that made peace precarious and an atmosphere of anxiety among the powers to mobilize rapidly should a new war threaten: a recipe, in short, for rupturing peace. Still, until the end of the nineteenth century, enough powers were sufficiently evenly matched to keep the peace for most of the time.

By then, however, the fear of revolution had so diminished, and the habit of short wars had become so familiar, that neither the fragility of peace nor the fear of war excited much alarm in Europe. The balance of power, on which peace depended, was beginning to tilt toward war because of the uneven distribution of heavy industry. By 1900, Germany produced vastly more coal, iron, and steel than all the other European powers combined. The Russian Empire, with its huge population, was beginning to show signs of being able to catch up. This fact—little noticed outside Germany—made a trial of strength seem urgent. In the arena of Europe, the sand that the changes of the nineteenth century kicked up was raked into new patterns of alliance, made with war in mind rather than to contain change or maintain the balance of power. The arena was ready for the gladiators.

PROBLEMS AND PARALLELS

1. What were the differences between European nationalism and nationalist movements outside Europe? What was the relationship between constitutionalism and modernization in the nineteenth century?

2. How did new states emerge in the nineteenth century? What roles did nationalism, constitutionalism, militarization, and bureaucratization play in state development?

3. Why did many nineteenth-century states emphasize centralization? Who benefited from centralization? Which groups lost power?

4. Why did religion and politics clash in the nineteenth century? Why did some clergy oppose the theory of revolution? Why was religion a "revolutionary force in the world" during the nineteenth century?

5. How did democracy become more widespread in the nineteenth century? What does the term *public sphere* mean? Why did new forms of political radicalism emerge in the nineteenth century?

DOCUMENTS IN GLOBAL HISTORY

- Joseph Mazzini on nationalism
- José Fernández, *El Gaucho Martin Fierro*
- José Rizal, excerpt from *El Filibusterismo (The Reign of Greed)*
- An Ottoman government decree defining the "modern" citizen, 1870
- The Constitution of the Empire of Japan, 1889
- Pope Leo XIII, *Rerum Novarum*, 1891
- Matthew Arnold, *Dover Beach*

- Alexis de Tocqueville, from *Democracy in America*
- Feng Guifen on Western strength
- Robert Owen, *Address to the Workers of New Lanark*, 1816
- Mikhail Bakunin, "Principles and Organization of the International Brotherhood, " 1866
- John Stuart Mill, from *On Liberty*

Please see the Primary Source DVD for additional sources related to this chapter.

READ ON

The opening story comes from J. H. Kerry-Nicholls, *The King Country* (1974). J. Belich, *The New Zealand Wars* (1988), and *Making Peoples* (1996) are gripping revisionist studies of New Zealand. B. Anderson, *Imagined Communities: Reflections on the Origin and Spread of Nationalism* (1991) is the fundamental starting point for contemporary thinking about nationalism. G. Wawro, *Warfare and Society in Europe, 1792–1914* (2000) is a solid introduction to the impact of militarization on European states and society. Lord Durham's *Report on the Affairs of British North America*, ed. by C. Lucas (1970), shows the thinking that went into the emerging political structure of the British Empire.

Nationalism and state-building beyond Europe is beginning to receive more attention in the literature. Among the many books by B. Lewis, *The Middle East* (1997) is a good introduction to the politics of the Arab world. F. R. Hunter, *Egypt Under the Khedives, 1805–1879: From Household Government to Modern Bureaucracy* (1984) is the foundational work on the emergence of the modern Egyptian state. H. S. Wilson, *Origins of West African Nationalism* (1969) analyzes the impact of colonial rule on the emergence of African nationalisms, while *West African Kingdoms in the Nineteenth Century*, ed. by D. Forde and P. M. Karberry (1967), studies the range of successes in indigenous African state-building. B. Farwell, *Prisoners of the Mahdi* (1967) recounts the story of three Western prisoners of the Mahdi in the Sudan and explores this religiously inspired revolt against colonial encroachment. M. A. Klein, *Islam and Imperialism in Senegal, 1847–1914* (1968) provides a more analytical account of the interaction of religion and imperial pressure. *José Rizal and the Asian Renaissance* (1996) sets a very broad context. His novels and many of Bankim's are available in English translations.

C. A. Bayly, *The Birth of the Modern World, 1780–1914* (2004) is indispensable for understanding the nineteenth-century state in global dimensions. D. Ralston, *Importing the European Army: The Introduction of European Military Techniques and Institutions in the Extra-European World, 1600–1914* (1996) studies several key examples of non-European states attempting to the new world of militarized centralization. D. Wyatt, *A Short History of Thailand* (1984) explores one of the few cases of successful Asian resistance to imperial pressures. R. Scheina, *Latin American Wars: Volume I, The Age of Caudillos, 1791–1899* (2003) gives a detailed military narrative that reveals the reasons behind the failures of Latin American state building. K. Pomeranz, *The Great Divergence: China, Europe, and the Making of the Modern World Economy* (2001) is excellent on the different paths taken by Britain and China after 1800, linking political regimes to economic development in unexpected ways.

PART
Ten

Chaos and Complexity: The World in the Twentieth Century

CHAPTER 27 The Twentieth-Century Mind: Western Science and the World 692

CHAPTER 28 World Order and Disorder: Global Politics in the Twentieth Century 718

CHAPTER 29 The Pursuit of Utopia: Civil Society in the Twentieth Century 748

Cyberspace. This map of the Internet looks a lot ▸ like the Milky Way. But each of the wispy strands represents millions of computer networks that crisscross the planet like a lattice. The reddish wisps indicate networks in East Asia and the Pacific. Europe, Africa, the Middle East, and Central and South Asia are green. North America's heavily wired landscape is evident in the predominance of blue, while the relatively few yellow fibers suggest the scarcity of connections in Latin America and the Caribbean. Sectors of the Internet that have yet to be mapped shimmer in white like distant galaxies.

ENVIRONMENT

since 1905, 1918, 1930
Relativity—Quantum machanics

CULTURE

1914–1918
World War I

1929–1939
Great Depression

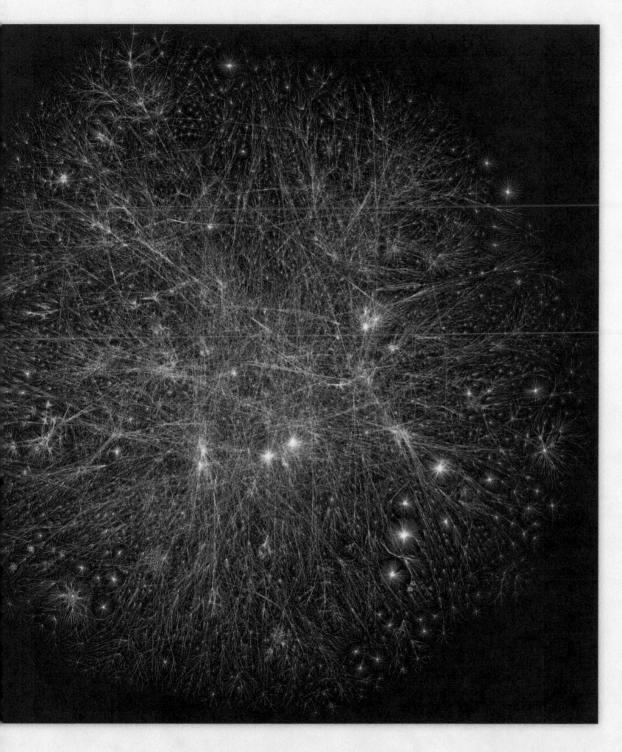

since 1950s
Global warming

since 1960s
Intensive deforestation

since mid–1980s
AIDS epidemic

since 1990s
Genetically modified crops

1936–1945
World War II

1945–1989
Cold War

since early 1950s
Television

since mid–1990s
Internet

CHAPTER 27

The Twentieth-Century Mind: Western Science and the World

Dr. Edward H. Hume taking a patient's pulse at the Yale-Hunan Clinic. Dr. Hume founded the clinic in the city of Changsha, in Hunan, China, in 1914 and was its dean until 1927. The presence of guards shows that this photograph was taken after the clinic began to attract socially elevated patients.

IN THIS CHAPTER

WESTERN SCIENCE ASCENDANT
China
India
The Wider World

THE TRANSFORMATION OF
WESTERN SCIENCE
Physics
Human Sciences

Anthropology and Psychology
Philosophy and Linguistics

THE MIRROR OF SCIENCE: ART

THE TURN OF THE WORLD

IN PERSPECTIVE: Science,
Challenging and Challenged

E dward H. Hume's heart sank when he saw the gateway to the city where he was to begin his new life. He arrived in China in 1905 from Yale University to start a clinic in Changsha, in remote Hunan province, where the Chinese government admitted foreigners as part of its policy to develop the interior. The city gate had been symbolically bricked up at the orders of the local gentry, who resented having foreign barbarians in their midst.

The notables of the town shunned him. For the poor, however, Hume's services were attractive. With backing from Yale alumni, he could afford to treat them for nominal sums. So they frequented his clinic, as well as visiting the shops of his Chinese rivals—an astrologer, a fortune-teller, a physiognomist who diagnosed illnesses by scrutinizing the faces of the sick, and an old soldier who had become a folk pediatrician.

For nearly three years, Hume had no patients from among the mandarins, the scholar-elite who monopolized authority in China. Then one morning, he heard harsh voices outside his clinic. "Stand aside, you brats! This is a mandarin's chair!" Apprehensive at first, the newcomer seemed pleased when Hume began to check his pulse. But when Hume dropped his patient's wrist and shoved a thermometer into his mouth, the mandarin was enraged. "Why," he said to the attendant who accompanied him, "did you let this foreigner put this strange, hard thing inside my mouth? Can't you see that he knows nothing of medicine?" Only subsequently did Hume learn how he had offended his patient. He had read his pulse by taking his left wrist, but Chinese tradition dictated that a doctor must also check pulse points on the right arm. By proceeding straight to taking the patient's temperature, Hume had exposed himself, in his patient's eyes, as an ignoramus.

It took years of painstaking work before Hume retrieved official confidence. His struggle was an episode in a long, slow, and fitful story of the assimilation of Western medicine in China, which was itself part of the spread of Western science—led by medicine and military technology, but extending to every kind of science and to scientific habits of thought—across the world. In no area was the rise of the West to world dominance more apparent.

● ● ● ● ●

- WHY DID Western science dominate the world during the first half of the twentieth century?
- WHAT FORMER certainties about the cosmos and human nature did science undermine during the twentieth century?
- WHY DID many people turn away from science in the late twentieth century?
- HOW DID styles in the arts mirror developments in science?
- WHY HAVE many people in the West come to rely on non-Western forms of medical treatment?

In the twentieth century, science set the agenda for the world. Whereas previously scientists had tended to respond to the demands of society, now science drove other kinds of change. In Europe and the Americas, a scientific counterrevolution exploded certainties inherited from seventeenth- and eighteenth-century science. Revolutions in psychology and social anthropology made people rethink cultural values and social relationships. A new philosophical climate challenged traditional ideas about language, reality, and the links between them. Ever larger and costlier scientific establishments in universities and research institutes served their paymasters—governments and big business—or pursued their own programs. New theories shocked people into revising their image of the world and their place in it.

Yet the lessons of Western science proved equivocal. New technologies raised as many problems as they solved: moral questions, as science expanded human power over life and death; practical questions, as technologies multiplied for exploiting the Earth. In the twentieth century, ordinary people and nonscientific intellectuals lost confidence in science. Uncertainty corroded the hard facts with which science was formerly associated. Faith that science could solve the world's problems and reveal the secrets of the cosmos evaporated.

In part, this was the result of practical failures. Though science achieved wonders, especially in medicine and communications, consumers never seemed satisfied. Every advance unleashed side effects. Machines fought wars and destroyed or degraded environments but could only make people happier in modest ways and did nothing to make them good. Even medical improvements brought equivocal effects. The costs of treatment sometimes exceeded the benefits. Health became a purchasable commodity. Medical provision buckled, in prosperous countries, under the weight of public expectations and the intensity of public demand.

As the power of science grew, more and more people came to fear and resent it and react against it. Science stoked disillusionment, even as it spread. It disclosed a chaotic cosmos, in which effects were hard to predict, and interventions went wrong. A century dominated by Western science ended with the recovery of alternative traditions that Western influence had displaced or eclipsed.

The stories of these changes fill this chapter—starting with the global diffusion of Western science, then turning back to the West to see how science changed from within, and how art mirrored the changes. In the remaining chapters, we can look at the effects of the changes on politics, culture generally, and the environment.

WESTERN SCIENCE ASCENDANT

The early twentieth-century world seethed with discontent at Western hegemony. Yet the allure of Western science (see Map 27.1) was twofold. First, it worked. Western military technology won wars. Western industrial technology multiplied food and wealth. Information systems devised in the West revolutionized communications, business, leisure, education, and methods of social and political control. Western medical science saved lives. Second, Western science offered infallibility:

knowledge that matched observation, fulfilled predictions, and withstood tests. Chinese revolutionaries called science a faith and represented "scientism" as an alternative to Confucianism.

China

The Chinese reception of Western science began in a continuous and systematic fashion in the 1860s, at the start of the "self-strengthening" movement (see Chapter 23). In 1866, Beijing's Foreign Language Institute opened a department "for the use of logical reasoning, methods of manufacturing and being practical.... This is the path to strengthening China." It was a promising beginning, but, as we have seen, Chinese self-strengthening was patchy in the nineteenth century, and the absorption of Western ideas was slow and subject to the mistrust of foreigners, whom Chinese often continued to see as barbaric or demonic.

Nor was the pace of change uniform in all the sciences. At first, medicine lagged behind mathematics and military and industrial technology. In 1876, for instance, a comparative study by Chinese physicians upheld the superiority of ancient Chinese methods over Western medicine. In 1883, however, the Beijing School of Medicine launched a Western-style curriculum. Chinese students began to go abroad to study medicine. By 1906 there were 15,000 Chinese students studying science abroad—13,000 of them in Japan, where the Western scientific curriculum was triumphant. Western doctors, meanwhile, acquired Chinese assistants and took advantage of Chinese interest in Western methods to move to China to practice. Dr. Hume was one of about 100 Western physicians in China in his day. In 1903, the University of Beijing acquired a medical department. Meanwhile, in essays published from 1895 onward, Yan Fu (yen foo) introduced Darwin's theory of evolution to China (see Chapter 25), and 20 or 30 Western scientific books were being translated into Chinese each year, with more reaching China via Japan.

The revolution of 1911, which made China a republic, brought intellectuals indebted to the West for many of their political ideas to power. They proclaimed what they called New Culture, in which science would play a prominent part, to modernize and "save" the country from Western and Japanese competition. In 1914, Chinese students in America met at Cornell University to found the Science Society of China. When they returned home, it became one of the most influential organizations in the country, dedicated to popularizing Western-style science and promoting scientific education. Science as Westerners understood it became part of the general curriculum, as well as the core of professional training. By 1947, for instance, China had 34,600 medical practitioners trained according to Western methods. By 2000, all Chinese physicians had at least some Western-style training.

In China, Western science had to rely chiefly on its inherent appeal. While the Qing had ceded a few small urban areas to foreign custody or control, in most of the country Western power was exercised only indirectly. Westerners had to buy or bribe their way into positions of influence. Yet Western science still exercised an irresistible fascination, even where it could not be forced on people. In parts of the world under direct Western rule the uptake was even greater, for European empires spread Western science. India, for instance, had a colonial government committed to promoting science and a native intelligentsia anxious to learn.

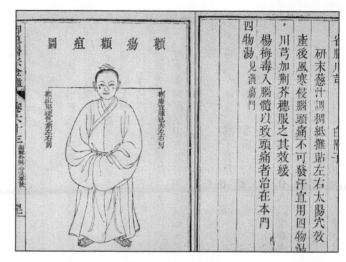

Chinese herbal medicine. In 1869, the emperor of China, Tongzhi, presented the U.S. government with 933 volumes of materials on Chinese herbal medicine and ancient Chinese agricultural techniques. This illustrated volume from the *Complete Survey of Medical Knowledge* demonstrates the proper usage of pertinent Chinese herbal medicine for illness.

MAP 27.1
Spread of Western Scientific Learning, 1866–1961

NORTH AMERICA

UNITED STATES OF AMERICA

1914 Science Society of China founded by Chinese students at Cornell University

Albert Schweizer s Western medicine West Africa in th mid-twentiet

SOUTH AMERICA

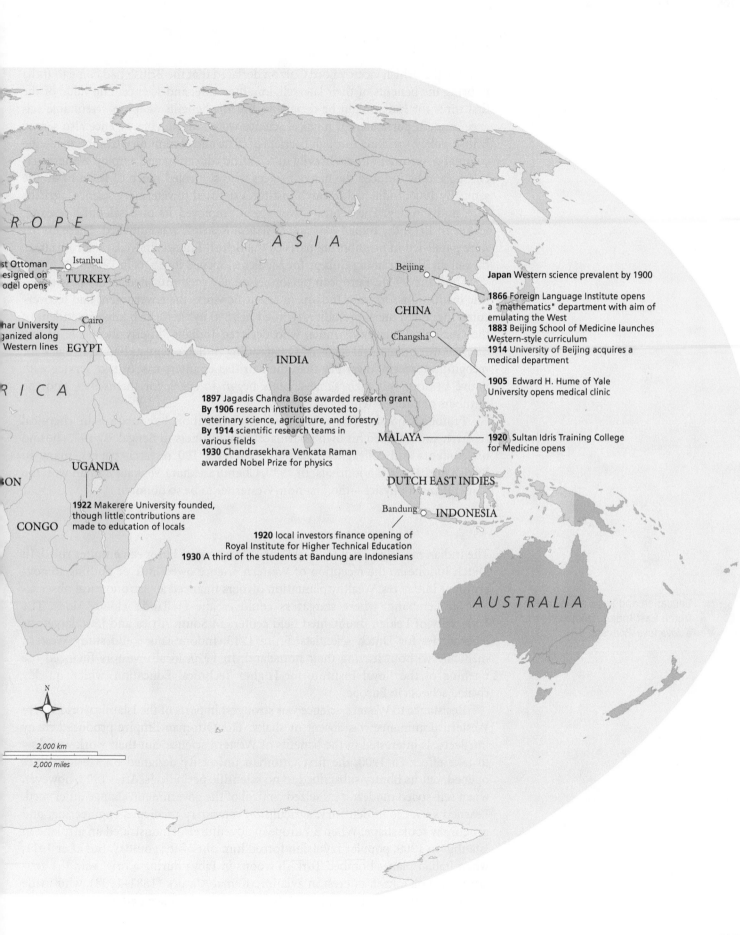

st Ottoman ___ Istanbul
esigned on
odel opens TURKEY

har University ___ Cairo
ganized along
Western lines EGYPT

RICA

ON

UGANDA

CONGO

1922 Makerere University founded,
though little contributions are
made to education of locals

R O P E

A S I A

Beijing

CHINA

Changsha

INDIA

1897 Jagadis Chandra Bose awarded research grant
By 1906 research institutes devoted to
veterinary science, agriculture, and forestry
By 1914 scientific research teams in
various fields
1930 Chandrasekhara Venkata Raman
awarded Nobel Prize for physics

MALAYA

DUTCH EAST INDIES

Bandung INDONESIA

1920 local investors finance opening of
Royal Institute for Higher Technical Education
1930 A third of the students at Bandung are Indonesians

Japan Western science prevalent by 1900

1866 Foreign Language Institute opens
a "mathematics" department with aim of
emulating the West
1883 Beijing School of Medicine launches
Western-style curriculum
1914 University of Beijing acquires a
medical department

1905 Edward H. Hume of Yale
University opens medical clinic

1920 Sultan Idris Training College
for Medicine opens

A U S T R A L I A

N

2,000 km

2,000 miles

India

In 1899, the British viceroy Lord Curzon declared that the British had come to India to bring the benefits of their law, religion, literature, and science. The value of the first three for India might be debatable, but the benefits of "pure, irrefutable science" and, in particular, of medical science were indisputable. Science also served British policy, breaking through barriers of caste and community. Curzon made the colonial government invest heavily in scientific education and employ Western scientists, and he induced the native princes who still ruled much of India to do the same. By 1906, India had research institutes devoted to veterinary science, agriculture, and forestry. The central government employed its own scientific research teams. In 1913, the Indian *Journal of Medical Research* was launched. These efforts were paralleled in neighboring parts of the British Empire. In Malaya, for instance, the Sultan Idris Training College for Medicine opened its doors in 1920.

Until the 1920s, European personnel hugely predominated in the new scientific institutions. To train Indians in scientific work, the government had to overcome ingrained racial prejudice, typified in 1880 by the British Superintendent of the Geological Survey of India, who declared Indians "utterly incapable of any original work in natural science." Outstanding Indian scientists had to struggle for recognition, accept lower pay than their British counterparts, or take service with native princes. But their achievements began to speak for themselves, and the numbers of native scientists multiplied.

Prafulla Chandra Ray established an international reputation in chemical research and founded his own pharmaceutical business in Bengal. By 1920, he and his students and colleagues had published over 100 research papers, many in British and American journals. In 1930, Chandrasekhara Venkata Raman won the Nobel Prize in physics—the first non-Westerner to be so honored.

The Wider World

The Indian model was not followed slavishly wherever European empires ruled. In Dutch Indonesia, the reception of Western science owed little or nothing to government initiatives. Wealthy plantation owners financed an astronomical observatory at Lembang, where stargazers could escape Holland's cloudy skies. The University of Leiden maintained field centers in South Africa and Java, largely as laboratories for Dutch scientists. From 1913, Indonesians could study Western medicine without leaving their homeland. In 1920, local investors financed the opening of the Royal Institute for Higher Technical Education, which quickly rivaled schools in Europe.

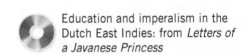
Education and imperalism in the Dutch East Indies: from *Letters of a Javanese Princess*

Resistance to Western science was strongest in parts of the Islamic world where Western dominance was absent or shaky. The Ottoman Empire produced many intellectuals interested in the benefits of Western science, but their work was slow to take effect. In 1900, the first Ottoman university designed on Western lines opened, but its library subscribed to no scientific periodicals. After 1908, however, when self-styled modernizers seized control of the government, change quickened. Learned societies in dentistry, agriculture, veterinary medicine, engineering, and geography took shape. When a European adventurer demonstrated an airplane in Istanbul in 1909, popular revulsion forced him out of the country. But after 1911, when Italian planes bombed Turkish troops in Libya during a brief war, the government took a keen interest in aviation. Kemal Ataturk (1881–1938), who made Turkey a secular republic in the 1920s, proclaimed "science and reason" to be his legacy.

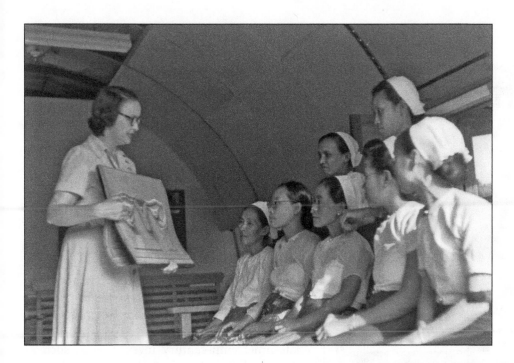

Colonial science. A British midwife instructs Burmese nurses in midwifery in the 1950s. The picture is posed to suggest Western superiority. The students—some older and presumably wiser than their teacher—are in Western-style uniforms, submissively listening to a lesson reinforced by simple diagrams.

On the fringes of the Ottoman Empire, and outside areas of Ottoman control, Muslim modernizers praised science as a proper occupation for a Muslim. One of the most influential modernizers, Jamal al-Dinal-Afghani, denounced religious establishments—Christian and Muslim alike—for hostility to science. The Lebanese Shiite scholar Husayn al-Jisr, who died in 1909, was the first great apologist for Darwin in the Islamic world. The Egyptian Ismail Mazhir (1891–1962) continued his work in a series of translations of Darwin, beginning in the 1920s. Scientific interpretation of the Quran was, at that time, one of the most popular types of literature in the Muslim world.

A survey of scientific research in the Middle East, conducted during the Second World War (1939–1945), found only a handful of Muslim scientists to consult. In 1952, a survey in Egypt counted 1,392 individual practitioners of science. By 1973, Egypt had 10,655 scientists. In 1961, the great Muslim educational center of Cairo, known as al-Azhar, was reorganized along the lines of a Western university. Similar changes were under way throughout the Arab world. Over the following two decades, at least 6 million Arabs studied Western-style science at universities.

In sub-Saharan Africa, meanwhile, Western science spread more slowly and selectively. While European empires lasted, racist assumptions inhibited colonial authorities from training African scientific elites. For most of the first half of the century, therefore, black Africans were the passive recipients of Western science, especially of medicine. Albert Schweizer (1875–1965), a Swiss theologian and doctor who devoted himself to the care of the sick in French West Africa for nearly 30 years, typified the spirit of the medical missionary, transforming the life expectancy of his patients not so much by his medical skill, which was never advanced, as by his efficient hospital buildings, emphasis on hygiene, and ability to dispense Western medicine. Thousands of idealistic Westerners followed similar vocations. From the 1930s until the 1980s, new pharmaceuticals, which were invented at a dizzying pace, slashed death rates and helped bring a population explosion to Africa. Medicine everywhere was the banner bearer of Western science.

 Al-Afghani on faith and reason

THE TRANSFORMATION OF WESTERN SCIENCE

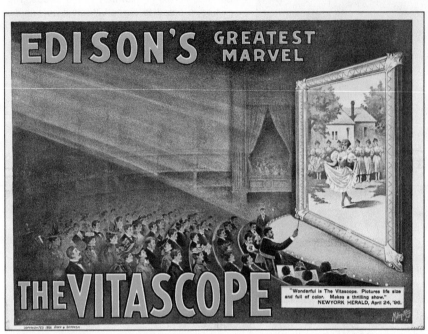

The vitascope was an early device for projecting cinematic images, displayed here showing the ballet *Giselle* in an advertisement of 1896. The gilt frame, prominent orchestra, and choice of theme all evoke the marketing context: a tasteful art form for the middle class.

Even while it achieved enormous influence and registered enormous effects across the world, conflicts changed Western science from within. Conventionally, historians represent the first decade or so of the twentieth century as a spell of inertia, a golden afterglow of the romantic age, which the real agent of change, the First World War, would turn blood red. But even before the war broke out in 1914, the worlds of thought and feeling were already alive with new colors. Technology hurtled into a new phase. The twentieth century would be an electric age, much as the nineteenth had been an age of steam. In 1901, Guglielmo Marconi broadcast by wireless radio across the Atlantic. In 1903, the Wright brothers took flight in North Carolina. Plastic was invented in 1907. The curiosities of late-nineteenth-century inventiveness, such as the telephone, the car, and the typewriter, all became commonplace. Other essentials of technologically fulfilled twentieth-century lives—the atom smasher, the steel–concrete skyscraper frame, even the hamburger—were all in place before 1914.

On the other hand, when the century opened, the scientific world was in a state of self-questioning, confused by rogue results. In the 1890s, X-rays and electrons were discovered or posited, while puzzling anomalies became observable in the behavior of light. In 1902, Henri Poincaré questioned the basic assumption of scientific method: the link between hypothesis and evidence. Any number of hypotheses, he said, could fit the results of experiments. Scientists chose among them by convention—or even according to "the idiosyncrasies of the individual." He compared the physicist to "an embarrassed theologian, ... chained" to contradictory propositions. Science usually affects society less by what it does or says than by how it is misunderstood. Readers misinterpreted Poincaré to mean that science could not disclose truths.

Physics

Thanks to the way Poincaré shook up perceptions, people became more willing to listen to radical theories. In 1905, Albert Einstein (1879–1955) emerged from obscurity to explode most educated people's image of the cosmos. According to traditional physics, the speed of a body ought to affect the speed of the light it reflects or projects, rather as a ball gains speed from the vigor with which it is thrown. Yet experimental data seemed to show that the speed of light never varied. Most people assumed an error in the measurements. Einstein proposed, instead, that the invariability of the speed of light was a scientific law and that the apparent effects of motion on speed were illusions. Rather, time and space change with motion. Mass increases with velocity, whereas time slows down.

Einstein's work broke on the world with the shock of genius: the sensation of seeing something obvious that no one had ever noticed before. The implications of a cosmos in which time was unfixed took getting used to. In Einstein's universe, mass and energy could be changed into each other. Twins aged at different rates.

Parallel lines met. The curvature of the trajectory of light literally warped the universe. Scientists hungered for an explanation that would resolve the apparent contradictions. Nonscientists were confused. "The spirit of unrest," the *New York Times* said in 1919, "invaded science."

While Einstein proposed a restructured universe, other scientists repictured the tiniest particles, or *quanta* of which the universe is composed. Ernest Rutherford's work in 1911 proved that atoms consist of masses and electric charges, including a *nucleus* surrounded by *electrons*. The basic structure of matter, it seemed, was being laid bare. But ever smaller particles, ever more elusive charges continued to come to light. Between 1911 and 1913, work on atomic structures revealed that electrons appear to slide erratically between orbits around a nucleus. Findings that followed from the attempt to track the untrappable particles of subatomic matter were expressed in a new field of study called **quantum mechanics**.

The terms of this new science were paradoxical—like those employed by Niels Bohr (1885–1962), who described light as consisting, simultaneously, of both waves and particles. By the mid-1920s, more contradictions piled up. When the motion of subatomic particles was plotted, their positions seemed irreconcilable with their momentum. They seemed to move at rates different from their measurable speed and to end up where it was impossible for them to be. Working in collaborative tension, Bohr and Werner Heisenberg (1901–1976) proposed a principle they called uncertainty or indeterminacy. Their debate provoked a revolution in thought. Interpreters made a reasonable inference—observers are part of every observation, and their findings can never be objective.

This was of enormous importance because other scholars—historians, anthropologists, sociologists, linguists, and even students of literature—were seeking to class their own work as scientific, precisely because they wanted to escape from subjectivity. It turned out that what they had in common with scientists, strictly so-called, was the opposite of what they had hoped—they were all implicated in their own findings.

Maybe it was still possible to pick a way back to certainty by following mathematics and logic. These systems, at least, seemed infallible, and they guaranteed each other. Mathematics was reliable because it was logical and logical because it was mathematical—or so people thought, until 1931, when Kurt Gödel severed mathematics from logic and showed that both systems, ultimately, must yield contradictory results.

Gödel inspired an unintended effect. He thought, like earlier philosophers, that we can reliably grasp numbers, but he helped make others doubt it. He believed that numbers really exist, objectively, independently of thought, but he provided encouragement to skeptics who dismissed them as merely conventional. The effect of Gödel's demonstrations on the way the world thinks, was comparable to that of termites in a ship that the passengers had thought was watertight. If mathematics and logic leaked, science would sink.

Meanwhile, practical discoveries and empirical observations upset the old picture of the cosmos. In 1929, thanks to a powerful telescope operated by Edwin Hubble, the universe was found to be expanding. It seemed so strange a finding that some physicists sought to explain it away for 50 years. By the 1970s, however,

Major Inventions, 1850–1914

1852	Gyroscope
1853	Passenger elevator
1856	Celluloid
	Bessemer converter
	Bunsen burner
1858	Refrigerator
	Washing machine
1859	Internal combustion engine
1862	Rapid-fire gun
1866	Dynamite
1876	Telephone
1877	Phonograph
1879	Incandescent lamp
1885	Motorcycle
	Electric transformer
	Vacuum flask
1887	Motorcar engine
1888	Pneumatic tire
	Kodak camera
1895	Wireless radio
	X-rays
1897	Diesel engine
1902	Radio-telephone
1903	Airplane
1911	Combine harvester

 Werner Heisenberg, "Uncertainty," 1927

Theoretical physicist **Albert Einstein** writes an equation on a blackboard while turning to his audience at the California Institute of Technology, ca. 1931. Einstein's distinctive looks—the ever-alert eyes, the deliberately disordered hair—became the universal image of a "typical," perhaps ideal, scientist.

most cosmologists took the view that expansion started with a **big bang,** an explosion of almost infinitesimally compressed matter that is still going on. For some interpreters, this was evidence of divine creation, or a description of how God did it. For others, it was a naturalistic explanation of change in the universe that made divine intervention an unnecessary hypothesis.

Contributions later in the century only seemed to put more space between science and certainty. In 1960, Thomas Kuhn argued that scientific revolutions were the result not of new discoveries about reality but of what he called paradigm shifts, changing ways of looking at the world, and new ways of expressing them. Most people drew an inference Kuhn repudiated—that the findings of science depended not on the objective facts but on the mind-set of the inquirer.

In the 1980s, **chaos theory** made the world seem hopelessly unpredictable. The idea emerged in meteorology as a result of the dawning awareness that weather systems are so complex that, ultimately, causes and effects are untraceable. A butterfly flapping its wings, according to a popular way to sum up the theory, can work up a storm. There is still, according to this way of thinking, some deep order in nature, some chain of cause and effect in which the whole of experience is linked—but we cannot see it whole.

Throughout these shake-ups, workers in theoretical physics never abandoned the search for a comprehensive way to explain the cosmos—a "theory of everything" that would resolve the contradictions of relativity theory and quantum mechanics. The way matter behaves—at least, the way it behaves when we observe it—is riddled with paradoxes that subtle thinking has to reconcile. By 2000, cosmologists were proposing terms for understanding the universe that described nothing anyone had ever experienced or could easily imagine: infinite dimensions, superstrings, supersymmetry, supergravity. No experiment validated any of these models of how the universe is structured.

Human Sciences

In some respects science did deliver measurable progress. Medicine registered spectacular advances. Doctors could control diseases ever more effectively by imitating the body's natural hormones and adjusting their balance. In 1922, they isolated insulin, which controls diabetes. Since the discovery of penicillin in 1931, doctors used *antibiotics* to kill microorganisms that cause disease. Inoculation programs and health education gradually became available almost everywhere.

Other advances in biology challenged people to rethink human nature. In 1925, in Tennessee, in the Scopes "monkey" trial an American court upheld the right of school boards to ban Darwin from the curriculum, on the grounds that evolution was incompatible with the Bible. Belief in creation and belief in evolution are not necessarily contradictory. Evolution, which is the most convincing description we have of how and why species change, could, to a religious mind, be part of God's creation and plan. But people on both sides of the debate kept picking fights with one another. Evolution became more controversial as its proponents' claims became more strident. Some late twentieth-century Darwinians claimed to have found an evolutionary explanation for morality, for instance, and even to be able to explain cultural change in evolutionary terms. These claims got headlines but left most people unconvinced.

While disputes about evolution rumbled, the new science of genetics posed even more searching problems. Beginning in 1908, T. H. Morgan at Columbia University demonstrated how genes transmit some characteristics. In 1944, Erwin

Schrödinger predicted that a gene would resemble a chain of basic units, connected like the elements of a code. A few years later, scientists in England built up the picture of what DNA (deoxyribonucleic acid) was really like. It soon emerged that genes in individual genetic codes were responsible for some diseases and perhaps for behavior that changing the code could regulate. The codes of other species could be modified to obtain results that suit humans: producing bigger plant foods, for instance, or animals designed to be more beneficial.

This discovery shed new light on an old controversy—the **nature versus nurture** debate. On one side are those who believe that "social engineering" cannot improve character and capability, which inherited genes determine. Their opponents believe that experience—nurture—produces these qualities and that social change can, therefore, improve us. Genetic research seemed to confirm that we inherit more of our makeup than we have traditionally supposed. Meanwhile, sociobiology, a new synthesis devised by Edward O. Wilson, created a scientific constituency for the theory that evolutionary necessities determine differences between societies and that we can rank societies accordingly. Two fundamental convictions survived in most people's minds: that individuals make themselves, and that society is worth improving. Nevertheless, genes seemed to limit our freedom. Genetic and sociobiological claims inhibited reform and encouraged a mood we shall examine in the next two chapters: the prevailing conservatism of the late twentieth and early twenty-first centuries.

By the 1990s, genetically modified plants promised to solve the world's food-supply problems. The potentially adverse economic and ecological consequences, as we shall see in Chapter 30, evoked a chorus of protest. Modification of human genes promised to eliminate genetically transmitted disease and enable infertile couples to have children. But it posed terrifying moral questions, best illustrated by the controversy over cloning of human embryos. This meant breeding human embryos to extract useful cells from them. A woman could produce as many embryos as she might wish and pick the specimens she most preferred. The rest would have to be discarded. In effect, this meant destroying human beings, since embryos, whatever their status in other respects, are human.

Less morally troubling methods of treatment would soon replace cloning to deal with infertility and treat inherited disease. But the prospect of "designer babies" selected for particular features of character or appearance was even more troubling. Children might be engineered with fashionable looks or exploitable talents, or along the lines once prescribed by eugenics—improving the human species through controlled breeding. Governments could legislate supposedly undesirable personality genes out of existence. States could enforce normality at the expense, for instance, of genes supposed to dispose people to be criminal or homosexual or just uncooperative. Morally dubious visionaries foresaw societies without disease or deviancy. In a world recrafted, as if by Frankenstein, humans could now make their biggest intervention in evolution yet: selecting according to what they happen to want at the moment. In 1995, a coalition of self-styled religious leaders in the United States signed a declaration opposing the patenting of genes on the grounds that they were the property of their real creator: God. The World Health Organization, UNESCO, and the European Parliament all condemned human cloning as unethical. Many countries banned it.

Meanwhile, the genetic revolution nudged people toward a materialist understanding of human nature. It became harder to find room for nonmaterial ingredients, such as mind and soul. Neurological research showed that thought is an

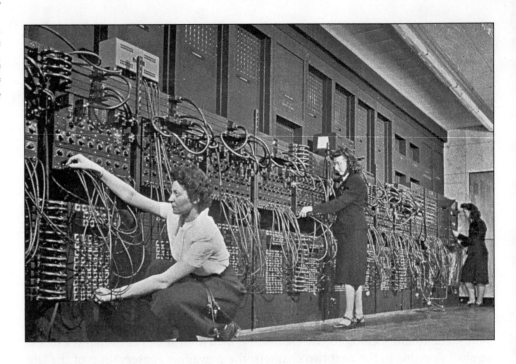

The Electronic Numerical Integrator and Computer.
One of the first electronic digital computers in the
United States was commissioned by the U.S.
Army and installed, at first, at the University of
Pennsylvania in Philadelphia. The choice of
female programmers was presumably dictated by
the public relations objectives of this photograph.

electrochemical process in which synapses fire and proteins are released. These
results made it possible to claim that everything traditionally classed as a function
of mind might take place within the brain.

Artificial intelligence (AI) research reinforced this claim—or tried to—with a
new version of an old hope or fear: that minds may be mechanical. Pablo Picasso
(1881–1973) painted a machine in love in 1917. In the second half of the century,
computers proved so dextrous, first in making calculations, then in responding to
their environments, that they seemed capable of settling the debate over whether
mind was different from brain. But people on either side were really talking about
different things. Proponents of AI were not concerned with building machines
with creative, artistic imaginations, or with intuitive properties, or with the ability
to feel love or hatred—qualities that opponents of AI valued as indicators of a truly
human mind.

Meanwhile, primatology and paleoanthropology also challenged human self-
perception. Paleoanthropologists discovered, among remains of humans' nonhuman ancestors and related primates, features formerly thought unique to *Homo
sapiens*. Neanderthal burials demonstrated that Neanderthals had ritual lives and
moral practices, including care of the elderly and reverence for the dead. This evidence proved that nonhuman species have existed who were morally indistin-
guishable from human beings. The question was important because, as we shall see
in Chapter 29, it emerged at a time when the notion of **human rights** became current—a notion based in part on the assumption that being human constitutes a
meaningful moral category that excludes nonhumans.

Animal rights movements challenged that assumption. So did improved
knowledge of apes and monkeys. First, scientists working with macaque monkeys
in Japan realized that these creatures, though modestly endowed with brains, have
culture. They can learn and transmit what they learn across generations. The
breakthrough discovery came in 1952, when a monkey was observed teaching her
community how to wash the dirt off sweet potatoes. The tribe took up the technique and continued to practice it, even when supplied with ready-washed potatoes, showing that washing had become a cultural rite, not a practical measure.

In subsequent decades, primatologists, led by Jane Goodall, found that chimpanzees have, albeit to a much smaller extent than humans, all the features of culture that were formerly thought to be peculiarly human, including toolmaking, language, war, rules for distributing food, and political habits. Further studies of other social animals—beginning with other great apes, such as gorillas and orangutans—showed similar results, suggesting that culture is only uniquely human as a matter of degree. Many observations and experiments cast doubt on the belief that humans have unique cognitive properties. Apes, for example, proved to be self-aware and showed sensibilities hard to distinguish in practice from the senses of morality and transcendence formerly thought to be human peculiarities. By the end of the twentieth century, some ethicists were campaigning for animal rights or for redefining the moral community to embrace great apes.

The discoveries of primatologists and comparative zoologists belonged in a broader context of scientific change: the rise of ecology, the study of the interconnectedness of all life and its interdependence with the physical environment. Ecologists' exposure of a vast range of new practical problems arising from human overexploitation of the environment became a major influence in the late twentieth century. We discuss them in Chapter 30.

Anthropology and Psychology

In anthropology, as in science, the early twentieth century was decisive. Among the West's supposedly scientific certainties was that some peoples and societies were evolutionarily superior to others: an image of the world stacked in order of race. Westerners used this picture to justify their rule over other peoples (see Chapter 25). But Franz Boas (1858–1942) showed that no race was superior to any other in brainpower. Societies could not be ranked in terms of a developmental model of thought. People, he concluded, think differently in different cultures not because some have superior mental equipment but because thought reflects the traditions to which it is heir, the society that surrounds it, and the environment in which it exists. Fieldwork piled up data to bury the crude hierarchical schemes of the nineteenth century.

The result was **cultural relativism**: the doctrine that we cannot rank cultures in order of merit but must judge each on its own terms. As we shall see in Chapter 30, this proved problematic. Should cannibals be judged on their own terms? Or cultures that licensed slavery or the subjection of women? Or those that practiced infanticide, head-hunting, or other abominations? Or even those that condoned milder offenses against values the West cherished—such as torture or female circumcision? Cultural relativism had to have limits, but anthropology compelled educated people to examine their prejudices and question their own convictions of superiority. "Primitive cultures" and "advanced civilizations" came to be labeled "elementary structures" and "complex structures." The long-standing justification for Western imperialism—the civilizing mission—lapsed, because conquerors could no longer feel enough self-confidence to impose their own standards of civilization on their victims.

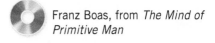 Franz Boas, from *The Mind of Primitive Man*

Psychology was even more subversive than anthropology, because it challenged the notions individuals had about themselves. In particular, the claim, first advanced by Sigmund Freud (1856–1939), that much human motivation is subconscious, challenged traditional notions about responsibility, identity, personality, conscience, and mentality. In 1896, Freud exposed his own *Oedipus complex*, as he called it: a supposed, suppressed desire—that he believed all male children had—to supplant his father. In succeeding years, he developed a technique he called **psychoanalysis** to make patients aware of their subconscious desires. Hypnosis or, as Freud preferred, free association could retrieve repressed feelings and ease nervous symptoms. Many patients who rose from his couch walked more freely than before.

Freud seemed able to illuminate the human condition. He claimed that every child experienced before puberty the same phases of sexual development. Every adult repressed similar fantasies or experiences. Women who previously would have been dismissed as hysterical malingerers became, in Freud's work, case studies from whose example almost everyone could learn. This contributed to the reevaluation of women's role in society (see Chapter 29). Freud's science, however, failed to pass the most rigorous tests. When Karl Popper asked how to distinguish someone who did not have an Oedipus complex from someone who did, the psychoanalytic fraternity had no answer. Nevertheless, for some patients, psychoanalysis worked.

Veterans of twentieth-century wars became patients of psychiatry. The nightmares of trench survivors in the First World War (see Chapter 28) were too hideous to share with loved ones. The guilt of those who missed the war echoed the shell-shock of those who fought it. Introspection—formerly regarded as self-indulgence—became routine in the West. Repression became the modern demon and the analyst an exorcist. The "feel-good society," which bans guilt, shame, self-doubt, and self-reproach, was among the results. So was sexual candor. So was the fashion of treating metabolic or chemical imbalances in the brain as if they were deep-rooted mental disorders. The good and evil that flowed from Freud's theory are nicely balanced and objectively incalculable. Psychoanalysis and other schools of therapy helped millions and tortured millions—releasing some people from repressions, condemning others to illusions or futile treatments.

The most profound influence psychology exercised was not, however, on the treatment of mental disorder but on how children were raised. In 1909, the feminist Ellen Key proclaimed the rediscovery of childhood. Children were different from adults. This was, in effect, a summary of the idea of childhood as it had developed in the nineteenth-century West (see Chapter 24). It was, perhaps, a valid observation. But it had questionable consequences. Children who were not treated as adults in childhood "never grew up," like the tragic hero of J. M. Barrie's play of 1911, *Peter Pan*, who withdrew into Neverland. Generations raised on the assumption that they could not face adult realities found themselves deprived of truths about their own lives and became fodder for the new therapies of psychiatry. Generational "hang-ups" became a new curse for Western children. People outside the West, where the new image of childhood arrived patchily and late, had fewer such troubles.

In the West, better treatment for childhood disease enabled more children to lead longer lives. So children became more suitable objects in whom to invest time, emotion, and study. Working on Freud's insights, educational psychologists in the West built up a picture of mental development in predictable, universal stages. School curricula changed in the 1950s and 1960s to match the supposed patterns of childhood development. Schoolchildren were deprived of challenging tasks because child psychology said they were incapable of them. While formal education got longer and longer, most children emerged from it with no experience of traditional elements of the curriculum that were now thought unsuitably difficult, such as calculus, foreign languages, sophisticated vocabulary, ancient authors, even grammar. Other developments, which belong in Chapter 29, stimulated this trend, including the economic changes that made vocational qualifications seem disproportionately important in education and the social pressures that made for "dumbing down."

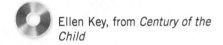

Ellen Key, from *Century of the Child*

Philosophy and Linguistics

To scientific uncertainty and cultural relativism, the opening decade of the century added philosophical unease. In combination with Einstein's disquieting revelations about the nature of time, the theories of Henri Bergson (1859–1941) proved both unsettling and inspiring. He formulated a concept he called "duration"—the new sense of time we get when consciousness "abstains from establishing a separation between present states and the preceding states." This difficult idea fortified educated people's faith in free will. Time is not a constraint that nature imposes on us, but a concept that we impose on nature. Bergson coined the term *élan vital* to express the freedom we retain to make a future different from the one that science predicts—a spiritual force with the power to reorder matter. Time, the way Bergson saw it, became not a sequence of atomized events, but a product of memory, which is different from perception and, therefore, "a power independent of matter."

Bergson's thinking infuriated scientists and inspired artists. Novels written in the **stream of consciousness** were among the results. He argued that evolution was not a scientific law but an expression of the creative will of living entities, which change because they want to change. Critics accused Bergson of irrationalism on the grounds that he was attacking science and representing objective realities as purely mental concepts. Indeed, consistent with his principles, he never tried to demonstrate the validity of his ideas by logical exposition or scientific evidence. This did not diminish their attractiveness or their effectiveness in liberating people who felt inhibited by the supposedly scientific determinism of the early twentieth century. Bergson reassured those who doubted whether, for example, history really led inevitably to the revolutions Marx predicted, or to the white supremacy "scientific" racism preached, or to the destruction the laws of thermodynamics predicted. Nature was unorganized. The chaos that made scientific minds despair offered hope to Bergson's readers.

Bergson's followers hailed him as the philosopher for the twentieth century. His first great rival for that status was William James (1842–1910). James wanted a distinctively American philosophy, reflecting the values of business and hustle. Seeking to make people share his belief in God, he argued in 1907 that "if the hypothesis of God works satisfactorily in the widest sense of the word, it is true." He called this doctrine **pragmatism.** But what one individual or group finds useful, another may find useless. James's claim that truth is not what is real but is whatever serves a particular purpose was one of the most subversive claims a philosopher ever made. James had set out as an apologist for Christianity, but by relativizing truth, he undermined it.

Linguistics produced similar doubts about the reality of truth and whether language could express it. Ferdinand de Saussure's lectures, published by his students after his death in 1913, contained a revolutionary idea: the distinction between social speech, the *parole* addressed to others, and subjective language, the *langue* known only to thought. Saussure seemed to say of language what Poincaré seemed to say of science—any language we use refers only to itself and cannot disclose remoter realities.

Mainstream philosophers were reluctant to pursue the implications of this idea. The dominant philosophy of the 1920s and 1930s, the years between the First and Second World Wars, was *positivism*, which asserted that what the human

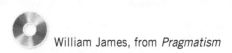

William James, from *Pragmatism*

Final passage from *Ulysses* (1922) by James Joyce, perhaps the most famous stream of consciousness novel in the twentieth century.

... serene with his lamp and O that awful deepdown torrent O and the sea the sea crimson sometimes like fire and the glorious sunsets and the figtrees in the Alameda gardens yes and all the queer little streets and pink and blue and yellow houses and the rosegardens and the jessamine and geraniums and cactuses and Gibraltar as a girl where I was a Flower of the mountain yes when I put the rose in my hair like the Andalusian girls used or shall I wear a red yes and how he kissed me under the Moorish wall and I thought well as well him as another and then I asked him with my eyes to ask again yes and then he asked me would I yes to say yes my mountain flower and first I put my arms around him yes and drew him down to me so he could feel my breasts all perfume yes and his heart was going like mad and yes I said yes I will Yes.

Existentialists. Jean-Paul Sartre (1905–1980) and Simone de Beauvoir (1908–1986) became icons of radicalism—she for her feminist classic, *The Second Sex*, he for the influence of his philosophy on postwar Western youth. At home in Paris, however, they seem like a model middle-class couple, stiffly sharing a newspaper in their underdecorated apartment.

senses perceived was real and that reason could prove that what our senses perceive is true. But developments in science and logic were undermining such confidence. In 1953, in *Philosophical Investigations,* Ludwig Wittgenstein argued that we understand language not because it corresponds to reality but because it obeys rules of usage. Therefore, we do not necessarily know what language refers to, except its own terms.

Equally disturbing, because of what it implied about human nature, was the work Noam Chomsky published in 1957. Chomsky was impressed at how easily children learn speech. They can, in particular, combine words in ways they have never actually heard. He also found it remarkable that the differences between languages appear superficial compared with the "deep structures"—the parts of speech, the relationships between terms that we call *grammar* and *syntax*—that are common to all of them. Chomsky suggested a link between the structures of language and the brain. We learn languages fast because their structure is already part of how we think. This suggestion was revolutionary. Experience and heredity, nurture and nature, it implied, do not make us the whole of what we are. Part of our nature is hardwired and unchangeable. As Chomsky saw it, at least at first, this "language instinct" or "language faculty" was untouchable—and, therefore, perhaps not produced—by evolution. Chomsky's views resonated in minds worried about the problems of using language and science to access reality.

Chomsky also argued that our language prowess, which some people claim is a uniquely human achievement, is like the special skills of other species: that of cheetahs in speed, for instance. "It is the richness and specificity of instinct of animals," he said, "that accounts for their remarkable achievements in some domains and lack of ability in others, so the argument runs, whereas humans, lacking such . . . instinctual structure, are free to think, speak and discover. ... Both the logic of the problem and what we are now coming to understand suggest that this is not the correct way to identify the position of humans in the world." This chimed in with the disarming discoveries of primatology and paleoanthropology.[1]

By the time Chomsky entered the academic arena, unease and pessimism were rampant, especially in Europe and parts of Asia, where the destruction of the Second World War had been most keenly felt. The most widely accepted response to the war had emerged from a group of German philosophers known as the Frankfurt School. They defined what they called alienation as the central problem of modern society. Economic rivalries and short-sighted materialism divided individuals and wrecked common pursuits. People felt dissatisfied and rootless. Martin Heidegger proposed a strategy to cope with this. We should accept our existence between conception and death as the only unchangeable thing about us and tackle life as a project of self-realization, of "becoming"—who we are changes as the project unfolds. This **existentialism** represented the retreat of intellectuals into the security of self-contemplation in revulsion from an ugly world.

Heidegger was discredited because he collaborated with the Nazis. In France, however, Jean-Paul Sartre (1905–1980) relaunched existentialism as a creed for the postwar era. "Man," he said, "is ... nothing else but what he makes of himself." For Sartre, self-modeling was more than an individual responsibility. Every individual action is an exemplary act, a statement about humankind, about the sort of species you want to belong to. Yet there is no objective way to put meaning into such a statement. God does not exist. Everything is permissible, and "as a result man is forlorn, without anything to cling to." "There is," he wrote, "no explaining things away by reference to a fixed ... human nature. In other words, there is no determinism, man is free, man is freedom."

In the 1950s and 1960s, Sartre's version of existentialism was used to justify every form of self-indulgence. Sexual promiscuity, revolutionary violence, indifference to manners, defiance of the law, and drug abuse could all be part of becoming oneself. The 1960s, to which we shall return in Chapter 29, would have been unthinkable without existentialism: beat culture and permissiveness—ways of life millions adopted or imitated—as well, perhaps, as the late twentieth-century's libertarian reaction against social planning. Existentialism was, briefly, the philosophical consensus of the West. But it never caught on in the rest of the world, and Westerners who saw more urgent problems than shaping one's personal future detested it. By the 1970s, a global reaction was in the making: conservative in politics, mistrustful of materialism, inclined to religion, anxious to recover tradition and rebuild social solidarity—especially through the family. It was particularly powerful in the Americas, while in Asia and Africa, revulsion from Western-dominated thinking strengthened the trend.

THE MIRROR OF SCIENCE: ART

Never more than in the twentieth century, artists represented the world not as they saw it directly but as science and philosophy displayed it for their inspection. The revolutions of twentieth-century art exactly match the jolts and shocks science and philosophy administered.

In 1909, Emilio Filippo Marinetti (1876–1944) proclaimed what he called **futurism.** At the time, most artists professed modernism: the doctrine that the new was superior to the old. Marinetti believed that what was traditional had not only to be surpassed but also repudiated and wrecked. He rejected coherence, harmony, freedom, conventional morals, and conventional language because they were familiar. Comfort was artistically sterile. Instead, futurism glorified war, power, chaos, and destruction, which would shove humankind into novelty. Marinetti and his followers celebrated the beauty of machines, the morals of might, and the syntax of babble. Sensitivity, kindness, and fragility were old-fashioned. Futurists preferred ruthlessness, candor, strength.

Painters inspired by Marinetti's lectures painted "lines of force"—symbols of coercion. The excitement of speed—attained by the new internal combustion engine—represented for Marinetti the spirit of the age, speeding away from the past. His movement united adherents of the most radical politics of the twentieth century: fascists, for whom the state should serve the strong, and communists, who hoped to incinerate tradition in revolution. They hated each other. But they agreed that the function of progress was to destroy the past.

Marinetti seems prophetic. The deepening destructiveness of wars and the quickening power of machines did indeed dominate the future. The speeding machines turned the world into a global village where every place was within, at most, a few hours' travel of every other place, and where information was accessible

The Diffusion and Transformation of Western Science

1842–1910	William James, American philosopher, developed the doctrine of pragmatism
1856–1939	Sigmund Freud, developer of psychoanalysis
1860s	China's "self-strengthening" program begins
1875–1965	Albert Schweizer, medical missionary to Africa
1879–1955	Albert Einstein, developer of the theory of relativity
1881–1938	Kemal Ataturk, founder of modern Turkey and proponent of secularism and Western science
1883	Western-style curriculum at Beijing School of Medicine
1885–1962	Niels Bohr, won Nobel Prize in 1922 for work on the structure of the atom
1891–1962	Ismail Mazhir, translator of Charles Darwin's work into Arabic
1901–1976	Werner Heisenberg, developed uncertainty principle
1902	Henri Poincaré questions the link between hypothesis and evidence
1903	Powered flight
1905–1980	Jean-Paul Sartre, French philosopher associated with existentialism
1907	Plastic invented
1912	Overthrow of the Qing dynasty increases pace of Westernization in China
1913	Indian *Journal of Medical Research* launched
1914	Science Society of China founded by Chinese students at Cornell University
1920	Royal Institute for Higher Technical Education founded in Indonesia
1931	Penicillin discovered
1944	Erwin Schrödinger predicts structure of the gene
1953	Ludwig Wittgenstein's *Philosophical Investigations* and Simone de Beauvoir's *The Second Sex* published

Emilio Filippo Marinetti, "Futurist Manifesto"

○ MAKING CONNECTIONS ○

TRANSFORMATIONS OF WESTERN SCIENCE AND THOUGHT IN THE TWENTIETH CENTURY

DISCIPLINE →	NEW THEORIES →	EFFECTS ON SOCIETY
Physics/Mathematics	Henri Poincaré: notes the elastic connection between hypothesis and evidence and how multiple hypotheses can fit results of experiments Albert Einstein: proposes and proves speed of light is a constant and time and space change with motion (theory of relativity) Ernest Rutherford: establishes basis of subatomic world Niels Bohr: light described as both waves and particles; links to Heisenberg's indeterminacy principle (uncertainty principle)	By mid–twentieth century, physics helped unleash the power of charged subatomic particles in practical technology including weapons (atomic bombs), communications (transistors, microprocessors, integrated circuits) The "new physics" also revolutionizes astronomy, chemistry, other physical sciences
Astronomy	Edwin Hubble: with large-scale telescopes, discovers that universe is expanding Development of radio telescopes, infrared and other means of examining distant stars	Combined with the "new physics" and jet propulsion, astronomical findings set the stage for exploration of solar system; they also challenge or confirm religious beliefs depending on religious standpoint; also raise new possibilities of extraterrestrial life
Biology	T. H. Morgan: demonstrates that genetic transmission influences physical characteristics Neuroscience demonstrates how mental functions operate within the brain	Advances in human biology lead to medical developments: controlling infections through use of antibiotics; controlling diabetes and developing large-scale preventive medical programs (inoculations, health education)

everywhere, instantly. The machines also achieved dazzling power to destroy. Toward midcentury, people devised massive gas chambers and incinerators that killed millions and disposed of their bodies economically and efficiently. Bombs obliterated thousands at a time and spread deadly radiation capable of killing millions more.

Other artists, meanwhile, preferred a vision that atomic theory suggested of an elusive, ill-ordered, uncontrollable world. In 1907, an artistic style called **cubism** began to hold up to the world images of itself reflected as if in a distorting mirror, shivered into fragments. Pablo Picasso and Georges Braque, the originators of the movement, denied they had ever heard of Einstein. But scientific vulgarizations reached them through the press. As painters of an elusive reality from many different perspectives, they were reflecting the science and philosophy of their decade. Marcel Duchamp (1887–1968) tried to represent Einstein's world. He called his painting *Nude Descending a Staircase,* of 1912, an expression of "time and space through the abstract presentation of motion." His notes on his sculpture *Large Glass* revealed how closely he had studied relativity. Meanwhile, in 1911, Vasily Kandinsky (1866–1944) had read Rutherford's description of the atom "with frightful force, as if the end of the world had come." After that, his paintings suppressed every reminder of real objects. The tradition he launched of entirely "abstract" art, which depicted objects unrecognizably or not at all, became dominant for most of the century. The new rhythmic beat of jazz and the noises of atonal music, developed in

DISCIPLINE →	NEW THEORIES →	EFFECTS ON SOCIETY
Genetics	Search for genetic codes begins in 1944, to establish basic building blocks of life in the 1950s, DNA is discovered and awareness follows that genetic codes could help solve medical problems	Fifty years of study leads to ability to manipulate genes of plants and animals to produce more beneficial results; more controversial is the focus on cloning and genetic engineering to develop most desirable humans
Primatology and paleoanthropology	Primatology: discovery that animals also have shared culture, language, toolmaking skills Paleoanthropology: discovery of features originally thought uniquely human (rituals, morality) among nonhuman ancestors	Widened research efforts in both disciplines; reinforced connection between all humans and led to deeper understanding of ecology, the study of interconnectedness of all life
Anthropology	Franz Boas: comparative study of societies shows that no race is superior to any other in brainpower, development of thought	New doctrine of cultural relativism focuses on studying communities in context of their traditions; widened appreciation for non-Western, native cultures (Native American, Samoan, etc.)
Psychology	Sigmund Freud: uncovered role of human subconscious in motivating actions; developed psychoanalysis to expose subconscious feelings, thoughts Development of new theories on child raising and education by Sigmund Freud and Ellen Key emphasizing childhood as a separate phase of life	Transformation of school curricula, child raising to conform with ideas of stages of child development; belief in subconscious strata of human mind leads to widespread interest in popular psychology including psychoanalysis and dream analysis
Philosophy and Linguistics	Henri Bergson and others reconceptualize time and causation as part of human-determined memory and experience F. de Saussure and others deconstruct language as human-constructed medium that cannot convey objective reality	New understandings of deep structures of language furthered by experiments of Noam Chomsky showing that language, speech, grammar, and syntax are linked to the brain, and are hardwired—debate widens on the usefulness of language and the accessibility of truth.

Vienna by Arnold Schoenberg from 1908 onward, subverted the harmonies of the past as surely as quantum mechanics began to challenge its ideas of order.

In art, the effects of the new anthropology were even clearer than those of the new physics. Picasso, Braque, and members of Kandinsky's circle copied "primitive" Pacific and African sculptures from museums of natural history, while artists in the Americas and Australia rediscovered the art of native peoples. As in science and philosophy, Asian traditions made a big impact in the West in the last four decades of the century, especially in music, architecture, and stage design. The vogue for primitivism ensured that craftsmen outside Europe had a market for their traditional arts. Yet whenever innovations occurred in art, as in science, Western initiatives predominated globally throughout the century.

As in so many areas of modernization, Japanese artists led the way in assimilating Western influences. Outstanding painters, such as Kuroda Seiki and Wada Eisaku, were already studying in Europe in the 1890s and the early 1900s. In China, influence radiated chiefly from Russia, especially from the late 1940s, as Russian-inspired Communists became all-powerful. Their characteristic subjects were stocky, heroic peasants and workers in poster-art style. This still dominated the art of Wang Guangyi (wahng gwang-yee) in the late twentieth century. Meanwhile, however, China had opened up to every kind of Western influence. The outstanding

Man as machine, speeding and striding into the future. The Italian artist Umberto Boccioní (1882–1916) captured the spirit of futurism in this sculpture of 1913. "Our straight line will be alive and palpitating," he wrote, aiming to "embed" the math and geometry of machines "in the muscular lines of a body."
Umberto Boccioni, Unique Form of Continuity in Space, *1913 (cast 1931). Bronze, 43 7/8 × 34 7/8" × 15 3/4" (111.4 × 88.6 × 40 cm). Acquired through the Lillie P. Bliss Bequest. The Museum of Modern Art/Licensed by Scala-Art Resource, NY*

young artist of the 1990s, Zhou Chunya (joe chwun-yah), was reported as saying, "Even though Western art dominates my painting style, I would say I am a Chinese painter ... because I maintain a Chinese lifestyle within myself." For painters working in the shadow of Western influence, this sentiment was typical.

Among artists who resisted or filtered Western influences, those from India were most conspicuous. At the end of the nineteenth century, Abindranath Tagore rejected his Western-style training as a painter to find inspiration in Mughal art (Chapter 19). His followers and successors—notably Nandalal Bose (1882–1966)—made anticolonialism part of the message of their work. Many artists around the world also turned to folk art to supply new styles. But even painters who loudly rejected the West could not escape altogether the magnetism of Western techniques, materials, and models.

The novel, modeled on the Western tradition, became a universal genre. Cinema, a new medium of Western origin, became the most popular art form in the world, and, although different cultures evolved their own schools of cinema, the "Hollywood" style dominated the global market. New initiatives in sculpture and architecture, and new genres, such as video art and computer-generated art, depended on technologies the West invented.

Paradoxically, it was in the West that the influence of Western art during the twentieth century declined. Though governments patronized conventional artists, the characteristic art of the First World War and its aftermath was **dada**—externalized disillusionment, deliberately brutal, ugly, and meaningless. The "Dada Manifesto" of 1918 celebrated World War I as the "great work of destruction." In Germany, Kurt Schwitters (1887–1948) scraped collages together from bits of smashed machines and ruined buildings. Max Ernst (1891–1976) exposed post war nightmares, often using hostile materials—barbed wire, rough wood. The artists who called themselves surrealists continued this trend in the 1920s and 1930s, reflecting psychology by creating paintings and films in which they aimed to externalize subconscious neuroses and desires. Their project overlapped with a school that established a more enduring tradition: Expressionists, most of whom were more concerned with color and texture than with form, reached inside themselves and their subjects to represent emotion and mood.

After that, art seemed to lose some of its power to make people see the world afresh. Plenty of great artists challenged onlookers' world picture, but none succeeded in changing it. In part, this was because propaganda seduced art, especially the most powerful new art of the twentieth century, cinema. Most of the great movie directors and music composers of the 1930s and 1940s in Europe, America, and Russia got caught up in the ideological conflicts of the time. Governments—even in democracies—victimized artists whose messages they disliked. More treacherously, art, like so much else in the twentieth-century West, became fodder for consumerism, commercialism, celebrity, and fashion. Artists escaped from political control by appealing to the mass market and to rich collectors. Salvador Dalí (1904–1989) was probably the most technically accomplished painter of the age. His paintings, film–set designs, and the marketing of his images in poster form communicated the spirit of surrealism to a worldwide public. But many of his fellow artists hated him for his dedication to self-promotion to boost the prices of his works. Picasso became the richest artist of the century by exhibiting uncanny business sense and becoming a celebrity, famous for being famous almost as much as for his art.

Art lost influence, too, because taste splintered. From the 1930s onward, the market lurched among fashions. Every school of artists had to repudiate every other school to attract buyers. Technology multiplied media exponentially from the 1960s onward, and the market responded by huddling in niches. From the 1960s, artists influenced by the new theories in philosophy and linguistics lost belief in the power of symbols generally. Images, some of them came to feel, like words, have no direct relation to reality.

Painting and sculpture yielded popularity to film and to mass entertainment. Arts suited to the new media—cinema, radio, photography, and the gramophone at first, television later, computers and video toward the century's end—spread second-hand experiences, received wisdom and hand-me-down values. The artists who really touched people were cartoonists. Walt Disney (1901–1966) became, perhaps, the world's most influential artist ever because his cartoon movies depicted the most commonplace emotions, morals, and character types in ways that people of all ages in all cultures could immediately grasp. Musical theater, sacrificing sophistication for melody, displaced opera. Pop music was to art what factory products were to crafts: cheap to make and capable of generating huge profits. In the second half of the century, when—for reasons we shall discuss in Chapter 29—masses of young people in the West acquired unprecedented spending power, the record industry became the home of the most socially revolutionary and subversive arts, a role writers had once filled. Now rock bands issued messages of political protest and sexual liberation. These messages proved less saleable, in the long run, than escapism.

By 2000, the most commercially successful genre was fantasy—the depiction of worlds that magic regulated or transformed, which suited computer-generated imagery. It seemed an ironic end to a century dominated by science, but it was symptomatic of the impatience with or revulsion from science that characterized popular responses. Meanwhile, the art form that attracted the most investment and, therefore, attained the highest technical standards was television advertising. Advertising jingles and images became the common artistic culture of the time—the only things you could rely on just about everyone to recognize. Sport, especially soccer, was the only rival—largely because it was broadcast all over the world.

Architecture ought to be the most popular art of all because people who never enter an art gallery live in some form of architecture. Indeed, after the Second World War, architecture replaced painting and rivaled cinema as the most socially powerful of the arts. The world had to be rebuilt after the destruction of the war and the neglect of colonialism. However, doctrines that proved hostile to most people such as functionalism and rationalism, which favored machinelike buildings, fashioned by necessity, stripped to their most elementary forms, angular, and unrelated to human scale, dominated the architecture of the period. So much had to be built so quickly that officialdom decided what and how to build, without giving much thought to the needs and feelings of the people who had to live in the huge apartment blocks, work in the offices, factories, and schools of the era, and recover or die in the hospitals. Only in the 1970s did

Bollywood. Few aspects of Indian life demonstrate the appropriation of Western culture so deeply as the Bombay (Mumbai) film industry, which has created its own imagery and values from a distant Hollywood model.

"Modern" Art

1866–1944	Vasily Kandinsky, Russian artist, launched tradition of entirely abstract art
1876–1944	Emilio Filippo Marinetti, proponent of futurism
1881–1973	Pablo Picasso, cofounder of cubism
1882–1966	Nandalal Bose, Indian artist, incorporated anticolonialism in his work
1887–1968	Marcel Duchamp, French artist influenced by Einstein's theory of relativity
Early twentieth century	Karoda Seiki and Wada Eisaku, Japanese painters, create works that assimilated Western influences
1918	Proclamation of the "Dada Manifesto"
1920s and 1930s	Emergence of surrealist and expressionist movements

architects and urban planners begin to heed popular demands, tear down some of the worst excesses of functionalism, and start again on a smaller scale and along more traditional lines.

THE TURN OF THE WORLD

In the second half of the twentieth century, a reaction set in. The West rediscovered "Eastern wisdom," alternative medicine, and the traditional science of non-Western peoples. Other cultures renewed their confidence in their own traditions. In the 1940s, J. Robert Oppenheimer, the American physicist who led the research team that developed the A-bomb, was one of many Western scientists who turned to the ancient Indian texts, the Upanishads, for consolation and insights, in a West disillusioned by war (see Chapter 28).

Then in 1956, Joseph Needham began to publish one of the momentous works of the twentieth century, *Science and Civilisation in China*, in which he showed that China had a scientific tradition of its own, from which the West had learned the basis of most of its progress in technology until the seventeenth century. Indian scientists, meanwhile, had made similar claims for the antiquity of scientific thinking in their own country. In the 1960s, India became a favored destination for young Westerners in search of values different from those of their own cultures. Zen Buddhism (Chapter 14) and Daoist descriptions of nature provided some Westerners with models to interpret the universe that seemed to match scientific discoveries.

Even in medicine, non-Western traditions gained ground. Westerners often came to respect and learn from the healers they met far afield. Edward Hume himself learned much from traditional Chinese herbalists during his years in Changsha. But it took a long time for such respect to become general in the West. In the 1980s, the World Health Organization began to realize the value of traditional healers in delivering health care to disadvantaged people in Africa. Nigeria, South Africa, and other African countries introduced alternative medicine to health-care centers.

Meanwhile, in the West, traditional healing arts of non-Western peoples attracted big followings. Researchers discovered the healing plants of Amazonian forest dwellers, Chinese peasants, and Himalayan shamans. Scientists began to appreciate that so-called primitive peoples had a cornucopia of useful drugs unknown to Western medicine. Traditional medicine had never died out in India and China. In a remarkable reversal of the direction of influence in the late twentieth century, Western patients seeking alternative medicines turned to Indian herbalism and Chinese acupuncture, along with other forms of traditional medicine in both countries. Westerners began to travel to China and India to study herbal treatments, just as Asian students had headed to the West for medical learning at the beginning of the century. Western demand for alternative medicine became an economic opportunity for Chinese and Indian physicians in the West. The world had come full circle since Edward Hume's day.

IN PERSPECTIVE: Science, Challenging and Challenged

In the first half of the twentieth century, the intellectual hegemony of science was linked with the global dominance of the West. All the major new scientific initiatives came from Europe and America. The rest of the world could only endure this supremacy or imitate it. In the 1960s, however, the pattern began to shift. Western scientists began to turn to non-Western, and especially to Asian, traditions of thought to help interpret some of the conflicting data their observations accumulated. These contradictions seemed, especially to nonscientists, to expose the imperfections of science as a system of knowledge that could explain the universe. Non-Western countries, especially in Asia, imitated Western technologies so well that they could afford their own scientific institutions.

Meanwhile, revulsion from science increased prestige for what came to be known as alternative methods. Some people, especially professional scientists, remained convinced of the all-sufficiency of science and scorned these trends. Their critics called them "scientistic." Toward the end of the century, divisions—sometimes called culture wars—opened between apologists of science and advocates of alternatives.

African healing cult. In Cape Town, South Africa, a ritual of initiation into Ngoma—a shamanistic cult widespread in Africa. Practitioners use music and dance to attain a trance-like state in which they communicate with spirits, usually to access powers of healing.

The search for the underlying or overarching order of the cosmos seemed only to lead to chaos. "Life is scientific," says Piggy, the doomed hero of William Golding's novel of 1959, *Lord of the Flies*. Other characters prove him wrong by killing him and reverting to instinct and savagery. Golding's novel seemed to be an allegory of its times. Science—in most people's judgment—soared and failed. It sought to penetrate the heavens and ended by contaminating the Earth. Among its most influential inventions were bombs and pollutants. The expansion of knowledge added nothing to wisdom. Science did not make people better. Rather it increased their ability to behave worse than ever. Instead of a universal benefit to humanity, science was a symptom or cause of disproportionate Western power. Under the influence of these feelings, and in response to the undermining of science by skepticism, an antiscientific reaction set in. It generated conflict between those who stuck to Piggy's opinion and the vast global majority who—as we shall see in Chapter 29—turned back to religion or even magic to help them cope with the bewildering world of rapid change and elusive understanding.

The revival of unscientific ways to picture reality surprised most observers. But by making the cosmos rationally unintelligible to most people, science stimulated religious revival. Motions we cannot measure, events we cannot track, causes we cannot trace, and effects we cannot predict all became familiar and seemed to license metaphysical and even supernatural explanations. Modern Japan is a land of high-tech Shinto, where spirits infest computers and an office tower of steel and plate glass can be topped off with a shrine to the fox-god. Some medical practitioners collaborate with faith healers. Even religious fundamentalism—one of the most powerful movements in the late twentieth century—mimicked science in seeking certainty.

The last wave of revulsion from science—or, at least, from scientism—in the twentieth century was a form of humanism: a reaction in favor of humane values. Science seemed to blur the boundaries between humans and other animals, or even between humans and machines. It seemed to take the soul out of people and substitute genes for it. It seemed to make freedom impossible and reduce moral choices to evolutionary accidents or genetically determined options. It turned human beings into subjects of experimentation. Ruthless regimes abused biology to justify racism and psychiatry to imprison dissidents. Extreme scientism denied all nonscientific values and became, in its own way, as dogmatic as any religion. The "new humanism" was much more, however, than an antiscientistic reaction. It

CHRONOLOGY

1856–1939	Sigmund Freud, developer of psychoanalysis
1858–1942	Franz Boas, anthropologist, proved that races are of equal intelligence
1860s	China's "self-strengthening" program begins
1866–1944	Vasily Kandinsky, Russian artist, launched tradition of entirely abstract art
1883	Western-style curriculum at Beijing School of Medicine
1871–1937	Ernest Rutherford, postulated concept of the atomic nucleus
1875–1965	Albert Schweizer, medical missionary to Africa
1876–1944	Emilio Filippo Marinetti, proponent of futurism
1879–1955	Albert Einstein, developer of the theory of relativity
1881–1938	Kemal Ataturk, founder of modern Turkey and proponent of secularism and Western science
1881–1973	Pablo Picasso, cofounder of cubism
1882–1966	Nandalal Bose, Indian artist, incorporated anticolonialism in his work
1885–1962	Niels Bohr, won Nobel Prize in 1922 for work on the structure of the atom
1891–1962	Ismail Mazhir, translator of Charles Darwin's work into Arabic
1901–1976	Werner Heisenberg, developed uncertainty principle
1902	Henri Poincaré questions the link between hypothesis and evidence
1903	Powered flight
1905–1980	Jean-Paul Sartre, French philosopher associated with existentialism
1906	15,000 Chinese study science abroad
1907	Plastic invented
1913	Indian *Journal of Medical Research* launched
1914	Science Society of China founded by Chinese students at Cornell University
1920s and 1930s	Emergence of surrealist and expressionist movements
1920	Royal Institute for Higher Technical Education founded in Indonesia
1925	Scopes "Monkey" Trial
1931	Penicillin discovered
1944	Erwin Schödinger predicts structure of the gene
1953	Ludwig Wittgenstein's *Philosophical Investigations* published
1956	Publication of Joseph Needham's *Science and Civilisation in China*

tended to blame religion—or, at least, religious conflicts—as much as science for the failures of history, and its thinkers and practitioners sought a morality based on universal values. More than either science or religion, the barbarities of the violent political history of the twentieth century stimulated the new humanism.

The story of politics in the twentieth century matched that of science. In politics, too, the new century opened with new departures. The world's first full democracies—in the sense that women had equal political rights with men—took shape in Norway and New Zealand. In 1904–1905, Japanese victories in a war with Russia foreshadowed the end of white supremacy. Independence movements arose in Europe's overseas empires. In 1911, the first great "rebellions of the masses" began. Contrary to the expectations of Karl Marx, these were not launched by urban workers but by peasant revolutionaries in Mexico and disaffected intellectuals and soldiers in China. In Mexico, the effect was to end the power of the two elements of society that had been dominant since colonial times: the church and the big landowners. In China, the Qing dynasty, which had reigned since 1644, was overthrown, the mandate of heaven abolished, and a republic proclaimed. This was an extraordinary reversal for a system that had survived so many convulsions for more than 2,200 years, and a sign that no form of political stability, however long-standing, could now be taken for granted. Both revolutions soured, turning into civil wars, breeding dictators. This too was an omen of the future. Most of the many violent regime changes of the twentieth century had similar consequences.

The future that the radicals of the nineteenth century imagined never happened. Ordinary people never really got power over their own lives or over the societies they formed—even in states founded in revolutions or regulated by democratic institutions. The progress people hoped for in the early years of the twentieth century dissolved in the bloodiest wars ever experienced. And just as Western science receded in the second half of the century, so did Western empires. To those stories we must now turn.

PROBLEMS AND PARALLELS

1. How did science come to set the agenda for the world in the twentieth century? How did Western empires affect the spread of Western science? How was Western science received in China, India, and the Islamic world?

2. How was Western science transformed in the twentieth century? What effects did uncertainty have on human self-perception and religious values?

3. Why is twentieth-century Western art a mirror of twentieth-century science? How did the revolutions in twentieth-century art match the jolts and shocks of science and philosophy?

4. Why did a reaction against Western science take hold in the second half of the twentieth century?

DOCUMENTS IN GLOBAL HISTORY

- Education and imperialism in the Dutch East Indies: from *Letters of a Javanese Princess*
- Al-Afghani on faith and reason
- Werner Heisenberg, "Uncertainty," 1927

- Franz Boas, from *The Mind of Primitive Man*
- Ellen Key, from *Century of the Child*
- William Jones, from *Pragmatism*
- Emilio Filippo Marinetti, "Futurist Manifesto"

Please see the Primary Source DVD for additional sources related to this chapter.

READ ON

T. Dantzig, *Henri Poincaré, Critic of Crisis: Reflections on His Universe of Discourse* (1954) is still the fundamental study of the thought of one of the founders of modern science, whose own philosophy of science is available in Henri Poincaré, *The Foundations of Science* (1946). Also valuable for the emergence of modern physics, and more recent, is G. J. Holton, *Einstein and the Cultural Roots of Modern Science* (1997).

On the history of psychology, see the very readable book by C. P. Bankart, *Talking Cures: A History of Western and Eastern Psychotherapies* (1996), which sets the different traditions in their cultural contexts. A good study of one of the founders of modern psychology is R. B. Perry, *Thought and Character of William James* (1935). The key work by a founder of modern anthropology is F. Boas, *Mind of Primitive Man* (1911), while a foundational work of modern linguistics is available as *Saussure's First Course of Lectures on General Linguistics (1907): From the Notebooks of Albert Riedlinger*, eds. E. Komatsu and G. Wolf (1996). For those willing to tackle one of the hardest of twentieth-century philosophers, L. Wittgenstein, *Philosophical Investigations*, translated by G. E. M. Anscombe (1953) is accessible. The quotation on page 708 is from N. Chomsky, *Knowledge of Language* (1986).

On the influence of Western science beyond the West, a number of fine works are available. E. H. Hume, *Doctors East, Doctors West: An American Physician's Life in China* (1949) is a first-hand account of the meeting of medical cultures, from which the story that opens the chapter comes. Li Yan and Du Shiran, *Chinese Mathematics: A Concise History* (1987), trans.

by J. N. Crossley and A. W. C. Lun, and L. A. Orleans, ed., *Science in Contemporary China* (1980) both illuminate the influence of Western science in China, while J. Reardon-Anderson, *The Study of Change: Chemistry in China, 1840–1949* (1991) examines the crucial transitional period of Chinese contact with Western learning. D. Arnold, *Science, Technology, and Medicine in Colonial India* (2000) does the same for the subcontinent, as does L. Pyenson, *Empire of Reason: Exact Science in Indonesia, 1840–1940* (1997) for southeast Asia. E. Ihsanoglu, *Science, Technology, and Learning in the Ottoman Empire: Western Influence, Local Institutions, and the Transfer of Knowledge* (2004) traces in detail the routes and methods of the transmission of Western science into the Ottoman world. A. B. Zahlan, *Science and Science Policy in the Arab World* (1980) brings elements of that story into recent times. *The Political Economy of Health in Africa* (1991), eds. T. Falola and D. Ityavyar, brings us into sub-Saharan Africa and back to medicine as a crucial vector of the spread of Western science globally.

P. Conrad, *Modern Times, Modern Places* (1999) is a sophisticated analysis of modern art globally as a reflection of changing social and cultural trends. The iconoclastic J. Waller, *Fabulous Science* (2002) debunks many scientific myths. W. Hung, ed., *Chinese Art at the Crossroads* (1991), examines the challenges posed by modernity to historical artistic traditions, with specific attention to China. D. Edgerton, *The Shock of the Old* (2006) is brilliantly revisionist on technology. T. Judt, *Postwar* (2006) helps explain the context of the new humanism.

CHAPTER 28
World Order and Disorder: Global Politics in the Twentieth Century

1931: News of the Manchurian Incident flashes around the globe, as imagined by the brilliant Belgian cartoonist Hergé. The Japanese propaganda version of the incident was false. Rogue Japanese agents, not Chinese "bandits," had blown up the railway track, and there were no casualties. The cartoon strip's boy hero, Tintin, discovers the truth and becomes entangled in the Japanese invasion of China for which the incident was a pretext. © Hergé/Moulinsant 2006

IN THIS CHAPTER

THE WORLD WAR ERA, 1914–1945
The First World War
Postwar Disillusionment
The Shift to Ideological Conflicts
The Second World War

THE COLD WAR ERA, 1945–1991

Superpower Confrontation

DECOLONIZATION

THE NEW WORLD ORDER
The European Union

IN PERSPECTIVE: **The Anvil of War**

I n Manchuria in the 1920s and 1930s, the brothels in the city of Harbin resembled clubs, where the regular clients became friends and met each other. On September 19, 1931, the Russian journalist Aleksandr Pernikoff arrived at his favorite haunt, Tayama's. The door was opened by a scholarly looking Japanese man with gold-rimmed glasses. As he shook hands with his friends, Pernikoff became aware of the tension in the atmosphere:

MANCHURIA

> "What's all this about?" Pernikoff asked in a whisper.
> "Didn't you hear?" replied one of the men. During the night, the Japanese had invaded Manchuria, claiming that the Chinese "tried to blow up a Japanese train."
> "Did they blow it up?" asked Pernikoff.
> "No," answered the man, with a half-smile. "The mine went off after the train had passed. But the Japanese troops were ready and waiting."
> A Japanese client of the brothel read out the official Japanese report of the incident. Miraculously, "by divine intervention," although thrust "up into the air" with the force of the explosion, the train descended back onto the rails, resumed its journey, and reached its destination without loss. "All of us in the room," wrote Pernikoff, "felt uneasy at hearing this childish account."
> "What will happen now?" he asked.
> "War."[1]

This episode, known as the **Manchurian Incident,** was the first in a series of crises that Japanese militants manufactured over the next six years—not always with the knowledge or approval of their own government. The first results were to convert Manchuria into a Japanese puppet monarchy. Then, in 1937, a tenacious Japanese attempt to conquer China began. It dragged on until 1945, merging with other struggles, in which all the world's potential super-powers—Japan, China, the United States, Russia, and Germany—were locked, together with the British, French, and Dutch Empires and most of the other sovereign states that then existed.

● ● ● ● ●

The war was part of a long series of global conflicts. Catastrophic warfare punctuated the first half of the century. A **cold war** between ideological antagonists dominated most of the second half, waged in local or regional outbreaks and in economic and diplomatic competition.

We can follow the story of politics in the twentieth century along a path picked between these conflicts. To make space for the cultural and environmental history of the century, we need to try to tell the political story briefly rather than dwelling, as textbooks usually do, on all the many twists and turns, and all the forgettable statesmen and generals whose legacy has not lasted. In the pages that follow, we divide the century roughly into three periods: first, that of the world wars, which ended in 1945; then, the era of superpower confrontation that began as world war ended. Finally, toward the end of the century, a "new world order" arose, as the United States outgunned or outlasted rivals.

FOCUS questions

- HOW DID the world wars weaken Europe's global dominance?
- WHY WERE totalitarian and authoritarian regimes so widespread during the twentieth century?
- HOW DID the United States become the world's only superpower?
- WHY DID the Cold War lead to the collapse of the Soviet Union?
- HOW DID decolonization affect Asia and Africa?
- WHY DID democracy spread around the world in the late twentieth century?
- ARE THE European Union and China likely to become superpowers in the twenty-first century?

THE WORLD WAR ERA, 1914–1945

One way to understand Japan's conflict with China is as a sort of civil war within a single civilization. Japanese usually represented the conflict as a decisive struggle to determine which country would be the "big brother" and which the "little brother" in a common empire or, as Japanese propagandists said, the Great East Asia Co-prosperity Sphere.

The European conflicts that merged with this intra-Asian war, and that overspilled Europe itself to become a global war, had similar characteristics. At first, in the episode known as the First World War, from 1914 to 1918, national and imperial rivalries triggered hostilities. The European powers disagreed about little except how to distribute power and territory among themselves. After the war had begun, to the great question of which country would dominate Europe, another greater question was added: Which ideology would dominate Europe? Would the common culture of European peoples in the future be religious or secular, liberal or authoritarian, capitalist or socialist, individual or collective?

The First World War

When the struggles began, all the belligerent states had more or less the same ideology. Except for France, they were all monarchies. Although most were not democratic, they all aspired to mobilize the allegiance of their peoples with the same rhetoric of chivalry, idealism, and crusade.

For Germany, the war was an attempt to resolve two obsessions: first, to strike a preemptive blow against Russia, before industrialization turned that country into a superpower; second, to break out of maritime containment by Britain, for Germany had no access to the ocean highways except through narrow seas easily policed by British naval power. For France, the war was an attempt to wreak revenge on Germany for humiliation in their last war in 1870–1871. For Britain, it was an exercise in traditional British grand strategy: pinning down a world-imperial rival—Germany—in a continental war.

For the Habsburg Empire of Austria-Hungary, striving to contain restless and violent national minorities, war was a desperate act of impatience with Serbian subversion, which threatened to detach the empire's southern Slavic provinces. For Italy, the objective was frontier snatching at Austria's expense. For the Ottoman Empire, fearing Russian expansion, it was a gamble to survive. For the Russian czar, war in defense of fellow Slavs in the Balkans was an obligation of honor. His ministers also feared that Germany had "a gigantic plan of world domination."

For all the belligerents, the war went wrong. On the Western Front, armies stuck in the mud in trenches from the English Channel to the Alps. In the east, Germans, Austrians, and Turks collided blunderingly with Russians in the vast terrain. In the Alps, Italians hurled themselves against Austrians who occupied the higher ground. The elites who had started the war could not control its course or its costs.

Russia dropped out in revolution and disorder toward the end of 1917—the first major belligerent to collapse. Germany could therefore switch its main effort to the west. The balance of forces, however, was already shifting against the Germans, for in April 1917 the United States joined the fray.

Soldiers' accounts of battle

This was a surprising development. It made sense for Americans to take the profits peace offered. This policy, known as **isolationism,** however, gradually became impractical, as "Uncle Sam," in the slang of the British press, had become "Brother Jonathan, a power among the powers."

America might have favored the Germans. There were millions of German immigrants in the United States. Many Americans viewed the British Empire with distaste. But Britain was America's biggest creditor and trading partner. Germany, meanwhile, offended against two of America's pet values: peaceful problem solving and freedom of the seas. Squeezed between France and Russia, the Germans practiced militarism partly as a survival technique. Once war in Europe broke out, Germany had to resort to submarine warfare—which, being sneaky and secretive, offended American sensibilities—to damage British commerce. In 1917, Germany announced that its submarines would sink any ships—hostile or neutral—in British waters. By then, the United States was already looking for a pretext to join the war against Germany. Its intervention was decisive because no belligerent could match America's power. American industrial output equalled that of the whole of Europe combined.

The United States entered the war to meet an American agenda: to crush militarism, free the seas, weaken European empires, lift American debts, consolidate America's growing superiority in wealth, liberate the Eastern European homelands of millions of American citizens, and make the world safe for democracy. But the war was a unifying experience for the powers that faced each other across the Atlantic. Three of the world's most powerful, resourceful, and predatory states—the United States, Britain, and France—were now in partnership. The rest of the world faced a source of cultural influence of peculiar force.

The First World War was a crucible, in which the world seemed to dissolve. It destroyed elites, empires, and traditional ways of life. Almost 10 million men died

A trench with wounded and dead, June 1915, on the western front in northern France during World War I. The apparently unposed photograph is shocking because of the standing soldiers' apathetic acceptance of the plight of their wounded comrade in the foul, brutalizing environment of the trenches.

Total Casualties in the First World War

Country	Dead	Wounded	Total Killed as a Percentage of Population
France	1,398,000	2,000,000	3.4
Belgium	38,000	44,700	0.5
Italy	578,000	947,000	1.6
British Empire	921,000	2,090,000	1.7
Romania	250,000	120,000	3.3
Serbia	278,000	133,000	5.7
Greece	26,000	21,000	0.5
Russia	1,811,000	1,450,000	1.1
Bulgaria	88,000	152,000	1.9
Germany	2,037,000	4,207,000	3.0
Austria-Hungary	1,100,000	3,620,000	1.9
Turkey	804,000	400,000	3.7
United States	114,000	206,000	0.1

Niall Ferguson, The Pity of War (New York: Basic Books, 1998).

in action. There were 25 million casualties in all. The war wiped out a generation of the natural leaders of Europe and provoked political revolution or transformation wherever its armies marched. Twelve new sovereign, or virtually sovereign, states emerged in Europe or on its borders (see Map 28.1). The Russian, German, Austro-Hungarian, and Ottoman Empires were felled at a stroke. Even the United Kingdom lost a limb, when revolution and civil war in Ireland ended with, in effect, independence for most of the island. Huge migrations redistributed peoples. After the war, more than 1 million Turks and Greeks shunted to safety across the new borders of their mutually hostile states.

MAP 28.1

Europe, the Middle East, and North Africa in 1914 and 1923

Europe, the Middle East, and North Africa, 1914

Europe, the Middle East, and North Africa, 1923

President Woodrow Wilson (1856–1924) appreciated the opportunity to recraft the world. He denounced imperialism. His country bought its last permanent acquisitions of territory (three of the Virgin Islands in the Caribbean) in 1917 from Denmark. Wilson did his best to discourage the imperialism of his allies and insisted, within Europe, on "self-determination." New nations sprang into being or reemerged at the rhythm of a State Department typewriter: first, what Wilson called "Czecho-slovakia," then "Jugo-slavia," Poland, Finland, Estonia, Latvia, and Lithuania.

On the other hand, the claims of Ukraine, Georgia, Armenia, Belarus, the Kurds, and the Muslim peoples of the Russian Empire were ignored. In Africa, the belligerents swapped colonies with no thought for self-determination. The aspirations of the Arab subjects of the Ottoman Empire were patchily treated. A leader of anti-Ottoman resistance in Arabia, Sharif Husayn (1856–1931), proclaimed himself King of the Arabs in 1917, with popular support, but the British and French divided his territory between them, leaving only what are now Jordan and Iraq to his heirs, and allowing an Islamist chieftain, Ibn Saud (1880–1953), to conquer what is now Saudi Arabia in 1924–1925. Meanwhile, in Libya, rebels against the Italians who had seized the country from the Ottomans in 1911–1912 proclaimed an Arab republic in 1918, but Italy suppressed them shortly afterward. From 1917, the British outraged Arabs by permitting—albeit halfheartedly—the creation in Palestine of what they called a "national homeland" for the Jews of Europe.

For Turkey itself, the loss of empire seemed a relief. The new, secular Turkish republic, founded by Mustafa Kemal in 1923 (he took the surname Atatürk, meaning "Father of the Turks"), had universal male suffrage in 1924 and women's right to vote from 1934. Atatürk made Friday, the Muslim Sabbath, a workday, imposed the Roman alphabet on a language formerly written in Arabic characters, and founded an opera, a university, and a symphony orchestra. His success inspired other Muslim secular nationalists. In Iran, for instance, an army strongman, Riza Khan, proclaimed himself shah in 1925 and imitated Atatürk's secularizing policies, abolishing the veil for women and banning Islamic religious schools.

Sir Henry McMahon, letter to Sharif Husayn, 1915

Finally, President Wilson proposed the **League of Nations** as a forum to resolve international disputes peacefully. But the United States Senate rejected Wilson's vision. Americans had no taste for world leadership. The costs of the Great War had been enough. When America refused to take part in the League and retreated into isolation, the new world order was doomed.

Covenant of the League of Nations

Or perhaps it was doomed anyway. The treaties the Allies imposed left too many dissatisfied states. Germany had been barely defeated, but the victors treated it with contempt: subject to massive reparations and loss of territory, with humiliating restrictions on the right to rearm. Italy remained discontented with its modest territorial gains. Japan, which had joined the Allies in 1914 expecting a free hand in East Asia, felt let down. Russia, stripped of its influence over Eastern Europe, was excluded from the postwar settlement and looked for ways to unpick it. Most of the new nation states included large, restive minorities. Faced with these resentments, the League was useless, its representatives—in the words of an English comedian—turning up for meetings "in taxis that were empty."

But the war changed expectations for the future. It was an experience of unmatched horror. The men who marched away expected another war like those of nineteenth-century Europe: short and glorious. What they got was more than four years of suffering. Soldiers on the Western Front lived in filthy trenches, contending with rats, lice, mud, and poison gas. While they cowered

Erich Maria Remarque, from *All Quiet on the Western Front*

Mohandas K. Gandhi, *Satyagraha in South Africa*

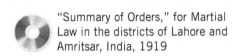
"Summary of Orders," for Martial Law in the districts of Lahore and Amritsar, India, 1919

underground, massive artillery barrages pounded their dugouts. When they charged, they faced machine guns and died, or watched their comrades die, in millions. Experiences too terrible to confide to loved ones back home became secret neuroses. Shell shock plagued the demobilized. The battlefield became soulless, desolate, a blackened, barbed-wired Golgotha. Tanks displaced cavalry. Machines crushed life out of the landscape and chivalry out of war. The war destroyed "even the survivors" of battle, said the German writer Erich-Maria Remarque (1898–1970) in *All Quiet on the Western Front*, the most influential of the war-born novels and memoirs.

Postwar Disillusionment

Optimism, however, survived in other places—especially where people resented European empires. The war was a collective humiliation for Europe. The United States was revealed as the world's leading power. Japan mopped up formerly German-owned islands in the Pacific and bases in China. Almost before the smoke cleared, nationalist movements got under way in the colonial empires. In Dutch-controlled Indonesia in 1916, the group known as Sarekat Islam mobilized a mass movement for self-government. In 1919, the Pan-African Congress demanded that Africans share in governing their own countries. In the same year, the Egyptian Wafd or Nationalist Party was founded to pressure the British into leaving.

In India in 1919, amid riots against the continuation of wartime measures, the British suspended civil liberties. Mohandas Gandhi (1869–1948) launched a movement he called **satyagraha**— "the force of truth"—relying on "passive disobedience": strikes, fasts, boycotts, and demonstrations. Other protesters derailed trains, battled police, and cut telegraph wires. The British responded nervously. In Amritsar, troops fired on demonstrators "to teach," their commander said, "a moral lesson": 379 unarmed people were killed and 1,200 wounded. Britain's hold—such as it was—on popular sentiment in India deteriorated rapidly. Much of the Indian intelligentsia was looking forward to dismantling Western hegemony and dismembering Western empires.

In the euphoria of peace, even some Western politicians were free with optimistic rhetoric. The war would "end all wars." Its survivors would return to "homes fit for heroes." Progress would resume.

In America, where no fighting took place, this was believable, at first. But war-scarred Europe found it hard to match this mood. Europeans were already becoming convinced of the imminent "decline of the West"—the title of the German historian Oswald Spengler's postwar blockbuster. For those who could afford it, the 1920s in Europe was an age of desperate pleasure seeking. For the rest, it was a time to try to salvage something from disillusionment. The results included labor unrest, extremist politics, economic failures, and impoverishing inflation.

Disillusionment hit America later. The war made the United States' economy boom. In "seven fat years" from 1922 to 1929, a spiraling stock market seemed to promise universal riches. In 1924, 282 million shares of stock changed hands on Wall Street. In 1929, that figure was 1.824 billion. That same year, the crash came. In three weeks, beginning on October 24, American stocks fell in value by $30 billion (almost $400 billion in today's money). The effects bounced the economy into recession, bounded across the Atlantic, and set off a string of bank failures. Meanwhile, ecological disaster struck farms in the American West. "Brother, can you spare a dime?" sang crooners in the character of a war hero down on his luck.

Disillusionment afflicted Latin America particularly deeply, because expectations there were so enormous. Argentina, Chile, Uruguay, Mexico, and Brazil were all self-styled lands of promise. In the early twentieth century, Argentina was the world's most desired destination for migrants. But Latin America's economies, after booming in the First World War, went into dramatic reversal after the war when demand for raw materials plummeted. Violent changes of government ensued. In 1930, in Argentina, Peru, and Brazil, army officers seized power or installed "emergency" governments with dictatorial powers. Guatemala, Honduras, Nicaragua, the Dominican Republic, and El Salvador soon followed suit.

The economic disasters of Europe and the Americas in the 1920s and 1930s seemed to show that the West was wormwood. It was an age of faultfinding with Western civilization. Some of the things people blamed were so fantastic as to be rationally incredible—yet miserable millions believed the rabble-rousers' claims and were susceptible to the appeal of "noisy little men" proposing easy and even "final" solutions. Anti-Semites, for instance, claimed that Jews controlled the world's economies and exploited gentiles. Advocates of eugenics claimed that unscientific breeding weakened society by encouraging inferior classes and races and degenerate individuals.

Marx's predictions seemed to be coming true. The poor were getting poorer. The failures of capitalism would drive them to revolution. Democracy was a disaster. Only authoritarian governments could force people to collaborate for the common good. Perhaps only totalitarian governments, extending their responsibility over every department of life, could deliver justice.

People who still believed in democracy and capitalism thought the system could be reformed from within. J. M. Keynes (1883–1946) advocated the most persuasive program. Governments could redistribute wealth through taxation and public spending, without weakening enterprise or infringing freedom. Well-judged interventions of this sort would stimulate the economy without stoking inflation (see Chapter 29). Britain, France, and Scandinavia adopted this solution to economic depression. So did President Franklin D. Roosevelt (1887–1945) in the United States.

Gandhi as he wished to be seen. He squats in a traditional position for Indian mystics, working calmly in a scholarly, reflective manner. His gaunt body, modest loincloth, and simply furnished home proclaim his selflessness and asceticism. He adopted a spinning wheel as the symbol of his movement for Indian independence to signify tradition, patience, constructiveness, self-sufficiency, and peace.

 J. M. Keynes, from *The End of Laissez-Faire*

Workers' demonstration. The Spanish painter Ramon Casas (1866–1932) specialized in meticulously painted scenes of bourgeois life of his native Barcelona, but he could also play the role of a social commentator. In 1902 he exhibited this scene of police dispersing a crowd of striking workers against a backdrop of gaunt factories. In the sky, there is gold beyond the industrial smog and perhaps a patch of hope.

The Shift to Ideological Conflicts

The alternatives were authoritarian or totalitarian. The right-wing or *corporatist* solution was to preserve private enterprise, but only on the understanding that individual rights, freedoms, and property were not to be allowed to exist for their own sake, but were at the disposal of the state. The state would force all citizens to collaborate and coerce or exterminate any groups thought to resist the common pursuit. Left-wing versions proposed to collectivize virtually all economic activity, seizing private property and eliminating "class enemies." This would have a morally, as well as economically, improving effect. The other main difference between Right and Left was that the Right was unashamedly nationalist, whereas the Left proclaimed internationalism, at least in its rhetoric. The Left was divided between those—usually called *anarchists*—who wanted collectives of workers to run economic activities, and *communists,* who wanted the state to own and control production, distribution, and exchange.

Long-accumulating class hatreds underlay ideological differences. Before the war, European elites talked themselves into expecting a showdown with the working class. Workers' demonstrations kindled fear and provoked massacres. On the eve of war in 1914, the British Foreign Secretary Sir Edward Grey predicted, "There will be socialist governments everywhere after this."

Such predictions were exaggerated. The first and, for a long time, the only successful revolution was hardly a workers' triumph. The Bolshevik uprising in Russia of October 1917 was a well-planned coup, which elevated the Communist Party to the role of an aristocracy and charismatic dictators—first Vladimir Ilyich Lenin (1870–1924), then Joseph Stalin (1879–1953)—to greater power than the czars'. What was left of the Russian Empire was renamed the "Soviet [meaning collective] Union." Copycat revolutions were defeated in Finland, Germany, Hungary, Bulgaria, and Italy. Socialists compromised with bourgeois rulers as the price of sharing power. But left-wing militancy kept up the struggle. Moscow encouraged and financed international communism.

Lenin on the Bolshevik seizure of power

Communists often attached more importance to suppressing left-wing splinter groups than to overthrowing capitalist regimes. It may seem odd that leftists fought each other under the guns of their common enemies, but it is worth remembering that most of them accepted the Marxist dogma that revolution was inevitable. For the communists it was more important to ensure their own leadership of the revolution than to provoke it prematurely.

In some places beyond Europe, in the 1920s and 1930s, conflicts over power were increasingly seen as clashes of classes or ideological showdowns. In China, for instance, the main contending parties called themselves Nationalist and Communist. Their conflict escalated in the 1930s, despite the menace of Japanese invasion. In parts of the British, French, and Dutch Empires, rebels and malcontents identified with socialism. They saw a similarity between the plight of their own peoples, oppressed by imperialism, and the worker-victims of capitalism, whom they got to know when they worked or studied in the metropolitan centers of the empires to which they, unwillingly, belonged. Ho Chih Minh (1890–1969), for instance, who later led a communist revolution in Vietnam, worked as a waiter in Paris after the First World War. Tan Malaka, leader of Indonesian communists, learned communism in the Netherlands. Thus, the West exported its ideological conflicts, along with so many other aspects of its culture.

Indonesian communists. In 1925, when this photograph was taken in Batavia (now Jakarta), the Indonesian communist party had just launched a new policy of armed insurrection, after a series of unsuccessful strikes and a growing sense of desperation, as the Dutch authorities expelled its leaders. The three languages of the placard tell a story. Chinese immigrants were prominent in the movement. Malay—written here in Arabic script rather than the Roman alphabet currently preferred—was the language of the masses. The elite who ran the party, however, used Dutch. The rebellion launched the following year was another failure.

Whether **fascism**—an extreme and violent corporatist movement—was another splinter ideology of socialism, an independently evolved doctrine, or a state of mind in search of a doctrine has been passionately debated. Stubbornly undefinable, its symbols best expressed its nature. In ancient Rome, the *fascis* was a bundle of rods with an axe through the middle of it, carried before magistrates as an emblem of their power to scourge or behead wrongdoers. Italian fascists adopted these bloodstained images of law enforcement as what we would call their logo. They appealed to a system of values that put the group before the individual, cohesion before diversity, revenge before reconciliation, retribution before compassion, the supremacy of the strong before the defense of the weak. They justified the enforcement of order by violence and the obliteration of misfits, subversives, deviants, and dissenters.

Communists tended to be as ruthless as fascists. Communists persecuted and massacred class enemies. Fascists victimized or exterminated "inferior" communities and races. The Nazis put more than 6 million people to death because they were Jews or Gypsies. In the Soviet Union, Stalin exterminated millions of peasants and ethnic minorities. Both sets of extremists believed in the omnipotence of the state. Fascism had, perhaps, wider appeal. Advocating policies that could be summarized as socialism without the abolition of private property, fascists could mobilize small property owners from among the inflation-impoverished bourgeoisie. The cults of violence were equally characteristic of the militants of both Left and Right. Both extremes recruited their street armies from the victims of economic slump and social dislocation. The same ideals of fraternal community kept parties at both extremes together.

Individuals moved between fascism and militant socialism as if through connecting doors. Benito Mussolini (1883–1945) who, as leader of the first successful Fascist Party—he coined the word *fascist*—seized power in Italy in 1922, began his political life as a socialist. The German Nazi Party—whose program was essentially fascist, with an anti-Semitic driving force—was officially called the National Socialist German Workers' Party. Britain's failed "man of destiny," Colonel Juan Perón (1895–1974), who took over Argentina in 1946

 Ho Chih Minh, "Equality!" 1922

Excerpts from the speeches of Juan Perón

Adolf Hitler, excerpt from *Mein Kampf*

The World War Era, 1914–1945

1914	United States industrial production equal to whole of Europe combined
August 1914	World War I begins
1915	Mohandas K. Gandhi, leader of Indian independence movement, returns to India from South Africa
1916	Sarekat Islam mobilizes mass movement for independence of Indonesia
1917	Russian Revolution begins; United States enters World War I
November 1918	World War I ends
1919	First meeting of Pan-African Congress
1919–1920	Paris peace conference
1922	Benito Mussolini's Fascist Party takes power in Italy
1923	Turkish Republic founded
1924	Vladimir Lenin, leader of Russian Revolution dies; Joseph Stalin emerges as new Soviet leader
1929	U.S. stock market crash
1930–1931	Army officers seize power in Argentina, Peru, Brazil, Guatemala, El Salvador, and the Dominican Republic
1931	Japan invades Manchuria
1933	Nazis take power in Germany
1936–1939	Spanish Civil War
1939	Germany invades Poland; World War II begins
1939–1945	Nazis carry out genocide of Europe's Jews
1941	Germany invades Soviet Union; Japan attacks Pearl Harbor
June 1944	Allied liberation of France begins
August 1945	United States drops atomic bombs on Hiroshima and Nagasaki; World War II ends

and founded a movement that remains influential there, promised employers that with "workers organized by the state, revolutionary currents endangering capitalist society can be neutralized." But he also used socialist demagoguery. His wife Eva (1919–1952), a former radio diva, became a proletarian goddess, "the faithful voice of the shirtless masses."

By 1933, when the Nazis took power in Germany, it was clear that in European politics, ideological defiance transcended national hatreds. But the conflicts that followed were not straightforward struggles of Left and Right. Old hatreds crisscrossed the killing grounds. Between 1936 and 1939, for instance, civil war in Spain seemed to project to the rest of the world images of a dress rehearsal for a global struggle of Left against Right. In reality, however, the fighting was between broad coalitions pursuing domestic Spanish agendas. The right-wing coalition partnered virtual fascists with awkward allies: traditional Catholics, who were defending the Church; old-fashioned liberal centralists, who were equally numerous on the other side; romantic reactionaries who yearned to reinstate a long-excluded branch of the royal house; constitutional monarchists, who wanted to return to the cozy, corrupt parliamentary system of the previous generation; worshippers of "the sacred unity of Spain," who thought they were fighting to hold the country together. On the other side, along with the mutually warring sects of the Left, were conservative republicans, liberal anticlericals, admirers of French and British democratic standards, and right-wing regionalists, who supported the republicans as the lesser evil.

Ideology, in any case, could still be sacrificed to national interest. The Nazi dictator, Adolf Hitler (1889–1945), regarded Jews and communists as his main enemies, but one of his chief aims was to crush Russia and conquer an empire of "living-space" and slave labor for Germany in Eastern Europe. In 1939, he made a nonaggression pact with his Soviet counterpart, Joseph Stalin. For both dictators, the pact was a temporary expedient. Hitler wanted to clear the ground for a knock-out war against France and Britain to free himself to deal with Russia in the future. Stalin wanted to get his hands on the resources of Finland, Romania, the Baltic states, and eastern Poland.

The pact wrecked the Western democracies' strategy for containing Hitler. Britain and France had attempted to buy time by conceding Hitler's demands and ignoring his provocations. Beginning in 1934, Hitler built up a massive military regime and reoccupied demilitarized parts of Germany. Then he forced German-Austrian unification and seized most of Czechoslovakia after trumping up a dispute over that country's German minority. The French and British hoped that Russia would keep him in check. The pact between Hitler and Stalin crushed those hopes and made war inevitable. The French and British had gambled that they could restrain Hitler by guaranteeing the integrity of his next target, Poland, even though geography made it impossible for them to offer Poland effective assistance. The German invasion of Poland, launched in September 1939, plunged them into a war that they had never wanted to fight and for which they were not ready.

The Second World War

In Europe, the Second World War (1939–1945) reran aspects of the First World War. This time, however, France crumbled, not Russia, and it was on their eastern front, rather than in the west, that the Germans became stuck. Hitler attacked Russia prematurely in June 1941, without first knocking Britain out of the war. Aided by "Generals January and February," and by Hitler's strategic blunders, Russia proved unconquerable. The decisive element was again American intervention—again procured despite American isolationism. Hitler made America's decision himself, declaring war in December 1941 in support of his ally, Japan.

Japanese society had become consecrated to war in the struggle to conquer China. The conflict escalated. Japan realized that it would have to procure the supplies its armies needed by conquering Dutch and British oilfields in southeast Asia. This was bound to become a global conflict. If Japan were to succeed, the United States would have to be intimidated into standing aside. In December 1941, Japan launched a preemptive strike against the American Pacific Fleet at Pearl Harbor in Hawaii. The attack was a success, but the strategy was miscalculated. The Americans were knocked out for long enough for Japanese forces to occupy French Indochina, overrun Dutch Indonesia and British Hong Kong, Malaya, and Burma, drive the United States from the Philippines and Guam, and fan out over the western Pacific. But a war of attrition began, in which the Americans, with help from Britain, Australia, and New Zealand and from the Chinese refusal to give up, gradually thrust the Japanese back (see Map 28.2).

Hiroshima, Japan, after the explosion of the atomic bomb. In August 1945, Japan's defeat was already manifest, but rather than negotiate a conditional surrender or sacrifice thousands of American lives by invading the Japanese islands, President Truman (1884–1972) decided on a terrible alternative: the incineration of the Japanese cities of Hiroshima and Nagasaki with atom bombs.

⊙ MAKING CONNECTIONS   ⊙

THE WORLD WAR ERA, 1914–1945

BELLIGERENTS →	CONFLICT →	CAUSES →	OUTCOMES
Germany, Austria-Hungary, Ottoman Empire versus Great Britain, France, Russia, Italy, other European powers	World War I, 1914–1918	Imperial and national rivalries	Defeat of Germany: dismantling of Austria-Hungary and Ottoman Empires; Bolshevik Revolution in Russia; Britain and France victorious but empires weakened and discredited; United States emerges as richest nation in the world; League of Nations formed; postwar disillusionment pervades Europe
Japan versus China	Second Sino-Japanese War, 1937–1945	Various incidents instigated by Japan lead to full-scale war in 1937 in an attempt to turn China into a subject territory	Japanese invade China and turn Manchuria into a puppet state (Manchukuo); conflict merges with World War II
Allies (Great Britain, United States, Soviet Union, other powers) versus Axis (Germany, Italy, Japan, other powers)	World War II, 1939–1945	Clash between different ideologies and forms of government (fascism, communism, democracy), and national/imperial interests	Germany, Italy, and Japan defeated; Eastern Europe falls under Soviet domination; Germany divided; Holocaust and forced migrations transform European society; Japanese Empire dismantled; European powers begin to decolonize; formation of United Nations; United States and Soviet Union emerge as nuclear superpowers

World War II

— maximum extent of Axis powers in Europe and Africa

— maximum extent of Japanese expansion in Asia/Pacific

Movement of troops

Axis

➡ German

➡ Japanese

Allies

➡ British

➡ British Commonwealth

➡ American

➡ Soviet

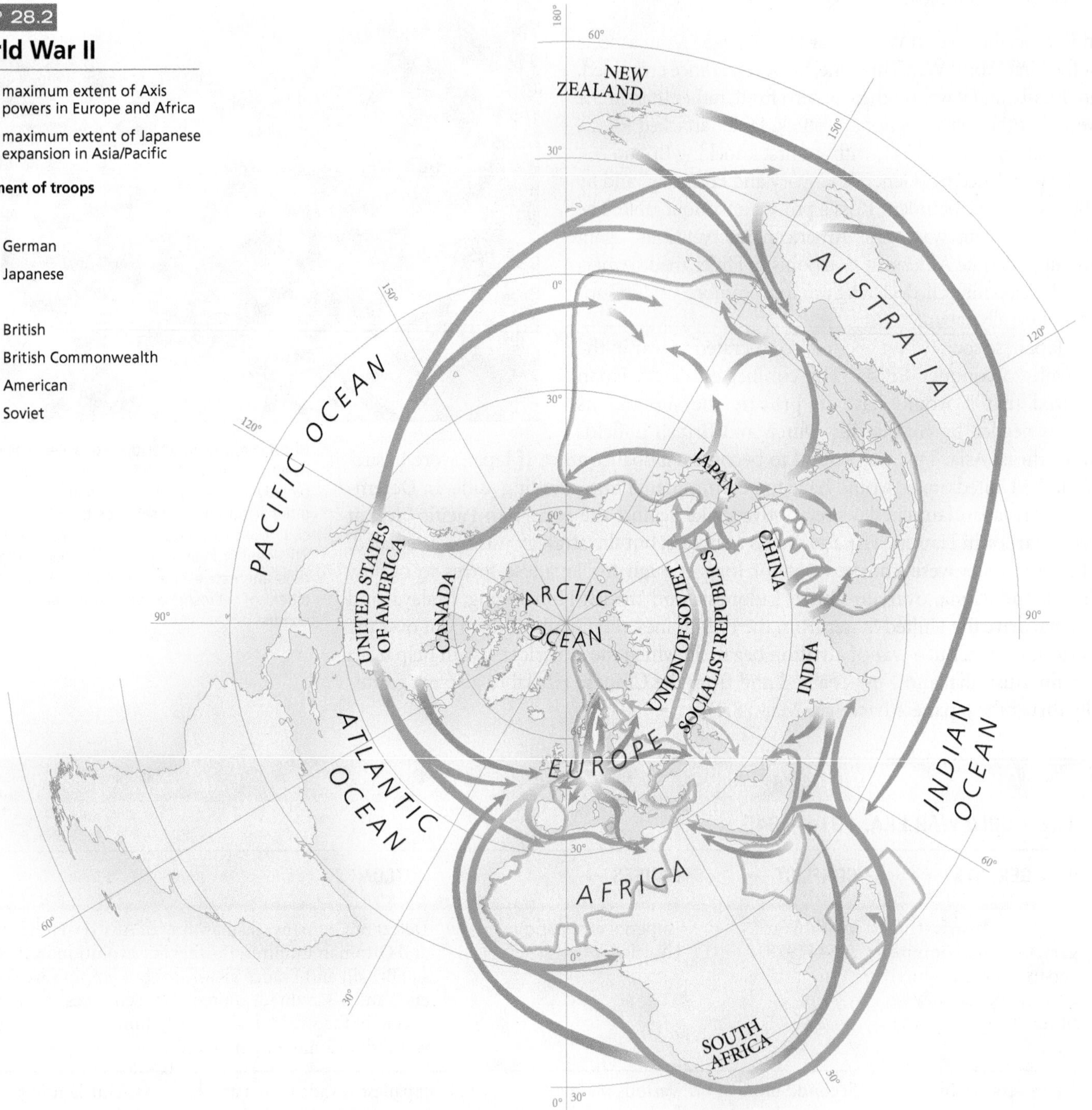

America and Britain constructed a vast coalition—known informally as the Allies and officially as the United Nations—to fight the war. In 1940, Italy joined Germany in what became known as the Axis. But Italians felt little enthusiasm for war. German troops became overcommitted pursuing Italian adventures in North Africa, where the British forces triumphed in 1943, and the Balkans. Meanwhile, the Russian campaign ground down the German armies. With the invasion and liberation of France that began in June 1944, Allied victory in Europe became irreversible. The Germans launched terrifying rocket bombs against Britain toward the end of the war, but these weapons made little difference. Germany was crushed between Russians from the east and the Allied forces from the west. By the time Hitler killed himself on April 30, 1945, aerial bombing had pulverized Germany, its armed forces were collapsing, and the Russians were in Berlin.

There was never any real likelihood of Japanese victory. Japanese leaders were aware of this. Their naval command compared war with the United States to a risky operation that might kill a critically ill patient. The Japanese ended up with too many enemies and overextended lines. Even so, Japan fought on, recoiling from surrender, which, in Japanese culture, was considered shameful. The end came only because the war stimulated research into devastating new technology. In August 1945, American planes dropped atom bombs on Hiroshima and Nagasaki, killing over 120,000 people and poisoning the survivors with radiation. The Japanese, who had no such bombs, surrendered.

THE COLD WAR ERA, 1945–1991

The peace was harder to win than the war. Franklin Roosevelt, like Wilson before him, had a vision of a new world order. In Roosevelt's version, Britain, Russia, and China would, in effect, divide the world among them and collaborate to police peace. But protracted conflict threatened from three sources: civil wars in "liberated" countries, the ambitions of international communism, and Russia's desire for security or power along its borders. Stalin seized or garrisoned much of Eastern Europe. In March 1946, Winston Churchill (1874–1965), who had led the British government for most of the war years, announced the descent of an "Iron Curtain" from the Baltic to the Adriatic, dividing Soviet-dominated Eastern Europe from the West.

 Winston Churchill, the "Iron Curtain" speech

 George C. Marshall, "The Marshall Plan," 1947

Superpower Confrontation

In 1947, America tried one of the most generous foreign aid programs ever, the **Marshall Plan** (named after Secretary of State George C. Marshall [1880–1959]), to seduce former enemies into dependence on the United States and "create the social and political conditions in which free institutions can exist." American taxpayers paid for European reconstruction, and Western Europe began to recover. But by choice, Russian occupation, or communist coups, the states east of the Iron Curtain became Soviet satellites. At Stalin's orders, they turned down Marshall aid. A ring of American client states faced a heavily fenced Soviet Empire.

So another opportunity to reconstruct world order had been lost. However, democracy did take root in countries American forces occupied. Japan was transformed into a demilitarized, democratic state and a staunch American ally. Italy also democratized without difficulty. Germany had to be partitioned. The Soviet zone in the east became a rigid dictatorship, but the American-, British-, and French-occupied zones in the west were combined to form another model democracy, the Federal Republic of Germany.

The world shivered under a nuclear cloud. British experimenters had noted the explosive properties of nuclear fission as early as 1911. In 1935, Frédéric Joliot, in his speech receiving the Nobel Prize for work on nuclear energy, warned that an atomic chain reaction could destroy the world. By 1939, European scientists had nearly overcome the technical obstacles to the manufacture of a bomb, but the more immediate

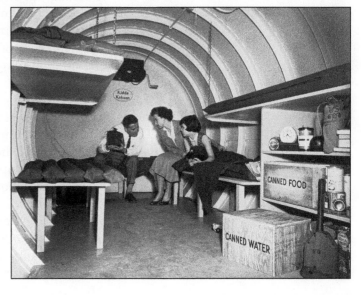

Bomb shelter. A U.S. public-information campaign photograph of the 1950s makes the "shadow of the bomb" seem almost comfortable with a family posed earnestly together around a radio in their well-stocked bomb shelter. But this reassuring propaganda was a sham. Only the elite had shelters, and if their shelters had survived an atomic bomb, these people would have emerged into a deadly, poisoned environment.

demands of the war effort distracted British researchers. Nazi conquest dispersed Joliot's team in France. In Germany, Werner Heisenberg (see Chapter 27) was unwilling or unable to put a bomb in Hitler's hands.

So the first bombs were made in America. Had the United States kept its monopoly of the weapon, it would have been permanently secure in the role of world arbiter. But Russia produced its own "A-bomb" in 1949.

Nuclear equivalency with the United States guaranteed Russia's free hand in territories it had already conquered or coerced. Yugoslavia broke free of Russian hegemony in 1947–1948 before the completion of the Soviet bomb. Afterwards, other East European satellite states tried to do the same and failed. Within a few years, technical improvements brought Russian and American firepower to the level of "mutually assured destruction." The balance of terror kept the peace between them.

Soviet and Western blocs confronted one another in a cold war that never quite reached boiling point. The Western allies ringed the Soviet world with alliances of anticommunist states in Europe, the Middle East, and Asia. The Soviet Union nurtured revolutionary allies among the poor countries of the world (see Map 28.3).

Depending on one's point of view, the conquests of international communism were battering rams pointing at Western Europe and the rest of the world, or giant buffers projecting the natural caution of a Russia that had barely survived the Second World War. Russian leaders' rhetoric wavered between defensive anxiety and aggressive bravado, reflecting struggles for supremacy within the Soviet elite. Stalin's eventual successor, Nikita Khrushchev (1894–1971), hammered loudly on the table at international conferences to distract attention from his weakness and practiced "brinkmanship"—periodically scaring the world with the threat of nuclear war—to deter the West from aggression. One of these crises—in 1962, over the housing of Soviet missiles in Cuba—nearly led to nuclear conflict. But both sides backed down. The Russians removed their missiles from Cuba, the Americans removed theirs from Turkey. Both powers recognized the need for co-existence, at least between themselves.

In retrospect, the Soviet phenomenon was bound to fail. Russia's postwar power reflected its natural endowments: a larger population than most of its neighbors, vast resources, and a heartland too big for enemies to conquer. On the other hand, the Soviet Empire was ramshackle, no more able than that of the czars to contain the national and religious identities of its subject-peoples. State-run economies tend to inefficiency. The Soviet elite compounded the problem by bad policies: collectivization of agriculture, which deprived farmers of any stake in the land; repression of the free market for goods and services, which led to nightmares of central planning and a chronic shortage of basic consumer goods; suppression of traditional cultures, which created festering resentment; and a horrific disregard for the environment, which wasted resources and polluted the landscape. The survival of the Soviet system to 1991 is more surprising than its collapse.

For a long time, however, it looked as if communism would win the ideological struggle and the Soviets would get most of the world on their side. In 1949, for instance, China appeared to join the Soviet camp when the Chinese communists defeated the nationalists. Since the overthrow of the Qing dynasty in 1911 (see Chapter 27), no Chinese government had been able to replace the legitimacy of the old imperial order or hold the country together. The Chinese communists succeeded where others had failed: mobilizing popular enthusiasm, unifying the country, creating a new elite—the Party—to replace the old mandarinate. Mao Zedong (mao dzeh-dohng) (1893–1976) was the most effective leader the Chinese

Harry S Truman, The Truman Doctrine, 1947

Nikita Krushchev, Speech to the Twenty-Second Congress of the Communist Party, 1962

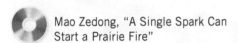

Mao Zedong, "A Single Spark Can Start a Prairie Fire"

MAP 28.3

The Alliances of the Cold War

U.S., allies, and satellite states

- U.S. and original NATO 1949
- later NATO
- NATO dependencies 1960
- other nations allied to the Western bloc by treaty

U.S.S.R. and allies

- U.S.S.R.
- Warsaw Pact 1955
- Communist satellite states
- China

Communist Party had, organizing its weak forces into an army that could never be defeated because it could never be pinned down.

At first China's revolution seemed a great addition to Soviet power. The United States struggled against communist encroachments in Korea. The country had been divided in 1945 because Soviet troops had occupied its northern half while

Atrocity. This 1973 Pulitzer Prize winning photo shows South Vietnamese forces casually walking behind terrified children, including Kim Phuc, center, as they head down a highway after a plane dropped napalm on suspected communist guerrilla hiding places. The terrified girl had ripped off her burning clothes while fleeing.

American forces had garrisoned the south. Supposedly, North and South Korea would be reunited after elections, but the rulers Russia installed in the north and those the United States backed in the south never held the elections. In June 1950, the north invaded the south. America stepped in, with military support from Britain and Australia. Despite Chinese intervention on the other side, the Americans and their allies drove the invaders back to the north. Korea remains divided.

In Vietnam, however, a similar situation led to a disaster for the United States. In the 1950s, after French imperialism in Indochina collapsed, a partition of Vietnam between communist and anticommunist regimes led to civil war. American troops poured into South Vietnam from 1961. The war of containment the Americans tried to fight proved impracticable against Vietnamese guerillas. The United States got trapped in rising costs, mounting casualties, plunging morale. American opinion would neither approve perseverance nor admit defeat. America entered a 12-year agony that dominated the world's media. No war had ever been so ruthlessly exposed on television and in the newspapers. Daily images of dead and wounded soldiers, atrocities, and ineptitude disturbed domestic audiences.

In response, peace movements spread across the West. "Flower power" celebrated "love, not war." Young men sought to evade serving in the military. In 1968, massive street demonstrations across Europe and America toppled some governments and shook others. The would-be revolutionaries mostly talked themselves into inertia or outgrew rebelliousness. Protest ebbed with the war. But the collapse of South Vietnam in 1975 wrecked American prestige and undermined America's moral authority. The insurgents' success encouraged America's enemies. Americans recoiled from responsibility for other people's liberty. The newly independent countries of the era were disinclined to take America's side. Communist takeover in Cambodia and Laos in the 1970s made the American rout seem worse. Cambodia's regime was one of the most brutal in a savage century, but its communism proved unique and demented. Pol Pot (1926–1998) proposed a return to a purely agrarian state, such as had supposedly prevailed in Cambodia's medieval golden age, by massacring the bourgeoisie, wrecking industry, and depopulating the cities.

As if these political setbacks were not enough, the West also seemed to be losing in the economic and scientific stakes against the Soviet system. In 1957, Russia launched the first successful spacecraft, *Sputnik I,* and in 1961 put the first man in space. Space exploration was expensive and brought virtually no useful economic or scientific returns. But America, in danger of forfeiting world prestige, was forced to play catch-up, which it did, putting the first man on the moon in 1969. Meanwhile Russia seemed ahead in the struggle to forge what a British prime minister called the "white heat" of technology.

However, the Soviet economy was not as strong as propaganda painted it. "Socialism is management," Lenin once said. But no Russian government managed the economy well. In 1954, for instance, Khrushchev launched a disastrous initiative known as the Virgin Lands scheme. He intended to turn vast areas of steppe into farmland—the way the great ecological revolution of the nineteenth century had transformed the North American prairie (see Chapter 23). In this case, however, intensive farming soon exhausted the soil of the grasslands the Russians plowed up. In all, an area greater than that of the entire farmland of Canada was lost.

In most respects, however, the era of Soviet economic success lasted until the world oil crisis of 1973, when oil-exporting countries, by hiking the price of fuel, triggered massive global inflation. The economies of Russia's satellite regimes in Eastern Europe slipped out of economic dependence on Moscow, which could not afford to subsidize them as lavishly as before, and into indebtedness to Western bankers who loaned them vast sums. Then, in the 1980s, after sending troops into Afghanistan to replace a ruler who was becoming too independent with a more pro-Moscow puppet government, Russia found itself embroiled in a hopeless war against fanatical Islamic guerrillas who were financed by conservative Arab regimes and armed by the United States. The costs in blood and cash were greater than Russians were willing to bear. President Ronald Reagan (1911–2004) stepped up the arms race, outstripping Russia's paying power. The Chicago economists (see Chapter 29) on whom Reagan relied for advice convinced the world that private enterprise made for prosperity and that economics was too important to be left to the state. The thinker who worked along ide them, the Austrian F. A. von Hayek (1899–1992), became the source of the era's fashionable idea: order in the service of freedom.

The pope helped dissolve Soviet power. In 1978, a Polish cardinal, Karel Wojtyla (d. 2005), became Pope John Paul II. He used his wide range of acquaintances among Catholics in Eastern Europe to build up resistance to Soviet domination. The Polish trade union Solidarity launched a series of strikes and demonstrations

"Each day of labor—a step toward communism!" Russian communists adopted the hammer and sickle emblem to symbolize the alliance of peasants and workers. In practice, however, landowning peasants remained hard to convince. Joseph Stalin had millions of them massacred and exiled in the 1920s and 1930s for refusing to join collective farms. As late as 1968, however, propaganda still featured images of steel and grain—the privileged products of Soviet economic planning.

REPORTING OUR HARVEST TO CHAIRMAN MAO

Mao Zedong's "Great Cultural Revolution" was meant to remake society by forcing the privileged to share the lives of peasants and workers. But by victimizing the educated and the enterprising, Mao wrecked the economy and impoverished China. Propaganda strove to conceal the truth—not least from Mao himself.

The bystanders and the little girl nestled protectively in Mao's arm represent peasants and youth—the groups Mao tried to mobilize against professionals and intellectuals, whom he saw as enemies.

Mao, godlike in stature and simple in dress, recites his "Thoughts" to implausibly smiling adorers.

The girl on the left wears the badge of the communist party on her peasant's wide straw hat. Under Mao, the party became the country's only permitted elite.

Peasants bring agricultural abundance to Mao—like tribute-bearers to a traditional emperor or worshippers to a god. In reality, there was no abundance of food or anything else in China. Mao's policies undermined productivity in agriculture as well as industry.

How does this painting differ from historians' accounts of China under Mao?

from 1980 onward, first against economic mismanagement by Poland's communist regime and then against the regime itself.

From 1985, the Soviet Union floated off the shoals and into the wake of the West, under a leadership that had ceased to believe in socialist rhetoric. Mikhail Gorbachev (b. 1931) dismantled the command economy, freed the market, introduced accountable government, and, eventually, submitted to demands for democracy and for self-determination by the Soviet Union's ethnic minorities. Moscow manipulated or permitted similar revolutions in the satellite states—the last act of a dying supremacy. Dissidents took over. Satellite states zoomed out of the Soviet orbit. The two European communist supranational states—the Soviet Union and the Yugoslav federation—splintered.

China, meanwhile, had become an enemy to both sides in the Cold War. Mao disappointed Moscow almost from the moment he took power. He admired the bandit heroes of Chinese romance more than he did Lenin or Stalin. He was a peasant by birth and developed his own theory of peasant revolution. "He doesn't understand the most elementary Marxist truths," said Stalin, who hated Mao. Under his rule, China remained as aloof from the Soviet Union as from the West. Mao denounced America for imperialism and the Russians for "bourgeois deviationism"—turning the Communist Party into a new kind of middle class. He competed with both for the friendship of the successor states of dismantled empires, while pursuing an aggressive policy toward neighbors. China overran Tibet, intervened in the Korean War, provoked confrontations on the Indian, Vietnamese, and Russian borders, and encouraged insurgents in Nepal.

Mao's domestic policies arrested China's development. He caused famine by communalizing agriculture and environmental disaster by absurd schemes of industrialization. He launched campaigns of mass destruction against a sequence of irrationally selected enemies: dogs, sparrows, rightists, leftists—even, at one point, grass and flowers. He outlawed romantic love as bourgeois and, proclaiming that vice was hereditary, reduced the descendants of ancient elites—scholars, landowners, officials—to the ranks of an underclass. In 1966, his regime proclaimed a **Cultural Revolution.** In practice, this meant forcing professionals—including teachers, scientists, doctors, and technicians, on whom the country relied—into manual labor or degrading them with humiliating punishments. For more than three years, intellectuals were brutalized, antiquities smashed, books burned, beauty despised, study subverted, work stopped. China's economy reverted to chaos.

Cultural Revolution: violence at Qinghua University, 1968

The long-term outcome of Mao's moral and economic failures was the reconversion of China to capitalist economics. Between 1969 and 1972, President Richard Nixon (1913–1994) abandoned America's traditional hostility, accepting China into the United Nations and opening American trade with it. It was an attempt to wedge Russia and China further apart, while mopping up some of the spoilage from the Vietnam War. Nixon's strategy worked, especially after Mao's death.

Deng Xiaoping on capitalism

Mao's successor, Deng Xiaoping (1904–1997), recommended Chinese "to get rich"—which neither Mao nor Confucius would ever have approved. After making trade agreements with America and Japan, Deng freed up the Chinese economy, gradually returning more and more production and finance to the private sector. In 1986, Vietnam, too, adopted a policy of market liberalization. By the 1990s, China's was the fastest-growing economy in the world. Early in the new century, Chinese demand was driving up the prices of energy and commodities worldwide. North Korea was the only state in the region, in the world, really, that remained inward looking, isolated, and hostile to economic freedoms.

DECOLONIZATION

Before the Cold War could end, the world had to endure the agonies of decolonization—the breakup of the old European empires in Asia and Africa (see Map 28.4). Between 1941 and 1945, Japan drove white rulers out of southeast Asia. After the war, the United States conceded independence to the Philippines. In other parts of Asia, nationalist resistance forced the colonialists to surrender power.

The Dutch "police operation" in the East Indies (1945–1949) was really a brutal war that ended in Dutch retreat and the independent Republic of Indonesia. The French suffered ignominious defeat in Indochina in 1954. The British managed to defeat communist insurgents in Malaya, but colonial rule ended there in 1957.

Meanwhile, in 1947, the British pulled out of India in haste, escaping horrific problems of famine control and ethnic and religious conflict. Partition of Britain's Indian Empire between Hindu and Muslim states—India and Pakistan, respectively—claimed at least 500,000 lives. The British bullied or blackmailed native princes into joining either India or Pakistan. Eventually the maharajahs were stripped of their powers.

European decolonization dismantled more than empire. In many places, colonial powers felt forced to abandon or sideline old elites—European settlers and native aristocracies—in favor of upstart leaders from the rising native middle classes. Usually the newcomers had been educated in Europe or mission schools at home. Once the colonial armies left, the new men, who commanded popular support, revolutionary armies, or help from abroad, stepped into leading roles, cutting out traditional elites or reducing the old aristocracies and monarchies to purely ceremonial functions. In India, which became the world's most populous democracy, the process worked exceptionally well. Pakistan was less successful and more typical. After about a generation of independence, it was defeated in two wars against India, partitioned to accommodate secessionists in what became known as Bangladesh, and subjected to long periods of military rule.

Frantz Fanon, from *The Wretched of the Earth*

Guerrilas, not rebels. In line with U.S. policy, which favored Indonesian independence and the end of Dutch colonialism in southeast Asia, the caption for this Associated Press photograph, in July 1947, identified these fighters not as rebels against Dutch colonialism, but as "non-uniformed combat guerrillas" of "supporting units to the regular military forces" of the "Republic of Indonesia." After bitter fighting, the Dutch finally ceded Indonesian independence in 1949.

Most Westerners assumed that Africa would take longer to decolonize than Asia, but the winds of change blew up a storm in that continent, too. Because sub-Saharan Africa largely escaped the Second World War, some forms of production—especially of rubber and food—were relocated there. As a result, an ambitious African middle class developed. Meanwhile, modern medicine produced a population boom. Uncontrollable numbers of needy people made empires unprofitable. Rather than shoulder escalating costs, it became cheaper for European powers to grant independence and foreign aid.

Egypt played the role in Africa that the Japanese played in Asia—uncovering the weakness of European empires and hastening their downfall. Britain and France, the two main colonial powers, were humiliated in a showdown with Gamal Abdel Nasser (1918–1970), an Egyptian nationalist whom an officers' coup elevated to power. When he seized the Suez Canal Company in 1956, Britain and France, joined opportunistically by Israel, invaded. For reasons of its own, the United States repudiated the Franco-British operation and, in effect, forced its allies to accept Egypt's case. A flight of colonial powers from Africa followed.

 Nasser, speech on the Suez Canal crisis

The cracks spread outward from Egypt. In the year of Suez, Britain evacuated Sudan, and France left Tunisia and Morocco. Algeria was more problematic. Although the vast interior of the country was a French colony, the parts of Algeria on the Mediterranean were considered an integral part of France, with over 1 million European settlers by the 1950s, many of whom were prepared to fight France, if necessary, to remain French. A savage war that broke out in 1954 between the French army and Muslim rebels settled the question in favor of independence by 1962, but not before mutinous generals and enraged settlers threatened to topple the government of France itself. Meanwhile, in 1957, Ghana in West Africa became the first sub-Saharan African state to gain independence. After that, the skirts of empire were lifted with indecent haste. In 1960, 14 new states came into being in Africa. Again, newcomers, schooled in resistance, replaced old elites. In Ghana, for instance, the independence leader Kwame Nkrumah (1909–1972) had "PG" for prison graduate embroidered on his cap. In Kenya, the first president, Jomo Kenyatta (1889–1978), had probably been the secret leader of the terrorists who had slaughtered white settlers and African loyalists under British colonial rule in the 1950s.

 Kwame Nkrumah, from *I Speak of Freedom: A Statement of African Ideology*

Postcolonial rulers in Africa adopted or affected secular programs, usually heavily influenced by socialism, and flirted with Moscow or Beijing, either out of ideological conviction or to maximize their freedom of maneuver and opportunities for graft or aid. The ease with which many of them slid into despotic habits, and reduced their countries to dictatorships and destitution, dismayed Western liberals who had hoped that decolonization would bring freedom and prosperity.

 Jomo Kenyatta, from *Facing Mt. Kenya*

Leader cults filled the gaps that the extinction or subversion of traditional loyalties left open. Nkrumah, who called himself the Redeemer, became prey to messianic delusions, as his troops sang, "Nkrumah never dies." Jean-Bedel Bokassa (1921–1996) declared the Central African Republic an "empire" and crowned himself its emperor in imitation of Napoleon. Idi Amin (1925–2003) used terror as a method of government and plunged Uganda into chaos. In Sierra Leone, Siaka Stevens (1905–1988) became preoccupied with justifying polygamy. In Congo, Joseph Mobutu (1930–1997) milked the economy of billions of dollars. Francisco Macías Nguema in Equatorial Guinea—executed by his own nephew after a coup in 1979—and Robert Mugabe (b. 1924) in Zimbabwe impoverished their countries and deployed armed gangs to terrorize opponents.

Decolonization left lands staggering under terrible burdens. Their populations were normally growing at an unprecedented pace, for which the colonial regimes had not prepared them. They were usually encumbered with irrational, indefensible borders that the departing colonialists had hastily outlined. The principle of national self-determination, which had guided, however imperfectly, the dismantling of imperialism inside Europe after the First World War, was ignored in the wider world. Colonial regimes crammed historically hostile communities into single states, or forced them into unstable "federal" superstates, or imposed borders between newly independent states that neither side found acceptable. International law treated postcolonial borders as inviolable, even where they were oppressive or unworkable.

MAP 28.4

Decolonization Since World War II

- before 1950
- 1950–1956
- after 1956

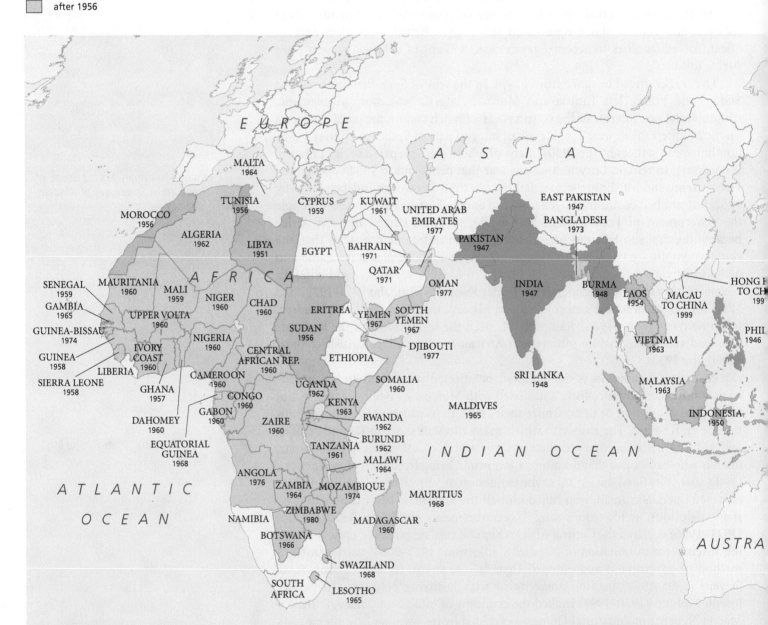

So civil wars commonly accompanied or followed decolonization, and disputes over the divisions of territory often remained unresolved into the twenty-first century: between new states, such as India and Pakistan; between Catholics and Protestants in Ireland; Jews and Arabs in Israel and Palestine; Turks and Greeks in Cyprus; Christians and Muslims in Nigeria, Sudan, Ivory Coast, and the Philippines; Tamils and Singhalese in Sri Lanka; centralists and secessionists in Congo, western Sahara, and Uganda; rivals for resources in Angola and Mozambique; and traditional elites and historically underprivileged groups in Liberia, Sierra Leone, Rwanda, Burundi, and other new countries in Africa and Asia.

All the ensuing wars multiplied the sufferings of the people who endured them, but the Palestinian conflict had the worst long-term effects on global history. In 1948, the British, who had occupied the country since the collapse of the Ottoman Empire in 1918, left

in the face of murderous conflict between Jews and Arabs. What swiftly emerged was a division of Palestine into a Jewish state and Arab enclaves. The Jews, who called their state Israel, were victorious in subsequent wars that left them in control not only of territory the British and the United Nations had assigned to the Arabs of Palestine, but also of land that Arab states had previously occupied. In the early twenty-first century, despite fitful progress, the resulting problems remained. Israel agreed in principle to recognize a Palestinian state, but its boundaries and nature were undetermined. Guarantees for Israeli security remained unsatisfactory. By choosing in effect to guarantee Israel's survival, the United States stoked Arab rage and alienated international opinion, especially in the Muslim world.

Meanwhile, the economic problems of decolonized lands mounted. In the 1970s and 1980s, the value of many primary products on the world market collapsed. This was the result of two so-called revolutions: the first, known as the green revolution, glutted the world with cheap grains (see Chapter 30). Simultaneously, an information revolution replaced many traditional industries and bore the West into a postindustrial age, in which services and information replaced manufacture as the main source of employment. The gap in wealth between the ex-imperialists and their former subjects became an abyss. Business imperialism was not easily thrown off. Even after colonies achieved political independence, their economic dependence frequently continued, often on the Soviet Union or the United States—the Cold War contenders whom newly independent governments sought to play off against one another. Cuba—always smarting under American economic control—played the game with some success after 1959, when revolutionaries, under Fidel Castro (b. 1927), threw out a dictatorship that had enjoyed Washington's support. Castro nationalized businesses—especially those Americans owned—and established an egalitarian welfare system. The United States took both offense and fright, and Castro became a client of the Soviet Union, while imposing authoritarian controls on Cuba. He even sent troops to Africa where the Soviets wanted to shore up regimes that favored them. The collapse of his Soviet ally in 1991 and the changing conditions of global trade obliged Castro to relax economic controls, but Cuba remained perhaps the only example of sustained socialism in the world.

Leader cult. When colonial powers rushed ill prepared to disengage from Africa in the 1960s, they left dysfunctional states behind, prey to ruthless dictators, sprung from the new elites that Europeans promoted to offset the power of traditional leaders. Idi Amin, for instance, of Uganda, who seized power there in 1971, had been a sergeant under the British. This photograph from 1975 captures an incident of his increasingly unbalanced behavior as ruler of his country, when he forced white subjects and employees into taking bizarre and humiliating oaths of allegiance to him, drafting them into the armed services, so that they would be under military discipline, and exacting vows to fight against the white-dominated South African regime.

 Palestinian Declaration of Independence, 1988

 Fidel Castro, *History Will Absolve Me,* 1953

Hamas supporters. A series of wars from 1948 to 1974 left Israelis in occupation of lands with a large and resentful Palestinian population, many of whom, rejecting the very existence of the State of Israel, resorted to resistance by terrorism. Even peaceful demonstrations—like this one in 2005 by supporters of the radical party Hamas—became exercises in martial discipline. Disputes over the distribution of land, water, jobs, and financial aid, and the exclusion by Israel of some Palestinian refugees from their former homes, inflamed the situation. Hamas won democratic elections—against rivals who favored accommodation with Israel—in 2006.

Nelson Mandela, from "The Struggle Is My Life" from *Freedom, Justice and Dignity for All South Africa*

THE NEW WORLD ORDER

At the end of the Cold War, the United States had no rival and could set the world's agenda. Most of the world willingly adopted the democratic principles long associated with America. In 1974, only 36 states could reasonably be called democracies. By 2000, 139 states were democracies. Democracy was the only political ideology universally praised, albeit often insincerely.

Authoritarian government disappeared from southern Europe. Between 1974 and 1978, Greece, Portugal, and Spain all made the transition to democracy. In much of Latin America, military dictatorships seized power in the 1970s, often with the connivance of U.S. administrations. By the 1990s, however, democracy was restored—shakily in some countries—in almost the whole of the continent. The Philippines experienced a democratic revolution in 1986, In 1994, South Africa embraced democracy. The white parliament dissolved itself, and the first democratic elections brought Nelson Mandela (b. 1918) to the presidency (see Chapter 29).

While much of the world democratized, most countries adopted **human rights** into their laws. These rights included guarantees of life, personal liberty, and dignity; freedom of expression, of religion, of education, and of equality under the law; and minimal standards of nourishment, health, and housing. The Helsinki Agreement of 1975, which pledged its signers to respect human rights, was particularly significant, because the Soviet Union signed it, along with most other European countries, Canada, and the United States. Dissident groups throughout the communist world were enormously encouraged. It was easier, however, to get assent in principle to the concept of human rights than to implement them. In practice, states ignored such rights whenever they wished. Even the United States found ways around its obligations in dealing with people accused of terrorist acts or of collaboration with the enemy during wars in Afghanistan and Iraq in the early twenty-first century. Some detainees captured in these wars were interned offshore in an attempt to exclude them from the protection of United States' laws. Others were subjected to torture by executive dispensation in defiance of the law or handed over to governments, such as those in Syria, Egypt, and Saudi Arabia, that abused prisoners.

Democratization made little impact in some states—especially in Africa and the Muslim world. Some post-Soviet republics fell into the hands of authoritarian leaders. Under Vladimir Putin, who became president in 1999, Russia itself attracted fears that democracy was in jeopardy. In South Asia, India and Sri Lanka preserved democracy, despite a secessionist war by the Tamil minority in Sri Lanka, while Pakistan and Bangladesh were often under military rule. In southeast Asia, a fault line divided nondemocratic Myanmar, Laos, and Vietnam from the more or less democratic states in the rest of the region.

In Latin America, Cuba remained a dictatorship, while some new democracies seemed fragile. Elected presidents of authoritarian inclinations—Hugo Chávez (b. 1954) in Venezuela, for instance—showed scant respect for democratic institutions. Most disturbingly, China continued to repress democratic opposition.

If there was an opportunity to fashion a more democratic, just, and peaceful world, the United States did not take it. American leaders from the 1980s onward lacked what President George H. W. Bush (b. 1924) called "the vision thing." They made no attempt to create international institutions to preserve world peace. They declined to accept the jurisdiction of an International Criminal Court. They kept aloof from efforts to establish a global environmental policy. They bypassed the United Nations when it suited them to do so. They intervened militarily on their own say-so in foreign countries. They exhibited what much of the world condemned as bias toward the Middle East.

In pursuit of its own national interests, the United States often sponsored antidemocratic regimes, especially in the Arab world. Nor were America's own democratic credentials perfect. Two presidents—John F. Kennedy in 1960 and George W. Bush in 2000—almost certainly came to power as a result of electoral malpractice. In 1974, President Nixon had to resign after revelations that he had attempted to obstruct justice by subverting investigations into a break-in in 1972 at Democratic Party headquarters. Elections have been bought with millions of dollars and abandoned by millions of voters.

United Nations Declaration of Human Rights, 1948

"Freedom for Bush." Graffiti in Baghdad in June 2004 satirize President George W. Bush's claim to have made war in Iraq to promote freedom. One graffito clothes the Statue of Liberty in the garb of violent U.S. racists; the other shows a tortured Iraqi. American soldiers had been caught photographing each other torturing and sexually humiliating Iraqi prisoners, including innocent noncombatants. Soon after, the U.S. government admitted that it had authorized other instances of torture beyond the jurisdiction of U.S. courts.

Most Americans wanted America to be a benevolent superpower, but the United States had cast itself in the role of world policeman, and the American taxpayer had to pick up the tab. This pleased no one. American governments, however, proved unwilling or unable to spread the burden, share power, or provide for a future in which America could no longer take care of the world.

The European Union

China was the most likely successor to the United States in the role of global hegemon. Although leaders talked of Pan-Arab or Pan-African unity, nothing meaningful ever came of it. But a chance to build loyalties across European frontiers arose from the ruins of the

Decolonization and the Post–Cold War World

1941–1945	Japanese occupation sets stage for postwar decolonization of southeast Asia
1947	Indian independence and partition into India and Pakistan
1948	State of Israel established
1950s and 1960s	Decolonization of most of Africa
1956	Suez Crisis
1959	Fidel Castro takes power in Cuba
1970s	Military dictatorships take power in much of Latin America
1970s and 1980s	Value of many commodities on world market collapses
1974	36 states have a democratic franchise
1975	Helsinki Agreement
1986	Democratic revolution in the Philippines
1990s	Under Deng Xiaoping China becomes world's fastest-growing economy
1994	Nelson Mandela becomes president of South Africa
1997	Hong Kong returns to Chinese control
1999	Vladimir Putin becomes president of Russia
2000	139 states are classifiable as democracies
2004	European Union enlarged to include 25 states

Treaty on European Union, 1992

Second World War. France, West Germany, Italy, Belgium, the Netherlands, and Luxembourg combined in the European Coal and Steel Community in 1952. The Messina Declaration in June 1955 proclaimed the goal of "... a united Europe, through the development of common institutions, ... the creation of a common market, and the gradual harmonization of social policies."

At every step, however, Europeans dragged their feet, partly because governments were jealous of their sovereignty and partly because peoples were protective of their national identities. The Council of Ministers that ran the **European Union (EU)** was deliberately an international rather than a supranational body.

The economic success of the EU complicated the problems, as the community enlarged from the 6 original member states to 25 in 2004. With each enlargement, consensus became more difficult. Some countries opted out of key initiatives, including the single European currency, the Euro, introduced in 2002. Divisions opened between countries, typified by Britain, that wanted power to stay with the member states and those that wanted a centralized European superstate. Reluctance to admit Muslim states—Turkey and Bosnia—was also obvious. Yet Europe needed to show that the EU could accommodate Muslims, if only because, as we shall see in the next chapter, Muslim minorities were growing rapidly throughout Western Europe.

IN PERSPECTIVE: The Anvil of War

War can almost be said to have determined global politics in the twentieth century. War strained the empires that Europeans had constructed in the nineteenth century. In the first half of the twentieth century, those empires barely endured, and in the second half, they collapsed. Decolonization was usually violent and economically disruptive. Much of the decolonized world, especially in Africa, was left impoverished and racked by instability. Only the United States emerged from global conflict richer and stronger.

Meanwhile, war stimulated the development of new military technologies that, by midcentury, had become so destructive that as President John F. Kennedy said in 1961, "Mankind must put an end to war, or war will put an end to mankind."

At one level, contending superpowers dominated the story of global politics in the twentieth century. At another, it was a tale of ideological conflicts, in which democracy contended with rival kinds of authoritarianism and totalitarianism.

If the great wars of the first half of the century were civil wars of Western and Eastern civilizations, the Cold War was the conflict of an increasingly globalized world—a struggle to decide what the common culture of the world would be. The end of the Cold War was part of a more general climax that spread democracy and capitalism. Yet efforts to establish a peaceful world order failed. By 2000, the world depended on the only remaining superpower, the United States, to act as a global policeman. No one would find this satisfactory for long. The chances increased that rivals would contest superpower status, as the European Union began to function and as China recovered, after a long period of unfulfilled potential. The prospect revived that global history would again unfold from the east as the era of Chinese disintegration and weakness ended.

In retrospect, the long-term significance of the Sino-Japanese war whose opening Aleksandr Persikoff witnessed, was boundless. Dominance in East Asia and the Pacific was at stake; over the twentieth century as a whole, this seems to have been the strategic area of greatest importance. For, as we shall see in the next chapters, during the twentieth century, the great shift of the balance of population, wealth, and power westward from Asia into European and North American hands—the dominant trend of global history in the nineteenth century— began to ease. The Pacific replaced the Atlantic as the world's foremost arena of long-range trade.

Americans, meanwhile, may have relished their country's role but did not choose it. They suffered resentment and hatred in return. In part, this was because the United States' exercise of global responsibilities seemed to many people to be unreasonable and unjust. On the one hand, the importance of the United States for the peace of the world was illustrated in 1990, when Iraq invaded Kuwait, and American-led forces restored the status quo. Some interventions, on the other hand, seemed poorly chosen. Under President Bill Clinton (1993–2001), military action in Somalia, Sudan, and Serbia seemed weakly justified and ill targeted. In 2002 and 2003, President George W. Bush's invasions of Afghanistan and Iraq appeared, to most of the rest of the world, to have little justification in the Afghan case and none at all in that of Iraq. Both adventures committed America to long-term interventions, without clear exit strategies. American power alone was not enough to preserve peace indefinitely. American administrations did little to build international institutions to share the burdens or take over the task.

It was not, however, solely American might that made the twentieth century "the American century." The magnetism of the United States was more a matter of what political scientists call *soft power:* cultural influence and the appeal of American institutions and ways of life. But for every admirer of American culture, others detested or despised it. To understand the context of these reactions, we have to turn to the social and cultural history of the twentieth century.

CHRONOLOGY

1914–1918	World War I
1917	Russian Revolution begins
April 1917	United States enters World War I
1919–1920	Paris peace conference
1922	Benito Mussolini's Fascist Party takes power in Italy
1929	U.S. stock market crash
1930–1931	Army officers seize power across Latin America
1931	Japan invades Manchuria
1933	Nazis take power in Germany
1936–1939	Spanish Civil War
1939–1945	Nazis carry out genocide of Europe's Jews; World War II
1941	Germany invades Soviet Union; Japan attacks Pearl Harbor
August 1945	United States drops atomic bombs on Hiroshima and Nagasaki
1947	Indian independence and partition
1948	State of Israel established; Soviet blockade of Berlin begins; Marshall Plan initiated
1949	North Atlantic Treaty Organization (NATO) formed; Soviet Union produces atomic bomb; communists take power in China
1950s and 1960s	Decolonization of most of Africa
1950–1953	Korean War
1955	Warsaw Pact formed
1959	Fidel Castro takes power in Cuba
1961–1973	U.S. involvement in Vietnam War
1966	Mao launches Cultural Revolution in China
1970s	Military dictatorships in much of Latin America
1973	World oil crisis triggers global inflation
1974	36 states have democratic franchises
1985	Mikhail Gorbachev takes power in Soviet Union
1989–1991	Collapse of Soviet control of Eastern Europe and of the Soviet Union itself
1990s	Under Deng Xiaoping China becomes world's fastest-growing economy
1994	Nelson Mandela becomes president of South Africa
2000	139 states are classifiable as democracies

PROBLEMS AND PARALLELS

1. Why can Japan's conflicts with China in the first half of the twentieth century and the European conflict of World War I be viewed as civil wars?

2. Why did the non-Western world view World War I as an opportunity to challenge European colonial control?

3. How did the United States emerge as the world's leading power after World War I? What effect did postwar disillusionment have on European society?

4. Why were conflicts over power in the 1920s and 1930s increasingly seen as ideological conflicts?

5. What effect did nuclear armaments have on world politics? How did the Cold War dominate world affairs from the late 1940s to the late 1980s?

6. What were the effects of colonization on decolonized lands? On former empires?

DOCUMENTS IN GLOBAL HISTORY

- Soldiers' accounts of battle
- Sir Henry McMahon, letter to Sharif Husayn, 1915
- Covenant of the League of Nations
- Erich Maria Remarque, from *All Quiet on the Western Front*
- Mohandas K. Gandhi, *Satyagraha in South Africa*
- "Summary of Orders," for Martial Law in the districts of Lahore and Amritsar, India 1919
- J. M. Keynes, from *The End of Laissez-Faire*
- Lenin on the Bolshevik seizure of power
- Ho Chih Minh, "Equality!" 1922
- Excerpts from the speeches of Juan Perón
- Adolf Hitler, excerpt from *Mein Kampf*
- Winston Churchill, the "Iron Curtain" speech
- George C. Marshall, "The Marshall Plan," 1947
- Harry S Truman, The Truman Doctrine, 1947
- Nikita Krushchev, Speech to the Twenty-Second Congress of the Communist Party, 1962

- Mao Zedong, "A Single Spark Can Start a Prairie Fire"
- Cultural Revolution: violence at Qinghua University, 1968
- Deng Xiaoping on capitalism
- Frantz Fanon, from *The Wretched of the Earth*
- Nasser, speech on the Suez Canal crisis
- Kwame Nkrumah, from *I Speak of Freedom: A Statement of African Ideology*
- Jomo Kenyatta, from *Facing Mt. Kenya*
- Palestinian Declaration of Independence, 1988
- Fidel Castro, *History Will Absolve Me*, 1953
- Nelson Mandela, from "The Struggle Is My Life" from *Freedom, Justice and Dignity for All South Africa*
- United Nations Delaration of Human Rights, 1948
- Treaty on European Union, 1992

Please see the Primary Source DVD for additional sources related to this chapter.

READ ON

The opening story comes from O. A. J. Pennikoff, *Bushido: The Anatomy of Terror* (1973). Good starting points for World War I include I. Beckett, *The Great War, 1914–1918* (2001), an overview of the military, political, social, economic, and cultural aspects of the conflict; M. Gilbert, *First World War* (1996); N. Ferguson, *The Pity of War: Explaining World War I* (2000), a controversial revisionist account of the war; and P. Fussell, *The Great War and Modern Memory* (2000), a cultural history of the Western reaction to the struggle and to its legacy. Probably the best introduction to World War II is W. Murray and A. R. Millet, *A War to Be Won: Fighting the Second World War, 1937–1945* (2000). Also solid is G. Weinberg, *A World at Arms: A Global History of World War II* (1995).

I drew on F. L. Allen's *The Lords of Creation* (1996) for the background to the Depression. S. L. Engermann and R. E. Gallman, eds., *The Cambridge Economic History of the United States,* vol. III (1996) is searching and comprehensive.

The historiography of the Cold War has not surprisingly proven ideologically contentious. J. L. Gaddis, *The Cold War: A New History* (2005) is a reasonably balanced and well-written overview that emphasizes the relationship between the superpowers, the United States and the Soviet Union. O. A. Westad, *The Global Cold War: Third World Interventions and the Making of Our Times* (2005), focuses instead on the global and Third World dimensions of the conflict and their complicated connections to decolonization. I found H. Thomas, *Armed Truce* (1986) helpful. A convenient introduction to decolonization itself is D. Rothermund, *The Routledge Companion to Decolonization* (2006), which presents both a detailed chronology and narrative and thematic analysis. P. Duara, *Decolonization (Rewriting Histories)* (2004) provides significant excerpts from the writings of major leaders of decolonization movements and presents the process from the perspective of the colonized.

Books on "The New World Order" tend to range from the partisan to the paranoid, but A. Slaughter, *A New World Order* (2005) is an original if dense reconceptualization. On the European Union, see J. McCormick, *Understanding the European Union: A Concise Introduction* (3rd., 2005). For a broad examination of the role of war and military power in shaping world orders, see J. Black, *War and the World: Military Power and the Fate of Continents, 1450–2000* (2000).

In war, atrocities breed atrocities. Chinese nationalist soldiers execute fellow countrymen accused of collaboration with the Japanese after the "Rape of Nanjing" in 1937.

IN THIS CHAPTER

THE CONTEXT OF ATROCITIES

THE ENCROACHING STATE

UNPLANNING UTOPIA: THE TURN
TOWARD INDIVIDUALISM

COUNTER-COLONIZATION AND
SOCIAL CHANGE

GLOBALIZATION AND THE WORLD
ECONOMY

CULTURE AND GLOBALIZATION

SECULARISM AND RELIGIOUS
REVIVAL

IN PERSPECTIVE: The Century of
Paradox

A few days before Christmas 1937, John Rabe found women and children, "their eyes big with terror," huddled in his garden in Nanjing. "Their one hope is that I, 'the foreign devil,' will drive the evil spirits away." Rotting corpses were piling up in the streets—torched or hacked to death, with a ferocity Rabe found impossible to understand. The victims of the atrocities could not believe their assailants were fellow human beings. But the perpetrators were Japanese soldiers, not evil spirits. Within a few weeks, more than 250,000 fugitives filled the Safety Zone that Rabe and his European friends—missionaries and businessmen—had set up to protect noncombatants from torture, rape, assault, and murder. The Japanese authorities, while nominally respecting the zone, were "content," Rabe wrote, "to let the refugees starve to death." He had witnessed one of the most intense massacres in history. Japanese soldiers who took part in the slaughter—such as Nagatomi Hakudo, who remembered "smiling proudly as I ... began killing people"—subsequently found their own behavior impossible to understand. But the **Rape of Nanjing**, as the episode was called, was by no means unusual. The most terrifying paradox of the twentieth century was that the advances of the era—in science, in technology, in the spread of education and knowledge, in the increased availability of information, and in progress toward worldwide prosperity—did nothing to avert moral catastrophe.

● ● ● ● ●

The paradox does, however, make a kind of hideous, warped sense. For people who experienced the unprecedented rate of progress in the twentieth century, **utopia** seemed attainable. A world improved or perfected seemed within reach. Massacre was just one way to get there: creating a world without enemies. The social history of the twentieth century is largely a story of failed utopian projects, as chaos overpowered progress.

THE CONTEXT OF ATROCITIES

The twentieth century was a century of atrocities, partly because it was a century of war. War is morally brutalizing. Propaganda, which portrays atrocities as excesses of the other side, often conceals that fact from the public. War blinds people to their enemies' humanity. As we saw in Chapter 28, when the Sino-Japanese War started in 1931, the belligerent peoples were inclined to be prejudiced in each other's favor—to see themselves as fraternally linked. But by the time of the Nanjing outrages, Chinese called the Japanese "evil spirits," while Japanese called the Chinese "insects," "pigs" or—in the case of women enslaved for military brothels— "public urinals." Japanese soldiers, according to their own later accounts, were taught to regard a Chinese victim as "something of rather less value than a dog or a cat."

FOCUS questions

- HOW WERE the atrocities of the twentieth century related to the attempts to create ideal societies or utopias?
- WHY DID the influence of the state increase and then decrease in the twentieth century?
- HOW IS globalization shifting the global patterns of wealth and power?
- HOW HAS migration from former colonies and underdeveloped regions affected social change in the West?
- WHY DID religion become more vigorous in the late twentieth century?

 Transcript from the Rape of Nanjing sentencing, 1947

 Eyewitness account of genocide in Armenia, 1915

The Holocaust. At the Nordhausen concentration camp, the Nazis spent nothing to build and operate the gas chambers they used in other camps. The inmates at Nordhausen—cataloged as too weak or ill to be useful as slave labor—were left to starve to death. In an attempt, apparently, to leave no witnesses, guards massacred the survivors when U.S. troops approached the camp in April 1945. This photograph shows some of the more than 3,000 corpses the Americans found, but a few of the inmates were still alive.
Art Archive/Picture Desk, Inc./Kobal Collection

Along with war, ideological and intercommunal hatreds stimulated inhuman behavior, which war conditions made worse. During the Second World War, Nazis consciously set out to exterminate groups they blamed for the ills of society: Gypsies, homosexuals, and, above all, Jews. Once they had perfected systematic, industrialized methods of genocide, the killers herded millions of Jews into death camps where they gassed them to death. The Nazi vision of utopia also demanded a world from which the physically weak or mentally sick had been gutted out and discarded. No case of genocide matched the Nazi campaign against the Jews, but comparable attempts to exterminate whole peoples continued throughout the century (see Map 29.1). Among attempts to eradicate political and economic communities, Stalin's dictatorship in Russia massacred independent peasants on a scale that equaled or excelled the Nazis', and Mao Zedong in China and Pol Pot in Cambodia also killed millions (see Chapter 28).

No level of civilization, education, or military discipline immunized people against barbarism, whenever war or fear ignited hatred and numbed compassion. During the Second World War, for instance, thousands of normally decent Germans, who prided themselves on their civilized attainments—including artists and intellectuals—helped massacre Jews and other alleged enemies, "deviants," and "subversives" without apparently realizing that they were doing anything wrong. On a lesser scale, soldiers who were raised in democracies and educated in humane values became corrupted. In the Vietnam War, for instance, in March 1968, nice, homey American boys massacred noncombatant peasants, women, and children in the village of Mai Lai, under the influence of fear-induced adrenalin. During war in Iraq in 2004, pictures of American soldiers of both sexes amusing themselves by torturing and sexually abusing Iraqi prisoners, almost all of whom proved to be innocent noncombatants, shocked the world. The perpetrators of these outrages did not even have the excuse of being depraved by combat. They were prison guards. Like some of the Japanese in Nanjing, they actually posed for souvenir photographs, smiling as they performed vicious and degrading acts.

THE ENCROACHING STATE

For most of the century, states seemed to be the likely agents of utopia, because they controlled more power and resources than ever before. Even in the liberal West, which had inherited from the Enlightenment the doctrine of social and economic laissez-faire (see Chapter 22), states took on ever more responsibility, for education, health, and welfare.

Social policy had to regulate increasingly complex and unwieldy societies. Planning—which meant, in effect, a huge surrender of individual liberty to public power and an extension of state interference into private life—seemed an irresistible cure-all. The example of the United States, where federal initiatives helped to dispel the misery of the Great Depression of the 1930s, was encouraging. The influence of John Maynard Keynes (1883–1946), who argued for the "end of laissez-faire," was, for some governments, decisive (see Chapter 28).

The Second World War (1939–1945) also encouraged regimentation and collectivism. The war accustomed citizens to take orders, produce by command, and accept rationing. Canada and Britain acquired command economies almost as heavily regulated as those under fascism and communism. Peace eased but did not end these conditions. In most of Europe, governments nationalized major industries on which the economic infrastructure depended, such as transport, communications, and energy supply. Even noncommunist states applied such measures.

Medicine and schooling illustrate the politicization of social issues. Compulsory, state-funded immunization ended the rapacious diseases that had regularly killed children, including polio, measles, mumps, and rubella. Health education, combined with fiscal measures, changed people's habits. Smoking—a universal relaxation in the early twentieth century—became a pariah activity in many Western countries by 2000. Addictive stimulants and narcotics increased in popularity as they became relatively cheap—including, especially, marijuana and coca-derived substances. But governments took tough countermeasures. Toward the end of the century, public health campaigns targeted alcohol and fatty foods.

States paid doctors and ran hospitals. Except for the United States, all rich countries acquired huge public health establishments. Millions of poor people were liberated from fear of neglect. Life, for the seriously sick, ceased to be a privilege confined only to those who could pay for treatment. But as the costs of medical care spiraled out of control, states struggled to pay the bills.

Meanwhile, education changed. Governments' priorities for schools were concerned with solid citizenship and economic efficiency. Like democracy, education was the cure-all of a former age—transforming dangerous masses into easily influenced, collaborative patriots. Theorists and practitioners in elite institutions pursued grander projects—such as enhancing the pleasure students take in life, acquainting them with their cultural heritage, and stimulating their critical responses. For most children, these remained postponed ideals. In the twentieth century, coarser objectives replaced them: curbing unemployment, manning technology, and keeping young criminals off the streets. More people got more education at greater cost than ever, yet almost everywhere parents and employers complained about the results. In practice, out-of-school education took up the slack: universities, in-work training, and continuing-education programs that enabled people to return to college during their working life.

No part of the world was exempt from "big government," but the United States experienced the phenomenon less than most other countries. The reasons are clear. The world wars left America unscarred. The American economy never suffered from the division of the world into primary and secondary producers. The United States always managed to perform both functions in a big way. Although budgets and bureaucracy grew as the federal government inaugurated public welfare programs, Americans took seriously their perception of their country as the land of the free. This was important in a world that looked increasingly to the United States for models to follow.

For a while, however, the Scandinavian countries were more widely admired, and the system they shared looked like it was becoming the model for the world. Scandinavians favored liberal law-and-order policies with a welfare state and a

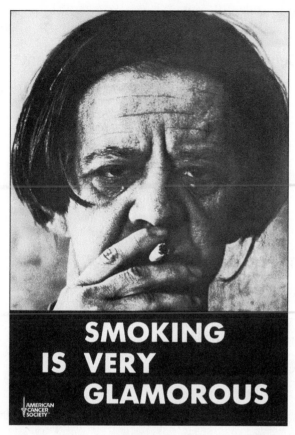

When antismoking campaigns began in the West in the 1970s, they were often privately funded and directed against the tobacco industry's own messages. Increasingly, as evidence accumulated that smoking undermined health, governments took over, combating smoking first with taxation and public health campaigns, then with outright prohibitions on smoking in public. In the mid–twentieth century, smoking was an almost universal indulgence. By the early twenty-first century in the United States, Canada, and parts of Western Europe, smokers had become a persecuted minority, forced to practice their habit furtively and in shame.
Reprinted by the permission of the American Cancer Society, Inc. All Rights Reserved.

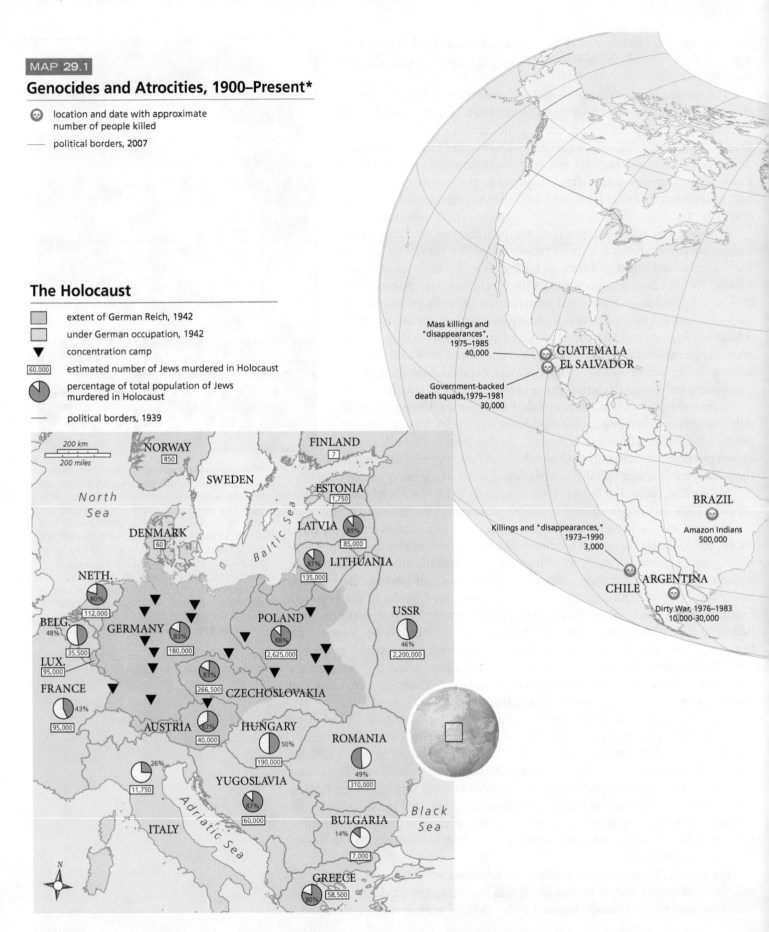

MAP 29.1

Genocides and Atrocities, 1900–Present*

☠ location and date with approximate number of people killed

— political borders, 2007

The Holocaust

▨ extent of German Reich, 1942

☐ under German occupation, 1942

▼ concentration camp

60,000 estimated number of Jews murdered in Holocaust

◐ percentage of total population of Jews murdered in Holocaust

— political borders, 1939

Mass killings and "disappearances", 1975–1985
40,000 — GUATEMALA

Government-backed death squads,1979–1981
30,000 — EL SALVADOR

BRAZIL
Amazon Indians
500,000

Killings and "disappearances," 1973–1990
3,000

CHILE — ARGENTINA
Dirty War, 1976–1983
10,000-30,000

200 km
200 miles

NORWAY 850
FINLAND 7
SWEDEN
ESTONIA 1,750
North Sea
DENMARK 60
Baltic Sea
LATVIA 89% 85,000
LITHUANIA 87% 135,000
NETH. 80% 112,000
GERMANY 83% 180,000
POLAND 88% 2,625,000
USSR 46% 2,200,000
BELG. 48% 35,500
LUX. 95,000
FRANCE 43% 95,000
CZECHOSLOVAKIA 83% 266,500
AUSTRIA 67% 40,000
HUNGARY 50% 190,000
ROMANIA 49% 310,000
26% 11,750
YUGOSLAVIA 87% 60,000
ITALY
Adriatic Sea
BULGARIA 14% 7,000
Black Sea
GREECE 80% 58,500

Forced famine, ethnic cleansing, and political purges, 1924–1953
20,000,000

Nazi extermination of Jews, gyspies, and other "undesirables," 1939–1945
12,000,000

UNION OF SOVIET SOCIALIST REPUBLICS
(to 1993)

Forced famine and purges, 1947–1987
1,600,000

MANCHURIA
biological warfare, 1943
400,000

NORTH KOREA

Central and Eastern Europe

CHINA

Rape of Nanjing, 1937–1938
250,000

Forced famine and political purges under Mao Zedong, 1958–1976
35,000,000

BOSNIA-HERZOGOVINA
ethnic cleansing
1992–1995
200,000

KOSOVO

Armenians in Turkey, 1915–1918
1,500,000

ARMENIA

KURDISTAN

EAST PAKISTAN

Ethnic cleansing, 1971
1,250,000

Systematic rapes and atrocities, 1995–present
3,000

TURKEY

Syria, 1980
25,000 massacred by government forces in Hama

SYRIA

LEBANON   IRAQ

Lebanon, 1982
1,000 Palestinian refugees massacred by Christian militias

Ethnic cleansing and germ warfare, 1980–1999
600,000

INDIA

Massacres associated with partition of India, 1947
500,000

BURMA

VIETNAM
Mai Lai, 1968
350

CAMBODIA
Khmer Rouge, 1975–1979
1,700,000

SUDAN

Darfur, 2003–present
400,000

NIGERIA

Biafra, 1967–1970
1,000,000

CONGO

1900–1908
3,000,000

RWANDA

BURUNDI

Ethnic cleansing, 1994
800,000

Ethnic cleansing, 1972
100,000

INDONESIA
Massacres, 1965–1966
400,000

EAST TIMOR
Ethnic cleansing, 1976–1998
500,000

*This map does not purport to be comprehensive, but to convey the global nature of genocides and other atrocities in the twentieth century.

mixed economy, heavily regulated and centrally planned. But the defects included "Scandisclerosis"—business restrained by regulation—where bureaucracy stifled initiative, and welfare provision cut the risk and zest out of life. Social engineering, however benevolent, did not deliver happiness. In the tawdry utopias modern architecture created (see Chapter 27), citizens recoiled from the dreariness of over-planned societies. By the 1980s, it became apparent to people all over the world that America's relatively underregulated economy was better at delivering prosperity.

Planning failed, not only because human beings love liberty but also because planners' assumptions were naïve. Societies and economies are chaotic systems, where unpredictable effects disrupt expectations. So the four- and five-year plans that were produced almost everywhere at some time up to the 1970s were almost

Terror alert. Secretary of Homeland Security Tom Ridge unveils a color-coded terrorism warning system on March 12, 2002, in Washington, D.C. Ridge said the nation was on yellow alert. The five-level system was in response to public complaints that broad terror alerts issued by the government since the September 11, 2001, attacks raised alarm without providing useful guidance. The vague categories—menacing without being informative—and the scary, angular graphics were part of the U.S. government's proclaimed "War on Terror," which justified the president in assuming, for an indefinite period, exceptional wartime powers of detention and surveillance that violated American traditions of civil liberties.

Excerpt from the 9/11 Commission Report

everywhere discarded. In the 1980s and 1990s, governments—even those nominally socialist—shed nationalized industries and made peace with market forces. The perfectly planned urban projects of the 1960s, which represented the fulfillment of the ideals of rationalist architects—creating functional, egalitarian, technically proficient environments—proved practically uninhabitable. After a generation or so, they had to be demolished. At about the same time, the mixed economies and command economies favored in the postwar period were dismantled, deregulated, and restored to private enterprise. By the mid-1990s, private enterprise was responsible for more than 50 percent of output in Europe, even in formerly communist states. This was a change that swept the world. By 2000, only North Korea remained implacably hostile to the private sector.

This did not mean that bureaucracies ceased to grow. The balance between the public and private sectors seemed impossible to get right. Whenever governments shifted responsibilities to the private sector, some communities and groups got left out of the benefits. Poverty gaps widened. Underclasses bred crime and rebellion. More government spending had to help pay for the consequences. More state welfare agencies appeared to try to remedy the effects. Toward the end of the century, most governments faced rising crime rates. Western governments exploited the threat by exaggerating it. In the early twenty-first century, terrorist-induced alarmism attained new heights, thanks to an entirely exceptional terrorist success that demolished the World Trade Center towers in New York and damaged the Pentagon in Washington, D.C. This was an unrepeatable attack, achieved with minimal weaponry—using razor blades to hijack aircraft that the terrorists employed, in effect, as missiles. Meanwhile, terrorism took its place alongside the hazards of modern life that demanded to be policed at the expense and inconvenience of the public—along with crime, drunkenness, drug addiction, and other antisocial behavior.

In consequence, even after the Cold War had ended, defense and internal security demanded more funds and more personnel. Public spending accounted for 25 percent of gross domestic product (GDP) in the world's seven richest countries in 1965, and 37 percent by 2000. The encroaching state pressed upon civil liberties, as police multiplied and surveillance became intrusive. Nor could governments shed welfare responsibilities, once they had undertaken them, without alienating voters and leaving citizens' health or welfare exposed. State-funded workers' pensions became barely affordable for many countries, because, as we shall see in the next chapter, life expectancy rose sharply in the late twentieth century. But somehow governments had to find ways to pay.

UNPLANNING UTOPIA: THE TURN TOWARD INDIVIDUALISM

In the last quarter or so of the century, the world turned away from social and economic planning, first toward a rival kind of utopianism, represented by confidence in **individualism** and freedom, then—when that seemed to fail, too—toward a search for a third way that would deliver both prosperity and social solidarity.

Marxists' explanations for the shift are worth hearing with respect, because Marxists have a profound need to explain the forms of radicalism with which they are out of sympathy. For them, the shift was economically determined. Like all rev-

◯ MAKING CONNECTIONS ◯

THE ENCROACHING STATE

AREA OF CONCERN →	STATE ACTIONS →	CONSEQUENCES
Medicine	Compulsory state-funded immunization programs; health education; public-health campaigns focusing on smoking, food, drugs; establishment of hospitals, medical care paid for by government	Control and elimination of once virulent diseases (polio, measles, mumps, rubella, etc.); decline of smoking; increase in life expectancy; health care becomes available to poor, elderly, and previously neglected groups
Education	Public funding of education through high school and new emphasis on college education and continuing education through grants, funding	Higher rates of literacy, increased science and technology education leads to innovations, social transformations; unemployment declines as education increases
Welfare	Assistance for children and poor via direct payments, education, and health programs	Increased life expectancy, educational achievement, and employment rates among poor; improved standard of living
National Insurance	Financing of retirement by compulsory contributions from employers, employees	Improved standard of living for elderly; drastic drop in poverty levels compared to pre-1940 era, better health care through specialized medical programs for elderly (e.g., Medicare in United States)

olutions, it accompanied a transition from one means of production to another: from industrial to postindustrial economies, from the energy age to the information age. It is true that the rise of information technology created a major new source of wealth and empowered a new class of businesspeople. At about the same time, growing prosperity increased demand for service industries, which displaced manufacturing as the big money spinners in the global economy, and especially in the richest countries and communities. Individualism, therefore, according to the Marxist argument, arose again as the ideology of a new "knowledge class," which now ran the world: the manipulators of information, who had replaced the puppeteers of production and the manipulators of the state.

The global turn toward conservatism may also have been connected with inflation. Inflation was a marked feature of the twentieth century. At times, it galloped uncontrollably, attaining rates of several thousand percent a year in Germany in 1923, for example, when the central bank deliberately printed as much money as it could. But, at historically unprecedented levels, it was a constant feature of life wherever money circulated. This fact is inseparable from the huge expansion of both resources and demand, which is part of the subject of the next chapter. If, however, one single influence drove prices upward more than anything else, it was governments' spending. As the number of governments grew, thanks to decolonization, and utopian projects gobbled up cash, global money supply got out of control. The situation became intolerable in the 1970s. In October 1973, oil-exporting countries attempted to influence American foreign policy by raising their prices. This triggered unprecedented worldwide inflation. Governments only succeeded in controlling it by curtailing their ambitions, cutting expenditure, reducing borrowing, and reining in the money supply.

Deeper, longer-term influences were also at work. Wartime solidarity was an emergency response for most of the societies that experienced it. It was bound to disappear into the generation gap that opened up in the 1950s and 1960s. As young people grew up without shared memories of wartime, they turned to libertarianism, existentialism, or mere self-indulgence. When postwar economic recovery created well-paid work, the young spent in ways calculated to offend elders and express independence: on fashions, for instance, that were first extrovert, then psychedelic. The growth of the generation gap was measurable in the 1960s. Pop bands discarded their uniforms and grew their hair. Health statistics began to register the effects of sexual permissiveness, with epidemics of sexually transmitted disease and cervical cancer. The contribution or response of the Catholic Church—the world's biggest and most influential Christian communion—is not often acknowledged. But in the Second Vatican Council, which convened in the 1960s, the Church relaxed its rules in favor of freedom. If the Church could not resist individualism, the state would not be able to either.

In extreme cases young rebels in the West turned to violence. Urban guerrilla movements were never numerically strong but they hoped that bombing, kidnapping, and shooting would spread terror, incite repression, and excite revolution. In Europe, they mounted spectacular operations against politicians, celebrities, businessmen, policemen, and service personnel, without provoking the intended reactions. They were most successful in Latin America. In Argentina in the 1970s, they provoked the authorities into horrifying countermeasures, involving at least 15,000 victims of abduction, torture, and murder by the army and police. In Brazil, from 1969 to 1973, the government waged war against a movement that specialized in kidnapping foreign diplomats. Uruguay's almost unbroken democratic tradition was suspended while the army broke the urban guerrillas. Even in these countries, however, outraged youth only succeeded in provoking reaction, never in launching revolution.

The generation gap opened almost as wide in communist countries as in the West. The failed revolutions that marked the coming-of-age of postwar youth in 1968 came nearest to success in Paris and Prague. Student revolutionaries on one side of the Iron Curtain denounced the crisis of capitalism, while those on the other called for a postcommunist "spring" or "thaw." In China, the ruling clique deflected youth rage into the Cultural Revolution (see Chapter 28). The revolutionaries' failures were part of a series of disillusioning experiences. In Russia, China, and other communist countries, no relief followed for the sufferings of ordinary people, no end to the tyranny of small elites. In the rest of the world, capitalism was spreading prosperity, fomenting democracy, winning the approval of working-class voters. The Left switched to soft targets: sexism, racism, elitism, the remnants of colonialism, traditional morality.

China: a Farmer's perspective, 2002

The trends of the next generation, when voters swung right, hair got shorter, fashion rebuttoned, and "moral majorities" found voice, were widely perceived as a reaction against "60s permissiveness." In reality, they represented the continuation in maturity of the projects of the young of the previous decade. Demands for personal freedom, sexual liberation, and existential self-fulfillment when one is young transform themselves naturally, when one acquires economic responsibility and family obligations, into policies of economic laissez-faire and less government. To "roll back the frontiers of the state" became the common project of those who rose to power in the West in the 1980s. Individual gratification—or *fulfillment*—replaced broader codes of conduct and dominated many people's decision making over whether to marry, to divorce, or procreate, or how to occupy one's time.

The triumph of liberation became inseparable from sex in Western minds. The development of reliable methods of contraception, and of fairly reliable methods of protection against sexually transmitted diseases, equipped people to lead undisciplined sex lives. Freedom to choose and change sexual partners proved incompatible, however, with the instinctive human tendency to feel sexual jealousy. Permissive sex

Warped Westernization? Brides and grooms standing in lines as the Unification Church weds 790 couples in a single mass ceremony in the 1970s in Seoul, South Korea. The sect, founded by Sun Myung Moon, and popularly called "the Moonies," was among the most successful new religious cults of the day. Its Christian roots were, at best, remote. Moon, not Jesus, was its messiah, and his followers believed him to be divine. The Unification Church exploited the appeal of Western fashion but suppressed individualism.

subverted some of the collective loyalties on which Western society traditionally relied. Families scrambled by sexual betrayal or boredom became typical. Even in the small nuclear families characteristic of Western society, individualism had a dissolving effect, as family activities diminished, and family members began to eat separately and scatter for entertainment to personal video monitors, computer screens, or friendships outside the household. In the United States, fewer than one child in five was born outside wedlock in 1980. By 2000, the number had risen to a third, and two-fifths of American marriages ended in divorce. What had once been normal—parents and children sharing the same household—became exceptional. Less than a quarter of households in the United States conformed to this pattern by 2000.

In the rapidly urbanizing environments of the world, family stability could not thrive as it had done in the rural communities from which the new town dwellers came. Street children crowded the streets of the developing world, becoming fodder for journalism and films, and the recruits of criminal gangs, warlords' armies, insurgents, guerrillas, and terrorists. The influence of Western lifestyles that movies, music, and broadcasting spread around the world created generation gaps everywhere. In Japan, commentators called the rootless young "new humans"—so profound was their rejection of traditional values and behavior. But the same sort of phenomenon could be observed everywhere. In the Muslim world, the young expected more freedom to choose marriage partners and careers. In Korea and parts of Africa and the Americas, millions joined new religions and cults. Of course, every change set off reactions and, while gaps opened between generations, chasms opened within them.

COUNTER-COLONIZATION AND SOCIAL CHANGE

The world shrank. Ever-cheaper, faster transport technologies meant that long-range migration became possible for many of the poor of the world. The huge and growing disparities in wealth between the West and the rest drew migrants. Wars, tyrannies, and political instability drove them. In the second half of the twentieth century, the population boom in colonial and ex-colonial territories reversed the demographic trends of the past. The long flow of migration from Europe to other parts of the

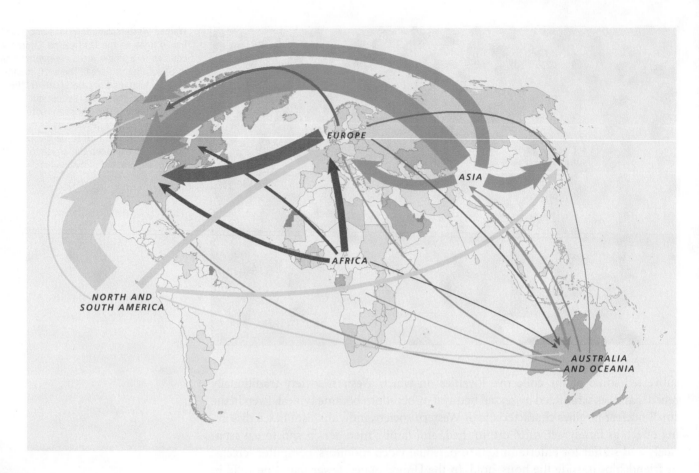

MAP. 29.2

Percentage of Noncitizen Population, ca. 2005

■	greater than 40%
■	18%–40%
■	8%–17%
■	2%–7%
■	less than 2%

International migration trend since 1990 (arrow width reflects number of migrants)

→ North and South American immigration

→ European immigration

→ Asian immigration

→ African immigration

→ Australia and Oceania immigration

world ended. Instead, **counter-colonization** began. Birth rates in the former imperial "mother countries" declined. Labor from the rest of the world filled the gap.

It happened quickly, in step with decolonization (see Chapter 28). In 1948, the first black Jamaicans to arrive in Britain were astonished to see white men doing menial work. Immigrants to Britain from the West Indies numbered tens of thousands by 1954. Those from India reached the same number the following year, and those from Pakistan two years later. By the end of the century, Britain had more than 2 million Muslims, and France had more than 4 million.

The exchange of population was most intense, at first, between former colonies and their European mother countries, but it soon became more general, as migrants shifted from relatively poor, overpopulated parts of the world to relatively rich, underpopulated regions (see Map 29.2). Migrants from Latin America and Puerto Rico became the largest minority in the United States—over 36 million strong by the early twenty-first century. This was a form of counter-colonization, since the United States had seized the territories most affected, California and the Southwest, from Mexico during its empire-building in the nineteenth century (see Chapter 25) and had exercised informal empire over much of Latin America for most of the twentieth century. In other places, the link between imperialist pasts and present immigration patterns was barely discernible. In Italy, Spain, and Scandinavia, most of the immigrants came from outside the old imperial territories. In the Netherlands, the numbers of Moroccans and Turks equaled or exceeded those of immigrants from former Dutch colonies. In Germany, whose overseas empire had disappeared in 1918, and Switzerland, which had never had an empire, Turks formed the biggest category of guest workers. The Philippines had been an American colony but supplied labor—much of it illegal—for many European countries.

Intercommunal tensions took on a new form, as communities of widely differing culture adapted to life alongside each other. One of the most remarkable changes of the late twentieth century was the way racism became socially and politically unacceptable in the West. This was, perhaps, another outcome of the Second World War. The Nazis had been racists, who regarded black people and Jews, in particular, as among the "subhuman" groups suitable for exploitation or extermination. The defeat of Nazism was, therefore, a victory for pluralism. The black and Asian soldiers who fought for Britain, France, and the United States demonstrated their credentials for equality. The decline of racism was also a consequence of scientific progress. The pseudoscience that justified nineteenth-century racism was discredited in the twentieth.

Immigrant community. A woman leaves a Turkish clothing shop in Berlin's Kreuzberg district, which has been called "little Istanbul." In 1961, the governments of West Germany and Turkey signed an agreement that allowed Turks to come to Germany as guest laborers. Many put down roots and never left. Today, Germany's Turkish community numbers over 2.5 million—the biggest minority group in the country.

Nevertheless, it took a long time to convince prejudiced people to accept and respect new circumstances and new science. The United States was the critical battleground, partly because it came to lead the world in just about everything, and partly because, with its huge black minority, it typified the problems. Many of the states had a history of exploiting and persecuting black people, and, in the mid–twentieth century, anti-black prejudice was still widespread. Beginning in the 1940s, African Americans fought a long series of legal cases, backed by political movements that organized demonstrations—especially those Martin Luther King, Jr. (1929–1968), led—and influenced voters to enshrine the principle of equality in the law. Only in the 1960s, thanks to pressure from the federal courts and Presidents Kennedy (1917–1963) and Johnson (1908–1973), did major breakthroughs occur. The federal government obliged reluctant and resisting states to desegregate schools and public amenities and enforce black people's right to vote. By the end of the century, it was still not clear that efforts to redress racial inequalities had gone far enough. Urban ghettoes, pockets of rural poverty, and inequalities in education remained.

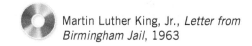

Martin Luther King, Jr., *Letter from Birmingham Jail*, 1963

Abolition in 1961 of the "white Australia" policy, which had restricted immigration to Australia to persons of European descent, was another landmark. Migration to the country became open to people of every hue. South Africa, meanwhile, was a sticking point. Its ruling class was white, and most white South Africans, isolated from the intellectual changes that had discredited racism in most of the rest of the world, clung to a conviction that black and white people should be consigned to exclusive spheres of *separate development*, which in practice supported white privilege. Increasingly, however, it became apparent that it was wiser for white South Africans to conserve their wealth and sacrifice their political power, rather than risk both in a catastrophic revolution. In the early 1990s, South Africa abandoned the policy of separate development. Black people were admitted to equality of rights, and a largely black political party assumed power peacefully, without either victimizing white South Africans or causing economic dislocation.

In response to unresolved tensions, people fell back on a reworked sense of their own identity. New forms of black identity were, perhaps, the most conspicuous example. Early in the twentieth century, Afro-Cuban scholars in newly independent Cuba began to treat black languages, literature, art, and religion on terms of equality with white culture. Coincidentally, white musicians discovered jazz, and

Black consciousness. In November 1970, four "Bush Negro" chiefs from Surinam—direct descendants of maroon communities established in South America in the sixteenth and seventeenth centuries (see Chapter 19)—toured West Africa to great acclaim. Here they are being received as dignitaries by Chief Apétor II of Togo. "The same wind that drove us against our will from Africa," one Bush Negro chief observed during the trip, "has now helped us to find the way back."

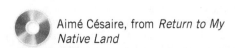
Aimé Césaire, from *Return to My Native Land*

Leopold Senghor on Négritude

white primitivist artists began to imitate African "tribal" art. In 1916, in the United States, the Jamaican immigrant Marcus Garvey launched the slogan, "Africa for the black peoples of the world." The idea that black culture embodied values superior to those of white culture emerged during the 1920s and spread wherever black people lived. In French West Africa in the 1930s, Aimé Césaire and Léon Damas became brilliant spokesmen for the black self-pride they called **Négritude**.

Counter-colonization changed the prevailing direction of cultural exchange. By the 1990s, in Leicester—the midmost city in England— people could listen to 40 hours a week of broadcasts in Gujerati, an Indian language. Australian public broadcasting services operated in 78 languages. Vietnamese and North African restaurants abounded in Paris. Indian and Indonesian dishes had joined the national cuisines of Britain and Holland, respectively.

But the spread of Asian influences in Westerners' tastes and thoughts also owed a lot to Western self-reevaluations. Under the weight of guilt about imperialism, postcolonial Westerners felt their own need for liberation from the legacy of the past. In the 1960s, travel to India became a compulsive fashion for Western intellectuals, along with Indian philosophy, mystical practices, music, and food. Political protesters in European and American streets in the same decade brandished copies of "little red books" containing thoughts of Mao Zedong. These fads waned, but Japanese, Chinese, and Indian art and thought became more important in the West. Zen became a widely revered intellectual tradition in the West. Buddhism, which had never attained the breadth of appeal of Christianity and Islam, began to attract converts in every clime. Black music and art, which had begun to influence the cultural mainstream in America and Europe in the earliest years of the century, captured the admiration of the white world.

The prevailing values of the late twentieth century were appropriate to a postcolonial, multicultural, pluralistic era. The fragility of life in a crowded, shrinking world and a global village encouraged or demanded multiple perspectives, as neighbors adopted or sampled each other's points of view. Hierarchies of value had to be avoided, not because they are false but because they led to conflict. Relativism—the doctrine that each culture and even individuals, can choose appropriate norms and, therefore, that no single set of norms is universally applicable (see Chapter 27)—displaced Westerners' confidence in their own superiority.

This doctrine, however, made it hard to argue for the universality of human rights. It also caused tension between cultural relativism and social norms. Conflicts arose when migrants brought with them cultural practices and values that conflicted with the laws of their new homelands. In Islamic countries increasingly influenced by Sharia, or Islamic law, for instance, Westerners found that they could be prosecuted for using alcohol or for not respecting traditional codes of dress and comportment for women. In the West, immigrants could not be allowed to continue traditional practices, such as female circumcision among African communities, or polygamy, or the marriage of minors. "Asian values" justified the use of the criminal law in, for example, Malaysia and Singapore, against practices the West tolerated, such as homosexuality and recreational drugs.

Equality before the law was so ingrained in the West that it would have been unthinkable to allow people of different cultural backgrounds to be treated separately in the courts or to be assigned separate jurisdictions, as had been usual, for instance, in the Middle Ages or under the Ottoman Empire. Most countries legislated for everyone to share the same civil rights, regardless of cultural background. Yet in practice, there were always cases of discrimination.

The status of women provoked some of the deepest difficulties. In 1900, no one expected different cultures to treat women the same. In the West, attention was riveted on the right to vote. In the Islamic world, controversy centered on the rights of women in the home: to choose their husbands, for instance, or to equality with men under marriage law and in property rights. The First World War (1914–1918), however, launched a profound revolution in the role of women in Western society. In practice, women were left to take command of their lives while so many men were away fighting. The dead of the war left gaps that societies were refashioned to fill. Meritocracies replaced hereditary aristocracies in power. Women replaced men in the workplace. Before the war, only a few marginal countries gave women the vote. After it, Russia, Germany, the United States, Britain, and most other Western countries enfranchised women. So did Japan and Turkey.

Women had to want to break out of domesticity, but it was not necessarily in their interests to do so. Many of those who competed with men suffered for it. To succeed, they had either to be *superwomen*—the term became current in the 1980s for a professional or working woman who managed her life so well that she could work outside the home and also discharge the traditional roles of wife and mother within it—or accept subordination. Although legislation to equalize opportunities became normal in the West, it was never fully effective. Many women accepted lower wages or worse contractual terms than men in corresponding jobs, so that they could move in and out of work as their family responsibilities demanded. Some workplaces, especially in traditional male preserves, such as the armed forces, the police, the construction industry, and industrial and financial boardrooms, had jock cultures that made it hard for women to fit. Nevertheless, the cause of equality for women became one to which all Western governments committed, at least in theory.

Westerners expected people in other cultures to reevaluate women's roles in the same way. This did not seem unattainable: Israel, India, Sri Lanka, the Philippines, Nicaragua, Dominica, Argentina, and even Muslim countries—Pakistan, Turkey, Indonesia, Bangladesh—all had female presidents or prime ministers between 1960 and 2000. But these were exceptional cases, and restraints on women's freedom or status remained in much of the world. China did not allow women to marry until they were 20 years old, and the growing preponderance of male over female children in China suggests that more infant girls than boys were

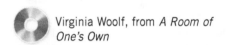

Virginia Woolf, from *A Room of One's Own*

The first woman to be elected an African head of state, President Ellen Johnston-Sirleaf of Liberia, photographed in November 2005 just after her victory. Johnston gave a new twist to feminist arguments in favor of political empowerment for women by suggesting that women had special nurturing and peacemaking talents that made them more suited to leadership in the modern world than men.

Timeline of Women's Suffrage

New Zealand	1893
Australia	1902
Finland	1906
Norway	1913
Denmark, Iceland	1915
Soviet Union	1917
Canada, Germany, Austria	1918
Poland, Czechoslovakia	1919
United States, Hungary	1920
Mongolia	1924
United Kingdom	1928
Turkey	1930
Spain	1931
Brazil	1932
Indonesia	1941
France	1944
Italy	1945
China, India	1949
Mexico	1953
Kenya	1963
Switzerland	1971
South Africa	1994
Kuwait	2005

http://www.nzhistory.net.nz/politics/suffrage-worldtimeline

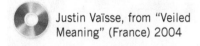

Justin Vaïsse, from "Veiled Meaning" (France) 2004

killed or aborted. It is hard to imagine fiercer discrimination than that. Opponents in Morocco and Iran interpreted government programs to establish female equality of employment and rights of freedom of marriage as infringements of parental rights and threats to the stability of home life. Female circumcision, a tradition in many African cultures, offended Western sensibilities. Women's educational opportunities remained restricted in much of the world outside the West, especially in rural areas. In India 87 percent of rural women were classed as illiterate in 2000. The corresponding figure for Bangladesh was 97 percent.

Problems associated with the status of women became acute with the mingling of cultures that accompanied the global migrations of the late twentieth century. Conflicts arose over arranged marriages and the rights of divorcees. In awarding custody of children, for example, Western courts tended to favor mothers, Islamic courts fathers. The disputes that best illustrate the difficulty of resolving conflicts between normative laws and cultural diversity concerned the issue of appropriate dress for women and girls. In some Muslim cultures, traditions of modesty enjoined garments for women that concealed most of the body and the whole of the face from male eyes. To some Westerners, these rules seemed to be male-imposed infringements on female liberty—although many women supported them. The potential for conflict with Western laws arose in schools, where these traditional Muslim dress codes conflicted with school regulations. In France, in the early twenty-first century, the courts banned Muslim girls from wearing headscarves over their heads, on the grounds that such scarves were religious symbols, incompatible with the secular nature of the French Republic.

Such disputes raised fundamental questions about the future of the world. The new multiracial societies in the West posed unprecedented problems. Existing populations became prey to alarmism about the adulteration of their identities or their cultures. Debate raged over whether integration in the host society—adopting its values, language, dress, manners, food, and even, perhaps, religion—best served new immigrants; or whether **multiculturalism** could work, in which people of divergent cultures agreed on a few core values, such as allegiance to the state and deference to democracy. Both responses had their disadvantages. Integration imposed on people's freedom. Multiculturalism, according to its opponents, created ghettoes and opened dangerous gaps in mutual understanding between neighboring communities. As the numbers of migrants began to reach critical thresholds, most Western governments began to encourage integration and tightened immigration controls as they lost confidence that multiculturalism could keep the peace. The Netherlands required immigrants to learn Dutch and submit to citizenship tests. Britain introduced allegiance tests. In the twenty-first century, multiculturalism was beginning to look like another utopian dream in danger of being discarded.

GLOBALIZATION AND THE WORLD ECONOMY

Not only were cultures getting more intermingled, but so were economies. In the last quarter of the century, in line with the worldwide withdrawal of the state from economic regulation, and the relaxation of controls on cross-border trade, businesses were able to operate internationally with greater freedom than ever before.

The growing interdependence of regional and national economies promoted peace, increased prosperity, and stimulated cultural exchange. The benefits of this **globalization**, however, were unevenly distributed. Relatively few vast business corporations, most of them centered in the United States, handled a disproportionate amount of the world's economic activity, shunting assets around the world, evading regulation by individual governments (see Map 29.3). Powerful countries—the United States above all—were able to demand free trade where it suited them but retain protective tariffs or subsidies for businesses they favored. To some extent, globalization perpetuated the old colonial pattern of the world economy—peasants and sweated labor in poor countries supplied rich ones with cheap goods, twisting the poverty gap into a poverty spiral.

Confrontation. Pim Fortuyn (1948–2002) confronts protestors in Rotterdam during elections for the Dutch parliament. Fortuyn's Livable Netherlands Party had a distinctly anti-immigration agenda. Fortuyn was assassinated by a white Dutch environmentalist in May 2002, shortly after this photo was taken. The slogan, "Stop the Dutch Haider," alludes to Jurgen Haider of Austria, another populist politician who successfully campaigned for tough immigration controls. The way Fortuyn caresses the demonstrator was part of his public image. He was a homosexual who appeared on campaign with Moroccan boys as evidence that his opposition to immigration was not based on racial discrimination.

Such defects, however, could probably be fixed. Some countries in Asia demonstrated that well-run communities could achieve prosperity and that globalization could make them as rich as the West.

Japan's was the exemplary case. After its defeat in 1945, Japan was ready for a makeover. No other country endured the A-bomb. But the Japanese, who live over seismic faults on typhoon-lashed coasts, are used to rebuilding after disaster. The psychological problems were harder to cope with. Japanese felt the shame of defeat more deeply than people of other cultures. Never before had their country surrendered or submitted to occupation. The emperor renounced his divinity. The people disclaimed superiority over other races and meekly accepted an American formula to remake their country into a democracy.

The abandonment of militarism helped conserve investment for industry. The big corporations—which the Americans had abolished—returned in the 1950s and 1960s. Workers sacrificed an independent social life and became infused with corporate loyalty. This was not Western-style capitalism, but it worked. In 1969, Japan overtook Germany to become the world's second biggest national economy. In the 1970s, despite the high price of oil, Japan caught up with the average European gross national product per capita. In 1985, Japan became the world's biggest foreign investor. Growth faltered toward the end of the century, but Japan remained in the premier league of world economic powers, with the highest per capita income in the world.

Other economies in Asia followed Japan toward European or North American levels of prosperity. In South Korea in the 1960s, collaboration between governments and huge corporations launched spectacular economic growth: 9 percent a year, on average, over the following three decades. The country became one of the world's major manufacturers of cars and electronic gadgets. South Koreans demonstrated that a country could industrialize itself out of poverty. By 2000, Japan and South Korea together—countries with only 3 percent of the world's population—accounted for 15 percent of its income and 10 percent of its trade.

Other "tiger" economies leaped in the same direction. The mid to late 1960s and early 1970s were bonanza years in southeast Asia because American military involvement in Vietnam created a huge demand for supplies, leisure facilities for troops, and all the infrastructure of a wartime baseline. Not everyone benefited. Cambodia, on Vietnam's flank, got sucked into the conflict and began a long, destructive civil war. But other neighbors were drenched in American investment. The biggest gainers were the already industrialized or industrializing economies of

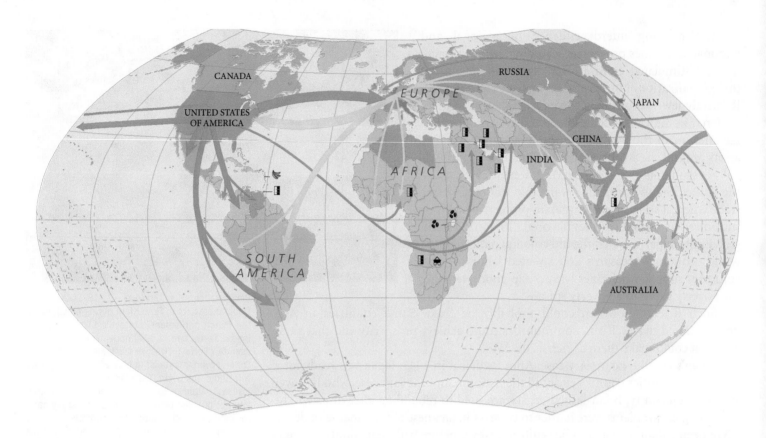

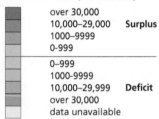

MAP 29.3

International Trade Flows, ca. 2004

Direct investment
(arrow width reflects level of investment)

→ from USA

→ from Europe

→ from Japan

Examples of countries reliant on a single export

🍌 bananas

☕ coffee

🛢 oil/petroleum

🔩 copper

Balance of trade (millions US$)

over 30,000	
10,000–29,000	**Surplus**
1000–9999	
0–999	
0–999	
1000–9999	
10,000–29,999	**Deficit**
over 30,000	
data unavailable	

MAP EXPLORATION

www.prenhall.com/armesto_maps

Japan, South Korea, Hong Kong, and Taiwan. In the mid-1960s, Singapore followed the same path. The accelerating trade of these tiger economies generated potential for investment all around the world. Most of their surplus money, however, went on projects around the shores of the Pacific. By 1987, the Pacific had displaced the Atlantic as the world's major arena of commerce. Communities and investments moved around the Pacific's shores with increasing ease and freedom.

Meanwhile, Latin American countries struggled to play catch-up with the rest of the West. The game began after the global economic crisis of the 1930s, when governments in Mexico, Argentina, and Brazil saw selective industrialization as a solution to the collapse of markets for their primary produce. As these policies spread through the continent, their effects proved mixed. Native industries continued to rely on machinery imported from North America and Europe. The falling prices of basic commodities made it hard for Latin American economies to accumulate capital to reinvest in industry. Mechanization increased unemployment. In the 1960s and 1970s, partly in response to these problems, authoritarian regimes took over most of the region. In most cases, authoritarian rule only protracted the economic disappointments, straining some countries' relations with trading partners elsewhere in the world, subjecting others to new forms of dependency on United States and European corporate allies and creditors. The military junta that took over Argentina in 1976, for instance, proclaimed Argentina's commitment to "the Western and Christian world" but alienated allies by repression at home and military adventurism abroad. For most Latin Americans, the period was impoverishing. Between 1980 and 1987, average personal income fell in 22 countries in the region. In Peru and Argentina, people were poorer on average in 1986 than they had been in 1970. Even Mexico, which stayed ostensibly democratic and avoided the worst of the region's economic problems, only survived by incurring massive debts—and defaulting on them in 1982.

Shanghai in the early twenty-first century emblemized China's promise and perils. Skyscrapers symbolized the stunning growth rates that enabled China to aim for superpower status and potentially resume its normal place as the world's richest country. The price was pollution and gaping disparities in wealth.

Still, the more enmeshed the global economy got, the more opportunities multiplied. More countries, more people were able to squeeze a share of the benefits. China's was the most spectacular case. The Chinese economy registered annual growth rates of nearly 10 percent in the 1990s and the early twenty-first century—enough, if those rates could be sustained, to enable China's economy to overtake that of the United States as the world's biggest by 2020. By 2004, more than 400 of the world's 500 biggest companies had branches or subsidiaries in China, overwhelmingly concentrated in regions bordering the Pacific. India became a leading player in high-tech industries, where many multinational companies located centers of computer manufacture and telecommunications services. In the 1980s, a dose of Chicago-style economics—the doctrine, advocated by economists at the University of Chicago, that low taxes and light regulation could unleash economic success—turned the Chile of the military dictator Augusto Pinochet into a prosperous country with a large middle class. Integration in the global economy shored up South Africa's delicate new democracy in the 1990s and helped to provide a capital-starved economy with the wealth the country needed to start rebuilding after centuries of injustice. Brazil, meanwhile, which had already become a major manufacturing economy with a lively high-tech sector, achieved, in the early twenty-first century, levels of growth not far short of China's. Even some economies that remained tied to primary production generated huge profits that their governments could invest in global markets. The oil-exporting countries on the Arabian shore of the Persian Gulf became major players in the global economy.

China: "A Harmonious Society," 2006

Even economists who acknowledged the benefits of globalization were prey to doubts about its stability. Some systems theorists argued that the more complex the world economy grew, the more fragile it would become, because, in an interdependent system, a local failure could cause widespread disruption. In fact the opposite happened. Early in the twentieth century, a local economic failure, such as the American stock market crash of 1929, could plunge much of the world into depression. In the 1980s and 1990s, markets reacted nervously to similar collapses of major stock markets in 1987, of the British currency in 1992, of the banking system in Argentina in 1999, and of the oil-pricing system and major commodity markets at irregular intervals. But none of these disasters had uncontrollable repercussions. Perhaps the greatest panic of all ensued in 2001, when terrorists destroyed the

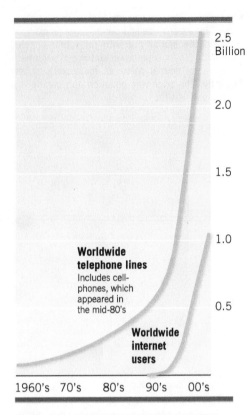

2.5 Billion

2.0

1.5

1.0

Worldwide telephone lines
Includes cell-phones, which appeared in the mid-80's

0.5

Worldwide internet users

1960's 70's 80's 90's 00's

FIGURE 29.1 TELEPHONE LINES AND INTERNET USERS, CA. 1960–2000
Worldwatch Institute, www.worldwatch.org

Pope John Paul II on consumerism, from *Centesimus Annus*

World Trade Center in New York. The economic consequences were slight. Even the firms worst hit by the attack were back at work within days. In practice, the globalized economy could endure terrible dislocations. Complexity made the system more robust, because multiple interconnections enabled it to bypass failures.

CULTURE AND GLOBALIZATION

Information traveled globally with even more freedom than trade. In 1971, the world's first microprocessor appeared. In combination with radio transmission, it made virtually every item of information from every part of the world universally accessible. There were over 2.5 billion telephones in the world by 2000 and over 500 million computers (see Figure 29.1).

The way people handled information changed. Miniaturization boosted individualism and enabled the like-minded to form cyberspace communities. The trend was unstoppable. China, for instance, tried to control Internet access, especially after demonstrators coordinated their activities by computer in what almost turned into a revolution in 1989. But China had 30 million Internet users by 2000. Worldwide censorship became difficult—at least for a while. But major servers have begun to impose filters.

The surfeit of data drove some consumers into narrow-minded retreat. Some cyber communities became cyber ghettoes, in which people spent their time with minds closed to the rest of the Web. Increasing information did not necessarily increase knowledge. Wider literacy helped. By 2000, just about everyone in the world was familiar with writing, and probably about 85 percent of them could make at least some use of it. But most consumers used the new technology for trivial entertainments rather than self-education. Professional intellectuals succumbed to specialization, partly in response to the proliferation of information. Students became reliant on data culled from the Internet, which changed constantly and was beyond verification. Cutting and pasting became a new form of literary activity, in which no text was stable and no work genuinely original. **Virtual reality** excited fears it would spawn a generation of "nerds"—introverted sociopaths who communed only with their computers.

Still, the Internet promoted globalization in the strongest sense of the word: the global spread of uniform culture. In a plural world, this was not a threat to cultural diversity, though people often perceived it as such. If there ever were to be a global culture, it would probably not replace diversity, but supplement it. What people really feared was global Americanization, the triumph of American popular culture, commonly called "McDonaldization" and "Coca-Cola colonialism" after two of the prevalent products of American industry. Hamburgers and sodas symbolized American cultural influence, because the world associated American lifestyles with what became the nearest thing to a common culture the world possessed: consumerism.

Consumerism is best defined as a system of values that puts the consumption and possession of consumer goods at or near the top of social values—as high as or higher than social obligations, spiritual fulfillment, or moral qualities. The best index of the growing importance of consumerism in the twentieth century is the sheer scale of consumption, which is among the subjects of Chapter 30. As we shall see, the late twentieth-century world was a battleground of consumerism against environmentalism. Consumerism nearly always won the battles. Products that best measure consumerism are those that can fairly be described as a waste of money. Consumption of tobacco, alcohol, and more addictive drugs makes the case. First on grounds of morality, then—as the century wore on and morality became unfashionable—on grounds of health, governments struggled to contain these extreme forms of consumerism. Nonetheless, by 2000, the alcohol industry world-wide turned over $252 billion annually, tobacco $204 billion. The term *drugs* is harder to define and the statistics fuzzier, but by the most widely respected esti-mates, the drug trade was worth about $150 billion by 2000, of which about $60 billion was spent in the United States.

Even those who condemned American cultural influence as trivial, trashy, and corrosive of traditional cultures found it hard to resist. American businesses dom-inated the major new media—cinema, television, and the Internet. So American images proliferated around the world (although the Indian film industry was beginning to shape up as a potential rival). Often those onlookers became admir-ers. The magnetism of American higher education was an important ingredient of America's soft power. American institutions educated a disproportionate number of the world's elites.

The most pervasive index of the global appeal of American culture was the adoption of American English as the universal language of business, politics, sci-ence, and study. This was a major reversal in the history of culture. While imperial, sacred, or trading languages had sometimes displaced or extinguished other tongues, never before had a single language achieved the role of a global common tongue. Mandarin Chinese, Spanish, and Portuguese also showed some potential. The extinction of minority languages became a conservation problem.

SECULARISM AND RELIGIOUS REVIVAL

Most of the really powerful utopian visions of the twentieth century were irreli-gious, even antireligious. Utopians who put their faith in the state often did so in conscious revulsion from religious establishments, which had failed to enhance virtue or spread welfare or justice. Communists usually regarded atheism as part of their own creed. Nazis wanted to sweep away the Church. Social planning relied for its appeal on a scientistic notion: that human agency alone could change societies like chemi-cals in a lab, and achieve predictable results, with no need for appeals to Providence or grace. The world—from these perspectives—would be better off without religion, which had caused wars, retarded sci-ence, and stifled reason with dogma. Religion was one of the first casualties of the skepticism that, as we saw in Chapter 27, was a major twentieth-century theme.

For most of the century, the demise of religion was widely fore-cast. The decline of churchgoing in the West, which lasted in America until the 1960s and still prevails in Western Europe and Canada, seemed to suggest that prosperity would erode faith. Religion had to face serious challenges and sometimes ferocious persecution from hostile political ideologies.

In response to secularism, however, people with religious identi-ties felt them more fiercely. In Egypt, for instance, the number of mosques increased nearly twice as fast as the population under the secular-minded rulers of the second half of the twentieth century. The most striking case occurred in Iran, where Shah Mohammad Reza Pahlavi (r. 1941–1979) imposed secularization on a reluctant country in the 1960s. He claimed to be ruling people who "resembled

Selling dreams. Garish signs of Western economic takeover and cultural invasion deface a traditional building on a prime commercial site in New Delhi, while child workers hope to make a few pennies by selling balloons to kids rich enough to feast on the fatty carbohydrates associated (in India) with U.S. fast-food businesses.

Globalization

1950s	Japan spends 2 percent of GDP on defense
1950s and 1960s	Big corporations return to Japanese economy
1960–1967	Japanese incomes double
1960s	Asian "tigers" (Japan, South Korea, Hong Kong, and Singapore) begin rapid eco-nomic ascent
1971	World's first microprocessor
1980–1987	Incomes fall in most Latin American nations
1982	Mexico defaults on national debt
1985	Japan becomes world's biggest foreign investor
1989	Tiananmen Square protests in China
1990s	China's economy grows at annual rate of almost 10 percent
Late 1990s	Economies of India and Brazil grow at rapid rate
1995	World Trade Organization (WTO) created
2000	30 million Internet users in China
2001	Terrorist attack on World Trade Center and Pentagon

Revolution's patron saint. After his death in 1989, Ayatollah Ruhollah Khomeini continued to influence Iranian politics. His shrine outside Tehran became a place of pilgrimage for followers who wanted to perpetuate Islamic revolution, like the women photographed here in 2001 on the twelfth anniversary of his death. His cult helped to mobilize voters for his unusual combination of agendas—communitarian, religious, populist, nationalist—and helped slow down and, at times, halt Iran's hesitant return to secular priorities and normal relations with the rest of the world.

Abu'l 'Ala Mawdudi, on the scope and purpose of the Islamic state

Americans" in the "France of Asia." He ignored the Muslim clergy. He seized religious endowments without compensation to redistribute the land among peasants. He also made himself unpopular in other ways—especially by spending on the armed services rather than on social welfare—but he lost his throne by alienating religious sensibilities.

A Shiite cleric, Ayatollah Ruhollah Khomeini (1900–1989) gradually emerged as the voice of outraged Islam. Broadcasting from exile, he attracted millions of followers by his incorruptibility and self-righteousness. The Shah's regime was, he proclaimed, literally the work of the devil and must be destroyed. Khomeini called for an Islamic republic—a welfare state that would enrich all its faithful and in which all the necessities of life would be free. In 1979, he inspired a revolution. His followers filled the streets, deserted the army, and paralyzed the government. The Shah went into exile. An Islamic republic dominated by Shiite clergy replaced the ancient Iranian monarchy. The Iranian experiment, which followed an Islamist experiment in Pakistan in 1977, encouraged similar movements all over the Islamic world.

Religion did decline in Western Europe. But in much of the rest of the world, traditional religion proved ineradicable, surviving, strengthened by persecution, after all the hostile ideologies collapsed. Far from outbidding religion, prosperity made spirituality marketable. In the United States, the world's richest country, people sought relief from materialism in religion. Yet religion never lost its appeal to the victims of poverty, for whom rewards in the next world compensated for being underprivileged here and now. Christian and Muslim propagandists found huge audiences in sub-Saharan Africa.

Traditional religions, especially Roman Catholicism, Islam, radical forms of Christianity, and Lamaist Buddhism, self-reformed successfully to confront secularism and widen their global appeal. The main challenge to traditional religions came not from atheism or secularism but from new religions. Most of these could be characterized as cults or folksy superstitions, or as personal religions concocted by individuals who did not see themselves as belonging in any particular communion but who picked and mixed from various traditions to create a menu of their own choice, like an Internet-surfing student plagiarizing a paper with the cut-and-paste facility.

Twentieth-century conditions favored cults in cities full of rootless, spiritually uneducated constituencies with excited expectations. Some fashions in belief were weird. Astrology was the starting point of the New Age movement, which, beginning in the 1960s, proclaimed the "dawning of the Age of Aquarius"—the doctrine that the astral prominence of the constellation Pisces is gradually being replaced, after about 2,000 years, with world-transforming effects. It is hard to believe that anyone could have taken such a doctrine seriously—but its success indicated how uneasy people felt. Toward the end of the century, sects predicting the end of the world achieved a brief vogue—even though the year 2000 had no particular significance, since our system of numbering years is purely arbitrary. Surprisingly, skepticism favored the proliferation of weird beliefs because, as the English writer G. K. Chesterton (1874–1936) reputedly said, "When people cease to believe in something, they do not believe in nothing; they believe in anything."

The biggest growth point was the kind of religion called **fundamentalist**. It started in a Protestant seminary in Princeton, New Jersey, in the early twentieth century in reaction to critical readings of the Bible. The idea was that the Bible contains fundamental truths that cannot be questioned by critical inquiry or scientific evidence. The name "fundamentalism" has been applied retrospectively to a similar doctrine, traditional in Islam, about the Quran. It can arise in the context of any religion that has a founding text or holy scripture. Karen Armstrong—one of the foremost authorities on the subject—sees fundamentalism as modern: scientific or pseudoscientific because it reduces religion to matters of undeniable fact. Apart from the bleakness of modernity, fundamentalism's other parent is fear: that the end of the world is imminent, of *Great Satans* (Iranian clerics' term for the United States and the West), of chaos, and above all, of the unfamiliar. To fundamentalists, all difference is subversive. These facts help to explain why fundamentalism arose in the modern world and has never lost its appeal. By 2000, fundamentalisms in Islam and Christianity, taken together, constituted the biggest movement in the world.

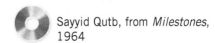

Sayyid Qutb, from *Milestones,* 1964

All fundamentalist movements are different but can be identified by the features they share: militancy, hostility to pluralism, and a determination to confuse politics with religion. Fundamentalists are self-cast as warriors against secularism. Yet, in practice, most fundamentalists are pleasant, ordinary people, who make their compromises with the world and leave their religion—as most people do—at the door of their church or mosque. The militant minorities among them, meanwhile, cause trouble by declaring war on society. Some sects, with their crushing effects on individual identity, their ethic of obedience, their paranoid habits, and their campaigns of hatred or violence, behaved in frightening ways like the early fascist cells.

When they got power, fundamentalists tended to treat people of other traditions with hostility. Bahais, Christians, Sunni Muslims, and Jews all suffered discrimination and persecution in Khomeini's Iran. In Afghanistan in the 1990s, the Islamic Taliban regime vandalized Buddhist monuments, smashed ancient art in the museums, suppressed Christian worship, ordered women out of school, and slaughtered homosexuals—of whom there were many since homosexual practice was a long-standing Afghan tradition. Saudi Arabia"s "religious police" imposed a rigid and uncompromising form of Islamic law even on non-Muslims. When a Christian fundamentalist general took power in Guatemala in 1982, the army persecuted Catholic churchmen and women for supposedly helping Native American rebels. Where Islamic fundamentalists took power nationally or locally, they usually imposed interpretations of Islamic law that often had dire consequences for women, whose freedoms were restricted, and for people who led supposedly irregular sex lives, who were liable to be put to death. Christian fundamentalists in the United States advocated laws to ban practices they considered objectionable on religious grounds, including homosexuality, the teaching of evolution, sex education in public schools, contraception, and abortion. Religious fundamentalism rarely managed to retain power for long, or to remain unseduced by the need for political compromise, but it continued to grow as a social movement, even when its political aspirations were frustrated or diluted.

Fundamentalism was one form of the religious response to secularism. Another was to imitate the secularists—to beat them at their own game. Traditional religions could do this by showing that they could make a difference to lives in the here and now, as well as in the hereafter, by organizing social services for worshippers and aid programs for the poor. New religions could try an alternative strategy. In developed countries, a lot of the new religion of the late twentieth century looked suspiciously like secularism—or even consumerism—in disguise. In South Korea, the Full Gospel Church promised its followers health and prosperity: bounding riches and bouncing bodies. In Japan, Soka Gakkai was a Buddhist prosperity cult that founded its own political party and spread to Europe and America. American churches increased their congregations by imitating the familiar world of trivial, middle-class lives, with coffee parties, muzak, casual clothes, and undemanding moral prescriptions. In Orange County, California, worshippers in the Crystal Cathedral believed that business success was a mark of divine election.

Some new religions were essentially healing ministries—offering a form of alternative therapy for a health-obsessed age in which, in the absence of shared moral values, health was the only commonly acknowledged good. Other new religious movements of the period were more political. The supposedly Buddhist Aum Shinrikyo cult in Japan waged war on the rest of society. A fashionable cult known as Scientology, which called itself a church, was instead classed as a political organization or as a business in many countries. The **Liberation Theology** movement in Latin America was concerned with justice for the poor and oppressed, arguing that sin was not just individual moral failure but also a structural feature of capitalist society.

IN PERSPECTIVE: The Century of Paradox

Traditions had to struggle to survive the quickening pace of change, which made social and political relationships unrecognizable to successive generations and bewildering to those whose lives spanned the transformations. Science drove change, inspiring new technology, reforging how people saw the world. The relentless growth of global population, which wars did not interrupt, increased the pressure on the world's resources. But, even more than population growth, spiraling desire—consumerism, as it came to be called, lust for abundance, impatience to enjoy the rewards of economic growth—made people exploit the planet with increasing ruthlessness.

Most of history had favored unitary states, with one religion, ethnicity, and identity. Large empires have always been multicultural, but they have usually had a dominant culture, alongside which others are, at best, tolerated. In the twentieth century, this would no longer do. The aftermath of the era of global empires, the range and intensity of migrations, the progress of ideas of racial equality, the multiplication of religions, and the large-scale redrawing of state boundaries made the toleration of diversity essential to the peace of most states. Those states that rejected toleration faced traumatic periods of "ethnic cleansing."

Vaclav Havel, "The Need for Transcendence in the Postmodern World"

An execution by guillotine in France in 1929. Revolutionary France began executing people by guillotine in 1792. The guillotine was supposed to be an efficient and humane death-machine because it killed quickly with a single blow without torture. But during the Revolution, it made a horrible spectacle of mass executions and became a symbol not of the Enlightenment but of barbarity. France continued to guillotine condemned criminals until 1977. Today, the laws of France, like those of almost every Western country, acknowledge that even criminals have basic human rights, of which the most fundamental is the right to live.

What was true of individual states was true of the entire world. "Shrinkage" brought peoples and cultures into unprecedented proximity. The peace and future prosperity of the world at the end of the century demanded an effort to accommodate religions, languages, ethnicities, communal identities, versions of history, and value systems in a single global community. Isaiah Berlin (1909–1997) explained, "There is a plurality of values which men can and do seek. . . . And . . . if a man pursues one of these values, I, who do not, am able to understand why he pursues it or what it would be like, in his circumstances, for me to be induced to pursue it. Hence the possibility of human understanding." Pluralism differs from cultural relativism. It does not say, for instance, that all cultures can be accommodated. One might exclude Nazism, say, or cannibalism. It leaves open the possibility of peaceful argument about which culture, if any, is best. It claims, in Berlin's words, "that the multiple values are objective, part of the essence of humanity, rather than arbitrary creations of men's subjective fancies." In a world where globalization made most historic communities defensive about their own cultures, it has been difficult to persuade them to coexist peacefully with the contrasting cultures of their neighbors. Still, pluralism is the only truly uniform interest that all the world's peoples have in common.

Human rights provided the key test of whether universal values could thrive in a plural world. Even in the United States, where public advocacy of human rights was as strong as anywhere, presidents seemed willing to ignore or circumvent them (see Chapter 28).

CHRONOLOGY

1933–1935	Restrictions placed on German Jews
December 1937	Rape of Nanjing
1939–1945	World War II
1939–1945	Holocaust
1950s	Japans spends 2 percent of GDP on defense
1950s and 1960s	Big corporations return to Japanese economy; generation gap emerges; civil rights movement in the United States
1960s	Second Vatican Council; Asian "tigers" (Japan, South Korea, Hong Kong, and Singapore) begin rapid economic ascent
1960–1967	Japanese incomes double
1961–1973	U.S. involvement in Vietnam War
1965	Public spending accounts for 25 percent of GDP of world's seven wealthiest nations
March 1968	Mai Lai massacre in Vietnam
1968	Prague Spring
1971	World's first microprocessor
1979	Islamic revolution in Iran
1980s and 1990s	Governments around the world move away from nationalized economies
1980–1987	Incomes fall in most Latin American nations
1982	Mexico defaults on national debt
1985	Japan becomes world's biggest foreign investor
1990s	China's economy grows at annual rate of almost 10 percent
Late 1990s	Economies of Brazil and India grow at rapid rate
Late twentieth century	Christian and Islamic fundamentalism on the rise; 30 million Internet users in China; public spending accounts for 37 percent of GDP of world's seven wealthiest nations; Muslim population: Britain, 2 million; France, 4 million; migrants from Latin America largest minority group in the United States
2001	Terrorist attack on United States

The problems went even deeper. The experiences of the century made human rights a lively issue but did not dispel moral confusion about the value of life. Almost everyone, for instance, by 2000, paid lip service to the rights to life and to equality of respect, but these values were more honored in theory than in practice. Many countries outlawed capital punishment. But this did not mean that they treated human life as inviolable. In some places, the lives of some criminals continued to be regarded as dispensable, even in most states of the United States. Many jurisdictions exempted unborn babies from the principle of inviolability of human life. The decriminalization of abortion in most of the West served humane ends: freeing women who felt obliged to have abortions, and those who helped them, from prosecution under the law. But the effects were morally questionable. Euthanasia became another focus of concern over the limits of human rights. Did the moribund and the vegetative have them? Did the incurably dying have a moral right to choose to end their sufferings by physician-assisted suicide?

By 2000, the world seemed to have tried everything. The "final solutions" and "inevitable" revolutions that extremists of Right and Left proposed had failed. Social planning went wrong. But the return to individualism failed to restrain the growth of government, widened the poverty gap, and bred terrorism and crime. The world was left looking for a "third way" between capitalism and socialism, in which freedom and order would coexist, governments would make society more equal without choking differences, and individual enterprise would thrive at the service of a wider community. These objectives were easier to state than to deliver.

The twentieth century was a century of paradox. Frustrated hopes coincided with unprecedented progress. Uncontrolled change left much of the world mired in stagnancy. Utopias nourished moral sickness, suicide, and crime. The century of democracy was the century of dictators. The century of war was also the century of pacifism. Rule by the aged survived the empowerment of the young. Globalization broke down some states and communities but encouraged others to recover historic identities. Science and secularism revived faith. As we shall see in Chapter 30, the twentieth century could also be called the century of ecology, but it was peculiarly destructive of nature.

PROBLEMS AND PARALLELS

1. Why did science, technology, education, and prosperity fail to avert moral catastrophies in the twentieth century?

2. The nation-state was the central actor in reorganizing societies after the economic disasters and wars of the twentieth century. Nation-states, however, were also the most efficient killers of tens of millions of people through war and misguided policies. What are the reasons for this paradox?

3. How did individualism manifest itself in both conservative and counterconservative ways?

4. How did the demands for personal freedom, sexual liberation, and existential self-fulfillment affect Western societies? Family structures? The status of women?

5. How did globalization affect economies and cultures in the late twentieth and early twenty-first centuries?

6. What does the term *counter-colonization* mean? How did people redefine the sense of their own identities in the twentieth century? Why did it take so long to dismantle the legacy of racism?

7. How did traditional as well as new religions respond to secularism? What features do fundamentalist movements have in common around the world?

DOCUMENTS IN GLOBAL HISTORY

- Transcript from the Rape of Nanjing sentencing, 1947
- Eyewitness account of genocide in Armenia, 1915
- Excerpt from the 9/11 Commission Report
- China: a farmer's perspective, 2002
- Martin Luther King, Jr., *Letter from Birmingham Jail*, 1963
- Aimé Césaire, from *Return to My Native Land*
- Leopold Senghor on Négritude

- Virginia Woolf, from *A Room of One's Own*
- Justin Vaïsse, from "Veiled Meaning," (France) 2004
- China: "A Harmonious Society," 2006
- Pope John Paul II on consumerism, from *Centesimus Annus*
- Sayyid Qutb, from *Milestones*, 1964
- Abu'l 'Ala Mawdudi, on the scope and purpose of the Islamic state
- Vaclav Havel, "The Need for Transcendence in the Postmodern World"

Please see the Primary Source DVD for additional sources related to this chapter.

READ ON

The study of wartime atrocities is ably represented by I. Chang, *The Rape of Nanking: The Forgotten Holocaust of World War II* (1997), which shows how Nanjing served as a training ground for further Japanese slaughter of civilians. *Good Man of Nanking: The Diaries of J. Rabe*, ed. by E. Wickert, translated from the German by J. E. Woods (1998) offers a firsthand account of the massacre by a German businessman who organized refuge for Chinese civilians.

D. Bell, *The Coming of Post-Industrial Society* (1976), predicted the coming of the Information Age and the social and cultural transformations it has wrought. It should be read in conjunction with F. Jameson, *Postmodernism or the Cultural Logic of Late Capitalism* (1991), a densely written but very sophisticated analysis of postmodernism as the artistic expression of its material milieu. The same author's *Marxism and Form* (1971) remains the basic manifesto of modern Marxist cultural analysis. J. Tomlinson, *Globalization and Culture* (1999) explores similar themes from a different perspective.

A. Musallam, *From Secularism to Jihad: Sayyid Qutb and the Foundations of Radical Islamism* (2005) is an insightful examination of the founder of modern Islamic political fundamentalism. T. Madan, *Modern Myths, Locked Minds: Secularism and Fundamentalism in India* (1997) looks at the intersection of secularism, religion, and politics for India's major faiths. S. Jacoby, *Freethinkers: A History of American Secularism* (2004) examines the paradox of the secular foundations of the United States very religiously tinged democratic culture.

N. Woods, ed., *The Political Economy of Globalization* (2000), explores key economic and political problems associated with globalization. R. Compton, *East Asian Democratization: Impact of Globalization, Culture, and Economy* (2000) uses detailed case studies of various East Asian countries to compare the political and cultural impact of globalizing economies.

Abolitionism Belief that slavery and the slave trade are immoral and should be abolished.

Aborigine A member of the indigenous or earliest-known population of a region.

Aborigines Indigenous people of Australia.

Afrikaans An official language of South Africa, spoken mostly by the Boers. It is derived from seventeenth-century Dutch.

Age of Plague Term for the spread of lethal diseases from the fourteenth through the eighteenth centuries.

Ahriman The chief spirit of darkness and evil in Zoroastrianism, the enemy of Ahura Mazda.

Ahura Mazda The chief deity of Zoroastrianism, the creator of the world, the source of light, and the embodiment of good.

Al-Andalus Arabic name for the Iberian Peninsula (Spain and Portugal).

Alluvial plains Flat lands where mud from rivers or lakes renews the topsoil. If people can control the flooding that is common in such conditions, alluvial plains are excellent for settled agriculture.

Almoravids Muslim dynasty of Berber warriors that flourished from 1049 to 1145 and that established political dominance over northwest Africa and Spain.

Alternative energy Energy sources that usually produce less pollution than does the burning of fossil fuels, and are renewable in some cases.

Alternative medicine Medicines, treatments, and techniques not advocated by the mainstream medical establishment in the West.

Americanization The process by which other cultures, to a greater or lesser degree, adopt American fashions, culture, and ways of life.

Anarchists Believers in the theory that all forms of government are oppressive and undesirable and should be opposed and abolished.

Animal rights Movement that asserts that animals have fundamental rights that human beings have a moral obligation to respect.

Anti-Semitism Hostility or prejudice against Jews or Judaism.

Arthasastra Ancient Indian study of economics and politics that influenced the Emperor Asoka. The *Arthasastra* expresses an ideology of universal rule and emphasizes the supremacy of "the king's law" and the importance of uniform justice.

Artificial intelligence The creation of a machine or computer program that exhibits the characteristics of human intelligence.

Arts and Crafts Movement Nineteenth-century artists and intellectuals who argued that the products produced by individual craftsmen were more attractive than and morally superior to the mass, uniform goods produced by industry.

Assassins A secret order of Muslims in what is today Syria and Lebanon who terrorized and killed its opponents, both Christian and Muslim. The Assassins were active from the eleventh to the thirteenth centuries.

Atlantic Slave Trade Trade in African slaves who were bought, primarily in West Africa, by Europeans and white Americans and transported across the Atlantic, usually in horrific conditions, to satisfy the demand for labor in the plantations and mines of the Americas.

Atomic theory The theory that matter is not a continuous whole, but is composed of tiny, discrete particles.

Australopithecine ("southern ape-like creatures") Species of hominids that occurred earlier than those classed under the heading "homo." Most anthropologists date australopithecines to 5 million years ago.

Axial Age A pivotal age in the history of world civilization, lasting for roughly 500 years up to the beginning of the Christian era, in which critical intellectual and cultural ideas arose in and were transmitted across the Mediterranean world, India, Iran, and East Asia.

Axial zone The densely populated central belt of world population, communication, and cultural exchange in Eurasia that stretches from Japan and China to Western Europe and North Africa.

Aztecs People of central Mexico whose civilization and empire were at their height at the time of the Spanish conquest in the early sixteenth century.

Balance of trade The relative value of goods traded between two or more nations or states. Each trading partner strives to have a favorable balance of trade, that is, to sell more to its trading partners than it buys from them.

Bantu African people sharing a common linguistic ancestry who originated in West Africa and whose early agriculture centered on the cultivation of yams and oil palms in swamplands.

Big bang theory Theory that the universe began with an explosion of almost infinitesimally compressed matter, the effects of which are still going on.

Black Death Term for a lethal disease or diseases that struck large parts of Eurasia and North Africa in the 1300s and killed millions of people.

Boers Dutch settlers and their descendents in southern Africa. The first Boers arrived in South Africa in the seventeenth century.

Bon Religion that was Buddhism's main rival in Tibet for several centuries in the late first millennium C.E.

Brahman A member of the highest, priestly caste of traditional Indian society.

British East India Company British trading company founded in 1600 that played a key role in the colonization of India. It ruled much of the subcontinent until 1857.

Bureaucratization The process by which government increasingly operates through a body of trained officials who follow a set of regular rules and procedures.

Business Imperialism Economic domination and exploitation of poorer and weaker countries by richer and stronger states.

Byzantine Empire Term for the Greek-speaking, eastern portion of the former Roman Empire, centered on Constantinople. It lasted until 1453, when it was conquered by the Ottoman Turks.

Cahokia Most spectacular existent site of Mississippi Valley Native American civilization, located near modern St. Louis.

Caliph The supreme Islamic political and religious authority, literally, the "successor" of the Prophet Muhammad.

Canyon cultures Indigenous peoples of the North American Southwest. The canyon cultures flourished between about 850 and 1250 C.E.

Capitalism An economic system in which the means of production and distribution are privately or corporately owned.

Caste system A social system in which people's places in society, how they live and work, and with whom they can marry are determined by heredity. The Indian caste system has been intertwined with India's religious and economic systems.

Centralization The concentration of power in the hands of a central government.

Chaos theory Theory that some systems are so complex that their causes and effects are untraceable.

Chicago economics The economic theory associated with economists who taught at the University of Chicago that holds that low taxes and light government regulation will lead to economic prosperity.

Chimú Civilization centered on the Pacific coast of Peru that was conquered by the Inca in the fifteenth century.

Chinese Board of Astronomy Official department of the Chinese imperial court created in the early seventeenth century that was responsible for devising the ritual calendar.

Chinese diaspora The migration of Chinese immigrants around the world between the seventeenth and nineteenth centuries.

Chivalry The qualities idealized by the medieval European aristocracy and associated with knighthood, such as bravery, courtesy, honor, and gallantry.

Chola Expansive kingdom in southern India that had important connections with merchant communities on the coast. Chola reached its height around 1050 C.E.

Christendom Term referring to the European states in which Christianity was the dominant or only religion.

Cistercians Christian monastic order that built monasteries in places where habitation was sparse and nature hostile. Cistercians practiced a more ascetic and rigorous form of the Benedictine rule.

Citizen army The mass army the French created during the Revolution by imposing mandatory military service on the entire active adult male population. The army was created in response to the threat of invasion by an alliance of anti-Revolutionary countries in the early 1790s.

Civilization A way of life based on radically modifiying the environment.

Civilizing mission The belief that imperialism and colonialism are justified because imperial powers have a duty to bring the benefits of "civilization" to, or impose them on, the "backward" people they ruled or conquered.

Clan A social group made up of a number of families that claim descent from a common ancestor and follow a hereditary chieftain.

Class struggle Conflict between competing social classes that, in Karl Marx's view, was responsible for all important historical change.

Climacteric A period of critical change in a society that is poised between different possible outcomes.

Code Napoleon Civil code promulgated by Napoleon in 1804 and spread by his armies across Europe. It still forms the basis for the legal code for many European, Latin American, and African countries.

Cold war Post–World War II rivalry between the United States and its allies and the Soviet Union and its allies. The cold war ended in 1990–1991 with the end of the Soviet Empire in Eastern Europe and the collapse of the Soviet Union itself.

Columbian Exchange Biological exchange of plants, animals, microbes, and human beings between the Americas and the rest of the world.

Commune Collective name for the citizen body of a medieval and Renaissance Italian town.

Communism A system of government in which the state plans and controls the economy, and private property and class distinctions are abolished.

Confraternities Lay Catholic charitable brotherhoods.

Confucianism Chinese doctrine founded by Confucius emphasizing learning and the fulfillment of obligations among family members, citizens, and the state.

Constitutionalism The doctrine that the state is founded on a set of fundamental laws that rulers and citizens make together and are bound to respect.

Consumerism A system of values that exalts the consumption and possession of consumer goods as both a social good and as an end in themselves.

Coolies Poor laborers from China and India who left their homelands to do hard manual and agricultural work in other parts of the world in the nineteenth and early twentieth centuries.

Copernican revolution Development of a heliocentric model of the solar system begun in 1543 by Nicholas Copernicus, a Polish churchman and astronomer.

Council of Trent A series of meetings from 1545 to 1563 to direct the response of the Roman Catholic Church to Protestantism. The council defined Catholic dogma and reformed church discipline.

Counter Reformation The Catholic effort to combat the spread of Protestantism in the sixteenth and seventeenth centuries.

Countercolonization The flow of immigrants out of former colonies to the "home countries" that used to rule them.

Country trades Commerce involving local or regional exchanges of goods from one Asian destination to another that, while often handled by European merchants, never touched Europe.

Covenant In the Bible, God's promise to the human race.

Creoles People of at least part-European descent born in the West Indies, French Louisiana, or Spanish America.

Crusades Any of the military expeditions undertaken by European Christians from the late eleventh to the thirteenth centuries to recover the Holy Land from the Muslims.

Cubism Artistic style developed by Pablo Picasso and Georges Braque in the early twentieth century, characterized by the reduction and fragmentation of natural forms into abstract, often geometric structures.

Cultural relativism The doctrine that cultures cannot be ranked in any order of merit. No culture is superior to another, and each culture must be judged on its own terms.

Cultural Revolution Campaign launched by Mao Zedong in 1965–1966 against the bureaucrats of the Chinese Communist Party. In lasted until 1976 and involved widespread disorder, violence, killings, and the persecution of intellectuals and the educated elite.

Culture Socially transmitted behavior, beliefs, institutions, and technologies that a given group of people or peoples share.

Cuneiform Mesopotamian writing system that was inscribed on clay tablets with wedge-shaped markers.

Czars (Trans.) "Caesar." Title of the emperors who ruled Russia until the revolution of 1917.

Dada An early twentieth-century European artistic and literary movement that flouted conventional and traditional aesthetic and cultural values by producing works marked by nonsense, travesty, and incongruity.

Dahomey West African slave-trading state that began to be prominent in the sixteenth century.

Daimyo Japanese feudal lord who ruled a province and was subject to the shoguns.

Daoism Chinese doctrine founded by Laozi that identified detachment from the world with the pursuit of immortality.

"Declaration of the Rights of Man and Citizen" Declaration of basic principles adopted by the French National Assembly in August 1789, at the start of the French Revolution.

Decolonization The process by which the nineteenth-century colonial empires in Asia, Africa, the Caribbean, and the Pacific were dismantled after World War II.

Deforestation The process by which trees are eliminated from an ecosystem.

Democracy Government by the people, exercised either directly or through elected representatives.

Demokratia Greek word signifying a state where supreme power belonged to an assembly of citizens (only privileged males were citizens).

Devsirme Quota of male children supplied by Christian subjects as tribute to the Ottoman Sultan. Many of the boys were drafted into the janissaries.

Dharma In the teachings of Buddha, moral law or duty.

Diffusion The spread of a practice, belief, culture, or technology within a community or between communities.

Dirlik (Trans.) "Wealth." The term applied to provincial government in the Ottoman Empire.

Divine love God's ongoing love for and interest in human beings.

Dominicans Order of preaching friars established in 1216 by Saint Dominic.

Druze Lebanese sect that regards the caliph al-Hakim as a manifestation of God. Other Muslims regard the Druze as heretics.

Dualism Perception of the world as an arena of conflict between opposing principles of good and evil.

Dutch East India Company Dutch company founded in 1602 that enjoyed a government-granted monopoly on trade between Holland and Asia. The company eventually established a territorial empire in what is today Indonesia.

Dutch East Indies Dutch colonies in Asia centered on present-day Indonesia.

The Encyclopedia Twenty-eight volume compendium of Enlightenment thought published in French and edited by Denis Diderot. The first volume appeared in 1751.

East India Trade Maritime trade between Western Europe and New England and Asia (predominantly India and China) between 1600 and 1800. Westerners paid cash for items from Asia, such as porcelain, tea, silk, cotton textiles, and spices.

Easterlies Winds coming from the east.

Ecological exchange The exchange of plants and animals between ecosystems.

Ecological imperialism Term historians use for the sweeping environmental changes European and other imperialists introduced in regions they colonized.

Ecology of civilization The interaction of people with their environment.

Economic liberalism Belief that government interference in and regulation of the economy should be kept to a minimum.

Edo Former name of Tokyo when it was the center of government for the Tokugawa shoguns.

El Niño A periodic reversal of the normal flow of Pacific currents that alters weather patterns and affects the number and location of fish in the ocean.

Elan vital The "vital force" hypothesized by the French philosopher Henri Bergson as a source of efficient causation and evolution in nature.

Empirical Derived from or guided by experience or experiment.

Empiricism The view that experience, especially of the senses, is the only source of knowledge.

Emporium trading Commerce that takes place in fixed market places or trading posts.

Enlightened despotism Reforms instituted by powerful monarchs in eighteenth-century Europe who were inspired by the principles of the Enlightenment.

Enlightenment Movement of eighteenth-century European thought championed by the *philosophes*, thinkers who held that change and reform were desirable and could be achieved by the application of reason and science. Most Enlightenment thinkers were hostile to conventional religion.

Enthusiasm "Religion" of English romantics who believed that emotion and passion were positive qualities.

Epistemology The branch of philosophy that studies the nature of knowledge.

Equilibrium trap Term coined by the historian Mark Elvin to refer to China in the eighteenth century, when industries were meeting demand with traditional technologies and had no scope to increase output.

Eugenics The theory that the human race can be improved mentally and physically by controlled selective breeding and that the state and society have a duty to encourage "superior" persons to have offspring and prevent "inferior" persons from reproducing.

Eunuchs Castrated male servants valued because they could not produce heirs or have sexual relations with women. In Byzantium, China, and the Islamic world, eunuchs could rise to high office in the state and the military.

European Union (EU) Loose economic and political federation that succeeded the European Economic Community (EEC) in 1993. It has expanded to include most of the states in Western and Eastern Europe.

Evolution Change in the genetic composition of a population over successive generations, as a result of natural selection acting on the genetic variation among individuals.

Examination system System for selecting Chinese officials and bureaucrats according to merit through a series of competitive, written examinations that, in theory, any Chinese young man could take. Success in the exams required years of intense study in classical Chinese literature. The examination system was not abolished until the early twentieth century.

Existentialism Philosophy that regards human existence as unexplainable, and stresses freedom of choice and accepting responsibility for the consequences of one's acts.

Factories Foreign trading posts in China and other parts of Asia. The chief representative of a factory was known as a "factor." Though the earliest trading posts were established by the Portuguese in the sixteenth century, the number of factories grew rapidly in the eighteenth and nineteenth centuries, with European and American merchants trading for silk, rhubarb, tea, and porcelain.

Fascism A system of government marked by centralization of authority under a dictator, stringent socioeconomic controls, and suppression of the opposition through terror and censorship.

Fatimids Muslim dynasty that ruled parts of North Africa and Egypt (909–1171).

Feminism The belief that women collectively constitute a class of society that has been historically oppressed and deserves to be set free.

Final Solution Nazi plan to murder all European Jews.

Fixed-wind systems Wind system in which the prevailing winds do not change direction for long periods of time.

Fossil fuels Fuels including peat, coal, natural gas, and oil.

Franciscans Religious order founded by Francis of Assisi in 1209 and dedicated to the virtues of humility, poverty, and charitable work among the poor.

Free trade The notion that maximum economic efficiency is achieved when barriers to trade, especially taxes on imports and exports, are eliminated.

French Revolution Political, intellectual, and social upheaval that began in France in 1789. It resulted in the overthrow of the monarchy and the establishment of a republic.

Fulani Traditional herdsmen of the Sahel in West Africa.

Fundamentalism Strict adherence to a set of basic ideas or principles.

Futurism Artistic vision articulated by Emilio Filippo Marinetti in 1909. He believed that all traditional art and ideas should be repudiated, destroyed, and replaced by the new. Futurists glorified speed, technology, progress, and violence.

Gauchos Argentine cowboys.

General will Jean-Jacques Rousseau's concept of the collective will of the population. He believed that the purpose of government was to express the general will.

Genetic revolution Revolution in the understanding of human biology produced by advances in genetic research.

Genocide The systematic and planned extermination of an entire national, racial, political, or ethnic group.

Ghana A medieval West African kingdom in what are now eastern Senegal, southwest Mali, and southern Mauritania.

Global gardening The collecting in botanical gardens of plants from around the world for cultivation and study.

Globalization The process through which uniform or similar ways of life are spread across the planet.

Glyph A form of writing that uses symbolic figures that are usually engraved or incised, such as Egyptian hieroglyphics.

GM Crops that have been *genetically modified* to produce certain desired characteristics.

Golden Horde Term for Mongols who ruled much of Russia from the steppes of the lower Volga River from the thirteenth to the fifteenth century.

Grand Vizier The chief minister of state in the Ottoman Empire.

Greater East Asia Co-Prosperity Sphere Bloc of Asian nations under Japanese economic and political control during World War II.

Green revolution Improvements in twentieth-century agriculture that substantially increased food production by developing new strains of crops and agricultural techniques.

Greenhouse effect The increase in temperature caused by the trapping of carbon in the Earth's atmosphere.

Guardians Self-elected class of philosopher-rulers found in Plato's *Republic*.

Guomindang (GMD) Nationalist Chinese political party founded in 1912 by Sun Yat-Sen. The Guomindang took power in China in 1928 but was defeated by the Chinese Communists in 1949.

Habsburgs An Austro-German imperial family that reached the height of their power in the sixteenth century under Charles V of Spain when the Habsburgs ruled much of Europe and the Americas. The Habsburgs continued to rule a multinational empire based in Vienna until 1918.

Haj The pilgrimage to Mecca that all faithful Muslims are required to complete at least once in their lifetime if they are able.

Han Dynasty that ruled China from ca. 206 B.C.E. to ca. 220 C.E. This was the period when the funda-

mental identity and culture of China were formed. Chinese people still refer to themselves as "Han."

Hanseatic League Founded in 1356, the Hanseatic League was a powerful network of allied ports along the North Sea and Baltic coasts that collaborated to promote trade.

Harem The quarters reserved for the female members of a Muslim household.

Herders Agriculturalists who emphasize the raising of animals, rather than plants, for food and products, such as wool and hides.

High-level equilibrium trap A situation in which an economy that is meeting high levels of demand with traditional technology finds that it has little scope to increase its output.

Hinduism Indian polytheistic religion that developed out of Brahmanism and in response to Buddhism. It remains the majority religion in India today.

Hispaniola Modern Haiti and the Dominican Republic.

Hohokam People Native American culture that flourished from about the third century B.C.E. to the mid–fifteenth century C.E. in south-central Arizona.

Holocaust Term for the murder of millions of Jews by the Nazi regime during World War II.

Holy Roman Empire A loose federation of states under an elected emperor that consisted primarily of Germany and northern Italy. It endured in various forms from 800 to 1806.

Homo erectus (Trans.) "Standing upright." Humanlike tool-using species that lived about 1.5 million years ago. At one time, Homo erectus was thought to be the first "human."

Homo ergaster (Trans.) "Workman." Humanlike species that lived 800,000 years ago and stacked the bones of its dead.

Homo habilis (Trans.) "Handy." Humanlike species that lived about 2.5 million years ago and made stone hand axes.

Homo sapiens (Trans.) "Wise." The species to which contemporary humans belong.

Human rights Notion of inherent rights that all human beings share. Based in part on the assumption that being human constitutes in itself a meaningful moral category that excludes nonhuman creatures.

Humanism Cultural and intellectual movement of the Renaissance centered on the study of the literature, art, and civilization of ancient Greece and Rome.

Hurons A Native American confederacy of eastern Canada. The Huron flourished immediately prior to contact with Europeans, but declined

rapidly as a result of European diseases such as smallpox. They were allied with the French in wars against the British, the Dutch, and other Native Americans.

Husbandry The practice of cultivating crops and breeding and raising livestock; agriculture.

Ice-Age affluence Relative prosperity of Ice-Age society as the result of abundant game and wild, edible plants.

Icon A representation or picture of a Christian saint or sacred event. Icons have been traditionally venerated in the Eastern, or Orthodox, Church.

Il-Khanate A branch of the Mongol Empire, centered in present-day Iran. Its rulers, the Il-Khans, converted to Islam and adopted Persian culture.

Il-khans ("subordinate rulers") Viceroys of the Mongols who ruled Persia and environs in the thirteenth and early fourteenth centuries.

Imam A Muslim religious teacher. Also the title of Muslim political and religious rulers in Yemen and Oman.

Imperator A Latin term that originally meant an army commander under the Roman Republic and evolved into the term *emperor*.

Imperialism The policy of extending a nation's authority and influence by conquest or by establishing economic and political hegemony over other nations.

Incas Peoples of highland Peru who established an empire from northern Ecuador to central Chile before the Spanish conquest in the 1530s.

Indian National Congress Political organization created in 1885 that played a leading role in the Indian independence movement.

Indirect rule Rule by a colonial power through local elites.

Individualism Belief in the primary importance of the individual and in the virtues of self-reliance and personal independence.

Indo-European languages Language family that originated in Asia and from which most of Europe's present languages evolved.

Inductive method Method by which scientists turn individual observations and experiments into general laws.

Industrial Revolution The complex set of economic, demographic, and technological events that began in Western Europe and resulted in the advent of an industrial economy.

Industrialization The process by which an industrial economy is developed.

Information technology Technology, such as printing presses and computers, that facilitates the spread of information.

Inquisition A tribunal of the Roman Catholic Church that was charged with suppressing heresy and immorality.

Iroquois Native American confederacy based in northern New York State, originally composed of the Mohawk, Oneida, Onondaga, Cayuga, and Seneca peoples, known as the Five Nations. The confederation created a constitution sometime between the mid-1400s and the early 1600s.

Isolationism Belief that, unless directly challenged, a country should concentrate on domestic issues and avoid foreign conflicts or active participation in foreign affairs.

Jainism A way of life that arose in India designed to free the soul from evil by ascetic practices: chastity, detachment, truth, selflessness, and strict vegetarianism.

Janissaries Soldiers in an elite Ottoman infantry formation that was first organized in the fourteenth century. Originally drafted from among the sons of the sultan's Christian subjects, the janissaries had become a hereditary and militarily obsolete caste by the early nineteenth century.

Jesuits Order of regular clergy strongly committed to education, scholarship, and missionary work. Founded by Ignatius of Loyola in 1534.

Jihad Arabic word meaning "striving." Muhammad used the word to refer to the inner struggle all Muslims must wage against evil, and the real wars fought against the enemies of Islam.

Joint-stock company A business whose capital is held in transferable shares of stock by its joint owners. The Dutch East India Company, founded in 1602, was the first joint-stock company.

Kaaba The holiest place in Islam. Formerly a pagan shrine, the Kaaba is a massive cube-shaped structure in Mecca toward which Muslims turn to pray.

Keynesianism Economic policy advocated by J. M. Keynes, based on the premise that governments could adjust the distribution of wealth and regulate the functioning of the economy through taxation and public spending, without seriously weakening free enterprise or infringing freedom.

Khan A ruler of a Mongol, Tartar, or Turkish tribe.

Khedive Title held by the hereditary viceroys of Egypt in the nineteenth century. Although nominally subject to the Ottoman sultans, the khedives were, in effect, sovereign princes.

Khmer Agrarian kingdom of Cambodia, built on the wealth produced by enormous rice surpluses.

Kongo Kingdom located in west central Africa along the Congo River, founded in the fourteenth century. The Portuguese converted its rulers and elite to Catholicism in the fifteenth century.

Kulturkampf (Trans.) "The struggle for culture." Name given to the conflict between the Roman Catholic Church and the imperial German government under Chancellor Otto von Bismarck in the 1870s.

Laissez-faire An economic policy that emphasizes the minimization of government regulation and involvement in the economy.

Latin Church Dominant Christian church in Western Europe.

Latitude The angular distance north or south of the Earth's equator, measured in degrees along a meridian.

Law of nations Political theory that serves as the foundation for international law, first theorized by Thomas Aquinas in the thirteenth century and further developed by the Spanish theologion Francisco Suarez (1548–1617).

League of Nations International political organization created after World War I to resolve disputes between states peacefully and create a more just international order.

Legalism Chinese philosophical school that argued that a strong state was necessary in order to have a good society.

Levant The countries bordering on the eastern Mediterranean from Turkey to Egypt.

Liberation theology Religious movement in Latin America, primarily among Roman Catholics, concerned with justice for the poor and oppressed. Its adherents argue that sin is the result not just of individual moral failure but of the oppressive and exploitative way in which capitalist society is organized and functions.

Little Ice Age Protracted period of relative cold from the fourteenth to the early nineteenth centuries.

Logograms A system of writing in which stylized pictures represent a word or phrase.

Longitude An imaginary great circle on the surface of the Earth passing through the north and south poles at right angles to the equator.

Lotus Sutra The most famous of Buddhist scriptures.

Low Countries A region of northwest Europe comprising what is today Belgium, the Netherlands, and Luxembourg.

Magyars Steppeland people who invaded Eastern Europe in the tenth century and were eventually converted to Catholic Christianity. The Magyars are the majority ethnic group in present-day Hungary.

Mahayana One of the major schools of Buddhism. It emphasizes the Buddha's infinite compassion for all human beings, social concern, and universal salvation. It is the dominant branch of Buddhism in East Asia.

Mahdi A Muslim messiah, whose coming would inaugurate a cosmic struggle, preceding the end of the world.

Maize The grain that modern Americans call "corn." It was first cultivated in ancient Mesoamerica.

Mali Powerful West African state that flourished in the fourteenth century.

Malthusian Ideas inspired by Thomas Malthus's theory that population growth would always outpace growth in food supply.

Mamluks Egyptian Muslim slave army. The mamluks provided Egypt's rulers from 1390 to 1517.

Mana According to the Polynesians, a supernatural force that regulates everything in the world. For example, the mana of a net makes it catch a fish, and the mana of an herb gives it its healing powers.

Manchurian Incident Japanese invasion of Manchuria in 1931, justified by the alleged effort of the Chinese to blow up a Japanese train. In fact, Japanese agents deliberately triggered the explosion to provide a pretext for war.

Manchus A people native to Manchuria who ruled China during the Qing dynasty.

Mandarins A high public official of the Chinese empire.

Mandate of heaven The source of divine legitimacy for Chinese emperors. According to the mandate of heaven, emperors were chosen by the gods and retained their favor as long as the emperors acted in righteous ways. Emperors and dynasties that lost the mandate of heaven could be deposed or overthrown.

Manichaeanism A dualistic philosophy dividing the world between the two opposed principles of good and evil.

Manifest destiny Nineteenth-century belief that the United States was destined to expand across all of North America from the Atlantic to the Pacific, including Canada and Mexico.

Manila Galleons Spanish galleons that sailed each year between the Philippines and Mexico with a cargo of silk, porcelain, and other Asian luxury goods that were paid for with Mexican silver.

Maori Indigenous Polynesian people of New Zealand.

Marathas Petty Hindu princes who ruled in Maharashtra in southern India in the eighteenth century.

Maritime empires Empires based on trade and naval power that flourished in the sixteenth and seventeenth centuries.

Maroons Runaway slaves in the Americas who formed autonomous communities, and even states, between 1500 and 1800.

Marshall Plan Foreign-aid program for Western Europe after World War II, named after U.S. Secretary of State George C. Marshall.

Marxism The political and economic philosophy of Karl Marx and Friedrich Engels in which the concept of class struggle is the determining principle in social and historical change.

Material culture Concrete objects that people create.

Matrilineal A society that traces ancestry through the maternal line.

Maya Major civilization of Mesoamerica. The earliest evidence connected to Maya civilization dates from about 1000 B.C.E. Maya civilization reached its peak between 250 and 900 C.E. Maya cultural and political practices were a major influence on other Mesoamericans.

Mercantilism An economic theory that emphasized close government control of the economy to maximize a country's exports and to earn as much bullion as possible.

Mesoamerica A region stretching from central Mexico to Central America. Mesoamerica was home to the Olmec, the Maya, the Aztecs, and other Native American peoples.

Messiah The anticipated savior of the Jews. Christians identified Jesus as the Messiah.

Mestizos The descendents of Europeans and Native Americans.

Microbial exchange The exchange of microbes between ecosystems.

Militarization The trend toward larger and more powerful armed forces and the organization of society and the economy to achieve that goal.

Military revolution Change in warfare in the sixteenth and seventeenth centuries that accompanied the rise of fire-power technology.

Millenarianism Belief that the end of the world is about to occur, as foretold in the biblical Book of Revelation.

Minas Gerais (Trans.) "General Mines." Region of Brazil rich in mineral resources that experienced a gold rush in the early eighteenth century.

Ming Dynasty Chinese dynasty (1368–1644) noted for its flourishing foreign trade and achievements in scholarship and the arts.

Mongol peace A period of history, from about 1240 C.E. to about 1340 C.E., when peace and order, imposed by the Mongols, fostered trade, communication, and cultural exchange across the Eurasian steppes.

Mongols Nomadic people whose homeland was in Mongolia. In the twelfth and thirteenth centuries, they conquered most of Eurasia from China to Eastern Europe.

Monocultures The cultivation of a single dominant food crop, such as potatoes or rice. Societies that practiced monoculture were vulnerable to famine if bad weather or disease caused their single food crop to fail.

Monroe Doctrine The policy enunciated by President James Monroe in 1823 that the United States would oppose further European colonization in the Americas.

Monsoons A wind from the southwest or south that brings heavy rainfall each summer to southern Asia.

Mound agriculture Form of agriculture found in pre-Columbian North America.

Mughals Muslim dynasty founded by Babur that ruled India, at least nominally, from the mid–1500s until 1857.

Multiculturalism The belief that different cultures can coexist peacefully and equitably in a single country.

Napoleonic Wars Wars waged between France under Napoleon and its European enemies from 1799 to 1815. The fighting spilled over into the Middle East and sparked conflicts in North America and India and independence movements in the Spanish and Portuguese colonies in the Americas.

Nationalism Belief that a people who share the same language, historic experience, and sense of identity make up a nation and that every nation has the right to assert its identity, pursue its destiny, defend its rights, and be the primary focus of its people's loyalty.

Natural selection The process by which only the organisms best adapted to their environment pass on their genetic material to subsequent generations.

Nature versus nurture Debate over the relative importance of inherited characteristics and environmental factors in determining human development.

Nazis Members of the National Socialist German Workers' Party, founded in Germany in 1919 and brought to power in 1933 under Adolf Hitler.

Neanderthal Humanlike species, evidence for whose existence was found in the Neander River valley in northern Germany in the mid–nineteenth century. Neanderthals disappeared from the evolutionary record about 30,000 years ago.

Negritude The affirmation of the distinctive nature, quality, and validity of black culture.

Nestorianism The Christian theological doctrine that within Jesus are two distinct and separate persons, divine and human, rather than a single divine person. Orthodox Christians classed Nestorianism as a heresy, but it spread across Central Asia along the Silk Roads.

New Europes Lands in other hemispheres where the environment resembled that of Europe and where immigrants could successfully transplant a European way of life and European culture.

New Rich Rich people whose wealth was acquired in the recent past, often in industry or commerce.

New World Term Europeans applied to the Americas.

Nirvana The spiritual goal of Buddhism, when a person ends the cycle of birth and rebirth and achieves enlightenment and freedom from any attachment to material things.

Noble savage Idealized vision that some people in the West held about certain non-Europeans, especially some Native Americans and Polynesians. It was based on the notions that civilization was a corrupting force and that these peoples lived lives more in tune with nature.

Northwest Passage Water route from the Atlantic to the Pacific through the Arctic archipelago of northern Canada and along the northern coast of Alaska. For centuries, Europeans sought in vain for a more accessible route to the Pacific farther south in North America.

Obsidian Volcanic glass used to make tools, weapons, and mirrors.

Old regime Term for the social, economic, and political institutions that existed in France and the rest of Europe before the French Revolution.

Old World Term for the regions of the world— Europe, parts of Africa and Asia—that were known to Europeans before the discovery of the Americas.

Ongons Tibetan images in which spirits are thought to reside. Shamans claimed to communicate with the ongons.

OPEC The Organization of Petroleum Exporting Countries, an alliance of the world's major oil producers.

Oracle A person or group that claims to be able to have access to knowledge of the future by consulting a god. Ancient rulers often consulted oracles.

Oriental despotism Arbitrary and corrupt rule. Eighteenth-century Europeans saw it as characteristic of Asian or Islamic rulers.

Orthodox Church Dominant Christian church in the Byzantine Empire, the Balkans, and Russia.

Ottoman Empire Islamic empire based in present-day Turkey, with its capital at Istanbul. At its height in the sixteenth century, the Ottoman Empire stretched from Iraq across North Africa to the borders of Morocco and included almost all the Balkans and most of Hungary. The empire gradually declined, but endured until it was dismembered after World War I.

Pampas A vast plain of south-central South America that supports huge herds of cattle and other livestock.

Pan-African Congress A series of five meetings held between 1919 and 1945 that claimed to represent all black Africans and demanded an end to colonial rule.

Pangaea A hypothetical prehistoric supercontinent that included all the landmasses of the Earth.

Partition of India The division in 1947 along ethnic and religious lines of the British Indian Empire into two independent states: India, which was largely Hindu, and Pakistan, which was largely Muslim. The division involved widespread violence in which at least 500,000 people were killed.

Paternalism A social or economic relationship that resembles the dependency that exists between a father and his child.

Patrilineal A society that traces ancestry through the paternal line.

Philosopher's stone A substance that was believed to have the power to change base metals into gold.

Physiocrats Eighteenth-century French political economists who argued that agriculture was the foundation of any country's wealth and recommended agricultural improvements.

Plantation system System of commercial agriculture based on large landholdings, often worked by forced labor.

Polestar Bright star used for navigation.

Positivism Doctrine that asserts the undeniability of human sense perception and the power of reason to prove that what our senses perceive is true.

Pragmatism Philosophy advocated by William James that holds that the standard for evaluating the truth or validity of a theory or concept depends on how well it works and on the results that arise from holding it.

Proletariat The working class, which according to Karl Marx, would overthrow the bourgeoisie.

Protectorate A country or region that, although nominally independent and not a colony, is in fact controlled militarily, politically, and economically by a more powerful foreign state.

Protestantism The theological system of any of the churches of Western Christendom that separated from the Roman Catholic Church during the Reformation. The advent of Protestantism is usually associated with Martin Luther's break from the Catholic Church in the 1520s.

Psychoanalysis Technique developed by Sigmund Freud to treat patients suffering from emotional or psychological disorders by making them aware of their subconscious conflicts, motivations, and desires.

Public sphere Sites for the public discussion of political, social, economic, and cultural issues.

Qing dynasty Last imperial Chinese dynasty (1644–1912), founded when the Manchus, a steppeland people from Manchuria, conquered China. It was succeeded by a republic.

Quantum mechanics Mechanics based on the principle that matter and energy have the properties of both particles and waves.

Quran The sacred text of Islam dictated from God to the Prophet Muhammad by the Archangel Gabriel. Considered by Muslims to contain the final revelations of God to humanity.

Rape of Nanjing Atrocities committed by the Japanese during their occupation of the city of Nanjing, China, in 1937.

Rastafarianism A religious and political movement that began among black people in Jamaica in the 1930s. Its adherents believe that former Emperor Haile Selassie of Ethiopia (r. 1930–1974) was divine and the Messiah whose coming was foretold in the Bible.

Rationalism The doctrine that reason by itself can determine truth and solve the world's problems.

Realpolitik Political doctrine that says that the state is not subject to moral laws and has the right to do whatever safeguards it and advances its interests.

Reformation The Protestant break from the Roman Catholic Church in the sixteenth century.

Renaissance Humanistic revival of classical art, architecture, literature, and learning that originated in Italy in the fourteenth century and spread throughout Europe.

Renewable energy Energy that is not derived from a finite resource such as oil or coal.

Rig Veda A collection of hymns and poems created by a sedentary people living in the area north of the Indus valley where northern India and Pakistan meet. The *Rig Veda* provides evidence for the theory that invaders destroyed Harappan civilization.

Romanticism Intellectual and artistic movement that arose in reaction to the Enlightenment's emphasis on reason. Romantics had a heightened interest in nature and religion, and emphasized emotion and imagination.

Rus A Slavic-Scandinavian people who created the first Russian state and converted to Orthodox Christianity.

Safavids Shiite dynasty that ruled Persia between 1501 and 1722.

Sahel A semiarid region of north Central Africa south of the Sahara Desert.

Saint Domingue A French colony on Hispaniola that flourished in the eighteenth century by cultivating sugar and coffee with slave labor. It became the modern republic of Haiti after a protracted struggle that began in the 1790s.

Samurai The hereditary Japanese feudal-military aristocracy.

Sati In Hinduism, the burning of a widow on her husband's funeral pyre.

Satyagraha (Trans.) "The force of truth." Nonviolent movement launched by Mohandas K. Gandhi, with the goal of achieving Indian independence.

Savanna (or "Savannah") A flat grassland of tropical or subtropical regions.

Scientific revolution The sweeping change in the investigation of nature and the view of the universe that took place in Europe in the sixteenth and seventeenth centuries.

Scientism The belief that science and the scientific method can explain everything in the universe and that no other form of inquiry is valid.

Scramble for Africa Late nineteenth-century competition among European powers to acquire colonies in Africa.

Sea Peoples Unknown seafaring people that contributed to the instability of the eastern Mediterranean in the twelfth century B.C.E., attacking Egypt, Palestine, Mesopotamia, Anatolia, and Syria.

Second Vatican Council Council of the Roman Catholic Church that convened at intervals in the 1960s and led to major changes in church liturgy and discipline.

Secularism Belief that religious considerations should be excluded from civil affairs or public education.

Self-determination Principle that a given people or nationality has the right to determine their own political status.

Self-strengthening Mid–nineteenth-century Chinese reform movement initiated in response to Western incursions.

Seljuks A Turkish dynasty ruling in Central and western Asia from the eleventh to the thirteenth centuries.

Serf Agricultural laborer attached to the land owned by a lord and required to perform labor in return for certain legal or customary rights. Unlike slaves, serfs could not usually be sold away from the land.

Shaman A person who acts as an intermediary between humans and spirits or gods. Such a person functions as the medium though which spirits talk to humans.

Sharia Islamic law. The word *sharia* derives from the verb *shara'a*, which is connected to the concepts of "spiritual law" and "system of divine law."

Shiites Members of the most important minority tradition in the Islamic world. Shiites believe that the caliphate is the prerogative of Muhammad's nephew, Ali, and his heirs. Shiism has been the state religion in Iran since the sixteenth century.

Shinto A religion native to Japan, characterized by veneration of nature spirits and ancestors and by a lack of formal dogma.

Shogun A hereditary military ruler of Japan who exercised real power in the name of the emperor, who was usually powerless and relegated to purely ceremonial roles. The last shogun was removed from office in 1868.

Sikhism Indian religion founded by Nanak Guru in the early sixteenth century that blends elements of the Hindu and Muslim traditions.

Silk Roads Key overland trade routes that connected eastern and western Eurasia. The route first began to function in the aftermath of Alexander the Great's expansion into Central Asia at the end of the fourth century B.C.E.

Sioux A nomadic Native American people of central North America who, with the benefit of horses introduced to the Americas by the Spanish, formed a pastoralist empire in the late eighteenth and mid–nineteenth centuries.

Social Darwinism The misapplication of Darwin's biological theories to human societies, often to justify claims of racial superiority and rule by the strong over the weak.

Socialism Any of various theories or systems in which the means of producing and distributing goods is owned collectively or by a centralized government.

Socialist realism An artistic doctrine embraced by many communist and leftist regimes that the sole legitimate purpose of the arts was to glorify the ideals of the state by portraying workers, peasants, and the masses in a strictly representational, nonabstract style.

Sociobiology The study of the biological determinants of social behavior.

Solidarity Polish trade union founded in 1980 that played a key role in bringing down Poland's communist regime.

Solomids Dynasty that seized power in Ethiopia in 1270 C.E. and claimed descent from the Biblical King Solomon.

Song dynasty Dynasty (960–1279) under which China achieved one of its highest levels of culture and prosperity.

Songhay An ancient empire of West Africa in the present-day country of Mali. It reached the height of its power around 1500 C.E.

Soninke West African kingdom on the upper Niger River.

Soviet Russian term for a workers' collective.

State system Organization of early modern Europe into competing nation-states.

Steppe A vast semiarid, grass-covered plain, extending across northern Eurasia and central North America.

Stoicism Philosophy founded on the belief that nature is morally neutral and that the wise person, therefore, achieves happiness by accepting misfortune and practicing self-control.

Stranger effect The tendency some peoples have to esteem and defer to strangers.

Stream of consciousness A literary technique that presents the thoughts and feelings of a character in a novel or story as they arise in the character's mind.

Subsidiarity Doctrine that decisions should always be made at the level closest to the people whom the decisions most affect.

Suez Canal Canal linking the Mediterranean and the Red Sea. It was built by French engineers with European capital and opened in 1869.

Sufis Members of Islamic groups that cultivate mystical beliefs and practices. Sufis have often been instrumental in spreading Islam, but Muslim authorities have often distrusted them.

Sundiata Legendary hero said to have founded the kingdom of Mali in West Africa.

Sunnis Members of the dominant tradition in the Islamic world. Sunnis believe that any member of Muhammad's tribe could be designated caliph.

Surrealism Literary and artistic movement that attempts to express the workings of the subconscious.

Syllogisms A form of argument in which we can infer a necessary conclusion from two premises that prior demonstration or agreement has established to be true.

Syncretic Characterized by the reconciliation or fusion of differing systems of belief.

Taiping Rebellion Rebellion (1852–1864) against the Qing Empire that resulted in tens of millions of deaths and widespread destruction in southern China.

Tang dynasty Chinese dynasty (618–907) famous for its wealth and encouragement of the arts and literature.

Taro a fibrous root indigenous to New Guinea, first cultivated 9,000 years ago in swamplands.

Tengri "Ruler of the sky." The supreme deity of the Mongols and other steppeland peoples.

The Mongol Peace Era in the thirteenth and fourteenth centuries when Mongol rule created order and stability in Central Asia and enabled goods and ideas to flow along the Silk Roads.

Theory of value The theory that the value of goods is not inherent, but rather determined by supply and demand.

Theravada A conservative branch of Buddhism that adheres to the nontheistic ideal of self-purification to nirvana. Theravada Buddhism emphasizes the monastic ideal and is dominant in present-day Sri Lanka and southeast Asia.

Third Rome Term Russians used for Moscow and Russian Orthodox Christianity. It expressed the belief that the Russian czars were the divinely chosen heirs of the Roman and Byzantine emperors.

Thule Inuit Indigenous Native American people who crossed the Arctic and arrived in Greenland around 1000 C.E.

Tillers Agriculturalists who emphasize the cultivation of plants for food and products, such as timber and cotton.

Tokugawa A family of shoguns that ruled Japan in the name of the emperors from 1603 to 1868.

Trading-post empires Term for the networks of imperial forts and trading posts that Europeans established in Asia in the seventeenth century.

Treasure Fleets Spanish fleets that sailed from the Caribbean each year to bring gold and silver from mines in the Americas back to Europe.

Tundra A treeless area between the ice cap and the tree line of Arctic regions.

Turks A member of any of the Turkic-speaking, nomadic peoples who originated in Central Asia. The Turks eventually converted to Islam and dominated the Middle East.

Uncertainty principle Niels Bohr and Werner Heisenberg's theory that because observers are part of every observation their findings can never be objective.

United Nations International political organization created after World War II to prevent armed conflict, settle international disputes peacefully, and provide cultural, economic, and technological aid. It was the successor to the League of Nations, which had proved to be ineffectual.

Universal love Love between all people, regardless of status, nationality, or family ties.

Upanishads The theoretical sections of the Veda (the literature of the sages of the Ganges civilization). The Upanishads were written down as early as 800 B.C.E.

Urbanization The process by which urban areas develop and expand.

Utilitarianism System of thought devised by Jeremy Bentham, based on the notion that the goal of the state was to create the greatest happiness for the greatest number of people.

Utopianism Belief in a system or ideology aimed at producing a perfect or ideal society.

Vaccination Inoculation with a vaccine to produce immunity to a particular disease.

Vernacular languages The languages that people actually spoke, as opposed to Latin, which was the language used by the Roman Catholic Church and was, for a long time, the language of scholarship, the law, and diplomacy in much of Europe.

Virtual reality A computer simulation of a real or imaginary system.

Wahhabbism Muslim sect founded by Abdul Wahhab (1703–1792), known for its strict observance of the Quran. It is the dominant form of Islam in Saudi Arabia.

Westerlies Winds coming from the west.

Westernization The process by which other cultures adopt Western styles or ways of life.

World system The system of interconnections among the world's population.

World War I Global war (1914–1918) sparked by the assassination of Archduke Francis Ferdinand of Austria by a Serb terrorist in June 1914.

World War II Global conflict that lasted from 1939 to 1945 and ended with the defeat and occupation of Fascist Italy, Nazi Germany, and Japan.

Zen A school of Mahayana Buddhism that asserts that a person can attain enlightenment through meditation, self-contemplation, and intuition.

Ziggurat A tall, tapering Mesopotamian temple. Ziggurats were the physical and cultural centers of Mesopotamian cities.

Zimbabwes Stone-built administrative centers for rulers and the elite in southern Africa. The zimbabwes flourished in the fifteenth century.

Zoroastrianism Iranian religious system founded by Zoroaster that posited a universal struggle between the forces of light (the good) and of darkness (evil).

A NOTE ON DATES AND SPELLINGS

In keeping with common practice among historians of global history, we have used B.C.E. (before the common era) and C.E. (common era) to date events. For developments deep in the past, we have employed the phrase "years ago" to convey to the reader a clear sense of time. Specific dates are given only when necessary and when doing so improves the context of the narrative.

Recognizing that almost every non-English word can be transliterated in any number of ways, we have adopted the most widely used and simplest systems for spelling names and terms. The *pinyin* system of Chinese spelling is used for all Chinese words with the exceptions of *Hong Kong* and *Yangtze*, which are still widely referred to in their Wade-Giles form. Following common usage, we have avoided using apostrophes in the spelling of Arabic and Persian words, as well as words from other languages—thus, *Quran* and *Kaaba* instead of *Qu'ran* and *Ka'ba*, and *Tbilisi* instead of *T'bilisi*. Diacritical marks, accents, and other specialized symbols are used only if the most common variant of a name or term employs such devices (such as *Çatalhüyük*), if they are part of a personal noun (such as *Nicolás*), or if the inclusion of such markings in the spelling of a word makes pronouncing it easier (*Teotihuacán*).

Throughout the text the first appearance of important non-English words whose pronunciation may be unclear for the reader is followed by phonetic spellings in parentheses, with the syllable that is stressed spelled in capital letters. So, for example *Ugarit* is spelled phonetically as "OO-gah-riht." Chinese words are not stressed, so each syllable is spelled in lowercase letters. Thus, the city of Hangzhou in China is rendered phonetically as "hahng-joh." For monosyllabic words, the phonetic spelling is in lowercase letters. So *Rus* is spelled as "roos." The table below provides a guide for how the vowel sounds in *The World: A Brief History* are represented phonetically.

a	as in *cat, bat*
ah	as in *car, father*
aw	as in *law, paw*
ay	as in *fate, same*
eh	as in *bet, met*
ee	as in *beet, ease*
eye	as in *dine, mine*
ih	as in *if, sniff*
o	as in *more, door*
oh	as in *row, slow*
oo	as in *loop, moo*
ow	as in *cow, mouse*
uh	as in *but, rut*

CHAPTER 26
1. H. S. Wilson, *Origins of West Africa Nationalism* (London, 1969), p. 167.

CHAPTER 27
1. N. Chomsky, *Knowledge of Language* (Wesport, CT: 1986), p. 14.

CHAPTER 28
1. D. A. J. Pernikoff, *Bushido: The Anatomy of Terror* (1943).

CHAPTER 29
1. I. Berlin "My Intellectual Path", *New York Review of Books*, 14 May (1998);
The Power of Ideas, ed. H. Hardy (Princeton, 2002), p.12.

CHAPTER 1: p. 4 Francisco Goya y Lucientes, Spanish, 1746-1828. Boy Staring at an Apparition (1824-1825) Carbon Black and watercolor on ivory (Black wash heightened with vermilion and brown) 6.03 x 6.03cm (2 3/8 x 2 3/8 in.) Museum of Fine Arts, Boston. Gift of Eleanor; p. 7 © The Natural History Museum, London; p. 8 Howard S. Friedman/Pearson Education/PH College; p. 12 The Jane Goodall Institute, www.janegoodall.org; p. 16 Charles & Josette Lenars/ © Charles & Josette Lenars/CORBIS All Rights Reserved; p. 17 Michael & Patricia Fogden/ © Michael & Patricia Fogden/CORBIS All Rights Reserved; p. 18 Peter/Georgina Bowater/Creative Eye/MIRA.com; p. 19 Novosti/Photo Researchers, Inc.; p. 22 AKG Images/Jurgen Sorges.

CHAPTER 2: p. 26 © Kevin Flemming/CORBIS All Rights Reserved; p. 28 Rostislav Ageev /Shutterstock; p. 30 Theya Molleson, Natural History Museum of London; p. 32 © Joe McDonald/CORBIS All Rights Reserved; p. 36 © Caroline Penn/CORBIS All Rights Reserved; p. 37 Ashmolean Museum, Oxford, England, U.K.; p. 39 Hittite Museum, Ankara, Turkey/ET Archive, London/SuperStock; p. 43 © Michael Holford; p. 44 Andrew McRobb © Dorling Kindersley.

CHAPTER 3: p. 50 © Copyright The British Museum; p. 54 M. Andrews/Ancient Art & Architecture Collection Ltd.; p. 57 TOP Erich Lessing/Art Resource, NY; p. 57 BOTTOM 57 bottom Werner Forman Archive; p. 58 Giraudon/Bridgeman Art Library; p. 62 Borromeo/Dancing girl. Bronze statuette from Mohenjo Daro. Indus Valley Civilization. National Museum, New Delhi, India. Borromeo/Art Resource, NY; p. 65 Michael Holford; p. 66 Royal Museums of Art and History, Brussels, Belgium. Copyright IRPA-KIK, Brussels, Belgium; p. 67 Lowell Georgia/Corbis/Bettmann; p. 71 Courtesy of the Library of Congress.

CHAPTER 4: p. 74 © CM Dixon/ HIP/The Image Works; p. 77 The Art Archive/Dagli Orti; p. 82 The Art Archive/Heraklion Museum/Dagli Orti; p. 84 © Erich Lessing/Art Resource, NY; p. 87 Eric Lessing/Art Resource, N.Y.; p. 88 The Art Archive/Dagli Orti; p. 91 Werner Forman/Art Resource, NY.

CHAPTER 5: p. 96 The Art Archive/Dagli Orti; p. 99 "Human-headed winged bull and winged lion (lamassu). Alabaster (ypsum); Gateway support from the Palace of AshurnasirpalII (ruled 883-859 BCE). Limestone. H: 10' 3/1/2". L: 9' 1". W: 2' 1/2". The Metropolitan Museum of Art, Gift of John D. Rockefeller, J; p. 104 Ronald Sheridan/ © Ronald Sheridan/Ancient Art & Architecture Collection Ltd; p. 105 The Art Archive/Museo Di Villa Giulia Rome/ Dagli Art; p. 107 The Art Archive/Archaeological Museum Sofia/Dagli Orti; p. 108 Lewandowski/Ojeda/Sarcophagus of a married couple on a funeral bed. Etruscan, from Cerveteri, 6th BCE. Terracotta. Lewandowski/Ojeda. Musee Louvre, Paris France. RMN Reunion Des Musees Nationeaux/Art Resource, NY; p. 109 AGE Fotostock America, Inc.; p. 116 116 Michael Holford.

CHAPTER 6: p. 124 Courtesy of the Freer Gallery of Art, Smithsonian Institution, Washington, D.C.; p. 127 © Tim Page/ CORBIS All Rights Reserved; p. 130 Erich Lessing/Relief, Israel, 10th-6th Century: Judean exiles carrying provisions. Detail of the Assyrian conquest of the Jewish fortified town of Lachish (battle 701 BC). Part of a relief from the palace of Sennacherib at Niniveh, Mesopotamia (Iraq). British Museum; p. 132 Courtesy of the Library of Congress; p. 134 "THE GOOD SHEPHERD", marble, Height: as restored cm 90, as preserved cm 55, head cm 15.5. Late 3rd century A. D. Vatican Musuems, Pio-Christian Museum, Inv. 28590. Courtesy of the Vatican Museums; p. 136 www.photos.com/Jupiter Images; p. 139 Christopher and Sally Gable © Dorling Kindersley; p. 141 Mark de Fraeye/Photo Researchers, Inc.; p. 144 Erich Lessing/Art Resource, N.Y.

CHAPTER 7: p. 150 Robert Clark/Robert Clark Photography; p. 157 The Art Archive/Picture Desk, Inc./Kobal Collection; p. 159 Bridgeman Art Library; p. 164 Romisch-Germanisches Museum der Stadt Koln/Rheinisches Bildarchiv; p. 165 © The Detroit Institute of Arts, USA/Bridgeman Art Library; p. 166 © Archivo Iconografico, S.A./CORBIS All Rights Reserved; p. 168 Adam Woolfitt/Robert Harding; p. 170 © Keren Su/DanitaDelimont.com; p. 172 Werner Forman Archive Ltd; p. 175 F9photos/Dreamstime.

CHAPTER 8: p. 180 © Justin Kerr; p. 184 Canali Photobank; p. 188 R. Sheridan/Ancient Art & Architecture Collection Ltd.; p. 189 Werner Forman Archive; p. 192 Ancient Art & Architecture/DanitaDelimont.com; p. 193 © Gallo Images/CORBIS All Rights Reserved; p. 195 The Art Archive/Dagli Orti; p. 197 Art Archive; p. 202 Dagli Orti/Picture Desk, Inc./Kobal Collection; p. 204 China Tourism Press. Wang, Jian Jun/Getty Images Inc.-Image Bank.

CHAPTER 9: p. 210 Fujita Museum Of Art; p. 215 The Art Archive/British Museum; p. 216 James Stanfield/NGS Image Collection; p. 217 © Michael Holford; p. 219 Natia Chakvetadze; p. 220 Picture Desk, Inc./Kobal Collection; p. 221 © Chris Lisle/CORBIS All Rights Reserved; p. 226 Scala/Art Resource, N.Y.; p. 229 Courtesy of the Library of Congress; p. 232 Reuters America LLC/ © Reuters/CORBIS.

CHAPTER 10: p. 236 © Carmen Redondo/CORBIS All Rights Reserved; p. 242 Sachsische Landesbibliothek p. 243 © Erich Lessing/Art Resource; p. 245 Werner Forman Archive Ltd; p. 248 Christopher Rennie/Robert Harding World Imagery; p. 253 © Luca Tettoni/Robert Harding; p. 254 Library of Congress; p. 256 National Museum of Ireland.

CHAPTER 11: p. 262 Kanai Morio/Tokyo National Museum/DNP Archives; p. 266 © Staffan Widstrand/CORBIS All Rights Reserved; p. 269 Courtesy of the Library of Congress; p. 271 © Kazuyoshi Nomachi/HAGA/ The Image Works; p. 272 Andrew Gunners/Getty Images-Digital Vision; p. 276 Japan Society; p. 278 Courtesy of the Library of Congress; p. 279 Bayerische Staatsbibliothek; p. 282 By permission of The British Library; p. 283 Rheinisches Bildarchiv, Museen Der Stadt Koln.

CHAPTER 12: p. 286 Library of the Topkapi Palace Museum; p. 288 Bibliotheque Nationale, Paris, France/Bridgeman Art Library; p. 289 By permission of The British Library; p. 293 Monasterio de El Escorial, El Escorial, Spain/Index/Bridgeman Art Library; p. 294 H. Lewandowski/Musee du Louvre/RMN Reunion des Musees Nationaux, France. Art Resource, NY; p. 297 Bridgeman Art Library; p. 300 Paul H. Kuiper/CORBIS-NY; p. 302 V & A Picture Library; p. 307 The Art Archive/Freer Gallery of Art; p. 308 The National Palace Museum.

CHAPTER 13: p. 314 © The Trustees of the British Museum; p. 317 The Bridgeman Art Library International/Bibliotheque Nationale, Paris, France/ The Bridgeman Art Library; p. 320 Akg-Images/VISIOARS/AKA-IMAGES; p. 321 Copyright Museum of Imperial Collections, Sonnomaru Shozo Kan; p. 323 The Metropolitan Museum of Art, Purchase, Bequest of Dorothy Graham Bennet, 1993 (1993.256) Photograph © The Metropolitan Museum of Art; p. 324 Linwendy/Dreamstime; p. 325 The Art Archive/Bibliotheque Nationale, Paris; p. 328 National Palace Museum, Taipei, Taiwan/ The Bridgeman Art Library; p. 329 Library of the Topkapi Palace Museum; p. 330 © George G. Schmid/Corbis All rights reserved; p. 333 Dallas and John Heaton/The Stock Connection; p. 335 Canali Photobank; p. 336 © National Maritime Museum Picture Library, London, England Neg. #E5555-3.

CHAPTER 14: p. 342 © Josef Polleross/The Image Works; p. 354 Museum of London; p. 349 © Bildarchiv Preussischer Kulturbesitz/Art Resource, NY; p. 351 Aka-Images/AKA-IMAGES; p. 354 Bibliotheque Nationale, Paris/Bridgeman Art Library; p. 360 SEF/Art Resource, NY; p. 362 © 1991 The Metropolitan Museum of Art; p. 365 The Granger Collection; p. 366 Frank Khoury/Museum purchase 86-12-2. Photograph by Frank Khoury. National Museum of African Art, Smithsonian Institution; p. 367 Dallas and John Heaton/The Stock Connection, p. 368 © Charles & Josette Lenars/Corbis All rights reserved.

CHAPTER 15: p. 374 Courtesy of the Harvard Map Collection, Harvard College Library; p. 376 Courtesy of the Library of Congress; p. 378 National Archives of South Africa; p. 379 Photograph © 1984 The Metropolitan Museum of Art; p. 382 Bodleian Library, University of Oxford; p. 390 Library of the Topkapi Palace Museum; p. 391 Courtesy of the Library of Congress; p. 399 Instituto Amatller de Arte Hispanico, Barcelona, Spain; p. 402 Courtesy of the Library of Congress; p. 404 © Michael Freeman/CORBIS All Rights Reserved.

CHAPTER 16: p. 410 By permission of The British Library; p. 414 By permission of The British Library; p. 417 Courtesy of the Library of Congress; p. 418 Copyright Rijksmuseum Amsterdam; p. 419 Courtesy of the Library of Congress; p. 421 Bibliotheque Nationale de France; p. 424 V&A Images/Victoria and Albert Museum; p. 428 Courtesy of the Library of Congress; p. 430 The Hispanic Society of America/Hispanic Society of America.

CHAPTER 17: p. 434 © Jonathan Blair/CORBIS All Rights Reserved; p. 437 Koninklijke Bibliothek, The Hague, The Netherlands; p. 440 Courtesy of the John Carter Brown Library at Brown University; p. 441 Musee des Beaux-Arts et d'Archeologie, Besancon, France/ Lauros/Giraudon/ The Bridgeman Art Library; p. 442 The Granger Collection, New York; p. 445 Courtesy of the Library of Congress; p. 448 Library of the Topkapi Palace Museum; p. 449 Charles Cavaliere; p. 450 The Art Archive/Mus[eacute]e Guimet Paris; p. 454 Courtesy of the Library of Congress; p. 457 Library and Archives of Canada website, www.collectionscanada.ca.

CHAPTER 18: p. 462 © Richard List/CORBIS All Rights Reserved; p. 465 Bildarchiv Preubischer Kulturbesitz; p. 466 Versucung Christi (1547), Gemalde, Bonn, Landschaftsverband Rheinland/Rheinisches Landesmuseum Bonn. Inv. Nr. 58.3; p. 467 Courtesy of the Library of Congress; p. 468 Jeffery Dykes/Photograph courtesy Peabody Essex Museum; p. 469 Courtesy of the Library of Congress; p. 470 © The National Museum of Denmark, Ethnographic Collection; p. 472 of the Library of Congress; p. 474 Courtesy of the Library of Congress; p. 475 Jerry Hardman-Jones/Art Quarterly; p. 478 The Bridgeman Art Library International; p. 481 © Erich Lessing, Art Resource, NY; p. 482 Courtesy of the Library of Congress; p. 484 Courtesy of the Library of Congress.

CHAPTER 19: p. 488 By permission of The British Library; p. 494 Courtesy of the Library of Congress. Rare Book and Special Collections Divisoin; p. 495 Archiv fur Kunst und Geschichte, Berlin; p. 497 Courtesy of the Library of Congress; p. 498 V&A Images/Victoria and Albert Museum; p. 499 Courtesy of the Library of Congress; p. 502 502 © The Metropolitan Museum of Art; p. 506 Breamore House, Hampshire, England; p. 507 Museo De America.

CHAPTER 20: p. 516 The Art Archive/Museo de Arte Antiga Lisbon/Dagli Orti; p. 519 Courtesy of the Library of Congress; p. 522 Courtesy of the Library of Congress; p. 523 Private Collection/ Agnew's, London, UK/ The Bridgeman Art Library; p. 526 Photograph courtesy Peabody Essex Museum; p. 527 Rijksmuseum,

A

Abahai, 502
Abbas I the Great, 499
Abbot Suger, 278, 283
ABC for Baby Patriots, An, 654
Abd al-Malik, caliph, *226*
Abd al-Rahman, 248
Abd-ar-Razzak, 375, 404
Abduction from the Seraglio, The
    (Mozart), 567
Abel, 309
Abelard, 283
Abolitionism, 548, G–1
Aborigine, 578, 630, G–1
    and rejection of agriculture, 28
Abortion, 771
Abrahamic religions, 133, *133*
Absolute sovereignty, 405
Abstract art, 710
Abu Simbel, 64, 93
Abul Fazl Allami, 424
Abundance theory and farming, 42–43
Academy of Athens, 144, *144*
Aceh, 646
Acupuncture, 714
Adam (Biblical), 135, *178–179*
Adam of Bremen, 266
Adario, 579
Adelard of Bath, 283
Adjara, *622*
Adowa, battle of, *647, 647, 649*
Adrianople, battle of, 185
Adulis, 237
Adultery, 511
Advertising, television, 713
Aegean civilization, 81–84
Afghanistan, 646, 655, 735, 742, 745,
    769
Africa, 338. *See also* East Africa,
    North Africa, South Africa,
    West Africa
    chronology, *118, 119*
    civilization of, *118*
    climate change in the fourteenth
        century, *348*
    cultural exchange, 113
    decolonization in twentieth centu-
        ry, 739–740
    developments in ancient, 116–118
    empires in fifteenth
        century, 377–380
    environmental problems, 775–776
    evolution of human species, 7–13
    in fifteenth century, *384*
    foreign imperialism, 653, *653, 654*
    in fourteenth century, *365*
    geographic obstacles, *254*
    geography impeding communica-
        tions, *238, 239*
    HIV, map of, *792*
    imperialism, 643, 651
    invasion by Almoravids, 283
    and Islam, 216, 331, 471
    life expectancy, 790
    map of, *239, 510*
        ancient, *117*
        fourteenth century states, *380*
        spread of Islam, *473*
        in twentieth century, *722*
    modernization, 677–678
    Muslim reform movements, *679*
    nationalism, 670
    and nomads, 309–310
    pastoral imperialism, 448
    population, 643, 646, 794
        in eighteenth century, *518*
    slaves/slave trade, 444–445, *509,
        509*–511, 548–553
        chronology, *509*

spread of agriculture in, 42
    in thirteenth century, 338
    and Western science, *715*
African Americans, 759
African bulge, 379
Africans
    as slaves, 444
Afrikaans, G–1
Afterlife, Egyptian, 64–65, *65*
Agaja, king, 509
Age of Plague, 522, G–1
Age of the Holy Spirit, 403
Agilulf, king, 195–196
Agrarianization, 612
Agriculture. *See also* farming
    by accident, 44
    in Africa, 42
    in the Americas, 38, 448–449
    in Asia, 38
    in China, 61–62, 250–253, 449–451
    chronology, *45*
    cult, 43, *43*
    domestication of animals, 659
    effect of climate change on, 345
    in Egypt, 56–58
    in eighteenth century, 531–536,
        532, 533, 534
    in eleventh century China, 307, *307*
    in eleventh century Europe, 279
    in Ethiopia, 193, 448
    in Europe, 38
    in fourteenth century Japan, 363
    in fourteenth century New
        Zealand, 367
    herding, *26*
    intensified, 54–55
    in Islamic world, 246–248, *247*
    in Japan, 248–249
    land reclamation, 456–457
    mechanization of, 622–623, *623*
    native Americans, 457, *457*
    in nineteenth century, 590–596,
        621–623, *622*
    in North American
        Southwest, 266–268
    in the Pacific Islands, 42, 253–255
    in Persia/Persian empire, 158
    plow technology, 451
    preagricultural settlements, 29–30
    prehistoric, 12
    problems of, 28–30
    rejection by Aborigines, 28
    in sixteenth century, 435–436
    in Southeast Asia, 250–253
    spread of, 38–42, *40–41*
        chronology, *42*
    in Tibet, 203
Agrochemicals, 781
Aguirre, Lope de, 476
Agyeman Prempeh I, *676*
Ahar, 315
Ahriman, 127, G–1
Ahura Mazda, 126, G–1
AIDS, 791–702
Aimi Fat Reduction Hospital, *784*
Ain Jalut, battle of, 331
Ainu, 417, 504
Ainu War, 449
Air pollution, 785
Aka River, 457
Akbar, 424, *424*, 477, *498*, 500
Akkad/Akkadians, 65, 70, 92, 157
Akrotiri, 82
Akwamu, 511
Al Biruni, 273
Alamut, 287
al-Andalus, 292, G–1
Alaska, 658
al-Azhar, 699

Alchemy, 481
Alcoholism, 619
Alejiadinho, 555, *555*
Aleutian Islands, 631, 658
Alexander the Great, *107*, 142, 143,
    156, 160–163, 166, 175, 191, 387
    hegemony of, 160
    map of empire, *161*
Alexandria, 162
    and industrialization, 620
Alexius IV, 302
Alfonso X, king, *293*
Alfred the Great, 214, *225*, 256
Algeria, 656, 739
al-Ghazali, 296
Algiers, 656
Algonquin Indians, 467
al-Hajj Umar, 226, *679*
al-Hajjaj, 226
al-Hakim, caliph, 287
al-Hallaj, 296
al-Hariri, *288, 354*
Ali, 200, 329, 500
Ali Mubarak Pasha, 671
Ali Pasha Mubarak, 671
Al-Idrisi, *260–261*
al-Istakhri, 277, *278*
Alienation, 708
All Quiet on the Western Front
    (Remarque), 724
Allies, 730
Alluvial plains, 33, G–1
    agriculture of, 37–38
Almanac, *522*
    Mayan, *242*
al-Mansur, 448
Almanzor, 293
al-Maqrizi, 349
Almohads, 293, 309
    chronology, *293*
    map of, *295*
Almoravids, 293, 309, G–1
    chronology, *293*
    map of, *295*
al-Mutawakkil, caliph, 225
Alp Arslan, 300
Alpha males, 12
Alphabet
    Greek, 104
    Phoenician, 99
al-Sarraj, *335*
Altai Shan, 322, 326
Altan Khan, 470
Alternative energy, 779–780, G–1
Alternative medicine, 714, G–1
Altigin, 224, *225*
Alvaro VI, king, *445*
Amarna, 64
Amarna Letters, *64*
Amazon, 455
America, colonial,
    independence, 556–558
American Indians. *See* Native Americans
American Samoa, 658
American Southwest
    climate change in the fourteenth
        century, *348*
    contending with isolationism, *280*
Americanization, 556, 766, G–1
Americas
    chronology, *92, 244, 458*
        of slave trade, *509*
    colonialism, 652–653
    empires, 426–429
        chronology, *431*
        map of, *427*
    expansion in eleventh and twelfth
        centuries, 264–270
    in fifteenth century, 381–385

geography, 239
imperialism
    chronology, *455*
    industrialization, 604–605
    land exploitation, 451–456,
        452–453
    map of, *559*
    nationalism, 670
    pastoral imperialism, 448–449
    population in eighteenth
        century, 517, *518*
    in sixteenth and seventeenth cen-
        turies, 505–509
    social classes/society, 507
    Spain, 549
    spread of agriculture in, 38
    state building, 88–92, *90, 92*
    in thirteenth century, 337
    urbanization, 519
Amin, Idi, 739, *741*
Amitabha Buddha, *228*
Ammianus Marcellinus, 185
Amritsar, 724
Amsterdam, 420, 519
Amu Darya, 780
Amun, 97
Amur River, 423
An Lushan, 203
An Lushan's rebellion, 203, 251
Anabaptism, 477
Anak, 192
Anarchists, 684, 726, G–1
Anatolia, 77, 297, 370
    trade, 77, *78–79*
Anatolian plateau, 79
Ancestor worship, *118,* 503
Andean civilization, *88,* 88–89
    art, *91*
Andes, 241, 442
    agriculture of, 35
    climate of, *381*
    expansion of, *246*
    map of, *240*
    in thirteenth century, 338
Andex, 35, 89
Angel of Death, 223
Angkor, 251, 271
Angkor Wat, 271–272, *272*
Anglo-Egyptian Sudan, 647
Angola, 509, 622
Animal husbandry, 30–31
Animal rights, 704, G–1
Animals, exchange among
    countries, 436–442
Anitta, king, 77
Ankara, 370
Anna Comnena, 300–301, 303
Anselm, archbishop of
    Canterbury, 283
Anthropology, 705, *711*
Antibiotic, 702
Anticlericalism, 574–575
Antimenes Painter, 104
Antiscientific reaction in the twenti-
    eth century, 714–715
Anti-Semitism, 356–357, 668–669,
    725, 728, G–1
Anti-smoking campaign, 751, *751*
Antwerp, 420
Anubis, 65
Anuradhapura, 96, 112
Anuruddha, king, 214, *225*
Apes, 705
    humanlike features, 5
Apétor II, *760*
Aphrodite (goddess), 104
Apollo (god), 227
Apollo of Miletus, 104
Appeasement policy, 171–172

Aquaculture, 442
Aqueduct, 241, *248*
Aquinas, Thomas, 333, 493
Arabia, 118, 193
  chronology, *118, 119*
  civilization of, *118*
  Muslim reform movements, *679*
Arabs, 309, 656, 741
  invasion of Roman
    Empire, 196–197
  against Persia and Rome, 197
  in World War I, 723
Aragon, 494
Aragonese, 494
Aral, 780
Araucanos, 554
Archimedes, 140, 334
Architecture, 713–714
  in the Americas, 454
  Christian, 478
  of early civilization, 56
  Greece, ancient, *144*
  Hittites, 77
  India, *333*
  Islam/Islamic, *236*
  Khmer kingdom, 271–272, *272*
  of Roman Empire, 164
  Tibet/Tibetans, *204*
Arctic
  climate change in the fourteenth
    century, 345, *348*
  contending with isolationism, *280*
  expansion in eleventh and twelfth
    centuries, 264–266
Arctic Circle, 564
Arganthonios, king, 109
Argentina, 622, 652, 655, 670, 683,
    756, 764
  and agriculture, 594
  industrialization, 605
  post World War I, 725
Aristocracy, 188, 356, 490, 495, 631,
    634–635
  British, 634, 650
Aristotle, 105, 131, 134, 135, 136,
    138, 140, 142, 143, 144, *146*,
    161, 283, 303, *402*, 566
Arkona, 196
Armenia, 218, 224, 418
  and Basil II, 298
Armenians, 215
Armstrong, Karen, 769
Arnhem Land, 28
Arnold, Matthew, 680
Arouet, Francois-Marie. *See* Voltaire
Arove, Don Francisco, *507*
Art, *2–3*
  abstract, 710
  American, *588*
  of the Americas, *506, 576–577*
  of ancient river valley
    civilizations, *62, 63*
  Andean civilization, *91*
  Assyrian, *99*
  Brazilian, *555*
  British, *532, 534, 562, 598, 646*
  Buddhist, *124, 210, 215, 215*
  Byzantine Empire, *302, 302–303*
  in Catalhüyü, 37
  cave, *16, 16–17, 17, 71*
  Celtic, *166*
  Cerro Sechín, *88*
  Chinese, *157, 170, 308, 308, 325,
    391, 450, 502, 526, 541,
    566–567, 568, 712*
  Chinese women, *202*
  Christian, *130, 132, 134, 256, 465,
    467, 468, 475*
  Christianity, *293*

Cretan, 82, *82*
Cuban, *670*
depicting
  industrialization, 616–617, *617*
Dutch, *417, 564*
early American, *682*
Egyptian, *50, 57, 65, 65*
in eleventh and twelfth
    centuries, *282, 282–283*
eleventh century Europe, *279*
Ethiopian, *193*
Etruscan, *108*
expressionism, 712
fifteenth century, *402*
Franciscan, *334–335, 335*
French, *564, 581, 598*
German, *279, 465*
Greek, ancient, *104*
Harappan, *58, 59, 62, 63, 68*
Hittites, *74*
Hungarian, *297*
Ice Age, *16, 16–17, 17*
Il-Khanate, *329, 329*
Indian, *712*
Japanese, *321, 591, 635, 711*
Java, *253*
Korean, *192, 220*
Kushanese, *124*
Mayan, *180, 242, 243*
Mesoamerican, *269*
Middle Ages, *286*
modern, *713*
Mongolian, *314, 320, 321*
morality, *626*
Mughals, *424, 498*
Muslim, *288*
naval, *597*
Nazca, 241
Nigerian, *116*
Olmec, *91*
Ottoman Empire, *424, 448, 498*
Persian, *159*
Peru, *368*
post World War I, *724*
prehistoric, *48–49*
primitive, *636*
religious, *210, 282, 283*
Revolutionary War, *674*
rock, *39*
Roman, *164, 166, 188, 189, 195,
    197, 217*
Romanesque, *283*
Russian, *710–711, 726*
Sarmatian, *172, 172–173*
Scythian, *171, 171–172*
seventeenth century, *417, 481*
in sixteenth and seventeenth centu-
    ry, *478, 478*
Song empire, *308, 308*
Spanish, *4,5, 91, 91, 441, 516*
surrealism, 712
Teotihuacán, 174
Thracian, *107*
in twentieth century, *709–714*
Vietnam, *87*
West African, *379*
Artemis (goddess), 147
Arthasastra, 166, 167, G–1
Arthaveda, 141
Artificial intelligence, 704, G–1
Artisans, 616
Arts and Crafts Movement, G–1
Asante, 672, 676, 676–677
Asceticism, 226
Ashanti, 511
Ashikaga shogunate, 362
  chronology of, *363*
Ashikaga Takauji, 362, *362*
Ashio copper mines, 626

Ashur, 62, 63, 76, 77, 84
Ashurbanipal, king, 99, 102
Ashurbanipal II, king, *99*
Asia
  climate change in the fourteenth
    century, *348*
  Enlightenment, 568–572, *570*
  exploitation of environment, *459*
  foreign imperialism, 642, 642–643,
    653, *653*
  imperialism, 449–451, 540–544
    chronology, *455*
  and imperialistic
    Portugal, 414–416
  and map of spread of religion, *471*
  and maritime
    imperialism, 416–419
  science, 714–715
  spread of agriculture in, 38
  and western science, 483–485
Asian values, 761
Asoka, 166–167, 174, 191, 214, 225
  emperor, 166, 167, *168, 168–169*
  chronology, *169*
  map of reign, *167*
Aspero, 53–54, 89
Assassins, 287, G–1
Assur (god), 84, 97, 98, 99
Assyria/Assyrians, 99–102, 157, 158
  Babylonian exile, 130, *130*
  chronology, *102*
  revival of, *103*
Asteroid, 788
Astrakhan, 326
Astrolabe, *335*
Astrology, 481, 768
Astronomy, 244, *335*, 336, 481–482,
    484, 484–495, *529*, 569, 698, *710*
Asturias, 256
Aswan High Dam, 780, *780*
Atahualf, king, 188
Atheism, 478, 572, 680, 768
Athens, 103, 105, 160
Atiba, 672
Atlantic Ocean
  map of European
    exploration, *400–401*
  navigation of, 376
  wind systems of, 395–398
Atlantic slave trade, 420, 440, G–1
Atomic bomb, 729, 731, 732
Atomic theory, 142, 147, 710, G–1
Augurers, 66
Augustus, 151, 164, 165, 478
Aum Shinrikyo, 770
Auracano, 631
Aurangzeb, 477, 498, 544
  emperor, 424, 661
Australia, 534, 535–536, 578, 591,
    622, 655, 656
  aborigines, 28
  convict labor, 626
  exploitation of environment, *459*
  Homo sapiens migration, 9
  racism, 759
  socialism, 686
Australopithecine, 6, G–1
Avars, 255
Aviation, 698
Avicenna, *141*
Avvakum, 467
Axial Age, 122–149, G–1
  aftermath of, 174–175
  chronology, *141, 146, 147, 175*
  definition of, 125–126
  map of, *127–128*
  math, 137–138

medicine, *141*, 141–142
political thinking, 134–137
reason, 138–139
religious thinking, 132–134
science, 139–141
skepticism, 142–143
structures of, 143–146
thinkers of, 126–131, *146*
thoughts of, 131–143, *146*
Axial zone, 237, G–1
Axis, 730
Axum, 193, 218, 271
Ayacucho, 241
Ayurvedic medicine, *141*
Ayutthaya, 543
Azerbaijan, 315, *658*
Azores, 395, *399*, 440
Aztec calendar stone, *556*
Aztecs, 382, 382–385, 403, 426, *428*,
    428–429, 442, 556, *556*, G–1
  chronology, *382*
  in fifteenth century, *383, 384*
  social nature of, 479–480

B

Baal (god), 98
Babur, 423–424
Babylon/Babylonians, 99
  chronology, *102*
  map of, *122–123*
  revival of, 102–103, *103*
Bach, Johann Sebastian, 576
Bacon, Francis, 482
Bacon, Nathaniel, 430
Bacon, Roger, 334
Bacteria, 594
Bactria, 158, 162
Baghdad, 248, 286, 287, 288, *743*
  siege of by Mongols, *320*
Bahais, 769
Bahía, *438*
Bahrain, 116
Bakeries, 597
Balance of trade, 157, G–1
Balearic islands, 333
Bali, *28*
Balkans, 480, 483, 544, 566, 658
Ballroom Guide, The, 651
Balmes, Jaume, 619
Banditry, 303
Bangladesh, 738, 743
Bankim, 671
Bankimcandra Chattopadhyaya, 671
Banks, Joseph, 535
Bantam, 421
Bantu, 34, G–1
Bantu languages, 42, 116
Baratieri, general, *647, 649*
Barbados, 440, 455
Barbarian invasions
  of China, 189–191
  chronology, *206*
  effects of, 206–207
  in Egypt, 84–85
  and fall of Roman
    Empire, 184–185, 188–189
  of India, 191–192
  of Roman Empire, 195–196
Barbarian West, 188–189
  map of, *190*
Barbarians
  and Byzantine Empire, 296–297
  invading China, 303–308
  map of, *190*
  and Roman Empire, 163, 164
Barbarossa brothers, 425–426
Barcelona, 350, 619, 683
Barghash of Zanzibar, *626, 648*
Barguzinsk, 449

Barley, 36, 61, 203
  in Greece, 103
Barrie, J.M., 706
Barroilhet, Carlos, 605
Basil II, emperor, 297–298
Baskore of Maradi, 676
Basra, 247
Bastille, fall of, 580, 581
Batavia, 417–419, 541, 542, 727
Battle of Little Bighorn, 646
Battle of Minato River, 362
Batumi, 622
Baybars, 331
Beans, 35
Beatus of Liébana, 178–180, 277
Beauvoir, Simone de, 708
Beavers, 457
Becker, Jerome, 626
Beckford, William, 549
Beef as food, 787
Beerage, 634
Beer-making, 57
Beethoven, Ludwig van, 583
Beijing, 317, 392, 484, 607, 641
Beijing School of Medicine, 695
Belgium
  imperialism, 643
  industrialization, 601, 603
Belgrade, 425
Belief in progress, 572
Bellerophon, 302
Belllunti, 463
Bence Island, 552
Bencon, 417
Benedict, St., 226–227
Beneficial and Beautiful
      Company, 524
Bengal, 332, 393, 451, 526, 527,
      545–546, 620, 622
Benin, 379, 379, 509
Benjamin of Tudela, 301, 355
Benson, Stephen A., 670
Bentham, Jeremy, 685–686
Benthamism, 686
Benxi, 778
Benxi steelworks, 778
Berbers, 196, 214, 292, 656
Bergson, Henri, 707, 711
Beriberi, 522
Bering Strait, crossing of, 19, 21
Berlin, Isaiah, 770–771
Bessemer, Henry, 598
Bessemer converter, 701
Big bang theory, 702, G–1
Bigamy, 465
Bingham, George Caleb, 682
Biology, 710
Bird flu, 791
Bird symbols, 245
Birth control, 590, 793–794
Bishops, 188
Bitter manioc, 34
Bizet, Georges, 629
Black America religion, 474–476
Black Bone Yi, 306
Black consciousness, 760
Black culture, 759–760
Black Death, 342, 343, 348, 349, 351,
      354, 369–371, 386, 444, G–1
  map of, 352–353
  moral and social effects, 351–358
Black Hills, 554
Black Land, 56
Blake, William, 132, 661
Blanc, Louis, 684
Blanco of Cadiz, Pedro, 624
Blast furnace, invention of, 333, 484
Bligh, William, 534
Blood, drinking of, 32

Bloodletting, 242, 243, 244
Blyden, Edward, 670
Board game, 66
Boas, Franz, 705, 711
Boccioni, Umberto, 712
Bodhisattva, 215, 228
Bodin, Jean, 492, 497
Boethius, 189
Bohème, La (Puccini), 629
Bohemia, 405, 478
  in fourteenth century, 370
Bohr, Niels, 701, 710
Boilly, Louis Léopold, 523
Bokassa, Jean-Bedel, 739
Bolivia, 241, 430, 670, 681
Bollywood, 713
Bolsheviks, 726
Bomb shelter, 731
Bombay film industry, 713
Bon, 222, 232, G–1
Boniface, 255
Bonobos, 12
Bon-po, 222
Boris, tsar, 256
Borlaug, Norman E., 781
Borneo, 540
Bornu, 339
Borobudur, 252, 253
Borommakot, king, 542
Bose, Nandalal, 712
Bosnia, 744
Boston, 519
Boston Tea Party, 556
Botanical Garden in Paris, 532
Botanical Garden of Madrid, 532
Botany Bay, 559, 560
Botticelli, 402
Bougainville, Louis de, 558
Bounty (ship), 534
Bourbon, 533
Bourbon dynasty, 566
Bourgeois, 726, 726
Bow and arrow technology, 16
Boy Staring at an Apparition
      (Goya), 4–5
Brahman, 111–112, 127, 132, 222,
      662, G–1
Brahmanism, 127, 133
Brahmins, 419, 567
Braque, Georges, 710, 711
Brattahlid, 266
Braun, Georg, 454
Brazil, 442, 533, 670, 683, 756, 765
  in the Americas, 454–455
  art, 555
  and black religion, 474–476
  coffee production, 440, 604, 604
  conquest by Portugal, 554–555
  dams, 780
  emancipation of slaves, 626
  independence, 558
  missionary activity in, 476
  nationalism, 670
  and slaves/slave trade, 445
  and sugarcane, 440, 440
Brazilian Catholicism, 476
Breadfruit, 534, 534–535
Bread-making, 57
Breeding of animals, 44–45
Bride, St., 232
Briggs, Henry Perronet, 562
Brigid, 232
Britain, 490. See also England
  commerce with India, 608–609
  constitutionalism, 672
  decolonization in twentieth centu-
      ry, 738–739
  empire, 644

imperialism, 642, 668
  in India, 648, 650
in India, 678
industrialization, 529–532, 597
  map of, 531
in Latin America, 652
and Maoris, 664, 665
nationalism, 668
Opium Wars, 638, 640–641
politics, 683
and Roman culture, 164
rule in Canada, 557, 656
social classes, 634
urbanization, 519
war with American
      colonies, 556–557
war with China, 639
war with Maoris, 647
World War I, 720, 723
World War II, 729–731
British East India Company, 525,
      528, 533, 545, G–1
British Guiana, 627
British Niger Company, 653
British North America, 455–456
Bronze Age, 73
Bronze making, 79, 87, 87
Brookes (ship), 548, 548
Brother Jonathan, 721
Brothers of the Sword, 330
Bruckner, Anton, 680
Brun, Cornelis de, 499
Brunel, I.K., 599
Bubonic plague, 349, 443–444, 791
Buddha/Buddhism, 112, 124, 127,
      127–130, 133, 134, 143, 144,
      147, 153, 157, 168, 212, 215,
      358, 361, 447, 678, 760
  art, 210, 215, 215, 253
  and Asoka, 168–169
  in China, 200, 219, 392, 469–470
  chronology, 221
  conflict and conversion, 214
  in India, 222
  in Japan, 204, 220–221, 469–479
  in Korea, 192, 219–220
  Mahayana, 221, 228, 233
  map of, 231, 471
  and Mongols, 470, 470–471
  monks, 227–228, 262
  persecution of, 192
  and politics, 219
  religious communities, 228,
      228–229
  revitalization of, 472
  in Southeast Asia, 272–273
  spread of, 225, 229, 232–233
    chronology, 471
  Theravada, 221, 233
  in Tibet, 221–222
  world view of, 514–515
  Zen, 362, 714
Buddhist, 167, 167
Buddhist clergy, 168
Buenos Aires, 455
  and industrialization, 620
Buffalo, 554
Buganda, 679
Bulgaria, 668
  and Basil II, 298
  intensified settlements of, 54
Bulgars, 196, 223, 256, 289
  and Basil II, 298
Bull of Heaven, 66
Bulliet, Richard W., 226
Bullion, 573
Bundu, 553
Burbank, Luther, 594
Bure, 365

Bureaucratization, 673–679, 677, G–1
  chronology, 678
Burgundians, 188
Burke, Edmund, 528, 583
Burkina Faso, 774, 775–776
Burma, 417, 451, 542–543, 646
  and Western science, 699
Bursa, 372
Bush, George H.W., 743
Bush, George W., 743, 743, 745, 788
Bush Negro, 760
Bushmen of Africa, 17, 22, 22
Business imperialism, 652, 652–655,
      G–1
Bustani, Butrus, 615
Buttons, 606
Byblos, 97, 98
Byzantine Empire, 194–195, 206,
      223–224, 296–303, 332–333,
      370, 390, G–1
  art and learning, 302, 302–303
  chronology, 302
  and the crusaders, 300–302
  map of, 299
Byzantium. See Byzantine Empire

C

Cabbalism, 481
Cabet, étienne, 684
Cabot, John, 398
Cacao, 244, 384, 431, 441
Cacapol, 554
Cadiz, 98
Caere, 108
Cahokia, 268, G–1
Cain, 309
Cairo, 287, 331, 342, 343, 354, 620,
      699
Calcutta, 620
Calendar, 2–3
  Ice-Age, 2, 18
Calendar stone, 556
Calicut, 398
California, 449, 454, 628
  in eighteenth century, 555
Caliph, 199–200, 332, G–1
Cambodia, 274, 734, 750, 763
Camel caravans, 216
Camera obscura, 572
Cameroon, 34
Canada, 558
  formation of nation, 655
  and French, 557
Canal workers in China, 392
Canal Zone, 658
Cañaris, 381
Canary Islands, 398, 532
Cancer, 791
Canda
  and industrialization, 604
Candra Gupta, 191
Candragupta, 166
Cane sugar, 440, 440
Cangapol, 554
Cannibalism, 479, 574
Canning of food, 594, 597
Canon of Medicine, The
      (Avicenna), 141
'Cantiga' of Alfonso X 'the Wise,' 293
Canton. See Guangzhou
Canyon culture, 266–268, G–1
Cape of Good Hope, 398, 448
  exploitation of environment, 459
Cape Verdes, 440
Capital punishment, 771
Capitalism, 419, 618, 684, 725, 727,
      756, G–1
Capitoline Hill, 184
Captives (Michelangelo), 478

Caravaggio, 466
Carbon dioxide emissions, 779, 779
Carbon in the environment, 779
Carchemish, 74
Caribbean, 440, 723
  exploitation of environment, 459
Caribbean Islands, 426
Carmen (Bizet), 629
Caroline Islands, 253
Cars, 778
Carson, Rachel, 781, 781
Carthage, 98–99, 162
Cartography, 260–261, 374, 564
  Buddhist, 514–515
  of world, 277, 277
Cartoonists, 713
Casa, Don Cristóbal Choque, 469
Casa Grande, 345, 348
Casas, Ramon, 726
Casimir the Great, 370
Cassava, 35, 436
Cassia, 153
Caste system, 167, 192, 222, 622, G–1
Caste War, 681
Castiglione, Giuseppe, 568
Castile, 333, 402–403, 490
Castilians, 666
Castro, Fidel, 741
Catalan Atlas, 363–364, 364
Catechism, 469
Catherine the Great, empress of Russia, 574
Catholic Church, 212, 756. See also Catholicism
Catholic Reformation, 466
Catholicism, 463, 464–466, 728. See also Catholic Church; Christianity
  black, 474–476
  Brazilian, 476
  Enlightenment, 571, 574, 574
  in Korea, 571
  missionaries in America, 474
  missionaries in Japan, 420
  persecution of, 415, 467
  response to industrialization, 619
  revival in eighteenth century, 576
  and Wars of Religion, 494
  in White America, 476–477
Cattle, in the Americas, 437
Caucasus, 543
Caucasus Mountains, 159
Cave art, 16, 16–17, 17, 71
Cellini, Benvenuto, 478
Celtic, art, 166
Celts, 166
Census, 456
Central African Republic, 739
Central Pacific Railroad, 628
Centralization, 673–679, 677, G–1
  chronology, 678
Cerro Sechín, 88, 88
Certainty and science, 701–702
Cervical cancer, 791
Césaire, Aimé, 760
Ceylon, 111
Ceylon tea, 629
Chabi, 320, 327
Chaco Canyon, 265
Chadwick, Edwin, 619
Chak Tok Ich'aak, 182
Chaldiran, battle of, 501
Cham kingdom, 251
Chambers, William, 567
Chan Chan, 368, 368–369
Chan Santa Cruz, 681
Chang Chueh, 190–191
Chang'an, 191, 303
Changchun, 321

Changsha, 692, 693
Changsu, king, 219
Changzhao, battle at, 327–328
Chaos theory, 702, G–1
Charaka, 141–142
Charlemagne, 214, 225, 255
Charles, king of Spain, 490
Charles I, king of England, 494
Charles the Great, 370
Charles V, 478
  map of dominion, 491
Chatham Islands, 254, 647
Chaucer, Geoffrey, 357
Chavagnac, Father, 568
Chávez, Hugo, 743
Chavín de Huantar, 89, 90, 91
Checa, 381
Chechnya, 658
Chekhov, Anton, 634
Chen-la, 251
Cheops, 70
Cherokee, 658, 672, 672
Cherry Orchard, The (Chekhov), 634
Chesapeake Indians, 443
Chesterton, G.K., 768
Cheyenne, 646
Chicago, 619
Chicago economics, 765, G–1
Chichén Itzá, 270
Chichicastenango, 474
Chiefdoms, 52
Children, 734, 793
  as laborers, 628
  perception of, 629, 706
Chile, 431, 555, 652, 655, 765
Chimborazo, Mount, 577, 577
Chimpanzees, 8, 705
  humanlike features, 5
  male domination, 12
  warfare among, 12, 12
Chimú, 43, 368, 368–369, 381, G–1
China, 257, 655, 743
  agriculture, 61–62, 250–253, 307, 307
  ancient chronology, 88
  ancient civilization, 61–62, 110
  ancient government, 67–68
  ancient politics, 69
  art, 157, 308, 325, 391, 450, 526, 709, 712
  barbarian invasions of, 206
  birth control, 793–794
  and Buddhism, 215, 469–470
  centralization, 674
  and Christianity, 467
  chronology, 157, 251, 310
  chronology of dynasties, 191
  cities of ancient, 61–62
  civilizing, 660
  climate change in the fourteenth century, 345, 348
  in Cold War era, 736, 737
  communism, 727, 732
  comparison with Rome, 191
  conquest by Manchus, 423
  conquest by Mongols, 326–329
  conquest of Taiwan, 450
  Cultural Revolution, 756
  dams, 781
  decline of ancient civilization, 86–88, 92
  ecology of civilization, 61, 63
  economy, 765, 765
  economy in eighteenth century, 524–526, 536, 537
  emigration, 417–418
  empires of, 423
  energy sources, 456
  Enlightenment, 566–567, 570, 571

environmental problems, 777, 778
epidemics, 443
expansion of, 250–251
expansion of ancient, 62, 70–71
expansion since 1949, 737
fish farming, 787
in fourteenth century, 371
government, 189–191
  in sixteenth and seventeenth centuries, 501–502
herbal medicine, 714
Homo sapiens migration, 9
imperialism, 169–172, 391–394, 404, 446–451, 541–542
indentured labor, 627
industrialization, 607–608
influence on Europe, 566–567
introduction of maize, 437
introduction of sweet potato, 437
invasion of, 189–191
Legalism, 135
Manchurian Incident, 719
map of, 110, 252
map of ancient, 61
map of in eighteenth century, 525
and maritime imperialism, 423
migration of labor, 628
Ming, 393
nationalism, 672
in ninth and tenth centuries, 303–308
obesity in, 784
Opium Wars, 638, 640–641
origins of medicine, 141
origins of science, 140–141
philosophers, 145
plague in, 343, 349, 350, 351, 443
political parties, 727
population, 789, 793–794
population in eighteenth century, 517
public sphere, 683
recovery chronology, 203
recovery of ancient civilization, 91
recovery of empire, 200–203
relations with Japan, 204, 277
religion, 130, 681
science, 140, 714, 716
in sixteenth and seventeenth centuries, 501–503
social classes, 634
social classes/society, 502–503
spread of Buddhism, 219
spread of Christianity, 467–468
stability and change, 505
and Steppelanders, 171–172, 189–191, 289
tea trade, 608
trade routes, 156–157
trade with Mongols, 323
war atrocities, 748
war with Britain, 639
war with Japan, 605, 748, 749–750
and western science, 483–484, 695–697
writing, 71
China, Tang, map of, 201
Chinese, as laborers in America, 627–628
Chinese and Gothic Architecture (Halfpenny), 567
Chinese Board of Astronomy, 484–485, G–1
Chinese Communist Party, 732–733
Chinese diaspora, 630, G–2
Chingú, 182
Chippendale, Thomas, 567
Chittorgarh, 424, 424
Chivalry, 282, 402–403, 676, G–2

Chocolate, 441, 441, 596
Ch'oe Sungno, 220
Chola Kingdom, 275, 284, G–2
  chronology, 275
  contending with isolationism, 280
Cholera, 443, 522, 590, 791
Chomsky, Noam, 708, 711
Chonae, 297
Chopin, Frédéric, 399
Christendom, 214, 222–223, 281, 289, 388, 464–467, G–2
Christianity, 147, 256, 463, 768. See also Catholicism; Latin Christendom
  art, 130, 132, 134, 256, 282, 282–283, 293, 379, 467, 468
  Byzantine Empire, 298–300
  and chivalry, 402–403
  chronology of conversions, 219
  chronology of spread, 219, 224
  and commerce, 419
  conflict and conversion, 214
  conversion of monarchs, 216–218
  development of, 133
  division of, into Eastern (Byzantine) and Western (Roman Catholic), 298–300
  early, 184
  in early Western Europe, 278
  in eleventh and twelfth centuries, 281–282
  Enlightenment, 574
  expansion chronology, 257
  expansion of, 255–256, 467–469
  in fifteenth century, 402, 405
  in Ireland, 256
  in Japan, 420, 567
  map of, 230, 471
  missionaries, 457
  monks, 226–228
  and Muslim relations, 291–292, 293
  and Native American influence, 476
  in the New World, 442
  in nineteenth century, 680
  persecution of, 467
  and philosophy, 478
  relations with Muslims, 198
  religious communities, 226–229
  revitalization of, 468, 472
  revival in Christendom, 464–467
  revival in eighteenth century, 575–576
  and the Rus, 223–224
  in Russia, 388
  in Scandinavia, 337
  schism, 466
  in Scotland, 231
  on the Silk Roads, 215
  spread of, 217–218, 222–225, 225, 231, 232–233
  in thirteenth century, 333–336
  view of plague, 354
Chronicles of Java, 472
Chronometer, 648
Chu, 145
Chukchi hunters, 18
Chulalongkorn, king, 676, 678
Church of the Holy Sepulchre, 226
Churchill, Winston, 731
Cinema, 712, 712, 713
Cisneros, Cardinal, 465
Cistercians, 278, G–2
Cities/towns, 519, 601, 620–621
  in the Americas, 454
  ancient Greece, 104
  growth of, prehistoric, 52
  in Italy, 281

Cities/towns, *(cont.)*
  population of, *620*
  Thrace/Thracians, 106
  in twentieth century, 784–785
Citizen army, G–2
City-states, 280
  Mayan, 182–183
  Mesopotamian, 65–66
Civil rights, 761
Civil War, 626, 674–675
Civilization, G–2
  chronology of great river valley, *68*
  definition of, 31
  early, 6–16
  ecology of, 55–56, *63*
  use of term, 56
Civilizing mission, 660–661, *661*, G–2
Clan, 616, 665, G–2
Class conflict, 684
Class struggles, 615–616, G–2
Clausewitz, Carl von, 596, 675
Clearances, 668
Clement VI, pope, 354
Clement XI, pope, 468
Clergy, 420, 464
Climacteric, 45, G–2
Climate, 787–789
  in Andes, *381*
  in fourteenth century, 343–348
    map of, *346–347*
  instability, 43
Clinton, Bill, 745
Clive, Robert, 545
Clockmaking, 336
Cloning of human embryos, 703
Clothing, *648*
Clovis people, 19, 222
Cnoll, Cornelia, *418*
Cnoll, Pieter, *418*
Coal production, 456, 529–530, 597
Coalbrookdale, *598*, 616
Cobbett, William, 618
Coca-Cola colonialism, 766
Cochabamba valley, 781
Cockerill, John, 601
Cocom, 270
Code Napoleon, 582, 662, G–2
Code of Hammurabi. *See* Hammurabi, Code of
Codex Mendoza, *382*
Coeman, Jacob, 417
Coen, Jan Pieterszoon, 417
Coffee, 440–441, *441*, 622, 652
  industry, 533, 604, *604*
Coinage, 164, *314*
Coke, Thomas, *532*
Colbert, Jean-Baptiste, 456
Cold War, 719, 731–738, G–2
  alliances, *733*
Collège Royal (France), 567
Cologne, 354
Colombia, 658, 670
Columba, 255
Columbian Exchange, 435–442, G–2
  chronology, *445*
Columbus, Christopher, 398, 403, 406, 426, 431, 436, 476
  and Native Americans, 479
Commentary on the Apocalypse (Beatus of Liébana), 277
Commerce, 151–157, 611, 620. *See also* Economy; Imperialism
  cane sugar, 440
  chocolate, 441, *441*
  chronology, *216*
  chronology of in eleventh and twelfth centuries, *284*
  coffee, 440–441
  in colonial New World, 430–431

of eleventh and twelfth century India, 273–274
  in Eurasia, 152–156, 274–276
  in Indian Ocean, 152–156
  and industrialization, *621*
  international flow, *764*
  and Islam/Islamic, 216
  Japan, 277
  land routes, 156–157, *158*
  Portugal, 414–416
  and religion, 419
  in Roman Empire, 164–165
  sea routes, *158*
  slave trade, 417
  and spread of religion, 212–216
  tea, 441, 641
  in thirteenth century, *337*
  Western Europe, 277–282
  Western superiority over China, 641
Commune, G–2
  in eleventh and twelfth centuries, 281
Communications, 337–338
Communism, 683, 726–727, *727*, 732, *736*, 756, G–2
  collapse of, 735, 737
Communist Party, 726, 732
Communists, 726, 727, *735*
Communities, growth of, prehistoric, 52–55
Comorão, 411
Compass, invention of, 333
Compendium of Chronicles (Rashid al-Din), 317
Complete Survey of Medical Knowledge, 695
Compostela, 256
Compressed-gas cooler, 594
Computers, *704*
Con, Jan, 417–418
Conciliarists, 405
Concubinage, 568, *568*, 651
Condorcet, Marquis de, 517, 572
Conficius, 146
Confraternities, 474, *475*, G–2
Confraternity of Our Lady of the Rosary, 475
Confucianism, 135, 139–140, 144–145, 170, 192, 200, 250, 308, 392, 483, 501, 503, 504, 566, 569, 571, G–2
  in China, 304, 394
Confucius, 56, 125, 131, 134, 135, 138, 139, 143, 144–145, 191, 320
Congo, *378*, 509, 650, 653, 739
Conimbriga, 164–165
Conquistadores, *631*
Conservation of resources, 785–787
Conservatism, 755
Consolation of Philosophy, The (Boethius), 189
Constantine, 185
Constantine IX Monomachus, *300*
Constantine the Great, 224, *225*
  religious conversion to Christianity, 217–218
Constantine VII, 223, 297
Constantinian model, 222
Constantinople, 185, 188, 194, 255, 296–298, 300, 301, 332, 386, 391
Constitution of the Cherokee Nation, 672, *672*
Constitution (U.S.), 583
Constitutionalism, 672–673, *677*, G–2
  chronology, *678*
Consuls, 165, 281
Consumerism, 766–767, G–2

Contraception, 9, 590, 756, 769
Convict labor, 626–627
Cook, James, 27, 534, 535, 578, *579*
Cook Islands, 255
Cookie production, 596
Cooking with fire, 9
Coolies, 627, G–2
Cooper, James Fenimore, 591
Copán, 242
Copernican revolution, 481, G–2
Copernicus, Nicolaus, 481
Cordova, 248
Corinth, 103
Corporatist, 726
Cortés, Hernán, 426, 476
Cosmos, 702
Costa Rica, 653, 670
Cotopaxi, Mount, 577
Cotton
  commerce of, 606, 608, *609*, 620
  production, 369, 525–526, 532, *642*
Cotton, John, 477
Cottonseed oil as energy source, 456
Council of Ministers, 744
Council of Trent, 464, G–2
Counter Reformation, 466, G–2
Counter-colonization, 757–762, G–2
Country trades, 430–431, G–2
Covenant, G–2
  in Jewish tradition, 131, 133
Crane catching, 316
Crawfurd, John, 527
Creation, *132*
Creation Oratorio (song), 659
Creation stories, 132
  Mixtec, *269*
Creation theory, 702
Creoles, 506, 670, G–2
Creolism, 555–556
Cresques Abraham, *325*, 364, 365
Crete/Cretans, 81, 82, *83*
  art, 82, *82*
  chronology, *84*
  decline of, *93*
Creux, Francois du, *457*
Crèvecoeur, Michel-Guillaume Jean de, 556
Crimea, 172, 426
Crimean War, 626, 658
Criminals as source of labor, 626–627
Critique of Pure Reason (Kant), 583
Crompton, Edmund, 530
Crosby, Alfred, 381, 535
Croton, 104
Crown of Reccesvinth, 233
Crown of St. Stephen, 298
Crucifixion (Cellini), 478
Crudetboeck (Dodens), 569
Crusades, 289–292, *291*, *292*, 423, G–2
  First, 301
  Fourth, 302
    invasion of Byzantine Empire, 300–302
Cruz, Francisco de la, 476
Crystal Cathedral of the Reverend Robert Schuller, 770
Crystal Palace (London), 620
Cuba, *374*, 507, 600, 658, 683, 741, 743, 759
  emancipation of slaves, 626, 627
Cuban missile crisis, 732
Cubans, black, 759
Cubatão, 784–785
Cubism, 710, G–2
Cult agriculture, 43, *43*
Cult of everyday abundance, 57
Cult of nature, 576–577
Cult of the Supreme Being, *574*, 575

Cult worship, 184
Cults, *757*
Cultural exchange, 112–113, *114–115*, 635–636, 662
Cultural relativism, 705, G–2
Cultural Revolution, 756, G–2
Culture, 22, G–2
  of ancient river valley civilizations, 71–72
  of animals, 705
  in eleventh and twelfth centuries, 281–283
  exchange of, 106–109, 635–636, 760–761
  and globalization, 766–767
  of Ice Age, 17–19
  of India in eleventh and twelfth centuries, 273–274
  and maritime imperialism, 375–376
  material, 17–18
  of Roman Empire, 164–165
Culture wars, 715
Cumberland, duke of, 567
Cuneiform, 71, *71*, G–2
Cupisnique, 89
Curacao, 445
Curled Dragon Town, 62
Curzon, Lord, 698
Cuzco, 381, *454*
Cyrus the Great, 158, 159
Czars, 422, G–2
Czech Republic, 601
Czechoslovakia, 728

D

da Gama, Vasco, 398
da Vinci, Leonardo, 478
Dacca, 519
Dacia, 164, 256
Dada, 712, G–2
Dada Manifesto, 712
Dahomey, 509–511, G–2
Daimyo, 504, 505, G–2
Dairy products diet, 32, *32*
Dalai Lama, 470
Dalí, Salvador, 712
Damas, Léon, 760
Damascus, 351
Dampier, William, 578
Dams, *780*, 780–781, *781*
Daoism, 130, 138, 139, 140–141, 192, 232, 483, 714, G–2
Dara Shukoh, 477
Darius I, 153
Darjeeling Railway, *599*
Darwin, Charles, 44, *659*, 659–660, 680, 699, 702
Daud, Bwana, 539
Daulatabad, *360*
David, *314*, 315
DDT, *781*
De Beers Mining Company, *623*
de Cárdenas, Juan, 436
De Gouges, Marie-Olympes, 573–574
de la Vega, Garcilaso, 506
de Quadros, Jeronimo, 411, 419
de Sade, Marquis, 581
Death/burial customs, 57, *57*, 192, 354, 442
  in Americas, 53–54, 116, 241, *245*, 245–246
  ancient Chinese, 68
  in Bulgaria, *54*
  Cahokia, 268–269
  Egyptian, 64–65, *65*, 164–165, *165*
  Etruscan, 108, *108*
  Greek, ancient, 105

Homo ergaster, 6
Homo neaderthalensis, 7
in Ice Age, *18,* 18–19, *19*
at Jericho, *37, 37*
Mesoamerica, 174
Neanderthal, 704
Peru, 241
Roman, *165*
Debra Hayq, 271
Debra Libanos, 271
Declaration of the Rights of Man and the Citizen, 580, G–2
Declaration of the Rights of Woman and of the Female Citizen (De Gouges), 573
Decolonization, G–2
chronology, *744*
in twentieth century, 738–741, *740*
Deficiency diseases, 522
Defoe, Daniel, 530
Deforestation, 38, 451, 533, 786, G–2
map of, *786*
Deism, *574*
Delhi, 331, 423, 527, *527, 543*
Delhi Sultanate, 331–332, *332*
Delhi sultans, 359–360
Delphi oracle, 104, *139,* 160
Democracy, 681–683, 742–743, G–2
after World War II, 731
chronology, *686*
Greek, ancient, 105, 135–136
post World War I, 725
Democracy in America (Tocqueville), 682
Democritus, 139, 147
Demokrateia, 105, G–2
Demon Master, 306
Deng Xiaoping, 737
Dengue fever, 791
Depression of 1929, 725
Descartes, René, 482, *482*
Desegregation, 759
Desertification, 780
Designer babies, 703
Dessalines, Jean-Jacques, 625
Devsirme, G–2
Dharma, 214, G–2
d'Holbach, Baron, 576
Diabetes, 702, 789
type-II, 783
Dialogue Between a Brahman and a Jesuit (Voltaire), 567
Diamond, Jared, 6
Diamond mining, 455, 620, 623, *623*
Dias, Manuel, 484
Diaspora, 130, 630
Dibble tool, 33
Dictators, 165
Diderot, Denis, 558, 566, 572, *572,* 574, 579
Diffusion, 38, G–3
Diffusionist theory of civilization, 92
Dike building, *450*
d'Incarville, Pierre Nicole le Chéron, 532
Diogo de Silves, *399*
Direct rule, 204, 658
Dirlik, 497, G–3
Diseases, 789–792
in the Americas, 506
and children, 703
deficiency, 522
ecology of (migration), 523–524
in Eurasia, 443–444
and health, 590
and Native Americans, 428, *442,* 442–443, 506, 518
during warfare, 646
Disney, Walt, 713

Diu, 425
Divination. *See* Oracles
Divine love, 134, *134,* G–3
Diviners, 80–81
Divorce in ancient river civilizations, 63
DNA, 703
Doctor Faustus, 480
Doctrines of superiority, 658–660
Dodens, Rembert, 569
Dome of the Rock, *226*
Domestication of animals, 659
Domingo de la Calzada, 279
Dominicans, 480, G–3
Doña Marina, *428,* 428–429
Dong Shou, 192
Dorset culture, 113
Dream of the Eastern Capital's Splendor (Master Meng), 307
Dresden Codex, *242*
Dreyfus, Alfred, 669
Drinking, 104
Drought of 1876–1878, 661
Drugs
illegal, 767
medicinal in eighteenth century, 522
Druze, 287, G–3
Dual role, 650
Dualism, *146,* 215, G–3
Duchamp, Marcel, 710
Duke of Connaught, *634*
Dunhuang, 156, 157, 215, *215,* 227
Duration concept, 707
Durum wheat, 248
Dust Bowl, 780
Dutch
conquest of Aceh, 646
in East Indies, 547–548
Dutch East India Company, 417, 418, *418,* 441, 448, *527,* 553, 567, 569, G–3
Dutch East Indies, 547–548, 651, 653, G–3
Dutch Indonesia and Western science, 698
Dvořák, Anton, 636
Dysentery, 443

E
Earth
and Ice Age, 13
revolution of, 481–482
shape of, 564–565, *565*
East, foreign imperialism, *642,* 642–643
East Africa, 403. *See also* Africa
contending with isolationism, *280*
in eighteenth century, 539–540
expansion of in eleventh and twelfth centuries, 270–271
in fifteenth century, 377, *384*
population in eighteenth century, 518
East India trade, 455, G–3
East Indies, 738
relations with Netherlands, 421
Easter Island, 254, 366–367, *367*
Easterlies, 413, G–3
Eastern Christendom, 466
Eastern Mediterranean, 84–85
chronology, *85*
map of, *83*
Eastern Orthodox Christians, 300
Ebla, 77, *77*
Ebola, 790
Ebu us-Suud, 497
Ecological alarmism, 787–788

Ecological exchange, 436–442, *438–439,* 533, G–3
patterns of, 441–442
Ecological imperialism, 381–385, G–3
Ecology, 705
Ecology of civilization, 55–56, G–3
Economic liberalism, 624, G–3
Economic refugees, 418
Economy. *See also* Commerce; Imperialism
of Africans, 116, 118
of ancient Middle East, 98–103
chronology, *535, 536*
in eighteenth century, 524–537
chronology, *528*
Enlightenment, 573
global, 762–766
Hittites, 77–79, *78*
Japanese, 605–606
map of in Anatolia and Mesopotamia, *78–79*
of Phoenicians, 98–99
post World War I, 725
Song empire, 306–307
South American, 627
Ecuador, *642,* 670
Edessa, battle of, *197*
Edo, 504, 505, *519,* G–3
Education, 680, 751, *755*
Greece, ancient, 144
in nineteenth century, 629
Edward VIII, king of England, 783
Edwards, Bryan, 534
Edwards, Jonathan, 575
Egalitarianism, 358, 624
Egg, Augustus, 620
Eggplant, 248
Egypt, 97, 162, 296, 425, 622
ancient civilization, *50,* 56–58, 62–63
ancient government, 64–65
ancient politics, 69
centralization, 674
cities of ancient, 62–63
conquest by Britain, 647
decline of, 92–93, *93*
decline of ancient, 84–85
decolonization in twentieth century, 739
ecology of ancient, 56–58, *58*
ecology of civilization, *63*
effect of plague, 357
emancipation of slaves, 626
expansion of ancient, 69–70
imperialism, 609–610
industrialization, 609–610
invasion by Ottomans, 425
map of ancient, *58*
nationalism, 671
plague in, *349*
religion, 767
survival of ancient, 92–93
in thirteenth century, 330–331
and Western science, 480, 699
writing, 71
Egyptian Book of Instructions, 63
Egyptian Wafd, 724
Eight-Deer Tiger-Claw, 270
Einkorn, 44, *44*
Einstein, Albert, 700–701, *702, 710*
Eisaku, Wada, 711
El Niño, 89, 241, 344, 369, 590, G–3
El Salvador, 670
élan vital, 707, G–3
Electrical technology, *601*
Electricity, 600, 778
Electromagnetic induction machine, 600
Electronic Numerical Integrator and Computer, *704*

Eliot, John, 467
Elites, 18, 23, 51, 52, *53,* 65, 68, 72, 76, 82, 83, 106, 136, 143, 165, 174, 181, 182, 192, 194, 198, 206, 216, 220, 225, 271, 298, 303, 308, 328, 356, 357, 360, 368, 392, 394, 451, 465, 497, 503, 507, 540, 544, 547, 557, 583, 604, 605, 607, 608, 611, 631, 634–635, 652, 685, 720, 767
Elizabeth I, queen of England, 494, *494*
Ellis Island, *630*
Elmina, fort, *552*
Elvin, Mark, 343, 526
Emancipation Proclamation (1863), 626
Embryos, 703
Emishi, 249
Emmer, 44
Emperor worship, *217,* 217–218
Empires
in the Americas, 426–429
chronology, *431, 558*
chronology, *172, 560*
dynamics of, 151–152, *153*
effect of, 411–412
land, *413*
map of American, *427*
maritime, 412–421, *413*
in the New World, 554–558
in sixteenth and seventeenth century, map of, *422*
trading-post, 415
transformation of, *199*
Empirical, 333, 701, G–3
Empiricism, 333, 482, G–3
Employment, 598
and industrialization, *621*
Emporium trading, 158, G–3
Encyclopeida (Reasoned Dictionary of the Sciences, Arts and Trades) (Diderot), 572, *572,* 660, G–8
Energy, 456
chronology, *600*
demand for, 589
and industrialization, 597
renewable, 779
Engineering
in eleventh century Europe, 277–278
in Roman Empire, 164
England, 490. *See also* Britain
in the Americas, 455–456
chronology, *430*
art, *532, 534*
colonies in North America, 505–509
imperialism, 449
in India, 544–547
industrial revolution, 529–531
land reclamation, 457
plague in, 350
relations with Netherlands, 421
and Revolutionary War, 556
English Civil Wars (1640-1653), 494–495
English East India Company, 421
English language, 767
Enki (god), 60
Enlightened despotism, 566, G–3
Enlightenment, 562–585, G–3
in Asia, 568–572
chronology, *580, 584*
in Europe, 572–575
religion and Romanticism, 575–580
Enlil (god), 70
Enthusiasm, 476, 530, G–3

Entrepreneurship, 599
Environment, 254, 8, 13, 22, 22, 32, 32–38, 43–45, 45, 63, 86–87, 240, 243, 245–246, 246, 247, 248, 345–348, 348, 437, 459, 775–795
Environmental disasters, 343–372
Ephesus, 147
Epic of Gilgamesh, 66, 71
Epicurus, 142, 143–144, 146
Epidemics, 522
Epistemology, 482, G–3
Equatoria, province of, 647
Equatorial Guinea, 739
Equiano, Olaudah, 548
Equilibrium trap, 526, G–3
Erasmus of Rotterdam, 478
Eratosthenes, 140, 140
Ernst, Max, 712
Erythraean Sea, 156
Esarhaddon, king, 99
Esmeraldas, 507, 508
Essay on the Principle of Population (Malthus), 517
Estado da India, 417
Estates General, 580
Ethics, 143
Ethiopia, 36, 193, 218, 225, 257, 270, 274, 385, 419, 448, 475, 553, 647, 647, 666, 677–678, 681
  chronology, 193, 377
  contending with isolationism, 280
  decline of, 237
  development of, 205
  in fifteenth century, 377, 379, 384
  rise of, 193–194
Ethne, 118
Ethnicity, 632
Etiquette and the Perfect Lady, 651
Etruscans, 108–109
Euboea, 103
Eucherius, 188
Eugenics, 703, 725, G–3
Eunuchs, 189–191, G–3
Euphrates River, 37, 55, 59
Eurasia
  chronology of empires, 172
  commerce, 153–156
  cultural exchange, 112–113, 114–115
  empires in fifteenth century, 385–391
  expansion of in eleventh and twelfth centuries, 275–284
  exploitation of environment, 459
  imperialism, map of, 447
  intensified settlements of, 54–55, 55
  plagues of, 348–358, 443–444
  trade routes, 154–155
Euro, 744
Europe
  chronology of sixteenth and seventeenth centuries, 492
  chronology of technology and growth, 281
  climate change in the fourteenth century, 348
  democracy, 682–683
  Enlightenment, 562–585
  expansion in South and Southeast Asia, 546
  imperialism, 411–412, 449–451
    chronology, 405, 455
    resistance to, 669
  industrialization, 601–603, 602
  map of in twentieth century, 722
  map of oceanic explorations, 400–401
  nationalism, 666–668, 667

political change in, 490–492
political extremism, 727
social transformation of, 493–498, 496
spread of agriculture in, 38
in thirteenth century, 332–336, 337
unification in sixteenth and seventeenth centuries, 490–492
European Coal and Steel Community, 744
European Union (EU), 743–745, G–3
Eusebius, 224
Euthanasia, 771
Evangelical Christianity, 576, 624
Evangelical Protestants, 466
Evans, John, 561
Eve (African), 7–8
Eve (biblical), 178–179
Evolution, 5–7, G–3
  in Africa, 7–13
  early migration, 9–13
  map of, 10–11
  theory of, 6
Evolution, theory of, 659, 659, 680, 695, 702–703
Examination system, 308, 674, G–3
Execution, 770
Existentialism, 708, 708–709, G–3
Exodus (Bible), 349
Expressionism, 712
Extinction of animals, 785–787
Ezana, king, 218, 225
Ezekiel, 98, 555

F

Factories, 616–617, 628, G–3
  in eighteenth century, 525
Faith of God, 477
"Fall of Makassar" (Woldemar), 421
Fallopio, Gabriele, 494
Family
  in ancient Greece, 105
  in China, 503
  in eleventh century, 298
  in sixteenth and seventeenth centuries, 494
  in twentieth century, 757
Famine, 590, 661, 782
Fantasy novel, 713
Fanti, 671, 672
Faraday, Michael, 600
Farmers, violence with herders, 33–34
Farming. *See also* Agriculture; Tilling/tillers
  compared to foraging, 31
  disadvantages of, 30
  origin of, 42–45
Fars, 157, 158, 197
Fascism, 727–728, G–3
Fascists, 727
Fast food, 783
Fat
  in prehistorical society, 16
  supply of, 589
Fatimid caliphate, 290
Fatimids, 287–288, 309, G–3
Fat-tailed sheep, 310
Faxian, 192
Fayyum portraits, 165
Feasting, 43
Federal Republic of Germany, 731
Feminism, 573–574, G–3
Feng Guifen, 683
Fenlands, 457
Ferdinand I, 478
Ferghana, 157
Fertility goddess, 39
Fertilization of land, 781

Fertilizer, 594
Feudal tenure, 506
Fezzan, 108
Fifteenth century, chronology of, 405
Film industry, 713
Final Cause (Aristotle), 142
Final Solution, 725, 771, G–3
Finland, 657
Firepower technology, 424
First Crusade, 301
Fish, depletion of, 786
Fish farming, 22, 533, 787
Fitzroy, Robert, 659
Fixed-wing systems, 156, G–3
Flagellants, 351, 354
Flintstones, The (television series), 16
Floodplains in ancient civilizations, 56–62
Florence, 349
  in fifteenth century, 402
Florida, colony, 430, 437, 454
Floris V, count, 278
Food
  chronology, 600
  exchange among countries, 435–436
  production, 590–596
  production in eighteenth century, 519, 522
  production in nineteenth century, 594–596, 595
  production in twentieth century, 780–784
  resources, 23, 783, 789
  shortages, 57–58, 776–777
  technology, 601
  and urbanization, 620
Foot binding, 503
Foragers, 9, 21–22, 28–30
  dates of settlements, 30
Foraging, 31
  compared to farming, 31
Foreign Language Institute (Beijing), 695
Forests, 612, 786
Fornication, 465
Fort Jesus, 538, 539
Fortuyn, Pim, 763
Fossil fuels, 597, 601, 778–779, G–3
Fourier, Charles, 684
Fourteenth century, chronology of, 372
Fourth Crusade, 302
Fouta Jalon, 679
Fouta Toro, 679
France, 490. *See also* French Revolution
  in British North America, 557
  in Canada, 557
  conquest of Indochina, 646
  decolonization in twentieth century, 738–739
  emancipation of slaves, 626
  imperialism, 643
  imperialism in Indochina, 628
  industrialization, 596, 603
  in Mexico, 652
  nationalism, 669
  in North America, 554
  plague in, 50
  population in eighteenth century, 519
  and Revolutionary War, 557, 558
  Seven Years' War (1756-1763), 557
  and territorial imperialism, 421
  World War I, 720
  World War II, 729
Francis Borja, St., 467
Francis I, king of France, 478

Francis of Assisi, St., 334–335, 336
Francis Xavier, St., 467
Franciscans, 335, 358, 392, 403, 467, 468, 469, G–3
  art, 335, 336
  and millenarianism, 476–477
Franco-Prussian War (1870-1871), 675
Frankfurt School, 708
Franklin, Benjamin, 522, 529
Franks, 188, 222, 255
Fraticelli, 392
Frederick the Great, king of Prussia, 576
Free association, 706
Free trade, 573, 604, 624, G–3
Free will, 707
Freemasonry, 574
Freemason's Lodge of Freetown, 634
Freetown, 634, 651
French Revolution, 531, 580–583, 596, 625, 642, 682, G–3. *See also* France
  Bastille, fall of, 580, 581
  chronology, 583
  Declaration of the Rights of Man and the Citizen, 580
French Royal Academy of Science, 564
Freud, Sigmund, 705–706, 711
Frisia, 419
Frobisher, Martin, 455
"Frozen Thames, The," 345
Fudo Myo-o, 362
Fuel resources, 778–780, 783, 789
Fujian, 437, 450
Fujiwara, 205
Fujiwara no Michizane, 276
Fulani, 553, 553, G–3
Full Gospel Church, 770
Fulton, Robert, 600
Funan, 193
  development of, 205
Fundamentalism, 769–770, G–3
Fur trade, 455, 457
  in the Americas, 431
  in Russia, 386, 422
Futa Jallon, 553
Futa Toro, 553
Futurism, 709, G–3

G

Gabriel (Archangel), 197
Gabriele de' Mussis, 354
Gage, Thomas, 441
Galápagos Islands, 659
Galdós, Pérez, 634
Galilei, Galileo, 484, 529, 529
Galvani, Luigi, 529
Gambling, 619
Gandhara, 162
Gandhi, Mohandas, 724, 725
Ganges Valley, 111–112, 166, 332
  chronology, 119
  civilization of, 118
Gansu, 171
Gao, 238, 378
Garamantes, 108, 116
Gardar, 266
Garden of Eden, 178–179
Garden suburbs, 599
Gardening, global, 532–536
Garneray, Ambroise-Louis, 588
Garrido, Juan, 436
Garum, 165
Garvey, Marcus, 760
Gaspard, Etienne Robert, 583
Gaspée (ship), 556
Gassed (painting) (Sargent), 724

Gauchos, 622, 670, *670*, G–3
Gaudi, Antoni, 619
Gaul, 222
Gautama Siddharta, 127, *146*
Gaza, 99
Gembo, 221
Gender. See Male dominance; Women
General will, 577–578, G–3
Generation gap, 756
Genes, 703
Genesis (Biblical), 135
Genetic engineering, 6
Genetic revolution, 782, G–3
Genetically modification, 702–703
Genetically modified crops, 782, *782*
    See also GM
Genetics, 702, *711*
Genghis Khan, 316, *317*, 317–318,
    320, 328, 329, 331–332, 387,
    446, 498
Genji, 283
Genoa, 279, 333
Genocide, 429, 750, G–4
    map of, *752–753*
Genoese, 403
Gentile of Foligno, 354
Genus, 5
Geoffrey of Monmouth, 283
Geography
    in fifteenth century, *376*, 402
    in thirteenth century, 337
Geography (Ptolemy), *376*
Geometry, 138
George II, king of England, 523, 576
Georgia, 445
Georgia (country), 218, *314*, 315, 319
Georgians, 218, *219*
Gerald of Wales, 279–280
Gerbert of Aurillac, 283
German Reich, *752*
Germanic tribes, 164
    and fall of Roman
        Empire, 184–185
    Lombards, 195
    Ostrogoths, 189
    Visigoths, 155, 188, 206
Germany, 490
    centralization, 674
    democracy, 683
    imperialism, 643
    industrialization, 603
    mob violence, 354
    nationalism, 666
    partitioning, 731
    socialism, 686
    World War I, 720–721, 723
    World War II, 729–731
Gero of Cologne, archbishop, 283,
    283
Gerrha, 153
Gettysburg, *674*
Geza I, king, *297*
Ghana, 238, 257, 293, 671, 672, 739,
    G–4
Ghazna, 331
Ghazni, 224
Ghost Dance, 681
Ghurids, 331
Gilani, 296
Gilgamesh, *66*, 66–67, 70
Giotto, *336*
Giraffe in China, 293
Giselle (ballet), *700*
Gisho, 262
Glacier growth in fourth
    century, 344–345
Glass making, 336
Global gardening, 532–536, G–4
Global trade, *604*

Global warming, 43, 788–789
Globalization, G–4
    chronology, *767*
    and culture, 17, 766–767
    and global economy, 762–766
Glorious Revolution, 490
Glyph, 174, G–4
GM, 782, *782*, G–4
Goa, 419, 420, 421
Göberkli Tepe, 30
Gobi Desert, 777
Gobineau, Count de, 660
Gobnet, St., 232
God
    belief in, 564, 702–703
    monotheistic, 132–133
Godaigo, emperor, 362
Gödel, Kurt, 701
Goede, C.A.G., 616
Goibhnin, 232
Gojam, 377
Gold, 365, 620
    technology, 89
    in West Africa, 398, 511
Gold rushes, 655
Golden Gate, *289*
Golden Horde, 329, G–4
Golden Number, 137
Golding, William, 715
Goldsmith, Oliver, 566
Goodall, Jane, 12, *12*, 705
Gorbachev, Mikhail, 737
Gordon, Charles, 661
Gorée, 552
Gorillas, 5–6
Gosse, Thomas, *534*
Government, 751
    absolute sovereignty, 405
    ancient Egypt, 64–65
    autocratic, 497
    Byzantine Empire, 296–297
    city-states, 106, 280
    democracy, 742–743
    despotism, 566
    early Chinese, 190–191
    in eleventh and twelfth
        centuries, 281
    Enlightenment, 566, 577–578
    imperialism, 166–172
    and industrialization, *621*
    Mesopotamia, 65–66
    monarchy, 165, 188, *496*, 555, 650
    Persian, 159–160
    post World War I, 725
    Roman Empire, 165, 184, 188, 189
    in sixteenth and seventeenth cen-
        turies China, 501–503
    sovereignty, 506, 580, 673
    state system, 490, 492–493, *496*
    in twentieth century, 712
Goya, Francisco, *4*, *5*, 583, *583*
Graham, Sylvester, 596
Graham cracker, 596
Grain elevators, 591
Grains, 64, 591
Grammar, 708
Gran Colombia, 670
Granada, 402
Grand Army, 596
Grand Canal (China), 200–201, 392
Grand Vizier, 497, G–4
Grapes, 436
Grasses, in the Americas, 437
Grasslands, map of, *339*
Gravity, 482
Great Cultural Revolution
    (China), *736*, 737
Great Depression (1930s), 750

Great Drowning (1362), 345
Great East Asia Co-Prosperity
    Sphere, 720, G–4
Great Jaguar Paw, 182
Great River Valley
    civilizations, 50–73
    chronology, *68*, *72*
    ecology of civilization, 55–56
    great floodplains, 56–62
    growing communities, 52–55
    map of, *55*
    society/social classes, 62–72
Great Satans, 769
Great Wall of China, *136*, 170
Great Zimbabwe, 377, *377*, *378*
    in fifteenth century, *384*
Greece
    ancient
        art, *104*
        chronology, *108*, *119*
        civilization of, *118*
        colonialism, 104–105
        democracy, 135–136
        education, 144
        environment, 103–104
        literature, 104–105
        medicine, 141
        origins of science, 139–140
        purity, 106
        society/social classes, *105*, 105–106
        war with Persia, 159–161
    and Basil II, 298
    and democracy, 683
    nationalism, 668
Greek purity concept, 106
Green revolution, 741, 782, G–4
Greenhouse effect, 779, G–4
Greenland, 265–266, 345, 369–370
    contending with isolationism, *280*
    expansion in eleventh and twelfth
        centuries, 264–266
Gregorian Reform, 282
Gregory the Great, pope, 226
Gregory the Illuminator, 218
Gregory VII, pope, 282
Grey, Edward, 726
Grey, Lord, 671
Gross domestic product (GDP), 754
Grotius, Hugo, 493
Grünewald, Matthias, 466
Gu Hongzhong, *308*
Gu Yanwu, 483
Guadalquivir River, 248
Guam, 658
Guanaco, 35
Guangdong, 450
Guangzhou, 519, 525, *638*, *641*, 672
Guangzhou massacre, 216
Guangxi, 450
Guano, 594, 605
Guanzhou, *526*
Guardians, 135, G–4
Guatemala, *246*, *474*, 670, 769
Guillotine, *770*
Guizhou, 450
Gujarat, 418
Gujerati, 760
Gulf Stream, 413
Gunpowder, 390, 447, 484
    invention of, 333
Guntur, 590
Guomindang (GMD), G–4
Gupta dynasty, 191–192, 250
    transformation of, *199*
Gyerspungs, 222
Gyoki, 249

H

Haber, Fritz, 781

Habsburg dynasty, *419*
Habsburg Empire, 626, 720
    imperialism, 643
    nationalism, *667*, 668
Habsburgs, 668, G–4
Hagia Sophia, 223, *300*
Haider, Jurgen, *763*
Haiti, 440, 629
    rebellion, 625
    revolution, 558
Haj, *372*, G–4
Hajj, 232
Hakudo, Nagatomi, 749
Halfpenny, William, 567
Hamadan, 157
Hamas, *742*
Hammurabi, 66
Hammurabi, Code of, 66
Han, 170–171, G–4
Han China, 170–171
Han dynasty, *157*, 170–171, 172, 189,
    191
    chronology, *171*
    transformation of, *199*
Han Feizi, 144, *146*
Han Shan, 469
Han Wudi, 170
Handel, George Fredrich, 576
Hangzhou, 524
Hanseatic League, 279, G–4
Harappa, 58, 62
    ancient politics, *69*
    decline of, *93*, 111
Harappan civilization, 58–59
    ancient government, 68–69
    decline of, 85–86, *86*, 111
    map of, *59*
    writing, *59*, 71
Harbin, 719
Hard labor, 627
Harem, 80, G–4
Hari Rai, 477
Harkhuf, 92–93
Harlan, Jack L., 30
Harold Bluetooth, 223
Harrison, John, 578
Harsha, 194
Harun al-Rashid, caliph, 225
Hasan al-Basri, 228
Hastayar, 75
Hatshepsut, Queen, 57
Hatti, 76
Hattusa, 80
Hattusili, 75–76
Hausa, 473, 651
Hausaland, 473
Hawaii, 254, 658
    in eighteenth century, 533
Hayan Wuruk, 361
Hayden, Joseph, 659
Hayek, F.A. von, 735
Hazlitt, William, 517, 610
Headlong Hall (Peacock), 684
Healing cult, *715*
Health care, 751
Health education, 751
Heart diseases, 783, 791
Hebei, 203
Hebrew Art of the Covenant, 133
Hegemony, 160, 694, 714
Heian, *276*
Heidegger, Martin, 708
Heine, Heinrich, 668
Heinz, Henry, 617, 618
Heisenberg, Werner, 701, 732
Helen of Troy, *302*
"Hell's mouth," 282
Helmont, J.B. van, 482
Helsinki Agreement (1975), 742

Henotheism, 132
Henry of Finland, 333
Henry VIII, king of England, 478
Hera of Samos, 104
Heraclitus, 147
Herbal medicine, 695, 714
Herbalism, 714
Herder, Johann Gottfried, 577
Herding/herders, 3–33, 26, 27–28, 448, G–4
  compared with tilling/tillers, 34
  map of environment, 29
  violence with farmers, 33–34
Heresies, 281–282
Hergé, 718
Hermes Trismegistos (Hermes Thrice-Blessed), 480
Herodotus, 172
Herrnhut, 575
Herto, 8
Hesiod, 104
Hideyoshi, Toyotomi, 416–417, 456
Hieroglyphs, 71, 71
Highlanders of Scotland, 668
High-level equilibrium trap, 526, 529, G–4
Hilda of Merschede, abbess, 229, 283
Hildebrand, 185
Hildebrandslied, 185
Hill, James, 600
Hindu/Hinduism, 222, 232, 271, 272, 360, 361, 388, 544, G–4
  in Chola Kingdom, 275
  and commerce, 419
  in India, 331, 477
Hine, Lewis, 630
Hino Meishi, 362
Hippocrates, 141, 142
Hippocratics, 141
Hippolytus, 302
Hiroshige, 591
Hiroshima, 729, 731
Hiru, 253
Hispaniola, 374, 426, 436, 442, G–4
History of Canada (Creux), 457
Hitler, Adolf, 728, 729–731
Hittites, 76–93
  art, 74
  chronology, 81
  decline of, 93
  military/weaponry, 80
  politics, 79–81
  society, 79–81
  trade, 77–79, 78
HIV, 790, 792
Ho Chih Minh, 727
Ho Xuang Huong, 571
Hogenberg, Franz, 454
Hohokam People, 345, 348, G–4
Hokkaido, 449, 456
Holland, 417, 419, 490
  agriculture, 441
  land reclamation, 456–457
Hollywood, 712, 713
Holocaust, 750, 750, G–4
Holy Roman Empire, 490, G–4
Holy Sepulcher, 289
Holy war, 212, 289
Homeland Security, 754
Homer, 104, 283, 303
Homestead Act (1862), 594
Homo erectus, 6, G–4
  migration of, 10
Homo ergaster, 6, G–4
Homo floresiensis, 7, 10
Homo habilis, 6, G–4
Homo neanderthalensis, 7
Homo sapiens, 6, 7, 704, G–4
  evolution from Africa, 8–13

migration of, 10
Homo species, 6–7
Honda Toshiaki, 656
Honduras, 670
Hong Kong, 640
Hongxi emperor, 394
Honshu, 457
Honshu island, 30, 249
Hooghly, 419
Hoogly, 527
Hooke, Robert, 529
Hopkins, Gerard Manley, 619
Horace, 151, 162
Hormuz, 410, 419
Horses, 337
  in the Americas, 428
  in art, 157
  domestication of, 54
  in Mongolian society, 324
Horton, James Africanus, 670, 672
Houdon, Jean-Antoine, 566
Houel, Jean-Pierre, 581
Housing, 789
Huaca de los Reyes, 89
Huaca del Dragón, 368
Huai River, 70, 250, 304
Huai valley, 350
Huang Chao, 303
Huang Zongxi, 502
Huari, 241
Hubble, Edwin, 701, 710
Hubei, 62
Hui Shi, 143, 145
Hui Shih, 138
Hui-te-Rangiora, 255
Hülegü, 320
Human, diversity of, 479–480
Human cloning, 703
Human nature, 134, 569
Human rights, 704, 742–743, 761, 771, G–4
Human sacrifice, 88, 88, 470, 479, 510
Human sciences, 702–705
Human species, 5
  chronology, 23
  dates of early migration, 8
  evolution of, 5–7
  first, 6–9
  Homo erectus, 6, 10
  Homo ergaster, 6
  Homo floresiensis, 7, 10
  Homo habilis, 6
  Homo neanderthalensis, 7
  Homo sapiens, 6–13
  map of early migration, 10–11
Humanism, 402, 715–716, G–4
Humbert, Cardinal, 300
Humboldt, Alexander von, 577, 577
Humboldt, Baron von, 560
Humboldt Current, 431
Hume, David, 575
Hume, Edward H., 692, 693, 695, 714
Humoral theory of medicine, 522
Hunan, 443
Hunan-Yale Medical College, 693
Hungary, 425, 478
  art, 297
  in fourteenth century, 370
  invasion by Ottomans, 425, 446
  nationalism, 668
Huns, 185, 189, 222
  invasion of India, 191–192
Hunters, 630–631
  in Ice Age, 16
Hunters-gatherers, 245
Hunting, 457
  and male dominance, 12
Huntsman, Benjamin, 526
Hurons, 430–431, 443, 457, 579–580,

G–4
Hurricane Katrina, 788, 788
Husain, 501
Husayn al-Jisr, 699
Husbandry, 27–28, 30–31, G–4. See also Animal husbandry; Plant husbandry
  geographic diffusion of, 30–38
Hybrid human, 6
Hyderabad, 544
Hydroelectric projects, 779
Hydroelectricity, 779
Hydrogen as energy source, 779
Hyeyong, 220
Hygiene in eighteenth century, 522
Hyksos, 84, 93
Hypnosis, 529, 706

I
Ibbitt, William, 616
Iberia, 219
Ibn Battuta, 342, 343, 351, 359–360, 365
  map of travels, 353
Ibn Hwqal, 248
Ibn Khaldun, 309, 364, 366, 369, 386
Ibn Khatib, 354
Ibn Saud, 723
Ibn Tughluq, 359–360, 360
Ibn Wahab, 211, 232
Ibrahim al Halabi, 497
Ibsen, Henrik, 629
Icaria, 684
Ice Age, 13–21, 786, 788
  affluence, 16
  art in, 16, 16–17, 17
  culture and society, 17–19
  dates of, 17
  hunters, 16
  life in, 16, 16, 17–19, 19
  map of, 14–15
  writing, 18
Ice-Age affluence, 16, G–4
Iceland, 222
I-ching, 251
Icon, 494, G–4
Ife, 379
Igel, 165
Il Quarto Stato (Pelizza), 685
Ilg, Alred, 678
Iliad (Homer), 104–105
Il-Khan, 325, 329, 329, 370, G–4
  art, 329, 329
Il-Khan art, 329, 329
Il-Khan Ghazan, 329
Il-Khanate, 329, G–4
Illusion, challenging, 137
Illyria/Illyrians, 106
Iltutmish, 331, 332
Imam, 287, 539, G–4
Imbalanga, 489
Immigration, 450, 630, 630, 757–762, 759
  to the Americas, 444–445
  and industrialization, 604
Immunization, 751
Imperator, 165, G–4
Imperialism, 411–412, 704, 723, 734, 737, G–4. See also Commerce
  in Africa, 653
  in Asia, 540–544, 653
    chronology, 543
  business, 652, 652–655
  in China, 169–172, 391–394, 404
  chronology, 455, 535, 658, 662
  ecological, 381–385
  in Europe and Asia, 449–451
  foreign in East and Southeast Asia, 642, 642–643
  in India, 166–169, 275, 404, 451,

544–547
Japan, 449, 656, 657, 658
  map of, 546
  map of in Eurasia, 447
  maritime, chronology, 405, 421
  methods of ruling, 648–651
  in the New Europes, 655–656
  in New World, 554–561
  oceanic, 395–398
    chronology, 398
  pastoral, 448–449
  rationales for, 658–661
  resistance, 669
  Russia, 657–658, 658
  steppeland, 390, 446–448
  and technology, 648
  United States, 658, 658
  white, 641–648
  world map of, 644–645
Imperialists, 623, 653
Inca Empire, 381–385, 454
  in fifteenth century, 383, 384
Incas, 403, 426, 429, 506, 556, G–4
  chronology, 382
Incest, 80
Indentured labor, 444, 626–628, 627
Indeterminacy principle, 701
India, 418, 738, 743, 762
  ancient civilization, 111–112
  architecture, 333
  art, 712
  barbarian invasions of, 206
  as British colony, 651
  census, 456
  chronology, 112
  chronology of dynasties, 191
  civilizing, 660, 661
  commerce, 153–159
  contending with isolationism, 280
  decolonization, 738
  dynasties, 191
  economy, 765
  economy and culture, 273–274
  economy in eighteenth century, 526–528, 527, 536–537
  Enlightenment, 567, 584
  expansion of in eleventh and twelfth centuries, 273–275, 284
  in fourteenth century, 369
  government, 167–168
  imperialism, 166–169, 404, 451, 544–547, 648, 650
  indentured labor, 627
  industrialization, 608–609
  and invaders, 289
  invasion of, 191–192
  life expectancy, 789
  and maritime imperialism, 414–415
  medicine, 141
  missionary effects in, 477
  Mughals, 423–424, 498
  Muslim, 331–332
  origins of medicine, 141
  and plague, 359–360
  population, 794
  and Portugal's trading posts, 417
  post World War I, 724
  railways, 599, 599, 600
  religion, 127, 477
  science, 714
  spread of agriculture, 42
  and spread of Buddhism, 222
  Western science in, 698
Indian Civil Service, 651
Indian National Congress, 671, G–4
Indian Ocean, 270, 284, 375, 376, 395
  expansion around, 270–275
  map of, 274

map of maritime imperialism, *416*
trade routes, 152–153, *154–155,* 156
Indigo planting, 622
Indios, 652
Indirect rule, 650–651, *651,* 656, G–4
Individual gratification, 756
Individualism, 686, 754–755, G–4
Indochina, *648,* 650, 653, 738
expansion of, 251
and France, 628, 646
Indo-European languages, 38, G–4
Indonesia, 643, 724, *738*
communists, *727*
Indra (god), 86
Inductive method, 482, G–4
Indus, 55, 111
Indus River, 37, 58, 86
Indus Valley, 55–56, 58–59, 86
ecology of civilization, *63*
Industrial Revolution, 530, G–4
Industrialization, 526, 528–532, *621,*
G–4
and agriculture, 594–596, *595*
Americas, 604–605
Canada, 604
China, 607–608
chronology, *610, 611, 623*
effect on environment, 615–620
Egypt, 609–610
in eleventh and twelfth
centuries, *281*
Europe, 601–603, *602*
India, 608–609
Japan, 605–607
Latin America, 604–605
in nineteenth century, 597–601
philanthropic, 616–620
United States, 604
Infanticide, 563
Inflation, 755
Influenza, 349, 442, 791
pandemic, 590
Information age, 755
Information revolution, 741
Information technology, 766, G–4
Ingvary Ingvarevitch, 330
Inkarrí movements, 477
Inquisition, 465, G–5
Insulin, 702
Intensified settlements, 54–55, *55*
Internal combustion engine, 601, 778
International Criminal Court, 743
Internet, *690–691,* 766
users, 766, *766*
Introspection, 706
Inuit, 21–22, 23, 32
contending with isolationism, *280*
Inventions, 700
chronology, *701*
in eleventh century Europe, *279*
Iran, 288, 655, 723, 767, *768.* See also
Persia/Persian Empire
religion, 126–127
and spread of Islam/Islamic, 226
Iraq, 425, 742, 745, 750
invasion by Ottomans, 425
Irawaddy, 251
Ireland, 449, 722
nationalism, 668
potato famine, 590
Irene (empress), 255
Irish cross, *255*
Iron Age, 73
Iron Bridge, 530
Iron Curtain, 731
Iron industry, 529–530
Iron making, 77, 79, 116, 598
Iron pyrites, 455
Iroquois, 457, G–5

Irrigation, 64, 780
Isaac II Angelus, 301
Isabella, queen of Spain, 406
Isaiah (prophet), 159
Isandlhwana, 646
Isfahan, 157, 499, *499*
Ishida Baigan, 569
Ishin Suden, 483
Isidore of Seville, 226
Islam/Islamic, 131, 147, 196–197,
206, 212, 257, 425, 769. *See also*
Muslims
and agriculture, 246–248, *247*
architecture, *236*
art, *242*
in Asia, 447
and Christianity
relations, 291–292, *293*
chronology of expansion, *200*
conflict and conversion, 212–214,
216
and Crusades, 289–292
in Egypt, 331
Enlightenment Age, 567–568
in fifteenth century, 386–391
food, 246
in fourteenth century, 360
in India, 477
map of, *231, 471*
map of in Africa, *473*
monks, 227–228
and neighbors, 287–295
in nineteenth century, 680
religious communities, 227–228, *228*
revitalization of, *472*
and Sahara invaders, 291–295
in Southeast Asia, 447
spread of, 224–225, *225,* 232–233,
471–473
and steppelanders, 288–289
on trade routes, 216
and Turks, 224
in West Africa, 378–379, 472–473
and Western science, 699
Island of Dr. Moreau, The (Wells), 6
Ismail I, 500, 501
Ismail Mazhir, 699
Isolationism, 263, *280,* 366, 721, G–5
Israel, 130
conflict with Palestine, 741, *742*
Istanbul, *497*
Isthmus of Panama, 431
Isvarcandra Vidyasagar, 662
Italica, 164
Italy, *434,* 490
centralization, 674
city-states, 281
democracy, 731
fascism, 727
imperialism, 643
industrialization, 603
nationalism, 666
war with Ethiopia, 647, *647*
World War I, 720
World War II, 730
Itzamnaaj B'alam, *243*
Ivan IV, czar, 422
Ivan the Great, 386
Ivory Coast, 741, *790*
Ixtilxochitl, Fernando de Alva, 506
Izmir, 620

J

Jabel Sahaba, battle of, 12
Jackson, Andrew, *682*
Jainism, 127, 144, G–5
Jains, 127, 134, 137
and commerce, 419
Jamaica, 507, 534, 549

Jamal al-Dinal-Afghani, 699
Jambedkar, Bal Shastri, 584
Jambudvipa, *514–515*
James, William, 707
James of Vitry, 315
James the Great, 256
Jamshid, 153
Janissaries, 390, 496–497, 674, G–5
Japan, 204–205, 419, 770
agriculture, 248–249, 532, 591
art, *321, 591,* 711
and Buddhism, 469–470
census, 518
centralization, 674
chronology, *171*
introduction of Buddhism, *221*
isolationism, *277*
civilizing, 660
commerce, 277, 420
constitutionalism, 673
contending with isolationism, *280*
democracy, 731
development of, *205*
economy in eighteenth
century, 536
emancipation of slaves, 626
Enlightenment, 567, 569, *570, 571*
expansion of, 257
expansion of in eleventh and
twelfth centuries, 276–277
fashion, *635,* 635–636
in fourteenth century, 362–363,
369
fourteenth century art, *362*
geographic obstacles, *254*
imperialism, 449, 656, 657, *658*
industrialization, 605–607
invasion of Korea, 417
isolationism, 283
land reclamation, 457
Manchurian Incident, 719
map of, *201*
fourteenth century, *363*
and maritime imperialism, 416
migration, 263
militarization, 674
nationalism, 671–672
population, 789
population in eighteenth
century, 518–519
post World War II, 763
public sphere, 683
railway system, *606*
relations with China, 204, 277
and religion, 467, 681
rice cultivation, *591*
in sixteenth and seventeenth centuries, 504–505, *505*
social classes, 634
spread of Buddhism, 220–221
spread of Christianity, 467, *467*
stability and change, *505*
study of Dutch language, 569, *569*
trade with Korea, 277
unification of, 172
war relations with China, *748,*
749–750
and western science, 483, 569
World War II, *729,* 729–731
Japan Current, 413
Japonisme, 636
Jasaw Chan Kaui'il, 242
Jatakas, 153
Java, 194, 252, 360–361, 393, 441,
472, *472,* 533, 591, 646
art, *253*
imperialism, 648
invasion by Mongols, 320
Jaxartes, 780

Jayavarman II, king, 251
Jayavarman VII, king, 272–273
Jefferson, Thomas, 556
Jenne-Jeno, 238
Jenner, Edward, 523
Jericho, 37, *37*
Jerusalem, 102, 130, *225*
pilgrimages to, 289, *289*
rebuilding of temple, 159
Jesuits, 464, 466, *467,* 467–468, 555,
567, 574, G–5
in China, *484,* 484–485, 566, 568
in India, 477
in the New World, 442–443
Jesus, 131, 133, 137, 144, *146,* 198,
199, 215, 228, 233, 464
Jews/Judaism, 134, 137, *146,* 198,
725, 728, 741
in ancient civilization, 130
blame for the plague, 354–356
and Crusades, 291–292
development of, 130
emancipation, *668,* 668–669
exile of, 130, *130*
Holocaust, 750, *750*
map of in Medieval Europe and
Middle East, *355*
monotheism, 133
nationalism, 668–669
social structure, 494
in White America, 476
Ji Yun, 541
Jiangnan, 607
Jiangxi, 524
Jiddah, 393
Jihad, 212, 216, *225,* 290, 291, G–5
Jihad of the sword, 472
Jihad of words, 472
Jin dynasty, 191
Jodhpur, 477
Johannesburg (South Africa), 620
Johansen, Dan, 6
John (apostle), 132
John of Piano Carpini, 321
John Paul II, pope, 735
John the Baptist, 227
Johnson, Lyndon B., 759
Johnson, Samuel, 536
Johnston-Sirleaf, Ellen, 761
Joint-stock company, 420, G–5
Joliot, Frédéric, 731–732
Jomon, 30
Jones, William, 567
Jordan Valley, 37
Jordanes, 185
Jorge de Mina, 379
Jornada de la Muerte, 268
Joseph (Biblical), 64
Journal of Medical Research
(Indian), 698
Joyce, James, *707*
Juan, Jorge, 576
Judah, 130
Julius Caesar, 163
Jumel, Louis-Alexis, 609
Juntas, 558
Jupiter (god), 227
Jurchen, 304–305
Justinian, emperor, 194–195, *195,*
200, 223, 296
Jute, 622
Jvari, *219*

K

Kaaba, 232, *232,* G–5
Kaempfer, Engelbert, 567
Kaibara Ekken, 569
Kaifeng, 307
Kalahari, 630

Kalahari Desert, 22
Kaleb, king, 193
Kalidasa, 191
Kalinga, 169
Kaliyuga, 191
Kamehameha I, 534
Kamikaze winds, 320, 321
Kandinsky, Vasily, 710
Kanem, 339
Kanes, 77
Kangaroos, 28
Kangnido, 312–313
Kangxi emperor, 446–447, 450–451, 503, 568, 569
Kaniska, king, 214, 225
Kant, Immanuel, 578, 583
Karakhanids, 224
Karakorum, 32, 321
Karnataka, 274
Karr, Alphonse, 684
Kasai, 518
Kashgaria, 329
Kashmir, 194
Kaska, 81
Kaskaskia, 457
Katsina, 676
Kava, 253
Kay, Philip, 619
Kazakstan, 658
Kazan, 422, 449
Keichu, 470
Kemal, Mustafa, 723
Kennedy, John F., 743, 744, 759
Kenniff art, 17
Kenya, 739
Kenyatta, Jomo, 739
Kepler, Johannes, 481
Kerala, 419
Kerry-Nicholls, James, 665, 679
Kertanagara, 361
Key, Ellen, 706
Keynes, John Maynard, 725, 751
Keynesianism, 725, 751, G–5
Khan, 313, 316, G–5
Khan Kuchum, 423
Khazaks, 631
Khazars, 219
Khedive, 609, G–5
Khedive Ismail, 610, 647, 648
Khitans, 304
Khmer, 251, 271–273, G–5
Khmer Kingdom
    contending with isolationism, 280
Khoi, 448
Khomeini, Ayatollah Ruhollah, 768, 768
Khrushchev, Nikita, 732, 735
Kiev, 223, 330
Kimberley (South Africa), 620, 623, 623
Kimonos, 635, 635–636
King, Martin Luther Jr., 759
King and I, The (musical), 676
King Country, 665
King David, 314, 315
King of Wei, 145
Kipling, Rudyard, 681
Kirgiz nomads, 631
Kittis, 564
Knossos, 82
Knowledge class, 755
Knox, John, 494
Kochi, 263
Koguryo, 172, 192, 219
    development of, 205
Kokura, 467
Kong Fuzi, 125
Kongo Kingdom, 379, 398, 445, 511, 552, G–5

in fifteenth century, 384
Konya, 288
Korea, 192–193, 504, 532, 656, 733–734
    art, 192, 220
    chronology
        introduction of Buddhism, 221
    Enlightenment, 571, 571
    invasion by Japan, 417
    relations with China, 204–205
    relations with Japan, 204–205
    in sixteenth and seventeenth centuries, 504
    and society/social class, 504–505
    and spread of Buddhism, 219–220
    trade with Japan, 277
    unification of, 172
    world map, 312–313
Korean War, 737
Kosa Pan, 571
Kosala, 147
Kosrae Island, 253
Kremlin, 281
Kubilai Khan, 320, 320, 323, 324, 329, 361
Kücük Kaynarca, treaty, 543
Kuhn, Thomas, 702
Kuk swamp, 33
Kukai, 249
Kulottung I, king, 275
Kulturkampf, G–5
Kumarajiva, 228
Kumasi, 511, 677
Kumbi-Saleh, 238, 293, 363
Kunta, 472, 553
Kupe, 255
Kur Valley of Fars, 157, 197
Kurdistan, 287
Kurnool, 526
Kurosawa, Akira, 614
Kush, 93
Kushanese art, 124
Kussara, 75, 79
Kuwait, 745
Kwanggaet'o, king, 192, 219
KwaZulu-Natal, 377
Kyoto, 358, 503, 504
Kyushu, 456, 519, 532

L
La Venta, 91
Labor
    in the Americas, 444–445
    in ancient river valley civilizations, 62–63
    child, 628
    chronology, 630
    criminals as source, 626–627
    in eighteenth century, 530
    female, 628–629
    forced, 548
    and industrialization, 621
    migration of, 627, 629–631
Lachish, 130
Lactose tolerance and dairy consumption, 32
Ladinos, 507
Lady of Elche, 109, 109
Lagash, 70
Lagos, and industrialization, 620
Lahontan, Sieur de, 579
Laissez-faire, 573, 750, 751, G–5
Lake Chad, 339, 345
Lake Titicaca, 35, 241
Lalibela, king, 270–271, 271
Lamaist Buddhism, 768
Lament of Lady Qin, 303
Lancelot, 403
Land

exploitation in Americas, 451–456, 452–453
    overexploitation of, 780–781
    reclamation, 456–457
Land empires, 413, 422–431
Landholding
    in eighteenth century, 531
    in eleventh century Europe, 279
Language faculty, 707
Language(s), 402, 584, 707–708
    Bantu, 42, 116, 238
    Latin, 296
    Phoenicians, 99
    Sanskrit, 557
    Slav, 297
    sociology of, 707–708
    Swahili, 539–540
Laos, 734, 743
Laozi, 130, 143, 146
Laplace, Pierre-Simon de, 483, 581
l'Arce, Louis-Armand de Lom de, 579
Large Glass (sculpture) (Duchamp), 710
Larsa, 64
Las Casas, Bartolomé, 480
Lassa fever, 790
Last Supper (Caravaggio), 466
Latin, 296, 567
Latin America, 742. See also Spain in the Americas
    and business imperialism, 652–653
    constitutionalism, 672
    democracy, 743
    economy, 764
    foreign imperialism, 643
    and industrialization, 604–605
    nationalism, 670
    population, 785
    post World War I, 725
Latin Christendom, 277, 278, 283, 332–333, 405. See also Christianity
    map of, 334
Latin Church, 281, G–5
Latitude, 335, G–5
Lavoisier, Antoine, 529
Law
    during Axial Age, 135
    in fifteenth century, 405
    Mesopotamian, 66
    Ottoman Empire, 497
    Sharia, 198
Law of nations, 493, G–5
Lazica, 219
Leader cult, 740
League of Nations, 723, G–5
Leaseholding, 372
Lebanon, 628
Lee Bo, 579
Leeuwenhoek, Anton van, 529
Legalists/Legalism, 135, 144, 169–170, 200, G–5
Legionnaire's disease, 791
Lehrer, Tom, 781
Leibniz, Gottfried Wilhelm, 481, 485, 572
Leicester, 760
Lembang, 698
Lenin, Vladimir Ilyich, 726, 735
Leo XIII, pope, 619, 680
Leopold II, king of the Belgians, 626, 650–651, 653, 661
Lepers, 356
Leprosy, 443
Lervac-Tournières, Robert, 564
Lesseps, Ferdinand de, 610
Letters of a Chinese Philosopher (Goldsmith), 566
Leutard, 281–282

Levant, 131, 289, G–5
Lhasa, 204, 204
Li, king, 110
Li family, 202
Li Hongzhang, 607, 608
Li Longmian, 307, 308
Li Qingzhao, 306
Li Yuan, 202
Li Zhi, 502
Liao, 304
Liberalism, 686
Liberation theology, 770, G–5
Liberia, 670, 672, 741
Libya, 674, 723
Liebig, Justus von, 596
Lienzo de Tlaxcala, 428
Liezi, 142
Life expectancy, 444–445, 789–790, 790
Life of an Ant, The (Montgomery), 12
Lifestyle diseases, 791
Ligouri, Alfonso Maria, 576
Lima, 454, 519
Limpopo River, 377
Limschoten, Jan van, 415
Lin, commissioner, 640, 641
Lincoln, Benjamin, 558
Lind, James, 522
Linguet, Simon-Nicolas-Henri, 567
Linguistics, 707–708, 711
Linnaeus, Carolus, 579
Linschoten, Jan van, 420
Lipit-Ishtar, King, 65
Lisbon, 516
Literature
    Byzantine Empire, 302–303
    Christian, 449
    Greek, ancient, 86
    Japanese, 276
    novel, 707
    Philippian, 671
    Song empire, 308
Lithuania/Lithuanians, 370, 404
Little Bighorn, battle of, 646
Little China, 628
Little Ice Age, 345, G–5
Little Istanbul, 759
Liu Bang, 170
Liu Guandao, 320
Livable Netherlands Party, 763
Liverpool, 624
Livestock, in the Americas, 437, 448
Livonia, 333, 464
Llamas, 369
Locke, John, 572, 575
Locomotive, 598
Loess, 63
Logic, 138
Logograms, 71, 71, 99, G–5
Lombard cross, 196
Lombards, 195
London, 164
    population in eighteenth century, 519, 521
Long, Edward, 549
Longitude, G–5
Lord of Hosts, 214, 217
Lord of the Flies (Golding), 715
Lotus Sutra, 228, 228, G–5
Louis IX, king of France, 333
Louis the Great, 370
Louis XIV, king of France, 456, 566
Louis XV, king of France, 574
Louis XVI, king of France, 580
Louisiana, 554, 643
Loutherbourg, Philippe-Jacques de, 598, 616
L'Ouverture, Toussaint, 625
Love, universal, 131–134

Loving cups, 87
Low Countries, 603, G–5
Lower Egypt, 70
Loyola, Ignatius, 466, 467
Lozi, 651
Lü Liuliang, 502
Luanda, 552
Lübeck, 279
Lucayos, 479
Lucy (australopithecine), 6, 7
Ludwig, Nicolas, 575
Lugal Zagesi, 70
Lugard, Frederick, 650
Lu-igisa, 64
Lukaris, Cyril, 466–467
Lukon-kashia, 552
Luther, Martin, 465–466, 466
Luzon, 467

M
Ma Huan, 394
Macaque monkeys, 704
Macaulay, Thomas, 660
Macaw dynasty, 242
Macedon/Macedonians, 106, 161–162
Machiavel, 493
Machiavelli, Niccolò, 493, 596
Machine guns, 646, 648
Machine-age imagery, 709–710
Mad cow disease, 791
Madagascar, 362
Madeira, 370, 440
Madinat al-Zahra, 293
Madonna, 468
Madrid, 620, 621
Maecenas, 151
Maes Howe, 54
Magadha, 147
Maghada, 191
Magic, 250
  and science, 480
Magic Flute, The (Mozart), 574–575
Magnetism, 780
Magyarization, 668
Magyars, 289, G–5
Maharajah, 251
Mahavamsa, 112
Mahavira, 127, 144, 146, 147
Mahayana Buddhism, 221, 228, 233, G–5
Mahdi, 553, 680–681, G–5
Mahmud, 331
Mahmud II, 673
Mahmud of Ghazni, 288
Mahreb, 218
Mai Lai, 750
Maitreya, 392
Maize, 35, 36, 38, 91, 436–437, 457, G–5
  cultivation of, 245–246
  in North America, 116
Majapahit, 361
Majorca, 399
Makassar, 421, 421
Makerere University, 696
Malacca, 393, 421, 472
Malaka, Tan, 727
Malal, 215
Malaria, 86, 537, 552, 643, 791
Malaspina, Alessandro, 523, 558
Malay, 727
Malaya, 275, 698, 738
Maldives, 275
Male dominance
  in ancient river valley
    civilizations, 63
  in Greece, ancient, 105–106
  Hittites, 80

in prehistorical society, 12
Mali, 363–366, 378–379, G–5
  map of, 364
Malta, 54, 55, 98
Malthus, Thomas, 517–518, 590
Malthusian, 517, 590, G–5
Mamluk Egypt, 330–331, 404
Mamluk sultan, 365
Mamluks, 330–331, 342, G–5
  chronology, 331
Mana, 253, G–5
Manado, 468
Manaus, 620, 621
Manchester (England), 618, 620
Manchu Qing dynasty, 541
Manchuria, 423, 450–451, 470, 503, 541, 629–630, 719
Manchurian Incident, 718, 719, G–5
Manchus, 423, 446, 450, 468, 502, 502, 503, 672, G–5
Mandan Indians, 561
Mandarins, 501–502, 503, G–5
Mandate of heaven, 71, 88, 109, 304, 305, 316, 328, 502, 607, G–5
Mandela, Nelson, 742
Manhattan, 620
  map of ethnicity, 632
Mani, 215
Manichaeanism, 215, 232, G–5
Manifest destiny, 71, 658, G–5
Manila, 416, 417, 418, 541, 542, 560
Manila Galleon, 431, 492, G–5
Manon Lascaut (Puccini), 629
Mansa Musa, 365, 365, 378, 379
Mansas, 365, 365, 366
Manufacturing output, 611
Manyoshu, 470
Manzikert, battle of, 300
Mao Zedong, 732–733, 736, 737, 750, 760
Maori, 535, 635, 647, 664, 665, G–5
Maori Wars, 647
Mapmaking, 254, 255, 578, 586–587
Mapuche, 555
Maqamat (Scales of Harmony)
  (al-Hariri), 288, 354
Maragha, 326
Marajó Island, 246
Marathas, 544–545, 545, 547, G–6
Marcellinus Ammianus, 185
Marcia Procula, 164
Marco Polo, 320, 321, 323, 324, 325
Marconi, Guglielmo, 700, 778
Marcus Aurelius, 184
Marcus Valerius Celerinus, 164
Margarine, 597, 603
Mari, 77
Marib, 118–119, 194
Marinetti, Emilio Filippo, 709
Maritime empires, 412–421, 413, G–6
Maritime imperialism
  and Asia, 416–419
  chronology, 413, 421
  map of, 416
  and Portugal, 410, 414–419
Maritime navigation, 252, 253–254, 419–421
  by Europeans, 395, 398
  in fifteenth century, 375–376
Maritime technology, 333, 412–413
Maroons, 506, 507, 507–508, G–6
  map of in the Americas, 508
Marquess of Bute, 634
Marriage, 680
  ancient Greece, 105
  ancient river valley civilizations, 63
  in China, 503
  in fourteenth century, 362–363

in imperialistic Portugal, 415
interracial, 549
in nineteenth century, 590
in sixteenth and seventeenth centuries, 506, 506
of slaves, 549
Marseillaise, 583
Marseilles, 524, 574
Marshall, George C., 731
Marshall Plan, 731, G–6
Martilineal, G–6
Martin, St., 227
Marx, Karl, 616, 618, 684, 707, 716, 725
Marxism, 726, 754, G–6
Mary, Mother of God, 293
Mary, Queen of Scots, 494
Mary of Hungary, archduchess, 478
Masai, 32, 518
Massachusetts, 477
Massacres, 418
Massaweh, 377
Master Meng, 307
Mastrillo, Nicolás de, 463
Mataka, chief, 636
Mataram, 472
Material culture, 17–18, G–6
Mathematics, 701, 710
  in Axial Age, 137–138
Maui, 255
Maupertuis, Pierre Louis de, 564, 564–565, 575, 576
Maurice, John, 441
Mauritius, 533, 533
Mauryan Empire, 169
Maxim gun, 646, 646
Maximilian II, 478
Maya/Mayans, 181–182, 241–244, 257, 269–270, 556, 681, G–6
  art, 242, 243
  contending with isolationism, 280
  expansion of, 246
  map of, 183
  trade, 431
  writing system, 243, 244
Mazhir, Ismail, 699
Mazzini, Giuseppe, 666
McAllister, Samuel Ward, 635
McDonaldization, 766
McDonald's, 767, 783
McNeil, John, 786
Mead, Margaret, 12
Meadowcroft, 21
Measles, 443, 518, 791
Meat processing industry, 594
Mecca, 232, 263
  pilgrimages, 232, 365
Mechanization, chronology, 623
Medici, Catherine de', 494
Medici family, 402
Medicine, 648, 695, 698–699, 755
  alternative, 714
  in Axial Age, 141, 141–142
  in China, 695
  chronology, 141
  in eighteenth century, 522–523
  Middle East, 714
  in twentieth century, 751
  Western, 702–703
    map of spread, 696–697
Meditations (Marcus Aurelius), 184
Mediterranean
  chronology, 108
  map of in eleventh and twelfth centuries, 290–291
  trade routes, 154–155
Mehmet Ali, 609, 631
Mehmet II, 391
Meiji Restoration, 606

Mekong River, 37, 251
Melaka, 540
Melbourne, 435, 620
Melville, Herman, 588, 589
Memphis (Egypt), 57, 70
Mencius, 136, 143, 145
Mendelssohn, Felix, 599
Menelik, 647, 649
Menelik II, emperor, 647, 649, 678
Menes, 69–70
Mental health, 791
Mercado, Tomás de, 573
Mercantilism, 205, 565, G–6
Mercator, 586–587
Mercy (Galdós), 634
Meroe, 116
Mersenne, Marin, 529
Meru, 271
Mesoamerica, 116, 442, G–6
  agriculture, 35
  ancient civilization, 89–92
  art, 269
  chronology, 268
  contending with isolationism, 280
  decline of ancient civilization, 98
  empire building, 173–174
  expansion in eleventh and twelfth
    centuries, 269–270
  expansion of, 246
  in fifteenth century, 381–385, 384
  growth of settlements, 53
  map of, 240
  map of in twelfth century, 267
  in thirteenth century, 338
Mesopotamia, 56, 59–61
  ancient government, 66
  ancient politics, 69
  ecology of civilization, 63
  expansion of ancient, 69–70
  map of, 60
  trade, 78–79
  writing, 71
Messiah, 131, G–6
Messiah (Handel), 576
Messiah of Portugal, 403
Messina Declaration (1955), 744
Mestizos, 507, G–6
Metallurgy, 53, 54
Mexico, 764
  and Christianity, 469
  conquest by Spain, 426
  exploitation of environment, 459
  industrialization, 605
Mexico City, 437, 454, 519, 785
Mi Fei, 307, 308
Miasmas, 522
Michael (archangel), 282, 297, 403
Michael IV, 300
Michael VII, 333
Michelangelo, 478, 478–479
Microbial exchange, 438–439, 442–444, G–6
Micronesia, 253
Middle East
  map of in eleventh and twelfth centuries, 290–291
  map of in twentieth century, 722
  preagricultural settlements, 29–30
  map of, 29
  trade and recovery, 99–103
  and Western science, 699
Midwifery, 699
Mieszko, 223
Migration
  in eleventh and twelfth
    centuries, 264–266
  of *Homo* species, 8–13
  map of early, 10–11
  map of world, 633

Migration, (cont.)
 to New World, 19, 20, 21–22
 in twentieth century, 721–722, 758
Migration of labor, 629–631
Mika'el Suhul, 553
Miletus, 160
Militarism, 721
Militarization, 673–679, 677, G–6
 chronology, 678
Military revolution, 447, 448, G–6
Military/weaponry, 496, 648,
  674–676
 bombs, 731, 732
 British, 646, 646
 Chinese, 171, 568
 Hittites, 80
 justification of, 495
 musket, 647
 of Native Americans, 428
 naval, 597
 in nineteenth century, 596–597
 poison gas, 724
 revolution, 447, 448
 Roman, 162
 Steppelanders, 189, 189
 submarine, 721
 World War I, 724
Mill, John Stuart, 686
Millenarianism, 357–358, 476–477, G–6
Millet, 36, 62
Milpas, 242, 244
Milvian Bridge, 217
Minamoto clan, 277
Minas Gerais, 455, 555, G–6
Mindanao, 467
Mineral phosphates, 604
Ming, 219, 225
Ming China, 393
Ming Dynasty, 356, 371, 391, 392, 446,
  450, 468, 483, 501–502, G–6
 chronology, 394, 503
Mining, 620, 621–623
Minoans, 81
Mir, Titu, 615
Miracles, 127
Missionaries, 216, 297, 463, 467
 in Brazil, 475–476
 in California, 555
 Christian, 420, 467, 467–469
Mississippi region, 266–268
 contending with isolationism, 280
Mitsubishi, 606
Mitsui, 606
Miura Baien, 569
Mixtec, 269, 270, 408–409
Moa, 367
Moais, 366–367, 367
Mobutu, Joseph, 739
Moby Dick (Melville), 588, 589
Moche, 239, 241, 368
 expansion of, 246
Moctezuma II, 426
Modern art, 713
Modernism, 709
Modernization, 665
 in nineteenth century, 676
Mogador, 98
Mogodishu, 270
Mohenjodaro, 62, 62, 68–69
 decline of, 93
Mohists, 144
Mojmir I, 256
Moldavia, 425
Mollusks, 45
Molucca Islands, 468
Mombasa, 538, 539
Monarchs, religious
  conversions, 216–224
Monarchy, 135–136, 165, 490, 650

Monasteries, 219, 221, 221, 250
Monasticism, 226–229
 chronology, 229
Monet, Claude, 636
Mongaku, 277
Mõngke Khan, 324
Mongkut, prince, 678
Mongo, 518
Mongol Peace, 321, G–6
Mongolia, 316, 450
 exploitation of environment, 459
Mongolian Peace
  travelers during, 326
Mongols, 370, 386–388, 446–447,
  G–6
 art, 314, 320, 321
 and Buddhism, 470, 470–471
 in China, 326–329
 chronology, 317, 340
 conquest of China, 326–329
 conquest of Persia, 329
 conquest of Russia, 329–330
 and Egypt, 330–331
 infected by plague, 350, 351, 356
 invasion of, 315–325
 map of campaigns, 318–319
 map of European travelers, 322
 peaceful period, 321–324
 religion of, 470
 in Russia, 329–330
 trade with China, 323
 uniqueness of, 336–339
Monks, 226–228, 262
 in Russia, 330, 330
Monocultures, 533, G–6
Monopolies, 416
Monotheism, 132–133
Monroe Doctrine, 652, G–6
Monsoons, 113, 153, 156, G–6
 and maritime navigation, 375
Montagu, Mary Wortley, 424, 523
Monte Albán, 174, 175
 map of, 173
Monte Cassino, 227
Monte Verde, 21
Montesquieu, 566, 567, 568, 573
Montgomery, Bernard, 12
Moonies, 757
Moral meterology, 343
Moral superiority, 659–660
Morales, Eduardo, 670
Morgan, T.H., 702, 710
Morinaga, Motoori, 470
Morning Star, 242
Morocco, 351, 404, 448, 647, 674, 739
Morse, Samuel, 600
Moscow, 386, 519
Moses, 349
Most, Johann, 684–685
Mound agriculture, 33, G–6
Mound clusters, 267–268
Mount Huascarán, 462
Mount Parnassus, 139
Mozambique, 377
Mozart, Wolfgang Amadeus, 567,
  574, 576
Mozi, 131, 134, 142–145, 146
Mugabe, Robert, 739
Mughal emperors, 456
Mughals, 421, 423–424, 477,
  526–527, 544–545, G–6
 chronology, 425, 547
 in India, 451, 498
 chronology, 501
Muhammad, 131, 133, 196–197, 198,
  206, 212, 216, 226, 228, 232,
  237, 247, 287, 296, 329, 329,
  500, 539, 680
Muhammad Ahmad, 680

Muhammad Ali, 674
Muhammad ibn Abd al-Wahhab, 544
Muhammad Shah, emperor, 544
Muhammad Touray Askia, 378–379
Mulay Hassan, 647, 648
Mullah Nasreddin, 658
Multaqa al-Abhur (Confluence of the
  Currents) (Ibrahim al
  Halabi), 497
Multiculturalism, 762, G–6
Mundigak, 69
Munjon, king, 277
Muqaddimah, 386
Murad IV, 497
Murillo, 466
Murray-Darling river, 781
Mursili II, 81
Muscovy, 386
Musi, 251
Music
 in eighteenth century, 576
 pop, 713
Musical theater, 713
Musket, 647
Muslims, 197–200, 214, 216,
  225–226, 229, 277, 287–288,
  314–316, 386, 424, 451, 477,
  544, 567, 681, 762. See also
  Islam/Islamic
 art, 288
 and commerce, 419
 in East Africa, 270
 in fifteenth century, 379
 map of, 198, 231
 migration, 263
 and missionaries, 467
 reform movements, 679
 in Russia, 658
 and sufism, 296
 in thirteenth century
  India, 331–332
 view of plague, 354
 in West Africa, 553
 and Western science, 699
 expansion of, 699
Mussolini, Benito, 727
Mutesa, king, 679
Mutis, José Celestino, 532
Muye, 87
Mwene Mutapa, 377, 379, 385, 403, 552
Myanmar, 743
Mycenae/Mycenaens, 81, 83, 83–84, 99
 chronology, 84
 decline of, 93
Mysore, 547
Mysticism, 302

N
Nabopolasar, 102
Nabta Playa, 30
Nadir Shah, 543
Naegamwalla, Jamsetji Dorabji, 600
Nagasaki, 420, 729, 731
Nahuatl, 442
Namibia art, 17
Nanak, 477
Nanjing, 524, 749
Nanjing, treaty of, 640
Napata, 116
Naples, 434, 519
Napoleon Bonaparte, 530, 581–583,
  583, 596, 642, 687
 map of empire, 582
Napoleonic Wars (1799-1815), 657,
  666, 668, 672, 682, G–6
Naqia, 102
Narrative of the Surveying Voyage of
  HMS Adventure and Beagle
  (Fitzroy), 659
Nasser, Gaml Abdel, 739

National Assemby, 580
National Health Service
  (Britain), 790
National insurance, 755
National Socialist German Workers'
  Party, 727. See also Nazis
Nationalism, 404–405, 666–672, 677,
  G–6
 beyond Europe, 669–672
 chronology, 678
 in Europe, 666–668
Nationalist Party (Egypt), 724
Nationalists, 723, 726–727
Native Americans, 631
 in Brazil, 555
 and Catholic
  missionaries, 468–469
 and Columbus, 479
 conquest by Spain, 426, 428–429
 contending with isolationism, 280
 and diseases, 428–429, 506, 518
 elimination in the United
  States, 429–430, 658
 human nature of, 479–480
 hunting, 457
 and New England
  colonists, 429–430
 population in eighteenth
  century, 518
 reactions to Europeans, 428–429
 and religion, 474, 769
 as slaves, 430
 and smallpox, 428, 442
Natural selection, 27, G–6
Nature, cult of, 576–577
Nature versus nurture, 703, G–6
Nature worship, 139
Naucratis, 104
Nautical maps, 413
Naval technology, 597
Naval warfare, 597, 597
Nawab, 545
Nazca, 239, 241, 245, 249
 expansion of, 246
Nazis, 708, 727, 728, 750, 750, 759,
  G–6. See also National Socialist
  German Workers' Party
Ndebele, 646, 651
Ndongo, 488, 489, 511
Neanderthal, 7, 704, G–6
Neanderthal Valley, 10
Neapolis, 172
Nebamun, 56
Nebaun, 50
Nebuchadnezzar II, 102–103
Needham, Joseph, 714
Négritude, 760, G–6
Nemesis (ship), 638
Nene, 664
Nenets, 23
Nepal, 194, 204
Nerchinsk, 449
 treaty of (1689), 423
Nestorianism, 329, G–6
Nestorians, 215, 225, 233, 326
Nestorius, bishop, 215
Netherlands, 483, 494, 758
 1550 map of, 419
 in the Americas, 444, 445
 decolonization in twentieth
  century, 738, 738
 emancipation of slaves, 626
 horticultural exchange, 441
 imperialism, 643
 industrialization, 603
 and maritime
  imperialism, 419–421
 and maritime navigation, 413,
  419–421

relations with East Indies, 421
relations with England, 421
relations with India, *527*
relations with Portugal, 421
in South Africa, 448
Neuroscience, *710*
New age movement, 768
New Christians, in white America, 476
New Conquests, 541
New Culture (China), 695
New Delhi, *767*
New England, 556
in the seventeenth and eighteenth centuries, 455–456
in the sixteenth and seventeenth centuries, 445
New Europes, 535, 630, G–6
imperialism, 655–656
New France, 445
New Guinea
and agriculture, 33–34
civilizing, *661*
New Harmony (town), 684
New Hebrides, 253
New Israel, 430
New Jerusalem, 271, *271*
New Mexico, 430, 555
New Order, 674
New Orleans, 554, 788, *788*
New Rich, 634, G–6
New Russia, 657
New South Wales, 535
New Spain, 469
New World, 505–509, G–6
demographic collapse, 442–444
early migration to, 19, 21–22
map, *20*
map of, *374*
in sixteenth and seventeenth centuries, 505–509
spread of Christianity, 468–469
New York, 445
New York City, 519, *590*, *630*
and industrialization, 620
New Zealand, 253, 535–536, 578, 591, 655, 656, 665
democracy, 716
in eighteenth century, 535
in fourteenth century, 367–368
Maori wars, 647
socialism, 686
Newfoundland, 266, *374*
Newspapers, 683
Newton, Isaac, 481, 482, 529, 564
Newton's laws, 482
Neyici Toyin, 470
Ngoni priests, 646
Nguema, Macías, 739
Ni Bozhuang, 328
Nicaea, 333
Nicaragua, 670
Nietzsche, Friedrich, 686
Niger, 653
Niger River, 116, 379
Niger Valley, 238
Nigeria, 331, 622, 672, 714, 784
art, *116*
population, *777*
Night Revels of Han Xizai, The (Gu Hongzhong), *308*
Nihongi, 249
Nile River, 37, 55–57, 69–70, *376*
Nile Valley, 42
Nineveh, 99
Ning-an, 451
Nino, St., 218, *219*
Nintu (goddess), 60
Nirvana, 127, G–6

Nitrates, 652
Nixon, Richard, 737, 743
Nizam al-Mulk, 544
Nkrmah, Kwame, 739
Nobel, Alfred, 676
Nobi plain, 457
Nobility, 490, 491, 493, 496
Noble savage, 578–580, G–6
Nomadism, *309*, 309–310, 554, 631
See also Pastoralists
Nootka Sound, 560
Nordhausen concentration camp, *750*
Normans, in eleventh century, 300
Norse, 368–370, 395
chronology, *265*
contending with isolationism, *280*
migration, map of, *265*
migration of, 265–266
North Africa, 404, 425, 543
and Islam/Islamic, 293
map of in twentieth century, *722*
plague in, 351
World War II, 730
North America
chronology, *113*, *119*, *268*
civilization of, *118*
climate change in fourteenth century, 345
developments in ancient, 113–116
expansion of, *246*
exploitation of environment, *459*
fur trade, 431
geographic obstacles, *254*
map of in twelfth century, *267*
North American Southwest, 266–267
North Atlantic, climate change in the fourteenth century, *348*
North Island, 665
North Korea, 734
North Vietnam, 734
Northern Kingdom, 304
Northmen. *See* Norse
Northwest Passage, *265*, G–6
Norway, 214, 223
democracy, 716
Nosso Senhor do Born Jesus de Matosinho, *555*
Novel, 671, 707
Novgorod, 256, 281, 330, *330*
Nubia, 58, 92–93, 116, 218, 331
Nüchunyu, 202
Nuclear fission, 731
Nuclear power, 779
"Nude Descending a Staircase" (Duchamp), 710
Nüjie, 202
Numancia, 166
Nunneries, 229
Nuns, 229
Nurhaci, 502
Nutrition and human population, 442
Nyaya, 131
Nyaya School, 138–139, *146*
Nzinga of Ndongo, queen, *488*, 489, 511

O

Oaxaca, 174
Ob River, 386
Obeah-men, 507
Oberá the Resplendent, 477
Obesity, 783, *784*, 791
Obs, *379*
Observatory, *484*
Obsidian, 182, G–6
Ocean of Death, 67
Oceanic imperialism, 395–398

chronology, *398*
Ocelotl, Don Martín, 476
Ocher, *2–3*
Ochre, 17, 18
Odyssey (Homer), 105
Oedipus complex, 705–706
Ogallala Aquifer, 781
Ogyu Sorai, 569
Oil as energy source, 456, 597, 778–779
Oil crisis, 735
Okayama, 532
Okinawa, 417
Oklahoma, 658
Olaf, *225*
king of Norway, 214
Old Believers, 495
Old regime, 580, G–6
Old San Juan, 454
Old World, G–6
agriculture of, 36
Olive growing industry, 103–104, *104*
Olive oil, 103, *104*
Olmec civilization, 35, 89, *90*, 91–92
Olof Skötkunung
king of Sweden, 223
Omai, 579, *579*
Oman/Omanis, 116, 416, 539–540, 560
Omdurman, battle of, 646, *646*, 681
Ongghot, 470
Ongons, 470, *470*, G–6
OPEC, 755, 779, G–6
Opera houses, 620, *621*
Opitz, G.E., 668
Opium, 525–526, 620, 640–641, *641*
Opium Wars, 608, *638*, 640–641, 660
Oppenheimer, J. Robert, 714
Opticks (Descartes), *482*
Oracle bones, 67, *67*
Oracles, 66–67, *67*, 87–88, G–7
Greek, 104
Orangutans, 6
Organ transplants, 789
Organization of Petroleum Exporting Countries. *See* OPEC
Oriental despotism, 566, 568, G–7
Origin of Species by Means of Natural Species (Darwin), 659
Orkney Islands, 54
Oromo, 518, 553
Orontes River, 248
Orthodox Church, 466, G–7
Osaka, *519*, 532
Oshio Heicharo, 626
Osiris, 65
Ostrogoths, 189
Ostyaks, 423
Otto I, emperor, 278
Otto III, emperor, 278, *279*, 283
Otto of Freising, 281
Ottoman Empire, 386–391, 424–426, 440, 622, 671, G–7
centralization, 673–674
chronology, *501*
constitutionalism, 672
democracy, 683
economy in eighteenth century, 528
emancipation of slaves, 626
Enlightenment, 571–572
imperialism, 416, 543–544
laws of, *497*
map of, *388–389*, *586–587*
nationalism, 668
population in eighteenth century, 519
in sixteenth and seventeenth centuries, 495–498

and Western science, 698
World War I, 720
Ottoman State, map of, *370*
Ottomans, 370, *370*, *390*
art, *448*, *498*
chronology, *425*
Enlightenment, 567–568
Our Lady of Guadalupe, 469
Outer Mongolia, 423
Ouyang Xiu, 305–306, 308
Overall Survey of the Ocean's Shore, The (Huan), 394
Overconsumption, 766
Overpopulation, 517–518, 758
Oviedo Cathedral, 256
Oxus, 658, 780
Oxus River, 85
Oyo, kingdom, 672
Ozette, 367–368

P

Pacal, king, 242
Pachamachay, 35
Pacific
colonization of, 253–255
in the eighteenth century, 578–579
in fourteenth century, 366–369, *369*
geographic obstacles, *254*
map of fourteenth century societies, *368*
Pacific Islands, spread of agriculture in, 42
Pacific Ocean
map of maritime imperialism, *416*
Paekche, 172, 192, 204, 220
development of, 205
Paganism, 217, *217*, 220, 232, 469
Pahlavi, Mohammad Reza, 766–767
Painting, 709–712
Byzantine Empire, 302–303
Chinese, 307, *307*, 308
cubism, 710
Dutch, *417*
Japanese, *570*
Mongolian, *316*
seventeenth century, *481*
Spanish, *4*, *5*
Paisley, 662
Paizi, *323*
Pakehas, 665
Pakistan, 738, 741
Palas dynasty, 222
Palembang, 251, 361
Palenque, 242
Paleoanthropologists, 6, 7, 8
Paleoanthropology, 704, *711*
Palestine, 162, 723
conflict with Israel, 741, *742*
Palmares, 508
Palm-oil production, 622
Pamir Mountains, 156
Pampa de Caña Cruz, 89
Pampas, 32, 431, 605, G–7
Pan-African Congress, 724, G–7
Panama, 431, 658
Pangea, G–7
Panlongcheng, 62
Pansophy, 481
Pánuco River, 382
Papago Native Americans, 44
Papal infallibility, 680
Paper, invention of, 333, 483
Paquimé, 345
Paradigm shifts, 702
Paraguay, 442, 670
dams, 780
Paraná, 780
Paranthropoi, 6

Paraquay, 555
Paris, 519, 620, 756
Paris, Matthew, 317
Paris Peace Conference (1919–1920), 728, 745
Parliament, 672
Parmenides, 138, 146
Parramatta, 535
Parthian shot, 189
Parthia/Parthians, 162, 189
Partition of India, 738, G–7
Passport, Mongolian, 323
Pastoral imperialism, 448–449
Pastoralism, 171, 288–289, 446–447, 448
Pastoralists, 324, 630–631
Paternalism, 623, G–7
   during industrialization, 616–618
Patna, 519
Patriarch of Constantinople, 466
Patrilineal, G–7
Patriotism, 653
Paul, Apostle, 214, 218
Paul III, pope, 479
Pavón, Hipólito, 532
Peacock, Thomas Love, 684
Pearl Harbor, 729
Peasants, 281–282, 493, 784
   in China, 502–503
   in fifteenth century China, 392
   in fourteenth century Japan, 363
   in nineteenth century, 622, 622
   and plague affecting land owner-
      ship, 357–358
   revolts, 626
      in fifteenth century China, 392
      in nineteenth century China, 607
      in sixteenth and seventeenth cen-
         turies, 493–495
      in sixteenth and seventeenth centu-
         ry Japan, 504
Peat as energy source, 456, 597
Pedra Pintada, 22
Pedro I, king, 558
Pedro IV, king, 552
Pelizza, Giuseppe, 685
Peloponnese, 81
Pencillin, 702
Peng Shaosheng, 470
Pennsylvania and Native
   Americans, 430
Pentagon, 754
Pepi, 93
Pepper as spice, 416, 421
Pequot War, 429
Pergamum, 162
Perm River, 386
Pernambuco, 440, 440, 455, 508
Pernikoff, Aleksandr, 719
Perón, Eva, 728
Perón, Juan, 727–728
Perry, Matthew C., 605
Persepolis, 159, 159
Perses, 104
Persian Letters (Montesquieu), 567
Persian-Greek Wars, 159–161
Persia/Persian empire, 147, 153,
   157–162, 370, 424, 440. See also
   Iran
   Arab invasion, 197
   art, 159
   chronology, 160
   conquest by Mongols, 329
   Enlightenment, 567–568
   government, 159–160
   imperialism, 543
   map of, 161
   population in eighteenth
      century, 519

religion, 132
Safavids, 499–501
   chronology, 501
   transformation of, 199
   war with Greece, 159–161
Persikoff, Aleksandr, 745
Peru, 239, 241, 426, 462, 605, 670,
   725, 766
   agriculture of, 35
   art, 368
   conquest of, 428, 431
   ecology in eighteenth century, 436
   independence, 556
   and pre-Christian devotions, 469
Perun (god), 224
Pescadores Islands, 656
Peshawar, 214
Petals Palace, 204
Peter Pan (Barrie), 706
Peter the Great, czar of Russia, 495, 495
Peter the Wild Boy, 579
Petrarch, 354
Phagspa, 323
Pharaohs, 64, 69, 93
Philadelphia, 519
Philip, king of Macedon, 161
Philip II, king of Spain, 456, 491, 494
Philip III, king of Spain, 507
Philip IV, king of Spain, 494, 497
Philippines, 418, 467, 541, 591, 658,
   738, 758–759
   democracy, 742
   map of Catholic missions, 471
   nationalism, 671
Philosopher's Stone, 482, G–7
Philosophical Investigations (Wittgen-
   stein), 708
Philosophy, 142–143, 707
   ancient Greece, 106
   in Axial Age, 131
   Chinese, 145
   and Christianity, 478
   of eleventh and twelfth
      centuries, 283
   Enlightenment, 572
   in fifteenth century, 385, 402
   Japanese, 569
   map of schools, 145
   nineteenth century, 684–686
   Song empire, 308
Philosophy of Christ, 478
Phocaea, 109
Phoenicia/Phoenicians, 98–99
   chronology, 99
   map of civilization, 100–101
   revival of, 103
Phosphate, 781
Photography, 572
Phuc, Kim, 734
Phyongrgyas, 204
Physics, 700–701, 710
Physiocrats, 531, 573, G–7
Picasso, Pablo, 704, 710, 711, 712
Pig, 535
Pig-iron production, 530
Pilgrim ship, 262
Pilgrimages, 262, 263, 288
   to Jerusalem, 289, 289
Pineapple, 436
Pinochet, Augusto, 765
Pisces, 768
Pitcairn, 534
Pithecanthropoi, 6
Piux IX, pope, 680
Plague, 194, 342, 348–358, 349,
   369–371, 435, 442, 523, 590, 789
   in Africa, 643
   in China, 392
   chronology, 372

course and impact of, 350–351
   in Eurasia, 443–444
   moral and social effects, 351–358
   treating, 351
Plant husbandry, 30–31, 703
Plantation system, 445, 507, 549, 624,
   G–7
Plants, exchange among
   countries, 436–442
Plassey, battle, 545
Plastic, invention of, 700
Plato, 106, 131, 132, 135, 137, 143,
   144, 146, 303, 478
Platonism, 478
Pliny, 157
Plow technology, 249, 451
Pluralism, 759
Plymouth, 445
Pneumonic plague, 349
Pocahontas, 441
Pohnpei, 253
Poincaré, Henri, 700, 707, 710
Poison gas, 724
Poivre, Pierre, 533
Poland, 404, 490, 728, 735
   in fourteenth century, 370
Poldi-Pezzoli, G., 619
Poleis, Greek, 118
Polestar, G–7
Polio, 751, 789
Political optimism, 135–137
Political pessimism, 135
Political radicalism, 681–683
   chronology, 686
Politicization of social issues, 751
Politics. See also Government
   in ancient river valley
      civilizations, 64
   of Axial Age, 134–137
   and Buddhism, 219
   chronology, 687, 745
   extremism in Europe, 724–725
   and farming, 43
   Hittites, 79–81
   and religion, 680–681
   in thirteenth century, 337
   in twentieth century, 664, 665–689,
      761
   Western Europe, 277–282
   Zhou dynasty, 87–88
Pollution, 778
   air, 785
Polo, Marco, 322
Polynesia/Polynesians, 253–255, 263,
   366–367
   chronology, 255
Polytheism, 133
Pondicherry, 421
Poor Richard's Alamack (Franklin), 522
Pop music, 713
Pope, Alexander, 482
Pophung, king, 192, 220
Popper, Karl, 706
Population, 376, 775–777
   in 1900, 620
   in the Americas, 441–442
   ancient China, 171
   in ancient river valley
      civilizations, 62–63
   in British North America, 556, 557
   in China, 257
   chronology, 528, 600
   and climate change in fourteenth
      century, 345
   control, 9
   decline in the Americas, 441–442
   early growth of, 9, 12, 13
   in eighteenth century, 517–524,
      518, 520, 521

of eleventh century Europe, 279
of European empires, 643
expansion during Song
   empire, 305
and farming, 42
foragers and farmers, 31
in fourteenth century, 371, 371
increase in world, 520, 589–590,
   592–593
map of, 785
in Mesoamerica, 182
migration, 630, 730, 757–758
in nineteenth century, 655
nineteenth century increase, 611
noncitizen, 758
and nutrition, 442
trends and migration of Homo sapiens, 9
in twentieth century, 789–790, 793
world, 776, 777
Porcelain, Chinese, 524
Pork industry, 534
Portugal, 333, 492
   in Africa, 538, 539–540, 552
   in the Americas, 436, 444, 445, 508
   in Angola, 622–623
   in Asia, 414–416
   in Brazil, 554–555
   democracy, 742
   in Egypt, 538
   exploration of Atlantic, 395, 398
   in Goa, 414, 414–415, 547
   imperialism, 643
   in India, 417
   introduction of potatoes, 437
   and maritime imperialism, 410,
      414–419
   in New World, 411
   relations with Netherlands, 419,
      421
   and territorial imperialism, 421
   in West Africa, 378, 378–379
Positivism, 707–708, G–7
Possession Island, 27
Postl, Karl, 682
Pot, Pol, 734, 750
Potala Palace, 204
Potato, 436, 437, 535
   domestication, 35
   famine in Ireland, 590
Potosi, 430
Pottery, 71, 104
Poverty Point, 113, 116
Power, alternative sources
   of, 779–780
Practical learning, 571
Pragmatism, 707, G–7
Prague, 756
Pragvata family, 274
Prairie, The (Cooper), 591
Prairies in North America, 437, 554,
   591
Praying towns, 467
Prazeros, 552
Preagricultural settlements, 29–30
   map of, 29
Primatology, 704, 711
Primitivism, 711
Prince, The (Machiavelli), 493
Prince Gong, 607
Prince Henry, 403, 406
Princeps, 165
Printing, 469, 483, 571
   press, 465
Procurement and agriculture produc-
   tion, 44–45
Progress of the Human Mind, The
   (Condorcet), 517
Proletarians, 684

Proletariats, 618, 631, 684, G–7
Propaganda, *734, 736,* 749
Prostitution, *62,* 628
Protectorate, 650, G–7
Protestantism, 477, G–7
Protestants, 466
   and black America, 476
   social structure, 494
   and Wars of Religion, 494
   in White America, 476
Prussia, 581, 675
Psellus, Michael, 303
Pskov, 281
Psychiatry, 706
Psychoanalysis, 706, G–7
Psychology, 705–706, *711*
Ptolemy, Claudius, *260, 376,* 402
Public health, 618
Public sphere, 683, G–7
Puccini, Giacomo, 629, 636
Puduhepa, 81
Pueblo Bonito, *267*
Puerto Rico, 658
Pump technology, 529
Punic Wars, 162
Punjab, 86, 194, 678
Punt, 57, *57*
Puritans, 505
Putin, Vladimir, 743
Pylos, 83
Pyrrho of Elis, 142
Pythagoras, 137, *146*

Q

Qianlong emperor, *502, 541,* 542, 568, *568*
Qin dynasty, 145, 169, *170*
   chronology, *171*
Qing dynasty, 423, 446, 483, 502, 607, 608, 630, 672, 681, 683, 695, 716, 732, G–7
   chronology, *503*
   map of revolts, *675*
Qizilbash, 499
Quadroon, *549*
Quakers, 430
Quantum mechanics, 701, G–7
Quebec, 560, 655
Queen mothers, 498
Queen of Sheba, 118, 271
Quesnay, Francois, 566
Qufu, 394
Quinine, 436, 646, *648*
Quinoa, 35
Quito, 382
Quran, 197, 212, 216, 228, 287, 390, 473, 567, 699, 769, G–7
Qusayr Amra, *236*
Qutb Minar, *332*

R

Rabban Bar Sauma, 326, *327*
Rabia al-Adawiyya, 228, 229
Racial intermarriage, *506*
Racism, 508–509, 629, 651, 715, 759
   scientific, 707
Radicalism, 581
Radio, 778
Radiyya, 332
Ragae, 157
Railway industry, *599,* 599–600, 631, 635
   in Japan, *606*
Rajasthan, 273
Raleigh, Walter, 436
Ralpachen, king, 222
Raman, Chandrasekhara Venkata, 698
Ramiro I, 256

Ramses II, 93
Ramses III, 84, *84*
Rape, John, 749
Rape of Nanjing, *748,* 749, G–7
Rapeseed oil as energy source, 456
Raratonga, 255
Rarity value, 530
Rashid al-Din, *317*
Rastafarianism, G–7
Rathenau, Walter, 669
Rationalism, 138–139, G–7
Ravenna, 189, 195, *195*
Ray, Prafulla Chandra, 698
Reagan, Ronald, 735
Realpolitik, 493, G–7
Reasoning, 138–139
Reccesvinth, king, 233
Recession (economic), 725
Record industry, 713
Reform Act (1832), 682
Reform Acts, 672
Reformation, 466, G–7
Regents, 202, *220,* 276, 494, 546
Reichstag, 683
Relativism, 705
Religion. *See also* Specific types of religion
   art, *210*
   Axial Age, 131–134
   Black America, 474–476
   Buddhism, 126–130
   in Catalhüyük, 37, *38*
   chronology, *216, 233*
      in sixteenth and seventeenth centuries, *485*
   conversions, 218–219
   cult agriculture, 43, *43*
   Daoism, 130
   in eleventh and twelfth centuries, 281–283
   and Enlightenment, 575–580
   fertility, 16, *39*
   forcible conversion, 212–216
   Hittites, 80
   in Ice Age, 17–18
   Islam, 131, 196–197
   Judaism, 130
   Mesopotamian, 66–67
   in nineteenth century, 680–681, *686*
   Persian, 159
   and politics, 680–681
   revitalization of, *472*
   revival, 354, 767–770
      in eighteenth century, 575–576
   rise of, *210, 213*
   in Russia, *495*
   in sixteenth and seventeenth centuries, 462–287
   syncretic features of, 474
   in thirteenth century, *337*
   tolerance of in Ottoman Empire, 388
   and trade, 214–215
   white America, 476–477
   Zoroastrians, 126–127
Religious communities, 225–229, *228–229*
Religious fundamentalism, 715
Religious map of Europe, *471*
Religious orders, 464, 466
Remarque, Erich-Maria, 724
Remezov Chronicle, *449*
Renaissance, 399, 402, 478–480, *496, 596,* G–7
Renewable energy, 779, G–7
Requiem Mass (Mozart), 576
Resettlement, 776
Revolutionary War, 556, 580

Reynolds, Joshua, *579*
Rhine River, 188
Rhodes, 425
Rhodes, Cecil, 623
Rhubarb, 420, 441
Rhyming Chronicle, 333
Ri, 569
Ricardo, David, 530, 573
Ricci, Matteo, *467,* 468
Rice, 33, *247,* 249, 623
   in the Americas, 455
   cultivation of, *33, 62, 271, 272,* 307, *307, 591*
   famine in Japan, 615
Richard II, king of England, 405
Ridge, Tom, *754*
Rig Veda, 86, G–7
Right to vote, 683, 761
Rindos, David, 45
Río Tinto, 109, 623
Rion, Edouard, *610*
River blindness, *774,* 775–776
River Plate, 431
Riza Khan, 723
Rizal, José, 671, *671*
Roca, general, 646
Rocket (Stevenson), 598
Rolfe, John, 441
Roman Catholicism, 768
   conflict with state, 680–681
Roman Empire, 295, 490
   architecture/art, 164–165
   art, *164, 166, 188, 217*
   barbarian invasions of, 184–185, 188–189, 195–196, 206
   changes within, 185, 188
   chronology, *165*
   commerce, 157, 164–165
   conquest of Celts, 166
   culture, 164–165
   eastern, 194–195
   government, 136, 165, 188
   invasion of Carthage, 99, 162
   map of, *163, 189*
      invaders, *186–187*
   rise of, 162–166
   transformation of, *199*
   western, 184–188
Romanesque art, *283*
Romania, 668, 672
   democracy, 683
   nationalism, 668
Romanticism, 575–580, *576–577,* 619, G–7
Romanus IV Diogenes, 300
Rome, 184, 187, 425
   Arab invasion, 197
   comparison with China, *191*
   rise of, 162
   and Steppelanders, 189
Ronin, 504
Roosevelt, Franklin D., 725, 731
Rooster in Islam, *329*
Rosario, 652
Rosary, 335
Rousseau, Jean-Jacques, 577–578
Rowntree, R. Seebohm, 620
Roy, Rajah Rammohan, *562, 563,* 584, 662
Royal Botanical Gardens, 532
Royal Institute for Higher Technical Education, 698
Royal Navy, 534
Royal Observatory, 635
Rudna Glava, 54
Rudolf II, emperor, 480–481
Rum, 455
Rumelia, 425
Rural capitalism, 358

Rus, 223–224, G–7
Ruse, James, 535
Ruskin, John, 684
Russia, 403, 404, 716, 743
   art, 710–711, *726*
   in Asia, 652, 654
   communism, 726
   conquest by Mongols, 329–330
   constitutionalism, 672
   emancipation of slaves, 626
   empire in fifteenth century, 385–386
   expansion chronology, *423*
   in fifteenth century, 385–386
   in fourteenth century, 358
   genocide, 750
   imperialism, 417, 449, *449,* 522–523, 643, *657, 657–658, 658*
   industrialization, 603
   map of, *387*
   migration of labor, 629–630
   modernization of, 495
   nationalism, 672
   and Ottoman Empire, 543
   plague in, 351
   population in eighteenth century, 519
   religion in, *495*
   states, 370
   technology and growth, 281
   World War I, 720, 723
   World War II, 729
Russian Orthodox Church, 467, *495*
Russification, 668
Rusudan, queen, *314, 315*
Rutherford, Ernest, 701, *710*
Ryazan, 330
Rye, 36
Ryukyu, 417

S

Saba/Sabaeans, 118–119
Sachs, Hans, 465
Sacred Heart of Jesus, 576
Sacrifices, human, 241–242, *243*
Sadism, 581
Safavid empire, 424, 446, *499,* 499–501, 543
   map of, *500*
Safavid Persia, 498, 498–501
   chronology, *501*
Safavids, 446, 499–501, G–7
Safflower, *247*
Sages, 126, 143–146, *146*
Sahara, 42, *216,* 292–293, 448, 647, 775, 780
Sahel, 32, 238, 337–339, 448, G–7
Sahid, Muhammad, 419
Said Barghash, 648
Saikaku, 504
Sailendra dynasty, 252–253
Saint Symeon the New Theologian, 302
Saint-Domingue, 440, 533, 548, 625, G–7
Saints, patron, 471
Sakhalin, 417, 560
Saladin, 290, 291, 330
Salarich, Jaume, 619
Salmonella, 791
Salt, *379*
Salvation by faith alone, 466
Samarkand, 423
Sami, 23, 32, 631
Sammuramat, 102
Samoa, 253
Samoyeds, 23, 32
Samurai, 504, *614,* 615, 626, 634, 635, 656, G–7
   rebellion, 626

Samye monastery, *221*
San (African), *17*, 22, *22*
San Antonio, 555
San Francisco, 620
San hunters, 630
San Ignacio, 182
San José de Moro, 241
San Juan Bautista, *455*
San Lorenzo, 91
San Pedro Mártir, 181
San Salvador, 479, 670, 725
San Vitale, 195, *195*
Sanchi, *168*
Sand, George, *399*
Sanitary Conditions of the Labouring Population (Chadwick), 619
Sanskrit, 567
Sanskrit College of Calcutta, 662
Santo Domingo, 507
São Jorge da Mina, 379, 398
São Paulo, 430, 670, 785
Saraswati River, 55, 58, 86
Saray, 330
Sardines, 594
Sardinia, 98
Sarekat Islam, 724
Sargent, John Singer, *724*
Sargon of Akkad, 70, 159
Sarmatians, 172
   art, *172*, 172–173
Sartre, Jean-Paul, *708*, 708–709
Sasanians, *197*
   transformation of, *199*
Sati, 222, G–7
Satsuma, 505
Satyagraha, 724, G–7
Saudi Arabia, 723, 769
Saussure, Ferdinand de, 707, *711*
Savanna, 62, G–7
Sawad, 248
Saxons, 255
Saxony, 255–256
Sayids, 539–540
Scandiclerosis, 753
Scandinavia/Scandinavians, 83, 751, 753
   imperialism, 643
   migration, map of, *265*
   migration of, 265–266
Schism, 466
Schoenberg, Arnold, 711
Schrödinger, Erwin, 702–703
Schurz, Karl, 616
Schweizer, Albert, 699
Schwitters, Kurt, 712
Science
   in Axial Age, 139–141
   chronology, *141*
   in the East, 483–485
   Indian, 714
   painting, *481*
   religion, 140, 714, 716
   rise of Western, 333, 480–483
   in sixteenth and seventeenth centuries, 462–487
   in thirteenth century, *337*
   Western, 694–709
   map of, *696–697*
   transformation, 700–709
Science, Western
   chronology, *485*, *709*, *716*
   in the East, 483–485
   transformation of, *710*
Science and Civilisation in China (Needham), 714
Science Society of China, 695
Scientific racism, 707
Scientific revolution, 335, 529, G–7
Scientism, 575, 695, 715, G–7

Scientology, 770
Scopes "Monkey Trial," 702
Scotland, 448, 531
   monarchy of, 490
   nationalism, 668
Scramble for Africa, 654, *654*, G–7
Sculpture, *116*, *555*, *566*, *712*
Scurvy, 522
Scythians, 32, 172
   art, *171*, 171–172
Sea charts, 413, *413*
Sea of Butter, 153
Sea of Milk, 153
Sea Peoples, *84*, 84–85, G–7
Seacraft, Inuit, *266*
Sechín Alto, 88
Second Sex, The (Beauvoir), *708*
Second Vatican Council, 756, G–7
Second World War. *See* World War II
Secularism, 681, 767–770, G–7
Sedentary peoples, *30*, *31*, 33, *44*, 84, 86, 164, 173, 203, *309*, *309*, 316–317, 449
Sehetep-ib-Re, 64–65
Seiki, Kuroda, 711
Self-determination, 723, 740, G–8
Self-strengthening, 607–608, 695, G–8
Seljuk Turks, 288, 315
Seljuks, 224, *225*, G–8
Senate, Roman, 165
Senegambia, 239, 379, 553
Sénghor, Leopold, *760*
Sennacherib, *99*, 102
Separate development system, 759
Septicemic plague, 349
Sequoia, *672*, *672*
Serbia, 668, 720, 745
Serf, 626, G–8
Serfdom, 626
Serra, Junípero, 555
Service industries, 755
Seth (god), 84
Settlement of land
   in ancient river valley civilizations, 62–63
   in eleventh century Western Europe, 277
Seven Samurai, The (movie), *614*
Seven Years' War (1756-1763), 557
Seville, 443
Sextus Empiricus, 142
Sexual economic specialization, 13
Sexuality
   candor, 706
   Hittites, 80
   in sixteenth and seventeenth centuries, 465
   in twentieth century, 756–757, *757*
Shaanxi, 61, 171, 250
Shaka, king, 676
Shaka dynasty, 192
Shakers, 477
Shaman, 18, *18*, 67, *67*, 91, *91*, 127, 324, *474*, G–8
Shamanism, *470*
Shams al-Din, 472
Shang dynasty, 62, 67, 68, 70, 71, 87, 110
   decline of, 93
Shanghai, *765*
   and industrialization, 620
Shapur I, *197*
Sharia, 198, 761, G–8
Sharif Husayn, 723
Sheep, 655
   in Australia, 536
Sheffield, 616
Shelian Africa, 379

Shell shock, 724
Shen Xu, 139
Shen-rab, 222
Shenyang, 470
Shi Huangdi, 169–170, *170*
Shi Jing, 62
Shia, 200
Shiba Kokan, *570*
Shibusawa, Eiichi, 606
Shield Jaguar, *243*
Shiism, 233, 329, 499–500
Shiite, 287, 290, 543, 544, G–8
Shikibu, Murasaki, 276
Shimazu, 505
Shinto, 220, 221, 232, 715, G–8
Shintoism, 680
Shipping, steam-powered, 600
Ships, ironclad, *597*
Shoa, 377, 647
Shoguns, 277, 362, *362*, 504, 505, G–8
Shoshone, 631
Shotoko, prince, *225*
Shotoku
   empress, 221, 229
   prince, 220, *220*
Shrines, map of, *290*
Shun Ti, emperor, 345
Siberia, 422, 443, 449, *449*, 629–630, 657
Sibir, 423
Sic et Non (Yes and No) (Abelard), 283
Sichuan, 306, 307, 450
Sichun, 423
Siegfried, Jules, 599
Sierra Leone, *634*, 651, 670, 739
Sigismund, emperor, 405
Sigmund I, 478
Sigmund II, 478
Sikhism, 477, G–8
Sikhs, 646, 678
Silent Spring (Carson), 781, *781*
Silk, 499, 606
   and commerce, 156–157
   reeling, 628
Silk Roads, *150*, 156–157, *157*, 171, 215, *215*, 225, 304, 325, *325*, 386, 447, G–8
   chronology, *157*
Silla, 172, *192*, 192–193, 219–220
   development of, *205*
Silver mining, *430*
   and Spain, 490
Silver Mountain, 430
Silver trade, 420
Simpson, Wallis, 783
Sinai, 58
Sine, 681
Singapore, 764
Sinhalese, 112
Sino-Japanese War, 608, *608*, 729, 745, 749
Sioux, 554, 646, 666, 681, G–8
Sitalkes, king, 106
Siyaj K'ak, 181–182, 206
Skateholm settlement, 21
Skeletons, *30*
Skepticism
   in Axial Age, 142–143
   chronology, *143*
Skull decorating, 37
Slave Coast, 509
Slaves/slave trade, 390, *549*, 615, 647–648
   abolishing, 623, 624
   African trade, *509*, 509–511
   in the Americas, 444–445, 451, 505, 507–509, 548–552

in ancient Egypt, 330–331
in ancient Rome, 105
Atlantic passes, description of, 548, *548*
and black Catholicism, 474–476
chronology, *558*, *625*
chronology of trade, *509*
in colonial America, 604
in East Africa, 271
emancipation, 626–628
and imperialism, 624, 653
and industrialization, 604
map of, *550–551*
Native Americans, 430
in New England, 455
in nineteenth century, 624–628
and population in eighteenth century, 518
and Portugal, 379, 623
revolts, 555, 625
trade and sugar cane commerce, 440, *440*
Slavs, 196, 223–224
Sleeping sickness, 643
Slovakia, 723
Slums, *590*
Smallpox, 349, 428, 518, 522, 523, *523*, 554, 590, 789
   and Native Americans, 442, *442*
Smiles, Samuel, 599, 617
Smith, Adam, 573
Smoking, 751, *751*
Snails, 45
Soapstone lamp, 21, 113
Soccer, 713
Social classes/society
   in the Americas, 454, 507
   aristocracies, 490–491
   art, *282*
   caste system, 167
   categories of, 53, *53*
   China, 502–503
   chronology, *503*, *636*
   configurations of, 62–73
   division of classes, 53, *53*
   farming, 22
   foragers and farmers, 21–22, *22*
   Greece, ancient, *105*, 105–106
   growth of, prehistoric, 53, *53*
   Hittites, 79–81
   in Ice Age, 17–19
   in Japan, 362–363, 504–505
   in Korea, 504
   in nineteenth century, 615–616
   peasants in fourteenth century Japan, 363
   and plague, 356
   in sixteenth and seventeenth centuries, *493*, 493–495
   social equality, 573–574
   working class, 726
Social Darwinism, 659, G–8
Social engineering, 703
Social equality, 573–574
Social speech, 707
Socialism, 616, 618, 684–686, *685*, 726–727, G–8
Socialist regime, 726, G–8
Socialists, 726
Sociobiology, 703, G–8
Socrates, 143, 144
Soft power, 745, 767
Soga clan, 220
Sogdiana, 162
Soka Gakkai, 770
Sokaku, *514–515*
Sokoto, 553, 679
Sokoto Fulani kingdom, map of, *553*
Solar energy, 779

Solidarity, 735, G–8
Solomids, 284, G–8
Solomon, king, 118, 271
Solomon Islands, 253
Solon, 104, 104
Somalia, 26, 745
Son of Heaven, 171
Song, king, 220, 225
Song dynasty, 392, G–8
Song empire, 304–306
   art, 308, 308
   economy, 306–307
   map of, 305
Songhay, 378–379, 385, 448, G–8
   in fifteenth century, 384
Songtsen Gampo, 203–204, 221
Soninke, 216, 238, G–8
Soothsayer, 76, 87
Soothsaying, 75
Sophists, 143–144
South Africa, 653, 759, 765
   democracy, 742
   exploitation of environment, 459
   imperialism, 655, 656
South America
   expansion of, 246
   exploitation of environment, 459
   in fifteenth century, 384
   in fourteenth century, 368
   geographic obstacles, 254
South Asia
   map of, 110
   in fourteenth century, 359
   recovery of ancient
      civilization, 111
South Carolina, 554
South Korea, 734, 770
   economy, 763
South Sea islands, 156, 534
South Vietnam, 734
South Wales, 597
Southeast Asia, 763
   agriculture, 250–253
   contending with isolationism, 280
   Enlightenment, 571
   expansion of, 252
      in eleventh and twelfth
         centuries, 271–273
   foreign imperialism, 642, 643–648
   in fourteenth century, 360–361,
      369
   and Islam/Islamic, 471–472
   map of, 252
      in fourteenth century, 359
Southern Kingdom, 304
Southonax, Léger-Félicité, 625
Souw Beng Kong, 417
Sovereignty, 506, 580, 673
Soviet, 726, G–8
Soviet Union, 726, 727
   Cold War era, 731–733
   decline of, 735, 737
Space exploration, 735
Spain, 333, 490, 536
   in the Americas, 426–429, 442,
      444–445, 451, 454, 506, 555
   chronology, 430, 455
   ancient civilization, 108–109
   art, 441, 516
   Christian missionaries, 464
   civil war, 728
   commerce in the Americas, 426
   democracy, 683
   dominance of in sixteenth and sev-
      enteenth centuries, 490–492,
      492, 496
   emancipation of slaves, 626
   government during eleventh and
      twelfth centuries, 281

imperialism, 643
industrialization, 603
invasion by Almoravids, 293
and maritime navigation, 413
monarchy of, 490–492, 492
Muslim influence, 293
nationalism, 666, 668
in the Philippines, 541
plague of, 443
in Spanish America, 578
urbanization, 281
Spallanzani, Lorenzo, 575, 594
Spanish America, independence from
   Spanish rule, 558
Spanish Inquisition, 465
Spanish tobacco, 441
Spanish War of Independence, 583
Spanish-American war, 646
Sparta, 105
Species extinction, 786–787
Spengler, Oswald, 724
Spice Islands, 414, 421
Spice trade, 414
Spirit of Laws, The (Diderot), 566
Spiritual Conquest of Spanish Ameri-
   ca, 469
Spots, 713
Sputnik I, 735
Squash, 35
Sri Lanka, 112, 275, 376, 393, 415,
   421, 468, 743
   chronology, 112, 119
   civilization of, 118
Srivijaya, 251–252, 275
St. Benedict, 474
St. Elesban, 474–476, 475
St. George, 421, 649
St. Iphigenia, 476
St. Lawrence River, 442
St. Paraskeva, 281
St. Petersburg, 495, 519, 603
St. Sophia cathedral, 330
St. Stephen, 298
St. Thomas, 474
Stalin, Joseph, 726, 727, 728, 731,
   735, 737, 750
Stanley, Henry Morton, 650
State, conflicts with Roman Catholi-
   cism, 680–681
State of Israel, 742
State system, 172, 278, 404–406, G–8
States
   effect on society, 750–754
   in government, 490, 492–493, 496
   society, 65–66
Statue of Liberty, 743
Steam power, 529, 597, 600, 601, 648
Steamship trade, 600, 630
Stedman, John, 549
Steel production, 526, 598, 648
Stela of Axum, 193
Stephen of Hungary, 223
Steppe, 152, 156, 171–174, G–8
Steppeland, 18, 32, 71, 339
   exploitation of environment, 459
   imperialism, 390, 446–448
   invasion of China, 171–172
   Mongolian, 321–324
   in thirteenth century, 337
Steppelanders, 171, 189, 189–192,
   206, 286, 288–289
   invasion of India, 191–192
   invasion of Roman Empire, 185
   map of, 190
Stess, 791
Stevens, Siaka, 739
Stevenson, George, 598
Stock market crash (1922), 725
Stoicism, 143, 478, G–8

chronology, 143
Strabo, 103, 402
Strait of Gibraltar, 279
Stranger effect, 429, 650, G–8
Stream of consciousness, 707, 707,
   G–8
Stress theory and farming, 42
Stroganoffs, 422
Stump speaking (painting), 682
Stupa of Sanchi, 168
Su Dongpo, 308
Suárez, Francisco, 493
Subconscious, 705
Subjective language, 707
Submarine warfare, 721
Sub-Saharan Africa, 257, 699
   civilization of, 118
   in fourteenth century, 369
   geographic obstacles, 254
   geography of, 238, 239
Subsidiarity, G–8
Sudan, 680, 739
Sudanese, 646, 646
Suez Canal, 610, 610, 643, G–8
Suez Canal Company, 739
Suffrage, 683, 723, 762
   timeline, 762
Sufis, 229, 332, 472, 472, G–8
Sufism, 228–229, 296
Sugar, 455
   cane, 248, 440, 440
   industry, 533
   production of, 398
Suger of Saint-Denis, abbot, 278, 283
Suicidal utopias, 749–750
Sulawesi, 468
Suleiman the Magnificent, 390, 425,
   426, 446, 497
Sultan Idris Training College for
   Medicine, 698
Sultanate of Aceh, 472
Sultanate of Delhi, 331–332, 332, 404
Sultaniyyah tomb, 342
Sultans, 495–497
Sulu Islands, 467
Sumatra, 194, 252, 393, 472, 540
   expansion of, 251
Sumer/Sumerians, 65, 68, 70, 71, 72,
   92
Sumpweed, 38
Sun Myung Moon, 757
Sun Pyramid, 174
Sundiata, 364, G–8
Sunflowers, 38
Sunghir, 19
Sun-god, 64–65
Sunkuru, 518
Sunni/Sunnism, 200, 233, 287, 290,
   296, 497, 543, 768, G–8
Supe Valley, 53
Superpower, 641
Superstring theory, 702
Superwoman, 761
Supe Valley, 53
Surinam, 440, 508, 549, 549, 601, 760
Surrealism, 712, G–8
Survival of the fittest theory, 659
Suryavarman II, king, 271–272, 272
Susa, 157
Susa-no-o (god), 249
Susutra, 141
Swahili, 539–540
Swampland for tilling, 33–35
Sweden, 223, 490
Sweet potato, 35, 42, 436–437, 532
Switzerland, industrialization, 603
Sydney, 534, 655
Syllogisms, 138, G–8
Sylvanus, Bernardus, 374
Synagogue, 668, 668

Syncretic, 474, G–8
Syncretism, 476
Syntax, 708
Syr Darya, 780
Syria, 162, 543, 628
Szigetvár, 446

T
Tabasco, 90
Tagore, Abindranath, 712
Tagus valley, 293
Tahiti, 534, 558, 559, 578, 579
Taiping Rebellion, 607, 641, G–8
Taipings, 607
Taira, 277
Taira clan, 280
Taiwan, 656
   conquest of, 450
Taizong, 202
Taizu Emperor, 306
Takla Haymanyot, 270
Taklamakan Desert, 157, 325
Tale of Genji, The (Shikibu), 276, 276
Taliban regime, 769
Talking Cross, 681
Tamati Waka, 664
Tamil, 743
Tamkaru, 77
Tana, 326
Tan-fu, 67
Tang China, map of, 201
Tang dynasty, 202–203, 250,
   303–304, G–8
Tanit (god), 98
Tanjore, 275
Taro, 366, G–8
   cultivation of, 33
Tartaria, 54
Tartessos, 109
Tasmania, 28
Tawhiao, 679
   king, 665
Tayama's, 719
Tbilisi, 658
Tea, 420, 441, 641
   industry, 599, 628, 629
Technology
   and imperialism, 648
   in nineteenth century, 700
Teff, 36, 36
Telegraph, transatlantic, 600
Tel-Eilat Ghasuul, 48–49
Telephone lines, 766
Telescope, 484, 529, 701
Television, 713
Temperature changes, 344, 788,
   788–789
Temple of Artemis, 147
Temple of Solomon, 289
Temujin, 316
Tench, Watkin, 535
Tengri, G–8
Tenochtitlán, 382, 382, 385, 428, 428
Teosinte, 35, 36
Teotihuacán, 174, 181–184, 206, 245,
   385
   art, 174
   map of, 173, 183
   transformation of, 199
Teotihuacáno, 181–183
Terra Australis, 578
Territorial imperialism, 421
Terror alert, 754
Terrorism, 754
Teutonic Knights, 330
Teutonic Orders, 370
Tewodros II, 681
Textile industry, 529–530, 619,
   642

Thailand, 623, 655, 678
  in eighteenth century, 542
  Enlightenment, 571
  and imperialism, 404, 643
  modernization, 676
  relations with China, 542
Thaisa, king, 542
Thaj, 153
Thames River, 345
Thanesar, 194
Thar Desert, 86
The Mongol Peace, 321, G–8
Theaters of the world, 481
Thebes, 69
Theodora, empress, 195, 195, 298
Theodoric, king, 189
Theodosius, 224
Theophilus, 217
Theory of progress, 522
Theory of the Leisure Class, The (Ve-
  blen), 635
Theory of value, G–8
Thera, 82
Theravada Buddhism, 221, 233, G–8
Third Rome, 386, G–8
Tholos, 139
Thomas Cook and Company, 635
Thorgeirr Thorkelsson, 222–223
Thrace/Thracians, 106, 107
Three Gorges Dam, 781
Thule Inuit, 370, G–8
  chronology, 265
  migration, 264–265, 265
  migration, map of, 265
Tiahuanaco, 241, 244, 257, 385
Tian Shan, 326
Tibet/Tibetans, 203–204, 204, 446,
  470, 541, 737
  chronology, 204
  development of, 205
  map of, 201
  and spread of Buddhism, 221–222
Tierra del Fuego, 659, 659
Tigris River, 37, 55, 59
Tikal, 181–182, 242
Tilling/tillers, 30–31, G–9. See also
  Farming
  compared with herding/herders, 34
  environment of, 33–38
Timber as energy source, 456
Time
  measurement of, 635
  perception of, 707
Timur, 423, 498
  map of, 388–389
Timur the Lame, 387
Timurids, 386–389
Tintin, 718
Tippu Tip, 626
Tipu Sultan, 547
Tisza, 54
Tlaxcala, 428
Tobacco, 436, 437
  in the Americas, 441, 455
Tobolsk, 449, 449
Tocqueville, Alexis de, 618, 656, 682
Tokaido Highway, 519
Tokugawa, 504, 504–505, 606, G–9
Tokyo-Yokohama railway line, 606
Tolstoy, Leo, 615
Tominaga Nakamoto, 569
Tomsk, 449
Tonatiuh, 556
Tonga, 253
Tongzhi, 695
Tonle Sap, 251
Tool-making technologies, 8
Topkapi Saray, 495–496
Torokawa, 473

Tosa Lady, 263, 277
Toshimichi, Okuba, 606
Total war, 596
Toulon, 390
Trade. See Commerce; Economy
Trading-post empires, 415, G–9
Trail of Tears, 658
Trajan, emperor, 256
Transoxania, 322, 446
Transportation, 522, 601
  in early civilization, 54
Trans-Siberian railway, 608, 630
Transylvania, 426
Traviata, La (Verdi), 629
Trdat, king, 218, 225
Treasure Fleets, 427, G–9
Treatise on Astronomy, A (Dias), 484
Trebizond, 315
Trent, Council of, 464
Trevithick, Richard, 599
Tribunes, 165
Tribute system, 382, 382, 384–385,
  422–423, 428
Trisong Detsen, 221, 221, 225
Tristram, 403
Trollope, Anthony, 594
Truman, Harry, 729
Trumbull, John, 558
Trundholm, 83
Tsu Jia, 67
Tuareg, 553
Tuberculosis, 443, 789, 791
Tudhaliya IV, 81
Tugaru, 456
Tukolor, 651
Tula, 182, 245, 257, 385
  expansion of, 246
Tundra, 16, G–9
Tunis, 351, 528
Tunisia, 650, 674, 739
Turkestan, 329
Turkey, 424, 440, 543, 698, 723,
  744
  Enlightenment, 567
Turkeys, 441
Turkish Military Engineering
  School, 586–587
Turkmenia, 85
Turkmenistan, 38
Turks, 288–289, 300, 360, G–9
  in Germany, 758, 759
  invasion of Balkans, 425
  Seljuk, 288
  and spread of Islam/Islamic, 224
Turner, Joseph, 599
Turnips, 594
Turtle ships, 417
Tut-mose I, 93
Twentieth century, chronology, 745,
  771, 793
Type-II diabetes, 783
Typhus, 349, 443, 522
Tyre, 98

Uganda, 739, 741
Ugarit, 77, 85
Uighurs, 215, 303, 320
Ukraine, 54
Ulloa, Antonio de, 576
Ulysses (Joyce), 707
Umar I, caliph, 225
Umar II, caliph, 225
Umma, 70
Uncertainty principle, 701, G–9
Uncle Sam, 721
Unification Church, 757
United Fruit Company, 653
United Nations, 730, G–9

United Provinces of Central
  America, 670
United Society of Believers in Christ's
  Second Coming, 477
United States
  business imperialism, 652–653
  centralization, 674
  Civil War, 597, 597
  democracy, 681–682
  immigration, 630, 630
  imperialism, 658, 658
    resistance to, 669
  industrialization, 600, 604
  militarization, 674
  nationalism, 670, 673
  post World War I, 725
  as superpower, 743
  World War I, 720–721, 723
Universal Exposition, 621
Universal love, 131–134, G–9
Universe, view of, 481–482
University Garden of Leiden, 532
University of Beijing, 695
University of Chicago, 765
University of Dunedin, 532
University of Leiden, 698
University of Paris, 333, 334
University of Pennsylvania, 704
Upanishads, 111–112, 127, 132, 139,
  144, 714, G–9
Uplands for tilling, 35–36
Upper Egypt, 70
Ur, 62, 70
  codes of, 65
Uranium, 779
Urban guerrilla, 756
Urban II, pope, 278, 289
Urban planning, 620
Urban projects, 751, 753–754
Urbanization, 454, 620, 784–785,
  G–9
  chronology, 623
  in eighteenth century, 519
  in eleventh and twelfth
    centuries, 279
  map of, 602, 785
  in nineteenth century, social
    effects, 620–621
  and spread of disease, 590, 590
Uruguay, 655, 670, 756
Uruk, 66, 66
Urumqi, 541
Usuman da Fodio, 553
Utilitarianism, 685, G–9
Utopia, 750
Utopianism, 686, G–9
Uzbek Empire, 351, 446, 499

Vaccination, 523, G–9
Vakatakas, 192
Valencia, 425
Valerian, emperor, 197, 197
Valley of Mexico, 383
Vandal Stilicho, 188
Vandals, 188
Vanderbilt, Cornelius, 599
Vardhaana Jnatrputra, 127
Vattagamani, king, 214
Veblen, Thorstein, 634–635
Veda, 127, 147, 232, 563
Velleius, 164
Veneral disease, 443
Venezuela, 431, 670, 743
Venice
  and Byzantium, 301–302
  plague of, 443
Venus, 242, 255
Venus of Laussel, 16, 16

Venus of Willendorf, 16
Verbiest, Ferdinand, 485
Verdi, Giuseppe, 629
Vernacular languages, 466, G–9
Vernes, Jules, 779
Veroli casket, 302
Viceroy, 507
Victoria, queen of England, 620, 650,
  651, 653, 664
Vicuñas, 35
Videha, 147
Vidyasagar, Isvarcandra, 662
Vieira, António da, 476
Vienna, 498, 519, 620
Vienna Codex, 269
Viet kingdom, 251
Vietnam, 646, 734, 734–735, 743
  art, 87
  in eighteenth century, 543
  Enlightenment, 571, 571
  invasion by Mongols, 320
  nationalism, 672
Vietnam War, 734, 734–735, 750
Vijayanagar, 360, 375, 404, 404
Vilcabamba, 506
Villani, Matteo, 350
Vindication of the Rights of Woman, A
  (Wollstonecraft), 574
Virgil, 164, 478
Virgin Lands, 735
Virgin Mary, 293, 464, 466, 477
Virgin of the Rosary, 681
Virginia, colony, 437, 442, 444
Virtual reality, 766, G–9
Viruses, 790–791, 791
Visigoths, 185, 188, 206
  art, 236
Vision, 482
Vitamin C, 523
Vitascope, 700
Vitis vinifera, 439
Vitoria, Francisco de, 493
Vladimir, 225
Vladimir of Kiev, 223–224
Vladivostock, 600
Volga River, 386, 422
Volta River, 238
Voltaire, 566, 566, 567, 572, 574, 576,
  580
Vora, Virji, 418
Voyages to Moscow, Persia, and the
  East Indies (Brun), 499
Vulci, 105

W
Wahhabbism, 544, 544, 553, G–9
Walcher of Malvern, 283
Walid I, caliph, 236
Walker, Thomas, 664
Wall Strett, 725
Wallachia, 426
Wang Anshi, 308
Wang Fuzhi, 483
Wang Guangyi, 711
Wangchong, 142
Wanli emperor, 501–502
War atrocities, 748, 749–750
War of 1812, 655
War on Terror, 754
Warfare, 674. See also
  Military/weaponry
  Almoravids, 293
  chronology, 216
  and Islam, 212–213
  Mongols, 316–320
  in nineteenth century, 674–675
  origin of, 12
  submarine, 721
Warring States, 118, 130, 170

Wars of Religion, 494
Watan, 671
Watermill technology, *248*
Watling Island, 479
Watteau, Jean-Antoine, 566
Wealth of Nations, The (Smith), 573
Wealth of world, 776–777, *778*
Weather
   in Andes, 381, *381*
   change in fourteenth
      century, 344–348
Weaving, 52
Weber, Max, 419
Weeds, in the Americas, 437
Wei, king, 145
Welfare, *755*
Wells, H.G., 6
Wenamun, 97
Wendel, Francois, 599
Were-jaguars, 89
Wesley, Charles, 576
Wesley, John, 576
West Africa, *364*, 398, 441, 622, 628
   See also Africa
   art, *379*
   conquest by Muslims, 553
   in fifteenth century, 378–379, *384*
   in fourteenth century, 363–364
   and Islam/Islamic, 472–473
   nationalism, 671
   slave trade, 552, *552*
West Germany and Turkish immi-
      grants, *759*
West Indies, 629
West Nile virus, 791
Westerlies, *154*, G–9
Western Europe
   chronology, *284*
   contending with isolationism, *280*
   economics and politics, 277–282
   in fifteenth century, 399–403
   map of pilgrim routes and
      shrines, *231*
   religion and culture, 281–283
Western Front, *721*, 723–724
Western science, 694–709
   in China, 695
   chronology, *485, 709, 716*
   in India, 698
   map of spread, *696–697*
   rise of, 480–483
   transformation, 700–709, *710*
Westernization, 634–635, 666, G–9
Westphalia, Treaty of, 490
Whaling industry, *588*, 589
Wheat, 36, 37, 38, 42, 44, 782
   in the Americas, 436–437
White America religion, 476–477
White Australia policy, 759
Whitfield, George, 575–576
Widow suicide, 503, 563
Widowhood, 494
"Wife of Bath," *357*
Wild Boy of Aveyron, 579
Wild children, 579
Wilfrid the Hairy, 256
Wilhelm II, emperor of
      Germany, 660
William of Conches, 283
William of Rubruck, 321–324, *323, 324*
William of Tyre, 301
Williams, Samuel, 605
Wilson, Edward O., 703
Wilson, Woodrow, 723

Wind, 111, 113, *114–115*, 153,
      154–155, 156, 328, 375,
      396–397, 400–401, 413, 779, *779*
Wind energy, 779, *779*
Wind map, *396–397*
Windmill-pumping
      technology, 456–457
Witchcraft, 464, *465*
Witsen, Nicholaas, 441
Wittgenstein, Ludwig, 708
Wojtyla, Karel, 735
Woldemar, Frederik, *421*
Wolf children, 579
Wollstonecraft, Mary, 574
Wolseley, Garnet, 651
Women
   Almoravids, 293
   in ancient Greece, *105*, 105–106,
      108
   in ancient India, 167–168
   in ancient river valley
      civilizations, 62–63
   in art, *202*
   in China, 202, 307, 503
   in eleventh century, 298
   Enlightenment, 573–574
   equal rights, 716
   Etruscan, 108
   feminism, 573–574
   in fourteenth century, 356–357
   in fourteenth century
      Japan, 362–363
   and Freud, 706
   Greece, ancient, *105*
   Hittites, 80–81
   and imperialism, 651
   Islamic, 332
   in Japan, 205
   labor in nineteenth
      century, 628–629, *629*
   in Mongolian society, 324
   Muslim, 198
   Persian, 159–160
   in prehistorical society, 12–13
   religious, 229
   right to vote, 723, 761
   role in twentieth century
      society, 761–762
   as rulers, *488*, 489, 494, *494*, 552
   in Russia, 495
   in sixteenth and seventeenth cen-
      turies, 494
   spreading Christianity, 216–217
Wonder chambers, 481, *481*
Won'gwang, 220
Wool industry, *532*, 536
Wordsworth, William, 577
World
   creation of, 334–335
   geography, 140
   map of, *586–587*
   map of migration, *633*
World Health Organization, 714,
      774, 782
World system, 406, G–9
World Trade Center attack, *754*,
      765–766
World War I, 642, 675, 700, 712,
      720–724, *721, 729*, 761, G–9
   casualties, *721*, 721–722
   chronology, *728*
World War II, *729*, 729–731, 750,
      G–9
   chronology, *728*

debt reparations, 723
   map of, *730*
   postwar disillusionment, 724–725
   postwar settlements, 723
Wounded Knee, 681
Wright brothers, 700
Writing, *71*
   Cherokee, *672*
   of Great River Valleys, *71*, 71–72
   Greek, 105–106
   Harappan, *58*
   in Ice Age, 18
   Mayan, *243*, 244
   Mesoamerica, 174
   Phoenician, 99
Wu, empress, 202, 229
Wu Ding dynasty, 67
Wu Zhao, 202
Wudi, 157
Wuwei, *157*
Wuyang, 71

X
Xhosa, 552
Xia, 304
Xia dynasty, 68
Xianbei, 191, 192
Xianjang and exploitation of environ-
      ment, *459*
Xing, 87
Xinjiang, 423, 541
Xiongnu dynasty, 171–172, 185
   chronology, *171*
Xiutecutli, *408–409*
X-rays, 700
Xuan, 110
Xuantong, 303
Xuanzang, *210*, 222, *225*
Xunzi, 134, 141, 144, *146*

Y
Yahweh, 133
Yahya ibn Khalid, 248
Yakuts, 423
Yale-Hunan Clinic, *692, 693*
Yamatai, 172
Yamato, 204
Yams, 28, 34
Yan Fu, 695
Yang Jian, 200, 219
Yang Tingyun, 467
Yangbans, 504
Yangdi, 200
Yangtze River, 70, 171, 200, 250, 450,
      781
Yangtze valley, 306, 350
Yao, 636
Yaqui Indians, 646
Yaxchilán, *243*
Yayoi, 172
Yellow Emperor, 68
Yellow fever, 443, 523, 552, 643, 791
Yellow Peril, 660
Yellow River, 55, 61–62, *62*, 70,
      86–88, 200
   map of, *391*
Yellow Temple, 470
Yemen, 116, 247, 440
Yi, 140–141
Yi Ik, 571
Yi Tinggao, 328
Yi T'oegye, 483
Yijing, general, 639, 640
Yodfo River, 457

Yohannes IV, 678
Yongle emperor, 392
Yongzheng emperor, 568
Yorktown, *558*
Yoruba, 238
Yoshimune, 569
Younghusband, Francis, 660
Yu the Great, 67, 201
Yucatán, 242, 257, 269, 431, 469, 681
   contending with isolationism, *280*
Yucca, 35
Yugoslavia, 732
Yukichi, Fukuzaw, 606
Yunnan plague, 444
Yurt, *324*

Z
Zaghawa, 238
Zagros Mountains, 38, 157
Zagwe, 271
Zakros, 82, *82*
Zambezi valley, 377, *378*, 552
   in fifteenth century, *384*
Zangi, 290, 291
Zanzibar, 270, 393, 648
   emancipation of slaves, 626
Zaoyin, 524
Zayinda Rud, 157
Zaynab al-Nafzawiya, 293
Zealand, 419
Zealots of Piety, 467
Zeker Baal, 97
Zen, 362, G–9
Zen Buddhism, 714, 760
Zeng Guofan, 608
Zeno of Citium, 143, 144, *146*
Zeno of Elea, 138
Zhang Qian, 156
Zhang Zeduan, 307
Zhanyinbao, *502*
Zhao, prince, 145
Zhen Ji, *307*
Zhen Yilao, 542
Zheng He, *393*, 393–394
Zhengde emperor, 501
Zhou Chunya, 712
Zhou dynasty, 71, 87–88, 92
   chronology, *88, 119*
   civilization of, *118*
   decline of, *93*, 109–110, *110*
Zhoukhoudian, *11*
Zhu Hong, 469
Zhu Shixing, 227–228
Zhu Wen, 303
Zhu Xi, 308
Zhu Yuanzhang, 392
Zhuangzi, 143
Ziggurats, 56, *60*, G–9
Zimbabwes, 377, 646, 739, G–9
Zinzendorff, Count, 575
Zoe, empress, 298, *300*
Zola, Emile, 675
Zoroaster, 126–127, *146*, 147
Zoroastrianism, 126–127, 147, 174,
      214, 215, 232, *329*, G–9
Zoroastrians, 126, *127*, 198, 225
Zulus, 646, 651, 676
Zumárraga, Juan de, *469*
Zurbarán, Juan de, *441*
Zuurveld, 553